The Seed and the Soil

Comparative Studies on Muslim Societies

General Editor, Barbara D. Metcalf

1. *Islam and the Political Economy of Meaning,*
edited by William R. Roff

2. *Libyan Politics: Tribe and Revolution,*
by John Davis

3. *Prophecy Continuous:*
Aspects of Ahmadi Religious Thought
and Its Medieval Background,
by Yohanan Friedmann

4. *Shari'at and Ambiguity in South Asian Islam,*
edited by Katherine P. Ewing

5. *Islam, Politics, and Social Movements,*
edited by Edmund Burke, III, and Ira M. Lapidus

6. *Roots of North Indian Shi'ism in Iran and Iraq:*
Religion and State in Awadh, 1722–1859,
by J. R. I. Cole

7. *Empire and Islam: Punjab and the Making of Pakistan,*
by David Gilmartin

8. *Islam and the Russian Empire:*
Reform and Revolution in Central Asia,
by Hélène Carrère d'Encausse

9. *Muslim Travellers: Pilgrimage, Migration,*
and the Religious Imagination,
edited by Dale F. Eickelman and James Piscatori

10. *The Dervish Lodge: Architecture,*
Art, and Sufism in Ottoman Turkey,
edited by Raymond Lifchez

11. *The Seed and the Soil:*
Gender and Cosmology in Turkish Village Society,
by Carol Delaney

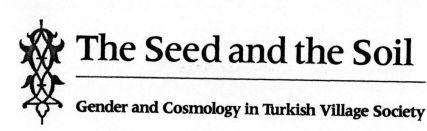

The Seed and the Soil

Gender and Cosmology in Turkish Village Society

Carol Delaney

University of California Press
Berkeley Los Angeles London

The poem on the facing page, from *Antarctic Traveller* by Katha Pollitt, © 1981 by Katha Pollitt, is reprinted by permission of Alfred A. Knopf, Inc. It originally appeared in *The New Yorker.*

University of California Press
Berkeley and Los Angeles, California

University of California Press, Ltd.
London, England

Library of Congress Cataloging-in-Publication Data
Delaney, Carol Lowery, 1940–
The seed and the soil : gender and cosmology in Turkish village
society / Carol Delaney.
p. cm. — (Comparative studies on Muslim societies : 11)
Based on the author's thesis (Ph.D.)—University of Chicago, 1984.
Includes bibliographical references and index.
ISBN 978-0-520-07550-4 (pbk.)
1. Childbirth—Turkey—Folklore.
2. Childbirth—Religious aspects—Islam.
3. Human reproduction—Social aspects—Turkey.
4. Human reproduction—Religious aspects—Islam.
5. Sex role—Turkey.
6. Sex role—Religious aspects—Islam.
I. Title.   II. Series.
GR450.D45   1991
302'.12—dc20   90-28545

Printed in the United States of America

08   07   06
10   9   8   7   6

The paper used in this publication meets the minimum requirements of
ANSI/ NISO Z39.48-1992 (R 1997) (*Permanence of Paper*). ∞

Archaeology

> Our real poems are already in us
> and all we can do is dig.
> —*Jonathan Galassi*

You knew the odds on failure from the start,
that morning you first saw, or thought you saw,
beneath the heatstruck plains of a second-rate country
the outline of buried cities. A thousand to one
you'd turn up nothing more than the rubbish heap
of a poor Near Eastern backwater:
a few chipped beads,
splinters of glass and pottery, broken tablets
whose secret lore, laboriously deciphered,
would prove to be only a collection of ancient grocery lists.
Still, the train moved away from the station
    without you.

How many lives ago
was that? How many choices?
Now that you've got your bushelful of shards
do you say, *Give me back my years,*
or wrap yourself in the distant
glitter of desert stars,
telling yourself it was foolish after all
to have dreamed of uncovering
some fluent vessel, the bronze head of a god?
Pack up your fragments. Let the simoom
flatten the digging site. Now come
the passionate midnights in the museum basement
when out of that random rubble you'll invent
the dusty market smelling of sheep and spices,
streets, palmy gardens, courtyards set with wells
to which, in the blue of evening, one by one
come strong veiled women, bearing their perfect jars.

Katha Pollitt
The New Yorker, June 22, 1981

Contents

List of Figures   ix

Acknowledgments   xi

Introduction   3

ONE   The Body of Knowledge   25

TWO   Marriage Practices and Wedding Ritual   99

THREE   Relatives and Relations   147

FOUR   Inside and Outside the Village   201

FIVE   The Embracing Context of Islam   283

Bibliography   325

Index   343

List of Figures

Poster: "How beautiful is the seed that bursts open the soil"   2

A weekly tea party at my house   44

Swaddling   66

Primary school children   89

Middle school class   90

Making mud-brick   113

Display of trousseau   126

Musicians from outside   132

Dancing at a wedding   136

Itinerant vendor   193

Lining copper pots with tin   193

A tea break for neighbors building a house   197

The structure of traditional authority relations   199

Anadolu: "filled with mothers"   203

Approaching the village   214

Map of the village   215

Girls getting water at the fountain   216

Karnıyarık: traditional house plan   234

Half a *karnıyarık*: plan of my house   235

New house plan   236

Separating the wheat from the chaff   241

Making bread   242

Boys herd, girls milk   244–45

Boy shearing   246

Evening meal on rooftop   249

Emekli: "the retired"   253

Putting final touches on a *yorgan*   261

Village tailor   263

Wall hanging: "Where do you come from? Where are you going?"   286

❦ Acknowledgments

At the end of a long journey it is easy to forget that one might never have begun, or, having once set out, might never have reached the destination. Here I wish to acknowledge certain people and institutions who "opened the road" at critical moments. Even when I was in the doldrums I was sustained by their unflagging encouragement, faith, and inspiration.

David Schneider, Bernard Cohn, Paul Friedrich, and Jean Comaroff, my professors at the University of Chicago, where this project first took shape, communicated not only their knowledge and wisdom but also a sense of the intellectual, existential, and deeply moral venture that anthropology can be. Each contributed in different ways and at different times; something of each of them is discernible in the text. Their different perspectives on my work enriched it immeasurably; knowing them has enriched my life. I am fortunate to have studied with them and thank each of them for their efforts on my behalf, for their wit and criticisms, and for their friendship. Margaret Fallers, whose last work with her late husband was in Turkey, shared my interest in the people and the place, as did Bob Dankoff, who patiently answered my odd and often obvious questions about the Turkish language and introduced me to a number of Turkish scholars.

I shall forever be indebted to the anonymous people who made the decisions to support this work through the Fulbright Cultural Exchange, the American Research Institute in Turkey, the National Science Foundation, the Fulbright-Hays Commission, and the Turkish Government, which gave the permission to carry it out.

In Turkey, hospitality is a national virtue. It would be impossible for me to thank all the people who befriended me—from the unknown taxi driver who returned the camera I left in his car, to all those in Ankara who gave generously of their time, their table, and their talk. Dr. Cağatay Güler let me accompany him on his rounds of villages during the winter of 1980 and first introduced me to the villagers with whom I would live for nearly two years. His trust and enthusiasm for my project smoothed the way for its implementation.

It is, however, to the villagers that I offer my deepest appreciation and affection. They opened their hearts as they did their houses, shared their lives as well as their food. Their acceptance of me, their generosity, and their sense of humor made my life there enjoyable and unforgettable. The symbolic dimension of their orientation to the world was compatible with my own and made for very satisfying fieldwork. Their letters still continue to come and make me aware that the anthropological encounter does not end. Out of respect for their privacy, I have disguised the names of people and places; but I must acknowledge the *muhtar*, the late Ali Yurtseven, without whose initial permission and abiding confidence this venture in mutual understanding would not have been possible.

I am also very grateful to several American, British, and Dutch friends living in Ankara who received me at a moment's notice when I came "from the mountain." Their kindnesses included dinner parties, concerts, hot baths, and the use of a washing machine.

The transformation from fieldnotes to dissertation to book demands space and time to put thoughts to paper. Several institutions—the University of Chicago, Harvard, and Stanford—have provided me that precious space. The completion of the manuscript would have been further postponed without a release from teaching and administrative responsibilities made possible by an Ellen Andrews Wright fellowship at the Stanford Humanities Center for the year 1989–90. A beautiful office, a cordial staff, and the lively fellowship of the Center helped me to see it through. A number of people gave graciously of their time and energy to read the manuscript and make suggestions for its improvement: Isen Arıcanlı, Eser Ayanoğlu, Jane Collier, Erika Friedl, Elvin Hatch, Michael Meeker, Unni Wikan, Sylvia Yanagisako, and my editors Lynne Withey and Jess Bell. If I have failed to incorporate their suggestions, it is because my own powers and energy failed.

Last, but most important, I wish to express my love and gratitude to my daughter, Elizabeth Bangs. She has endured the hardships of a journey she did not plan and whose purpose she did not at first understand.

She has been at turns an inspiration, my toughest critic, my staunchest supporter, comic relief, and over the long haul, the most resilient traveling companion.

Whatever friends I have failed to thank, whatever debts I have failed to acknowledge, the omission is unintentional—let it not be held against me. This sentiment was also expressed by the villagers when we parted:

Helal olsun!

The Seed and the Soil

toprağı çatlatan tohum ne güzel

MUSTAFA PALA

dizayn umut poster ● fotoğraf ibrahim demirel ● izmir caddesi 33/34 ankara ● tel 17 77 16

"How beautiful is the seed that bursts open the soil." Photo/poster:
Ibrahim Demirel.

Introduction

This book explores the way the theory and symbols of procreation are key to understanding the values and organization of Turkish village society. In defining procreation, I include such matters as how life comes into being; what it is composed of; who or what the agents are; what the person is, both male and female; and how persons are related to one another, the nonhuman world, and the cosmos. This definition includes far more than is generally attributed to "reproduction" and questions the usefulness of that category. In the village, procreation is the human analogue of divine creation; between these intimate and ultimate contexts a whole world is symbolically engendered and integrated. Specifically, I suggest that a "monogenetic" theory of procreation is correlative with the theological doctrine of monotheism. Both are concerned with genesis, albeit at vastly different levels; the principle of creation at both levels comes only from one source, and that is symbolically masculine.

The ethnographic focus may be Turkey, but the implications are directly related to debates in anthropology, religion, and contemporary Western society about gender, the body, and power. This study suggests that although gender definitions may be related to procreation, procreation is not just about sex and biology. Indeed, the major contribution of this work may lie in the challenge it presents to commonsense assumptions and conventional lines of anthropological inquiry. Religion and reproduction are generally held to be quite separate and distinct, if not mutually exclusive, areas of human experience and study. Reproduction is felt to be about sex and biology, considered to be matters of nature, whereas religion is usually thought to be about things set apart from ordinary life, about the sacred, the supernatural, and matters of the spirit (*pace* Durkheim 1965: 62). Rarely do these domains impinge upon each other except insofar as religion attempts to codify what kinds of sex and reproduction are legitimate. This division of experience and intellectual labor replicates, I suggest, the spirit-matter dichotomy inherent in our culture. Indeed, I argue that these gendered oppositions have their roots in the predominant folk theory of procreation, in which one aspect is felt to be natural and the other spiritual. The assumptions embedded in this division have fettered our thinking about gender and power in our own or any other culture.

Questions about coming-into-being are ultimately questions about origins. "Who are we? Where do we come from? Where are we going?" The question of origins is one that all peoples must contend with, as is evidenced by the universality of origin myths. Yet not all origin myths are the same; for example, not all origin myths are stories of creation. In other words, although the questions may be universal, the answers are not. Yet it is the answers that lead directly to the logic of specific sociocultural systems. Origins are simultaneously physical, social, and cosmological, and the way they are *represented* profoundly affects a person's or a people's identity. I see no reason to separate these levels a priori; instead, by means of similar or analogous categories, concepts, substances, agencies, and processes, I suggest that in any given culture they are related symbolically. At the same time, these are not merely philosophical questions and conceptual systems, for the answers are deeply embedded in values, attitudes, structures, and practices that motivate and orient everyday life and give that life its particular style. An ethnography is an evocation of that life.

Each person's work is, to some extent, an excavation of his or her own history. The intellectual problems one chooses to dig into, the tools one employs, and the perspective one takes up are rooted in that history, or, more precisely, in the questions raised by that history. So, too, are the sources of inspiration that keep one going. The poem that opens this book, which I found toward the end of my anthropological research in Turkey, spoke not only to my immediate concerns but also to themes that have resonated throughout my life—dreams, archaeology, and the Near East. It also raised once again the question that every anthropologist, perhaps even more than the typical archaeologist, confronts—namely, "What on earth am I doing here?" One doesn't just stumble into a "Near Eastern backwater"; it would be irresponsible not to give some account of how and why one got there.

The questions that have motived my work have to do with gender, power, and religion but were much more concretely framed. Very simply, they were these. First, why in the three monotheistic religions (Judaism, Christianity, and Islam) is God explicitly or implicitly symbolized as masculine? How does this affect the way we think about men and women, the nature of authority, and the structures of power? Second, why is reproduction so devalued in our society? It might have been thought about some other way; it might even have been considered divine. Intuitively, I felt there was a connection between what seemed to be totally unrelated phenomena, if only because God's creation so overshadowed that of women. Indeed, women's activity was called "reproduction," a term more appropriate for the assembly line or photocopy machines than for the production of unique, sentient human beings.

So why that word? Why that particular valuation? Is the word merely a label attached to something that exists in the world, or does the word constitute that something as a topic for thought? Is there something inherent in the processes of reproduction that automatically assigns it, and women associated with it, low status? Or is the low status the result of a particular way of conceptualizing the process? Where does that understanding come from? The more I began to dig into those questions, the more they turned up material that related not just to my own history but to the wider culture. This is to emphasize that the point of departure for any ethnographic exploration is always one's own culture; so, too, is the return.

Laius-Abraham

In my youth, I dreamed of becoming an archaeologist and working in the Near East. A well-meaning but ill-informed teacher told me "Girls can't be archaeologists." That was my first conscious awareness of the restriction of gender. That dream was buried, and my life took a different direction. Many years later I became interested in the interpretation of dreams conceived as a kind of archaeology of the psyche. Both Freud and Jung were interested in dreams, both believed that they represented the hidden landscape of the mind, and both thought that the way to excavate this terrain was through the interpretation of dream symbolism. I was more attracted to Jung's approach because of his insistence on the specific content of dreams. Regardless of whether or not dream material may reflect universal themes such as an archetypical "Oedipus complex," which I find questionable, we need to take seriously the specific content and the images—why this and not that? That kind of attention, rather than the theory of psychoanalysis, was to greatly influence my anthropological style.

In the meantime, I studied with a Jungian psychoanalyst and proceeded to have a number of archaeology dreams, in one of which beehive-domed houses figured prominently. That dream was to prove prophetic. During this time my daughter's dreams also demanded my attention, for she had several in which her father was trying to kill her. He wasn't, of course, but the dreams may have expressed a feeling that he was sacrificing his relationship with her. Several months later, reading a book of Greek myths supposedly adapted for children, we noticed that the same theme was repeated in all of the first set of myths. That recognition served to exhume a memory from my own childhood.

When I first heard the biblical story of Abraham and the intended sacrifice of Isaac, I was outraged. How could any father, regardless of the reasons, think of killing his own child? What kind of God would ask such a thing? My teacher punished me for that "sacrilegious" question; the question and the punishment were repressed, only to return twenty-five years later. Then, I came to realize that my daughter's dreams, the story of Abraham, and certain Greek myths were the obverse of the Oedipus complex, Freud's name for the allegedly universal unconscious desire of the (male) child to kill his father so he can have his mother all to himself. Anyone familiar with the ancient Greek version of the myth knows that the father, Laius, first tried to dispose of Oedipus. Why had Freud neglected the other side? Why did he not even entertain the idea of a "Laius complex," or at least the possibility that there might be some relationship between the destructive wishes of both father and son and that these might have something to do with a particular understanding of fatherhood? Why in his analyses of religion, and especially of monotheism, did Freud go only to Moses and fabricate a story of the sons killing the father? Why did he not instead turn to Abraham, whose willingness to sacrifice his son is integral to his position as the father of faith in the three monotheistic religions?

What blindness prevented Freud from seeing the relation? I began to see the Oedipus complex as only one aspect of a much broader complex, another, unexamined, aspect being the story of Abraham. At the same time, I began to suspect that these themes and complexes, although widespread, were not universal, but were generated by and relevant within a particular cultural framework.

Meanwhile, the story of Abraham consumed my time and energy at Harvard Divinity School, where I focused on its historical context as well as its hermeneutic (Delaney 1977). It was there I learned that the beehive-domed houses were at Harran, allegedly Abraham's home after the migration from Ur but before the migration to Palestine. To go to Harran became another dream, even an obsession. Learning that Harran is now a village in eastern Turkey, I inquired whether any archaeological excavations had been conducted there and found to my surprise that very little had been done. In the course of those researches, however, I was invited to join an archaeological project in central Turkey. Thus by a circuitous route an ancient dream was fulfilled. Our dreams are in us; all we have to do is dig. (Ten years later, I even became a member of a team to excavate Harran, an excavation that has not taken place because the Turkish government rescinded permission.)

At the end of that first archaeological project, I made an "antipilgrimage" to Harran and learned that the stories of Abraham, known as Ibrahim in Islam, still live. More important, I learned that the most holy day of the Muslim calendar, Kurban Bayramı, commemorates the Abraham story. On that day every male head of household sacrifices a sheep, and every male child is reminded that, but for the grace of God, he might have been the one sacrificed. While seeming to mitigate patriarchal power, the ritual reinforces it on a cosmic scale.

On my return to the British Institute of Archaeology in Ankara, someone gave me a copy of "Religion as a Cultural System" by Clifford Geertz (1973). I found his theoretical approach to the interpretation of religious/cultural symbolism very sympathetic. Unfortunately, Geertz had moved to the Institute for Advanced Studies in Princeton by the time I arrived at the University of Chicago to study anthropology; but I had the fortune to study with David Schneider instead. His theory of culture as a system of symbols and meanings and his work on kinship theory shaped my thinking substantially. In particular, he introduced me to the Gordian knot known as the "Virgin Birth debate," where many of the issues I had been struggling with were entangled. In trying to untangle them, I began to pull together the threads of my own argument.

Seed and Soil

Some of those threads, however, have been drawn from another part of my life, and I wish to pick them up before returning to the anthropological debate. These have to do with reproduction, and once again my daughter's questions opened memories that were to direct my search. When she asked the perennial question, "Where do babies come from?" I began to repeat what I had been told as a child, an answer commonly given to small children: "The daddy plants a seed inside the mommy." I stopped in mid-sentence, shocked by what I was saying, and revised the explanation. I remembered my indignation on first being told that as a girl I would be merely the medium for a creation not my own, that my contribution to the procreative process was perceived as supportive, not generative. This sentiment was exactly what I was to encounter among girls and women in Turkey, and for the same reason.

I suddenly became aware of the power of verbal imagery, not to gloss reality, but to shape it (cf. Langer 1979; Sapir 1951: 162; Friedrich 1979). Seed and soil, seemingly such innocent images, condense powerful meanings: although they appear to go together naturally, they are categorically different, hierarchically ordered, and differentially valued. With seed, men appear to provide the creative spark of life, the essential identity of a child; while women, like soil, contribute the nurturant material that sustains it. This has been the predominant folk theory of procreation in the West for millennia. Inscribed in the Bible and other influential texts from Aristotle to Freud that are read and reread each generation, embedded in poetry, song, and theological language, the theory and symbols permeate the attitudes, values, laws, and institutions that shape our everyday lives.

Some of these meanings are quite apparent in the terms "to father" and "to mother," as well as in "paternity" and "maternity." The perceived creative, life-giving ability of men allies them symbolically with God, whereas the material sustenance provided by women associates them with what was created by God, namely the earth. In other words, there is a cosmological dimension to gender, and conversely there are gendered aspects of cosmology. The simple terms "father" and "mother" were no longer so simple or self-evident; they embodied *meanings* relating to beliefs about procreation, beliefs that drew upon a much wider system of meanings. Would it be appropriate or accurate to use such terms for peoples who have different theories of procreation, different cosmological systems? Perhaps it is a theory of procreation, symbolically understood, rather than religion, as Geertz claimed, that "tunes human action to an envisaged cosmic order and projects images of cosmic order onto the plane of human experience" (1973: 90).

Procreation Beliefs

Although such a relation, once articulated, seems obvious, I learned that anthropologists had rarely investigated procreation beliefs except among peoples whose views differed significantly from their own, and that their investigations had done little to change their (or our) cultural categories. Spencer and Gillen (1899) had briefly noted that certain Australian groups did not seem to have a notion of paternity, but this possibility did not really come to scholarly attention until Malinowski (1927, 1929) noted the same thing among the Trobriand Islanders with whom he worked during World War I. His discovery reopened an earlier debate that most had considered closed. Speculations about procreation were integral to nineteenth-century theorizing about the evolution of the forms of social organization; but these speculations did not lead to theories that could be investigated empirically.

A primary assumption was that procreation is always and everywhere the stuff out of which the genealogical web of kinship is spun. The differences in kinship terminology systems (and social forms) were generally attributed to differences in *knowledge* (or lack of it) about the facts of procreation, and these differences, in turn, were felt to be related to the form of marriage practiced. Although McLennan argued that kinship terminology systems were merely systems of address, he like all the others believed that kinship itself was established by procreation defined as sexual and biological. Although a number of major theorists in the nineteenth century (Bachofen, Frazer, Smith, Durkheim, Morgan, McLennan) attempted in varying degrees to relate stages of knowledge of procreation and kinship structures to forms of religion, they construed these relations developmentally, as evidence of various stages of social evolution rather than simply different cultural systems. It was assumed that by the nineteenth century most peoples had learned the necessary facts and agreed on what they were. Malinowski's discovery that the Trobriand Islanders appeared not to recognize paternity accordingly came as a surprise, sparking a new debate that has flickered intermittently ever since.

Even though that debate is about paternity, it came to be known as the Virgin Birth debate, an indication, perhaps, of the way attention was deflected from what was truly problematic. Trobriand beliefs about conception and birth were classified with other tales of miraculous or supernatural conceptions and births, of which the Virgin Birth was considered typical. Among Trobrianders, however, virgins neither conceive nor give birth; the so-called supernatural conception is, in fact, what they consider the normal, dare I say "natural," way of doing things. The Virgin Birth, by contrast, is seen by Christians as a unique event in human history.

By assimilating their beliefs to our categories, the anthropologists lost an opportunity to explore the ways such beliefs are constructed in and relevant to particular systems of beliefs about the world, their own as well as others'. I often wonder what the shape and structure of anthropology would be if the focus of attention had been beliefs about the process of coming-into-being rather than the static system of kinship terms and the stages or types of religion. In restructuring the discipline, it is important to be aware of the junctures where wrong turns were taken so as not to travel the same road again. My work returns to one such juncture and travels a little way along the road not taken. In order to get some sense of where that road may be leading, we need to understand more of what was involved in the Virgin Birth debate.

The central question of the debate was "whether certain primitive peoples . . . were or were not ignorant of the facts of physiological paternity" (Leach 1967: 39). The simplicity of the question is deceptive, for it involves very complicated issues about language, translation, reference, and fact. Like its nineteenth-century counterpart it was construed as a question of knowledge: either people knew the "facts" or they didn't. But is the question really of an either/or type, and what exactly constitutes the facts? Minimally, anthropologists assumed that anyone aware that sexual intercourse was related to pregnancy must know the facts of paternity; what they did not consider was that there can be several interpretations of the male role, that the meaning of it is not obvious. For example, it may be (1) that in intercourse the male is thought to open the path for a fetus that comes by other means; (2) that intercourse stops menstruation, which allows for (1); or that the product of ejaculation (3) feeds the fetus or (4) contributes in some other way to its formation. As a corollary one must ask whether one act or several are considered necessary to complete the process. None of these notions, however, is the same as the notion of "paternity."

The Meaning of Paternity

Paternity has not meant merely the recognition of a physiological link between a man and a child analogous to that held to exist between a woman and the child she bears. Paternity has meant begetting; paternity has meant the primary, creative, engendering role, and it *means* the same thing whether the male is a human or God the Father. If there is any difference between the two, that difference has to do with the difference between the human and divine realms, not the meaning of paternity. The theory of conception and the conception of the deity are, I believe, two aspects of the same system.

Malinowski came very close to this understanding and was far more aware than his critics of the intricacy of the problems involved in the Virgin Birth debate. He warned, for example, of the danger of using a term such as "father" in discussing other cultures: "The term 'father,' as I use it here, must be taken not as having the various legal, moral and biological implications that it holds for us, but in a sense entirely specific to the society with which we are dealing" (1982 [1929]: 4). Malinowski also recognized, however fleetingly, the interrelationship between our concept of paternity and our religious-cosmological system: "The whole Christian morality . . . is strongly associated with the institution of a patrilineal and patriarchal family, with the father as *progenitor* and master of the household" (ibid.: 159, emphasis mine). Indeed, he went on to say, "We cannot then wonder that Paternity must be among the principal truths to be inculcated by the proselytising Christians" (ibid.), and to affirm that this was in fact one of the chief points made by the missionaries. This definition of paternity was a laying of the ground, so to speak, for the reception of the *logos spermatikos*, the seminal word of God, and the values entailed.

But what were the "truths" of procreation and paternity for Malinowski? The facts of procreation could be represented, he said, "by the simile of a seed being planted in the soil and the plant growing out of that seed" (1954: 223). In other words, the "true facts" of procreation were none other than those of the folk theory we have been discussing. The natives were understandably curious and "asked whether this was the white man's way of doing it" (ibid.)!

Malinowski's explicit endorsement of the Western folk view, astutely referred to by Trobrianders as "missionary talk," should have been a clue to those involved in the Virgin Birth debate, but no one picked it up. Because the anthropologists did not question their own beliefs about the meaning of paternity, they did not realize how unreasonable it was to assume that primitives should know the facts of physiological paternity—the more so since, as Barnes has rightly pointed out, "physiological paternity is a fact that until recently no one could have known scientifically" (1973: 69). Anthropologists' beliefs about paternity were not dependent on scientific discoveries; they had existed for millennia. Moreover, the anthropologists, like the missionaries, believed not only that a man was physiologically related to a child but also that his was the creative role in bringing that child into existence. The importance of the scientific discovery (the union of sperm and ovum viewed under a microscope), which was thought to confirm the first belief, obscured but did not eradicate the second. The focus on that discovery also obscured the possibility of a transformation in the meaning of the female role.

The Meaning of Maternity

Although a woman is considered necessary for procreation, the woman's role has been imagined as secondary and supportive, not that of a creator or co-creator. The discovery of the ovum in 1826 raised the possibility of a different interpretation; and throughout the rest of the nineteenth century the nature and function of the ovum were debated in scientific circles. In general, however, the ovum was believed to be primarily nurturant material; in other words, the dominant meanings were perpetuated, albeit on a different scale (cf. Martin 1987; Stolcke 1986; Tuana 1988). Nevertheless, some women were coming to see themselves not merely as vessels for the male seed, not merely as nurturers and supporters of life, but as co-creators. This growing sentiment, I believe, was related to women's growing demands for rights: the right to control their bodies, the right to vote, the right to education, to linguistic representation, to property, to satisfying work.

With the rediscovery of Mendel's genetics in the twentieth century, it was understood that the ovum contained half the genetic contribution of the child. Some women learned that their contribution was of the *same* kind as that of men; that they were in fact equal or more than equal contributors to the *creation* of a child. Yet this understanding of the process is relatively recent (not widely assimilated in the West until the mid-twentieth century), is known only among the educated classes, and is used only in certain specific contexts. The older images are suffused throughout the culture, are used in a variety of contexts, and continue to affect us on another level. Here, as elsewhere, the revelations of science do not in and of themselves bestow meaning; they are resources bound up with and utilized within a wider system of meaning and value. Since our notions of gender are so deeply involved with assumptions about procreation and biology, one would think that any change in our scientific understanding of procreation or biology would immediately affect our notions of gender. The fact that changes have been much slower suggests that science is already implicated in cultural projects laden with value (cf. Keller 1985; Harding 1986; Tuana 1989), as well as that gender cannot be reduced to biology and sex role.

Kinship and Gender

Despite the fact that Malinowski's own material gave ample evidence of the relation and integration between beliefs about coming-into-being on both the human and superhuman planes, he channeled the material about procreation into a discussion of "kinship." The opening paragraph of *The Father in Primitive Psychology* makes this quite clear: "The dependence of social organization in a given society upon the ideas, beliefs and sentiments current there is a fact of which we should never lose sight. . . . In particular the views held about the function of sex and procreation, about the relative share of father and mother in the production of the child, play a considerable part in the formation of kinship ideas" (1927: 7).

In turn, "kinship" reduced procreation to sex and biology, and that is where it has stayed for the most part. Because kinship was the central focus of anthropology since its inception, and since a number of assumptions were embedded in it, it bequeathed a set of issues to which later scholars were heir (see D. Schneider 1972, 1984; Coward 1983; Yanagisako and Collier 1987, for excellent discussions of these issues).

Tenaciously, David Schneider has been pulling these assumptions apart. Could it be, he asked, that kinship is not really about biogenetic relations, that "the biological elements are symbols and that their symbolic referents are not biology as a natural process at all" (1972: 45)? After all, he points out, a physical-biological element such as blood is a symbol for conceptualizing differences between groups of people and ways of treating them, what he calls a "code for conduct"; it is even "difficult at times to convince an American that blood as a fluid has nothing in it which causes ties to be deep and strong" (1972: 48). The ties that bind are not *in* the blood but in culture; they are symbolically constructed within an entire system of meanings about the world.

But the assumption that kinship is established by sexual reproduction led Yanagisako and Collier "to realize that assumptions about gender lie at the core of kinship studies. Moreover, not only are ideas about gender central to analyses of kinship, but ideas about kinship are central to analyses of gender . . . we cannot think of one without thinking about the other. In short, these two fields of study are mutually constituted" (1987: 31–32). In our society and in anthropological theory generally, genital difference, sexuality, and sex role are generally held to be an indissoluble and natural unity that both composes gender definition and derives from or at least is influenced by the roles of each sex in reproduction. Despite the fact that sex roles vary significantly across cultures, they are still held to be the particular culture's construction of the facts of nature. Yanagisako and Collier question that assumption and "argue against the notion that cross-cultural variations in gender categories and inequalities are merely diverse elaborations and extensions of the same natural fact" (1987: 15). In other words, they raise the question of whether definitions of male and female are always and everywhere explained by the role the sexes are assumed to have in sexual reproduction.

My question, although related, is a little different: Is procreation always and everywhere considered natural and sexual? Ashley-Montagu raised the same issue some time ago, but few have followed up on it:

In Australia *maternity* and *paternity* are viewed as essentially non-biological, exclusively *social* concepts. There is an absence of any notion of blood relationship between mother and child as well as between father and child—a fact which has generally been overlooked. . . . While our own system of beliefs tells us that a child is the immediate product of the fertilized ovum of the woman who bears it—its physiological mother—among the Aborigines there is no such recognition of any essential physiological relationship between the woman and the child that "comes out of her." The child born of a woman is believed to be a being much older than anyone living in the tribe at the time of its birth, the incarnation of an ancestral being or sage, and, thus, an entity perfectly independent *in origin* of any physiological causes operating at the time of its incarnation or birth into the tribe. (1974: 327)

In this context, it is perhaps even a misnomer to speak of concepts of maternity and paternity as if they are empty forms to be filled rather than themselves terms with specific meaning. In the societies Ashley-Montagu discusses it seems clear that sex in the sense of sexual behavior is one thing, procreation quite another. (Ironically, this is increasingly true of our own society, but for different reasons.) His discussion, like mine, is meant to point out that the conclusions we draw about procreation are not self-evident. Not even is maternity self-evident; instead it incorporates beliefs that hook into a metaphysical/cosmological system. Ashley-Montagu was aware of this with regard to Australian Aboriginal beliefs: "It is clear that the procreative beliefs of the Aborigines constitute the foundation stones of their cosmogony, kinship system, religion and social organization and possess a significance the ramifications of which far exceed in importance any question of whether or not the Aborigines are in some cases ignorant of the fact of procreation" (1974: 230).

Schneider has challenged conventional notions of kinship, and Yanagisako and Collier have demonstrated how theories about kinship are implicitly theories about gender. My work, concerned with the relationship between gender and cosmology or religion, is an attempt to direct attention away from the physical and social, where it has primarily been riveted, to the cosmological systems within which both gender and the study of gender have been constructed. As we have seen, Schneider concluded that kinship must be regarded not as a system of blood relations, but as a symbolic domain. Why, then, take kinship as foundational? Schneider himself raised that question in his later work; in American society, at least, he discovered that the symbols and meanings of kinship cannot be confined to a specific domain but escape those boundaries and overlap with those of other artificially circumscribed domains, in particular nationality and religion. That is, symbols and meanings similar to those used to define kin are also employed to define what makes one a citizen and a member of a religion (Schneider 1977: 67ff).

Relations of power, authority, and hierarchy, however, were not explained. Why is it that the head of the family, the state, the church, is symbolically and normatively male? Are we to assume this is merely accidental rather than an inherent part of the system of meanings? If Schneider had asked not about kinship but about procreation—not about a state of being, but about the process of coming into being—a whole new range of questions would have come into view. Then we would ask who the agents are and what they contribute, what male and female mean, and whether or how sexual intercourse is involved. We would learn that even in our own society, human procreation is not simply about the natural processes of sex and biology. At the very least, the concepts of "nature" and the "natural" are inextricably bound up with a specific religious/cosmological system that, while widespread, is not universal (cf. Strathern 1980). More specifically, however, the folk theory of procreation designates both a creative, divine aspect (symbolically male) and a nurturant, material aspect (symbolically female); it is the latter aspect that, in certain contexts, is today meant by "reproduction." "Reproduction" is, therefore, not a reflection of reality but a particular construction of it. Indeed, the term was considered a quaint figure of speech, a metaphor, when it was first introduced at the end of the eighteenth century. The common terms at that time—"generation," "procreation," or simply "begetting and bearing"—conveyed a notion of a creative rather than reiterative activity; and the creative aspect was masculine. The idea that human generation should be more closely associated with plant and animal processes than with divine activity was not, therefore, a "natural" conclusion naturally arrived at, but a cultural one. This metaphoric shift perpetuated women's association with the natural world and simultaneously transferred male (procreative) power to other (productive) spheres of activity.

Religion and Reproduction

Because of the way fields of study are bounded, only certain topics are considered legitimate; only certain kinds of questions can be asked and certain connections perceived (cf. Coward 1983: 1). Other topics and questions have no place; they are out of bounds. Because it is assumed that "religion" and "reproduction" are universal domains of human experience and culture, these categories become objects of study that tend to be mutually exclusive. Clearly such a division has theoretical as well as social consequences.

Social theorists have reified the notion of reproduction so that it functions to concretize a specific domain of activities (the domestic) having to do with the physiological processes of the female body (Ortner 1974; Rosaldo 1974). What is natural is by definition universal and therefore is thought to have little relevance for culture, even less for religion. Yet the very fact that reproduction involves at least two persons makes it automatically social and an arena wherein different interests intersect and possibly conflict.

Some Marxist analyses of reproduction have been illuminating. Socialist feminists have criticized the static nature of the concept in their analyses of the social relations of reproduction. They have pointed out ways in which the productive domain is dependent on the reproductive one, as well as the ways the domestic domain is itself deeply productive (cf. O'Brien 1979, 1981; Edholm, Harris, Young 1977; Harris and Young 1981; Mackinnon 1981; Mackintosh 1977; Moore 1988). Some of the problems of analysis are attributed to the conflation of various meanings and uses of the term "reproduction": social reproduction, reproduction of labor, and biological reproduction (cf. Harris and Young 1981). Yet all these writers take for granted the commonsense meanings of biological reproduction.

Others have focused on the social or cultural dimension of reproduction (cf. Jordan 1978; Ortner 1974; Weiner 1976, 1978), and a few culturally oriented feminist anthropologists have begun to explore understandings of reproduction in contemporary American society, where they find contradictions between women's perceptions and those of the medical establishment (e.g. Martin 1987; Rapp 1988). Although their analytical scheme is useful for understanding the structures and divisions in contemporary American society, their retention of the category "reproduction" unwittingly perpetuates some of the divisions they wish to overcome.

When Geertz asserts that he will confine his efforts to the cultural dimension of religion (1973: 89), he runs into a similar difficulty. Hard as he may try to get away from studying religion as some kind of "unusual object" (1975: 97), his use of the category "religion" to circumscribe something specific and distinct perpetuates that category. "In all approaches religion as a universal form of human experience and of Islam as a particular instance is presupposed" (el-Zein 1977: 227). This is as true of contemporary studies (e.g. Abu-Lughod 1986; Antoun 1989; Eickelman 1989; Loeffler 1988) as it is of those el-Zein reviewed, but it is particularly inappropriate for Islam. Islam, according to Muslims, is not one religion among many, any more than God is one among many; it purports to be the one true faith or way given in the beginning. The classification of it as one instance of a type of phenomenon focuses attention on Islam as *a* religion, a concept many Muslims reject.

The study of religion has generally focused on religious beliefs and practices, rituals and ritual specialists, and religious institutions specific to each religion. But where does religion leave off and ordinary life begin? How can we know what are specifically religious practices and what are not? As we shall see, precepts of Islam affect even daily hygiene. But if Islam does not make the same distinction between the sacred and secular, between the things belonging to God and to the world, as is made in Christianity, for example, or in Western nations, how can we use categories from one religion or society to study the other?

This question was implicit in Geertz's suggestion that we ought to think of "religion" as "a way of looking at the world" (1975: 97). Worldviews, he says, provide "conceptions of a general order of existence" (1973: 90) or the "assumed structure of reality" (1973: 129); in other words, they provide the conceptual context within which— against which, but nevertheless in relation to which—meaningful human action takes place. Nevertheless, he would have us believe that these worldviews are optional, that they are relevant only for believers and then only some of the time. In the words of Santayana, whom he quotes, they are "another world to live in." In contrast, I suggest that religious worldviews overflow the boundary of a community of believers and enter the cultural mainstream; that such worldviews profoundly affect people's everyday lives, regardless of whether they are believers and despite degrees of devoutness, and influence even seemingly secular conceptions. And I think this is as true of our own society as it is of any other.

For Geertz, religions are composed not only of a worldview but also of an "ethos" (an echo perhaps of the distinction between theology and ethics as it has developed in Christianity); the first frames conceptions of reality, the second modes of action appropriate to that frame. Although he notes the importance of worldview, his own work tends to focus on the ethos side of things (cf. Munson 1986; Ortner 1984). In *Islam Observed,* for instance, he is concerned to illustrate the contrasting styles of religious observances in two Muslim countries. A few scholars have taken such differences to extremes and suggested that there are as many islams as there are muslims (e.g. el-Zein 1977), a perspective that denies any meaningful function to the term Islam. In addition it betrays the social realities of Muslims, "the natives' point of view" (Geertz 1976) that Geertz thinks anthropologists should be trying to comprehend. For the Muslims I know, and in much Islamic writing, Islam is One and to suggest otherwise is blasphemy. Does the variety of practices that the anthropologist comes in contact with justify the omniscient observer's perspective, or is that another form of cultural imperialism?

Bourdieu, critical of the observer's stance in the construction of anthropological knowledge, may have gone to another extreme. Although he says that "the objects of knowledge are *constructed,*" he asserts that "the principle of this construction is practical activity oriented towards practical functions" (1977: 96). At the same time practical activities and interests are themselves symbolically mediated (if not symbolically constructed) and become meaningful in relation to a particular cosmological context (cf. Sahlins 1976), in this case Islam. Bourdieu seems not to have considered the impact of Islam in constructing habits of mind as well as of the "habitus." In *Outline of a Theory of Practice* (1977) for example, there is no mention of Islam in the text or in the index, where "religion" is listed under magic. There is no discussion of the influence of Islam on notions and practices related to honor, authority, inheritance, kinship and parallel cousin marriage, personal hygiene, or orientations in time and space. He would have us believe that the structures, values, and attitudes of everyday life arise out of the ground, in the exigencies of the seasons, and in the sexual division of labor, which is seen to lie in the givenness of sexual difference.

If Geertz's approach is too culture-bound, Bourdieu's is at once too local and theoretically too universalistic. There is something recognizable within the varieties of Islam that gives Muslim societies a specific cast. Perhaps our sights have been focused on the wrong things; perhaps we should look less at the observable "ethos" and "practice" side of things, and more at worldview. For despite local and regional variations, practical activities evolve in relation to a worldview that is far more than a local construction; yet universalistic theories about the transformation of life through practical activity cannot take into account the meaning and place of work in a specific worldview. People do change their societies and their lives over time. How does this happen? Where do we situate the motive forces of change, as well as the forces of resistance not only against the dominant system but also against the forces of change? We must ask whether an approach to the study of human culture that is grounded on universalistic premises about work, the division of labor, and the transformation of society is appropriate for all cultures, including Muslim cultures.

In Islam the focus of attention is not on the transformation of society but on its recuperation. History does not refer to "the ever changing creation of new meanings of human life but to the struggle to recapture and immobilize an eternal experience" (el-Zein 1977: 247). The Muslim ideal is a return to the pristine pattern of society and model of behavior as conveyed by God through Muhammed and inscribed in the Qur'an and Hadith. This point is made by Muslims and Orientalists alike (cf. Ahmed 1986; Hodgson 1974; von Grunebaum 1946).

Although I do not deny the possibility of a cultural distinction between the human and divine realms, I suggest that they are interrelated, that a symbolic exchange is going on between them, that metaphors of one are utilized in the conceptualization of the other and vice versa. I do not assume that "religion" and "reproduction" are two readily identifiable, relatively autonomous, and universal domains of human experience and culture. I assume instead that domains and the terms used to define them must emerge in empirical investigation. Perhaps each culture constructs its categories and domains of life differently. As a way of getting into this question, the investigation of notions of coming-into-being is, I suggest, very appropriate.

Turkey

From my previous visit to Turkey, I knew that having children was very important. Turkey was a pro-natalist state until quite recently, and it still has one of the highest birth rates in the world. "Do you have children?" is one of the first questions put to a new acquaintance, or to a candidate for public office. I did not know what the *theory* of procreation was, but I knew I would be able to find a place where modern, Western scientific theories had not yet fully penetrated. Turkey is a Muslim country, and Islam is one of the three monotheistic faiths in the Abrahamic tradition. Therefore Turkey was arguably a good place to explore the symbolic relationship between procreation and Creation, between genesis at the human and the divine level.

There are more than thirty thousand villages in Turkey. With a rural medical team, I visited more than fifty of them on the central Anatolian plateau, looking not for a "typical" village but for one with enough material resources to be viable, enough people of both sexes and all ages so that I could observe a number of life-cycle rituals of birth, marriage, and death, and a population of the predominant ethnic and religious group, that is Anatolian Turk and Sunni Muslim. The village I finally chose, which I will refer to as Gökler for reasons that become clear in Chapters 3 and 4, consisted of approximately 850 people (it was larger than the usual 200–400), who were evenly divided by sex and of all ages, and who considered themselves to be true Anatolian Turks and professed to be Sunni, rather than Alevi, Muslims.

The village in which I was to spend nearly two years of my life was also aesthetically appealing, which, although not a requirement, is not to be discounted. It was about thirty kilometers off a paved road and high on a mountainside. Although it was only a few hours from the capital, Ankara, its physical situation made it relatively remote. The roads leading down to the highway were treacherous at certain times of the year and were occasionally impassable; their condition prevented anyone from regularly commuting outside for work. The few who worked outside remained away for varying lengths of time and returned to the village periodically.

The village was not one whose population had been depleted by the outmigration of working-age people to urban centers in Turkey or to Europe. Villagers make a living primarily by wheat cultivation and animal husbandry: sheep, goats, and cows. Wheat provides flour for bread, the staple of the village diet; surplus wheat is sold for profit. Sheep are raised for their wool and goats for their world-famous Angora (Ankara) hair, and both are also sold as meat. Along with cows they provide villagers with occasional meat, but they are valued especially for their milk; milk products (yoghurt, cheese, and butter) form the second major component of the village diet. The village when I was there was prosperous but not rich. There was a considerable difference in wealth between the richest household and the poorest one, but the distribution of wealth formed a continuum and most households fell in the middle. There were no class differences within the village. Status and prestige differences did not necessarily or only depend on wealth.

Personally, I was attracted to this particular village aesthetically and emotionally. Its location on the mountain commanded a majestic view of the vast steppe of the surrounding countryside and gave a feeling of expansiveness to the spirit, at least to mine. But it was the people who attracted me most. Turkish villages differ not only in their location and physical attributes but in the way their people present themselves. Sometimes one can tell immediately whether a village is friendly or hostile, whether there is some almost palpable malignancy of body or spirit or whether a village is open and healthy. These rather categorical judgments are not just my own perceptions, but reflect the ways Turkish medical personnel and villagers themselves perceived and described various villages. Even on my first visit to the village I chose, which was in fact the first one I visited, I felt that the people had a healthy pride and appeared basically content. Also some that I talked to possessed a sense of humor, which can be an important consideration for an anthropologist. An outsider is bound to make mistakes and shock people by behavior that violates their expectations; and such mistakes can prove fatal—if not to the anthropologist, at least to the work. It is difficult to be the object of jokes and laughter, but preferable to being excluded by silence or actively persecuted. Once I decided on that particular village, I had to wait for the villagers to decide whether to allow me to live among them.

The first night that I was settled in my own house, September 11, 1980, was the night General Kenan Evren led a bloodless military coup and took control of the government. For several years the government had been unable to stem the rising tide of civilian bloodshed; and because of internal fighting between various political parties and their inability to form workable coalitions, the business of running the country had all but come to a halt. For the rest of my stay in Turkey (until July 1982), and for more than a year after I left, all overt political activity was suspended. There were no elections, political parties were disbanded and new ones could not be formed, all political organizations were closed down, and all government jobs were frozen. This context unquestionably affected the kind of fieldwork I could do. There could be no discussion of politics in the conventional sense, and for some this may appear to give a timeless quality to the book. On the other hand, life was not put on hold; and an examination of the intimate relation between sex and religion in the micropolitics of everyday life reveals a dimension that helps to comprehend macro-level politics.

Structure and Orientation of the Book

The book is divided into five chapters—an allusion both to the five "pillars" of faith that together support Islam and to the division of the Muslim day into five parts. Five times a day, Muslims are called upon to think about the oneness of God and the relationship between the earthly and the divine. The day is not evenly divided, nor are the chapters. One of the longest periods is that between dawn and noon, and in the book the first chapter is one of the longest. It discusses the theory and symbols of procreation as they construct notions of embodied persons both male and female. Notions of gender and generativity as they are expressed in attitudes and practices relating to the care of the body, sexual relations, birth, and childrearing are taken up to and including puberty, when the whole cycle can be repeated. The second chapter uses the symbols and meanings of procreation to review the concept of Mediterranean marriage, which in turn entails the complex of attitudes and practices known as the honor code. The most important event in the life of an individual, a family, and the village—a wedding—is also analyzed in detail.

The third chapter uses the symbols and theory of procreation to illuminate the villagers' notions of how people are related to each other through time (descent) and space (nearness and distance), and the ways these time and space relations are expressed in the structure of affective and authority relations. The symbols and meanings of procreation are also embodied in the conceptualizations of lived space (the house, the village, the nation, and the world), the division of labor for the reproduction of the household, and the rhetoric of nationalism. All these subjects are taken up in the fourth chapter. The fifth chapter discusses the most encompassing frame in which life is lived—Islam. The symbols and meanings of procreation are deeply embedded in the cosmological system of Islam and exemplified in a number of rituals and practices.

I rejected various other structures before deciding on this one. In particular, I considered beginning with the last chapter and ending with the first, a strategy that would discuss village life from its most ultimate parameters to its most intimate. But since the symbols of procreation are utilized in the Islamic conception of both life and death, procreation is logically prior. If a book could be constructed so that the end could be folded around and attached to the beginning, that would be a gratifying solution. It would also be Islamic, for in Islam the ultimate origin and end are the same. What takes place in between—that is, life in the world—is imperfect, mutable, and transitory. Yet it is this very embeddedness and specificity that captures the imagination of the anthropologist and that the writer of an ethnography tries to capture.

Our dreams are in us; the digging externalizes them. What started out as an excavation of my own history has become part of that history. At the same time, the deeper one digs, the more likely is the possibility of revealing something of more than personal meaning. The hours put in, not in a museum basement, but in offices in Chicago, Cambridge, and Stanford, are uncounted. I may not have uncovered the bronze head of a god, but I believe I have discerned the outline, at least, of a pattern that has far more general relevance and opened up new vistas for excavation.

ONE The Body of Knowledge

An encounter with lived Islam challenges conventional definitions of religion as consisting primarily of beliefs and practices set apart from everyday life. In the Turkish village where I spent nearly two years, Islam penetrates daily life as the call to prayer five times a day, penetrates one's being heedless of whether one is a believer. There is no escape; it is the very context in which daily life unfolds. Although Islam does formulate a conception of a general order of existence (cf. Geertz 1973), it is more than a conceptual system: it regulates and integrates every aspect of corporeal existence. "Islam Embodied," after Geertz's *Islam Observed*, might be an alternative title for this chapter, for the meaning of Islam is mediated through the meanings and comportment of the body in everyday life. Islam prescribes in minute detail how the body in its myriad activities must be presented; indeed, every aspect of bodily existence has been discussed at length in a voluminous literature both legal and erotic. Says one contemporary Muslim scholar:

Islam is a constant attention paid to one's own body. A Muslim upbringing is a training that makes one permanently aware of the physiological side of life. Eating, drinking, urinating, farting, defecating, having sexual intercourse, vomiting, bleeding, shaving, cutting one's nails. All of this is the object of meticulous prescriptions . . . of formulas to be recited before, during and after each act. There are ways in which the acts are to be performed, certain gestures to be carried out . . . it comes very close to an obsession. (Bouhdiba 1985: 55)

Such practices are particularly important for illiterate villagers, for bodies signify, they mean things. The way one comports one's body is a sign to others that one recognizes and submits to God's order; it is the way one demonstrates that one is Muslim. Wilfred Cantwell Smith characterizes Islam as a religion of "orthopraxy" in contrast to "orthodoxy" because of its concern not so much with correct beliefs (which, in any case, are relatively simple) as with correct practice (1957: 28). Understanding the body from the point of view of the villagers is prerequisite to understanding the structure and relations that compose their world—the family, kinship, the village, the nation, this-world and other-world—all of which will be taken up in the subsequent chapters.

We enter the world embodied; that is what human existence means. Each of us has/is a body; there are certain aspects of bodiliness that we all share such as flesh, blood, and bones and a susceptibility to illness, aging, and death. Yet how we got here, how and of what we are made and what our purpose is, are matters of cultural variation and affect the meaning of the body. Our natural and therefore universal characteristics do not determine the meaning of the body, since the same characteristics are not universally emphasized. Bodies do not exist outside of culture, but are shaped physically and figuratively within culture. Each culture appears to choose or highlight certain aspects of the human bodily repertoire while ignoring others. Although the body may be a rich source of "natural symbols" (Douglas 1970), we cannot assume that the symbolization is naturally determined or universal.

But even to speak of the "body" or "bodiliness" is to miss the crucial point that in all cultures a distinction is made between bodies that are male and those that are female. Each type of body has different meanings and may be related to the notion of bodiliness differently. In Turkey, for example, it is the female body that represents corporeality *par excellence*. This seems natural to us because we too assume that women are more immersed in the physical aspects of existence, owing to their reproductive function and role, and therefore more identified with the body (de Beauvoir 1949; Ortner 1974).

In contrast, I suggest that these meanings of the body, male and female, are not self-evident, are not derived from the "facts" of reproduction, but are instead intimately related to a theory of procreation, and that this theory is itself embedded in a wider corpus of beliefs about the world. It is true that babies come only from the bodies of women (at least at this point in time), but the processes involved and the significance of this truth are differentially understood, symbolized, and represented in the consciousness and activities of particular societies. In the village I studied, the theory of procreation is what I have called "monogenetic" (Delaney 1986) because, as we shall see, it is the male who is imagined as the creative, engendering person, in which character he is symbolically allied with God.

In this view of procreation, it is men who give life; women merely give birth. Giving life and giving birth are not synonymous. This subtle but extremely important distinction has been overlooked by social scientists as well as feminists; as a result, there has been a great deal of confusion about the relations between reproduction and women's inferior status, especially when the former is viewed as the cause of the latter (de Beauvoir 1949; Ortner 1974, etc.). It may not be procreation that is devalued but only women's culturally perceived role in the process.

The absence of a developed vocabulary to discuss these issues and distinctions adds to the difficulty. Anthropologists use the term "gender" to refer to the cultural construction of sex or, more accurately, of anatomical differences; but there is as yet no term established to refer to culturally constructed notions of the process by which life comes into being. Generally "reproduction" is used to refer to the physiological "natural" process, and it is generally assumed that this categorization is universal. Yet our notions of what is natural, including scientific notions, are intimately related to and derived from a religious-cosmological system that is not universal. Since "procreation" retains something of the cosmological dimension, this is the term I use to mean the folk theory of coming-into-being at the human level. I do not assume "procreation" is a native category, as "reproduction" has become for us; that it circumscribes a domain of activity, for example the private or domestic; that the processes are considered natural; or even that the female is the primary actor (indeed in Turkey she is not). Nor do I assume that "procreation" refers to the symbolic aspects of an already presupposed domain (Weiner 1978: 175); that is what needs to be established empirically in each case. A phrase such as "beliefs about coming into being" would be more accurate, but is too awkward to use repeatedly. "Procreation" is meant as a shortcut to express that idea.

Although I use "procreation" to refer to the villager's understanding of the process by which a child comes into being, the village itself has no comparable word. Villagers use terms reminiscent of Biblical notions: *uremek* and its synonym *coğalamak*, both meaning "to increase and multiply." These two words are used interchangeably to refer to the processes that social scientists have divided into "production" and "reproduction." In Turkish academic and medical usage two new words have been coined as equivalents: *ureme* for reproduction and *uretim* for production. However, this merely adds to the confusion, for *ureme* is a verbal noun that literally means "increasing and multiplying," whereas *uretim* is formed from the causative of the verb *uremek* (*uretmek*), which means to "breed and raise"! In any case, these are not the words in use in the village, and are thus of little use in understanding village conceptions (in both senses of the term).

For villagers, the distinction between male and female roles/functions in procreation also defines their roles in "increasing and multiplying" the household more generally. In other words, the salient distinction is not between "reproduction" and "production" but between male and female. The activities of both men and women are necessary and complementary though differentially valued; in short, it is not "reproduction" that is devalued in relation to "production," but the female role in relation to that of the male. Male and female roles are not only complementary, but of a completely different order. In the village, male and female roles/functions in the procreative process exemplify not only the division of labor but the division of the universe.

Learning the meanings of the body, male and female, leads one into that universe. Because the body is common to us all, it can serve as a useful reference with which to reflect upon the somewhat different but often familiar perceptions and symbolisms in the Turkish village. It provides a sensuously rich entrance into another culture at the same time as it parallels the entrance of the anthropologist. For no matter how much one knows intellectually about another culture, the lived reality of it is something else. The anthropologist's own visceral reaction to the people and place must be taken into account as well as their reaction to him or her. It would be naive to claim that one's gender, age, race, personality, and physiognomy did not affect the way one is incorporated into a community. Each anthropologist, whether he or she is aware of it, is assigned a position that gives access to certain types of knowledge and hinders access to other types. Some people, by virtue of a combination of characteristics appropriate to the particular context in which they find themselves, are able to negotiate a wider range of possibilities than others.[1]

---

1. Because I was an adult woman with a child, even though she was not with me, I was allowed to live in my own house and was much freer to walk about the village than a male anthropologist would have been (cf. Papanek 1964).

In order to learn about Turkish village culture and to be accepted into the community, I had to abide by their rules and live as they did. I had to learn how to dress, walk, sit, sleep, cook, eat, drink, bathe, relieve myself, and keep house as they did. I do not know to what extent I became a villager, but I surely had to live like one. Through such bodily training I learned, at least to some extent, what it was to be a Turkish-Muslim-villager-woman. But since definitions are always relational, I also learned what it might mean to be a Turkish-Muslim-villager-man; and from the perspective of a villager I was more able to understand the villagers' view of city dwellers, Europeans, Christians, and Jews.

It is important to make clear that in what follows I shall be discussing villagers' notions of the body, of gender, and of procreation; their ideas accord with or diverge from those elaborated in Muslim philosophical or juridical texts (as is true in any society). The differences do not make them any less Muslim, or the agreements more so. In other words, I do not hold up such texts as a standard against which to measure villagers' degree of "muslimness," but consider their beliefs and practices an authentic expression of it.

Although Islam is a textually based faith, Muhammed was illiterate and most of the people caught up in its sway have been illiterate. Attending to the words and images that move villagers may provide clues to help us understand the formation and transmission of powerful ideas. Villagers revere "The Book," but they have a different relation to and understanding of it than people whose entire life is mediated by written texts (cf. Ong 1982; Eickelman 1978). Words are signs that have power; the word for "sign" (T. *ayet*) is found throughout the Qur'an and is the word that means a verse in a *Sura* (chapter) of the Qur'an. *Ayet* also means wonder or miracle, and the Qur'an itself is considered a miracle.

But there are other kinds of signs, and the world is a different kind of book in which God's message is inscribed. Each sign speaks to and is related to others; there is system. With proper study the outward signs reveal their deeper meaning, and these deeper meanings in turn reveal the presence of the Creator. The sign of signs is thought to be male-female polarity; or, in villagers' terms, begetting and giving birth.

For villagers, procreation is a God-given sign that properly interpreted is key to understanding the order and meaning of the universe. If we are to gain entrance into that world, we need to understand what *they* mean by procreation.

Symbols of Conception

Analytically the notions of body, gender, and procreation are separable, but to villagers they are inseparable. Male and female are defined by their perceived role in procreation, and procreation defines what they are. "Perceived" is the key term here because what I wish to stress is their view of the process—a view that cannot be reduced to sex and biology. If it is true, as Boas claimed long ago, that "the seeing eye is the organ of tradition," meaning that people see pretty much what they are trained to see, then we need to readjust our focus. If we wish to understand villagers' perceptions, we need to learn to see as they do. Because perception is not direct but is mediated by symbols that are themselves embedded in a wider cultural system, we need to attend to the symbols with which they describe the process.

The different roles of men and women are most vividly expressed in their theory of conception. Villagers characterize the different roles of male and female in this process in terms of seed and field (*tohum ve tarla*). The man is said to plant the seed (*tohum*), and the woman is like the field (*tarla*) in which it is planted. Occasionally they would refer to the Qur'an to legitimize their view. There it is written: "Kadınlarınız sizin için ekilecek birer tarladır. Öyleyse onları dilediğiniz gibi ekin" (Sura 2: 223). "Women are given to you as fields to be sown, so go to them and sow [your seed] as you wish." This directive from God to men establishes them as intercommunicating subjects in an I-thou relationship from which women are excluded and in which they are objectified. God talks to men about women. The *tohum ve tarla* theory has been noted in a number of ethnographies of Turkey (Engelbrektsson 1978; Erdentuğ 1959; Magnarella 1974; Meeker 1970), but its place in a broader system of beliefs and values has nowhere been elaborated.

This neglect points to important distinctions between conventional sociologically oriented anthropology and more symbolic approaches. In the former, figurative language tends to be considered an embellishment. As in the physical (hard) sciences, the goal has been to strip away the decorative veils of language to reveal the naked truth. Thus, since there is nothing intrinsic about women that resembles a field and nothing about semen that resembles seed, *tohum ve tarla* can easily be dismissed as a quaint figure of speech, a metaphor having nothing to do with the "true facts" of reproduction.

Others believe that the metaphor *reflects* the natural resemblances. Paul Ricoeur, who is influential in theories of interpretation and metaphor, states, quite uncharacteristically I think, that "there is a correspondence between the tillable soil and the feminine organ and . . . between semen and seed"! (1976: 62). He feels the "correspondence" is given in nature; I feel that it is culturally constructed, and only for that reason appears to reflect reality. One need only think about peoples who do not or did not have agriculture to realize that the analogy is not given naturally. What about a people whose livelihood is derived from fishing or from hunting and gathering, or whose gardening did not involve seed? Is it likely their notions of procreation would involve seeds and fields?

The fact is that this particular way of conceptualizing the process of procreation has a long history in cultures that have been dominated by the Greco-Roman/Judeo-Christian traditions. Although dismissed as metaphor, the images of seed and soil are part of the cultural heritage of the researchers and thus no doubt seemed to have little to say specifically about Islam or Turkey. In contrast, I believe they may illuminate aspects of our culture that have been previously hidden from view.[2] Benveniste pointed to something like that when he said: "Sometimes an expression which becomes so commonplace that it no longer arouses the attention, is illuminated by the beliefs associated with the ideas it expresses" (1971: 267). It is not just that a "dead metaphor" is brought to life, but rather that a missing link is found that connects certain contemporary beliefs to their source. What then do these images imply?

Although no villager would confuse a woman with a field or semen with seed, it does not follow that the metaphor is a euphemism or a cover-up for some more accurate theory. Villagers do not have an alternative theory with which to contrast the seed-field image; instead, this representation constitutes their symbolic understanding of the pro-

---

2. This is not to deny that the images of seed and soil/field exist elsewhere, for example in Bengal (Fruzzetti and Östör 1984), but one cannot assume identical meaning *a priori*. Their meanings and connections with a wider symbolic scheme need to be investigated in each context.

cess. These images epitomize male and female nature, and these meanings are then elaborated in numerous ways. They are key symbols in both the summarizing and elaborating senses described by Ortner (1973); that is, they condense and epitomize certain values that ramify throughout the culture.

The production of a child is a central concern for both men and women in Turkey generally, not just in the village; but the ways it is understood furnish a key to understanding a whole range of attitudes having to do with sexuality and gender, honor and shame, authority and submission, time and space, inside and outside, open and closed. In addition the symbols and meanings by which procreation is understood and represented provide a means for understanding relationships between such seemingly disparate elements as body, family, house, village, nation, this-world, and other-world. They go beyond gender and embrace the cosmos. These "key symbols" are hardly embellishments to reality. Rather, I believe, they are key to a particular conception of it;[3] they illuminate the symbolic connections that give some coherence to social life. Instead of dismissing the images as fanciful metaphors, we need to learn to see with them. Rather than covering up reality, they disclose it. Tracing the meanings embodied in these images leads into all areas of village life and reveals a pattern that is distinctly Turkish; at the same time, they lead directly to the sources of some of our own deeply held assumptions and values. Let us turn to the beliefs expressed by these images.

"Tohumdan çocuk gelir," the child comes from the seed; "erkekten çocuk gelir," the child comes from the man. When I suggested to villagers that you couldn't have a child without a woman, they made it clear to me that I had missed the point. Men supply the seed, which encapsulates the essential child. A woman provides only the nurturing context for the fetus.[4] The luxuriant climate of her body is a generalized medium of nurture, like soil, which any woman can provide. It affects the physical growth and development of the fetus, but in no way affects

3. This is an allusion to Suzanne Langer's much used but rarely cited formulation of the nature and function of symbolization in human life: "It is not the essential act of thought that is symbolization, but an act *essential to thought,* and prior to it. Symbolization is the essential act of mind" (1979 [1942]: 42, emphasis in the original).

4. This, I suggest, is the rationale behind Şeriat law that permits marriages between Muslim men and non-Muslim women but not between non-Muslim men and Muslim women. The Turkish civil code now permits both.

its autonomy or identity. As another villager put it: "If you plant wheat, you get wheat. If you plant barley, you get barley. It is the seed which determines the kind (variety) of plant which will be grown, while the field nourishes the plant but does not determine the kind. The man gives the seed, and the woman is like the field." (Meeker 1970: 157)

The difference between seed and field is radical. Different seeds can grow in a field; what actually grows is defined by what is sown. The theory is borne out by the word used to describe the male role in the process: *döllemek* (to inseminate). *Döllemek* incorporates the word *döl*, which means seed, fetus, child. *Döllemek* is thus almost the exact equivalent of the English "to inseminate," literally "to put the seed in." *Döllemek* implies that the man's role is primary, that he is the one who creates. The *döl* is inserted into the *dölyatağı* (literally seedbed, meaning womb; also referred to as *rahim*, which is derived from Arabic) by way of the *dölyolu* (literally seedpath, meaning vagina). In other words, female anatomy is defined in terms of the male. *Döllemek* does not mean to fertilize the ovum or to provide half the genetic constitution of a child. Villagers do not know about the ovum and genetic theory; such knowledge was absent when the folk beliefs were formed and is still absent among much of the world's population. Even those of us who know about these things keep alive the older images by the use of such words as "inseminate." It is anachronistic as well as a mistake to read back into the past modern theoretical ideas as does Farah, when she states: "Coitus interruptus, or withdrawal prior to ejaculation in the hope there will be no sperm present to fertilize an ovum, was a practice of the ancient Arabs" (1984: 33). In our own society knowledge of these facts did not become widespread until the mid-twentieth century.

The creative, life-giving ability of men is felt to be godlike; villagers say the father is the second god after Allah. A prominent Muslim scholar reiterates this view: "The Muslim family is the miniature of the whole of Muslim society. . . . The father['s] . . . authority symbolizes that of God in the world" (Nasr 1985 [1966]: 110).

The male role in procreation was felt to reflect on the finite level God's power in creating the world.[5] As God is author of the world, so too are

5. I believe this is true in Judaism and Christianity as well—in fact, that it is a central tenet of both. Regarding Judaism, Mopsik (1989: 53) says: "By reproducing, religious man imitates the divine work of the original organization of the cosmos and his pro-creative act is perhaps considered as the ritual reenactment of cosmogony."

men of children, and upon this their authority rests. What I suggest is that there is a correlation between the "monogenetic" theory of procreation and the theological doctrine of monotheism; rather than cause and effect, I believe they are two aspects of the same revelation and a means for the symbolic integration of a world. This is not official doctrine; it is a method of interrogating such doctrine, a way of getting behind what the tradition *says* about men and women to understand what is meant by male and female and how these meanings extend beyond the physical boundaries of men and women.

Thus I am not convinced that the opinions of Muslim scholars, whether medieval or modern, are relevant for understanding either villagers' views or the origins of monotheism, which predated Islam by millennia. Although Muslims are opposed to the familial symbolism of Christianity, they share much of the history and heritage of Biblical religion. In particular, they believe that Islam is a recall to the one true faith given to Abraham, to whom all three monotheistic faiths (Judaism, Christianity, and Islam) attribute their origin. It is with Abraham that the concept of monotheism is alleged to enter the world; it is through Abraham that God establishes his covenant—specifically through the penis, which was thought to be the instrument of human procreation. Particular notions of paternity were integrally related to monotheism from the start.

The Turks I studied accepted the analogy between a "monogenetic" theory of procreation and the theological concept of monotheism. In Islam, however, the analogy may be more metaphoric than metonymic. In Islam, God is not imagined as father but as Creator, and the human male in his procreative role appears to be metaphorically analogous to God. In Christianity, God the Father is substituted for the human male in an extraordinary act of procreation. God the Father and Jesus the Son are One; they are of the same essence. Mary, the mother, is not; she is the means through which that relation is established. God does not literally inseminate her, but does so with the "seminal" word.[6] The difference in emphasis may be important for doctrinal differences; but

6. The symbolic equation, however, is perpetuated in popular imagination, for example in the film "The Last Temptation of Christ." At the critical moment, when the nature of Jesus is being discussed, it is said that he is not of the seed of Joseph but of God. See also First Epistle of John 3:9.

for the purposes of understanding the concept and meaning of paternity, it is negligible.

Among Sufis, who represent and elaborate the mystical tendencies in Islam, some of the meanings appear to coincide. In Sufism, Maryam (Mary) is a symbol of the kind of spiritual receptivity needed to receive divine inspiration (Schimmel 1975: 429). Similarly, Austin states that there "is the Muslim notion of the community of faith, in Arabic *al-umma*, a word closely related to the word *umm* meaning mother. Thus the Muslim community is seen in its relationship with God, as essentially receptive, open to receive the deposition of the Divine Word" (1983: 43–44). This could be interpreted as a positive identification for women, but transparent in these associations is the notion that the seminal word (like seed) is whole, is transcendent, and comes only from one source, whereas the feminine symbolism is associated with the temporal and physical aspects of existence. These images only further confirm the seed-soil theory of procreation we have been discussing. They may glorify the receptivity of the female, but they deprive her of creativity.

The seed-soil theory of procreation cannot, I suggest, be confined to physiological reproduction and the relation between men and women, for it expresses a fundamental aspect of the universe. In the projection of creative power onto God, it becomes omnipresent and invisible—a power animating the universe. Because of the structural and symbolic alliance established between men and God, men partake of this power; as a result, their dominance seems natural and given in the order of things. This association is part of the power behind these patriarchal systems, for it is the glorification, not just of the male, but of the male as "father." That, to me, is what patriarchy is all about. The widespread use of the term "patriarchy" to refer to other systems of male dominance seems to me intellectually sloppy, for the term "father" derives its meaning from an entire system of beliefs about procreation that are not universal. Such usage has confused the discussion of the variety of forms of male dominance. The domination of an emperor and that of a patriarch may be felt as equally oppressive, but the symbols that present and legitimate them and by which they can be transformed will be different. We cannot assume that the place and role of the gods is the same in each culture, any more than we can assume that male and female are universally defined by their role in biological reproduction. We need to know in each culture how the world is divided and how it comes into being, what male and female mean and how life comes into being.

In the villagers' theory only men are able to transmit the spark of life, and it is theoretically eternal as long as men continue to produce sons to carry it down the generations. From father to son, father to son, this spark is transmitted. The importance of sons is not therefore something separate from the ideology of procreation but an integral part of it, as is the notion of lineage. Unmarried men or married men who have not yet produced children are hardly considered full adults and have little say in village affairs. The man who has produced children, especially sons, shows that he is a "true" man, that he has the power to call things into being. Because the father is perceived as the one who gives life, he is referred to as *çocuk sahıbı* (literally, child owner), and this is the rationale for why, in case of divorce,[7] the children belong to him.

Regardless of whether lineages exist as defined social groups, the notion of lineage is extremely important for notions of identity and gender. The notion of lineage is also—at least according to Al-Ghazali (1058–1111), a famous Muslim theorist—integral to Islam.[8] On the first page of his manual about marriage and in the context of Creation, he says that one of God's "marvelous favors is creating human beings [and] causing them to be related by lineage and marriage. . . . Glory be to Him who . . . placed seeds in the soil of wombs and raised therefrom creatures" (Farah 1984: 45). Lineage, at least in this case, is very much related to ideas about seed and is synonymous with patrilineage; not surprisingly, the Turkish word for lineage, *sülale*, is derived from Arabic and means something like reproductive semen.[9]

The creative spark of life is identified with something divine, an association not unique to Islam. Seed or semen has been symbolically associated with fire, light, and the sun in a number of religious traditions. According to Eliade, "Light is an expression of divinity and of the human soul (or spirit) and at the same time, of divine creativity, and

---

7. In Europe and America until the early part of this century, children belonged to and stayed with their father in cases of divorce. Only "illegitimate" children—those without a father to name and claim them—remained with their mother.

8. The preoccupation with lineage is also very obvious in the Bible—especially in Genesis, with its long lists of who *begat* whom. Rather than assuming these are merely expressions of an already patrilineally organized society, one might just as easily interpret them as a way of establishing and legitimating a new conception of social organization.

9. Fazlur Rahman (1980: 17) and personal communication.

thus of cosmic and human life; . . . a series of identifications and hom-
ologizations beginning with godhead and ending with *semen virile*"
(1971: 3). But why does he begin with the most abstract, the godhead,
and end with the most concrete? Rather than trying to ascertain cau-
sality, I suggest they are both expressions of the same thing: a particular
theory of coming into being. The belief that semen is a kind of creative
life force that partakes of divinity is a widespread belief. The difference
between its occurrence in other traditions and in monotheism is that
creativity comes to be *the* characteristic of the one God; it is his creativity
alone that brings the world into being. In monotheistic traditions God
has no divine partner; instead the feminine element is subordinated and
becomes symbolically equated with what is created rather than with
the creative power. It is not only that the feminine is totally excluded at
the level of the divine, but that the exclusion becomes attached to
women, who are then imagined as lacking that kind of power.[10]

Women become symbolically associated with the world. "The body
of a woman is the microcosm of the work of God" (Bouhdiba 1985:
135). This equation is reciprocal—the world is also symbolically identified with woman—and has ramifications beyond the life of any particular woman. Discrete individuals are caught in a web of gender
meanings that they have not spun and often do not try to trace. Since
these meanings seem to be part of the lived world, they are difficult to
see.[11] In order to begin to untangle them, let us turn again to the images
and consider that of soil or field as it constructs notions of what a
woman is.

Like soil, women are basically all one substance. Their identity is
somewhat amorphous, and their bodily boundaries more fluid and
permeable. Mary Douglas has called the body "a model that can stand

10. Aristotle's *Generation of Animals* is an example of this. Women are defined by virtue
of an inability: they lack the power to "create" life. They provide the material out of which
it is formed, but men provide the form and the soul, that part of human beings that allies
them with the divine. I was not aware of this work until after my fieldwork, but on reading
it I was amazed how closely villagers' views corresponded to Aristotle's. Interestingly, this
book was apparently first translated into Arabic in Baghdad in the ninth century, and
the villagers believe their traditions derive from Baghdad. The historical research necessary to document such a pattern of influence would be extremely difficult and far beyond my expertise. The parallels are nevertheless worth noting.

11. Hallowell tried to say something similar when he said "the most fundamental
assumptions of any religious system are those least transparent" (cited in Ashley-
Montagu 1974: 387). It is also possible to imagine them as the most transparent, the
most closely coinciding with "reality."

for any bounded system" (1966: 115). Yet the perception in Turkish society is that only the male body is self-contained; the female body is relatively unbounded, and social measures are needed to bind and contain it. The female body is perceived as "naturally" open, and this is interpreted as a sign that it must, like fields, be socially closed. Women too must be enclosed. In this context it will be useful to clarify the differences between soil and field.

Toprak is the common word for soil. Soil is characterized as either fertile or barren; and these concepts are also used to describe women, but not men. Comparable terms for men are potent or impotent, implying agency and power (or lack thereof) rather than a passive intrinsic quality. Although a field is made of soil, soil does not make a field (*tarla*).[12] A field is still a field whether it is being cultivated, being harvested, or lying fallow. What distinguishes a field from soil is that a field has been defined, enclosed, and "covered" by ownership. Without that there is nothing to distinguish it from ordinary soil. The idea of land held in common, except for the *mera* (pasture for animals), is anathema to villagers, for it would confuse the rights of ownership to the produce.

Like land, women must be "covered"; a woman must always be under the mantle of a man (whether father, husband, brother, or son), and this is symbolized by wearing the headscarf. A woman who wears the headscarf is referred to as *kapalı* (covered, closed) as opposed to *açık* (open, uncovered). A woman who walks around *açık* is open to sexual advances from men; it is as if she were openly exhibiting her private parts. Women without cover, without a headscarf, indicate that they are without protection and are considered loose, immoral, and common property.

The vigilance with which the "protection" of women is carried out has often been remarked as a distinctive feature of Middle Eastern and Mediterranean societies. The system of behavior has been referred to as the honor/shame complex, or simply the honor code, about which there is a vast but unsatisfactory literature.[13]

Not all contributors to this literature would agree that honor and

12. I have been told that *tarla* (field) is derived from the old Turkish word *tarigla:g*, meaning "a place of seed." Rather than a thing in itself, it is the matrix or ground for the creation of something else.

13. See, for example, Campbell 1964; Peristiany 1966; Pitt-Rivers 1966, 1977; Davis 1977; DuBoulay 1974; Gilmore 1982, 1987; Herzfeld 1980; Blok 1981; Boissevain 1979; Bourdieu 1966, 1977.

shame are rooted in sexuality, but all would agree that sexuality is a prominent aspect of this system. Yet most attempts to explicate the system have focused on social structure, politics, economics, and ecology rather than on sexuality. All these factors may contribute to an explanation of how the system works, but none explains why honor is primarily an attribute of men and shame of women, or why male honor is, or at least has been, so inextricably tied to women.

Part of the problem is due, I believe, to an excessively general use of the term "sexuality," which has rendered any precise identification of its meaning difficult and which also betrays the Western preoccupation with sex detached from the entire process, let alone theory, of procreation. The protection of women in Muslim societies is, I believe, intimately and essentially related to the protection of seed; in other words, it is an integral part of the theory of conception we have been discussing. A man's power and authority, in short his value as a man, derives from his power to generate life. His honor, however, depends on his ability to guarantee that a child is from his own seed (Delaney 1987). This in turn depends on his ability to control "his" woman.

Michael Meeker, who has also worked in Turkey, has suggested that honor is essentially concerned with the legitimacy of paternity,[14] but he has not unraveled its full meaning. The meanings of "paternity" and "maternity" have been taken for granted as reflections of reality and have been relatively unexamined. As we have seen, maternity is not the equivalent but obverse of paternity: maternity is associated with nurture, paternity with the essential life-giving role.[15] Paternity is overdetermined, and in proportion so too are the social measures constructed to ensure the legitimacy of paternity. In the Middle East these

14. See Meeker (1976: 264). Antoun (1968: 688–89) has argued that legal rather than physiological paternity, however conceived, is the important issue. But Yalman (same article) and Abu-Zahra (1970) strongly disagree. Furthermore, Antoun's view is in contradiction to evidence from the lowest (rural) and highest (Ottoman court) strata of Muslim society. In the latter, sons of concubines on a number of occasions displaced sons of legitimate wives in succession to the throne. These sons were legitimate not because they were sons of legitimate wives but because the Sultan's seed was legitimate and guaranteed by the institution of the harem and eunuch guards. Monogenesis implies monogamy, at least for women.

15. Social or legal fatherhood does not necessarily deny the importance of biological creativity. In the new reproductive technologies, for example, the traditional notions of male and female role are being reinforced. The child must be the man's own, whereas the woman, especially in the case of the surrogate mother, is imagined as merely the carrier for seed. See also Stolcke 1986.

have ranged from infibulation and clitoridectomy, harem and eunuchs, veiling and seclusion, early marriage, and even murder to less dramatic but no less effective means. The practices vary from region to region and even within one region, and their logic must be worked out within each society as I am doing in this work. At a more general level, however, I believe they can be interpreted as various methods to enclose the human fields, like the earthly ones, in order that a man may be assured that the produce is his own. Not surprisingly, a threat to the boundaries of either field provokes a similar response.

Women by their created nature are already shameful, for they do not have within them the seeds of honor, that is the power to create and project themselves. Their shamefulness is basically a kind of indiscriminate fecundity, which can be redeemed only by putting limits around it. A woman's value in Turkish village society depends, therefore, not only on her fertility, which is a generalized medium of nurture that any woman can provide, but more importantly on her ability to guarantee the legitimacy of a man's seed. In other words, it is not her intrinsic nature or natural endowment for which she is primarily valued. To focus only on women's reproductive potential as a valuable resource over which men compete, as do many economic anthropologists, Marxist or otherwise, is to miss this crucial point. Although fertility is important, it cannot be assumed that always and everywhere it has uniform value. If fertility were the most important issue, one might expect less emphasis on women's virginity and purity. In this context, fertility is not the central issue, since all women are presumed fertile until proven otherwise. The primary issue is a woman's ability to guarantee the seed of a particular man; it is this that makes her valuable. The value of a woman depends on her virginity before marriage and her fidelity after marriage; this is socially recognized by her conformity to the code of behavior and dress.

The "modesty of women" (Antoun 1968) is accomplished by externally imposed restraints rather than by the development of internal qualities. Because it is believed that women do not have the power of self-restraint, these measures must be imposed. Mernissi (1975) has argued that in Arab culture female sexuality is viewed as inherently insatiable and therefore needs to be constrained; if she is correct, the external constraints can be interpreted as a way of protecting women from themselves. In Turkey, by contrast, the enclosure of women is thought to be a way of controlling male sexuality. For example, hair is thought to be especially erotic. One neighbor told me "If a man sees your hair, he will immediately want you." It is thought to trigger uncontrollable sexual desire in men. Another young man told me "Showing of the hair is the ruination of families."

Women as fields are the ground on which male sexuality is played out. Female sexuality is not so much insatiable as it is indiscriminate; indeed it is questionable whether a woman has an agentic sexuality of her own. Left to herself she has no resistance; she is open to men. The externally imposed constraints are her only shield. For example, I was told that if a woman and man are alone together for twenty minutes, it is assumed that they have had intercourse and this is grounds for divorce. It is not that the woman has been overpowered by the man, or by her own desires, but that she is thought to have no power of discretion or resistance. As one close neighbor explained to me: "Women are as easily seduced as Eve was by Satan in Cennet [Paradise]." It is because women are thought to be so vulnerable, so open to persuasion, that they must be socially closed or covered. The slightest shadow of doubt about a girl's sexual activity diminishes if not negates her marriage value because it casts doubt on the potential security of her husband's seed.

Sexual intercourse is the most extreme way a woman's body can be penetrated and defiled. Sex is said to take place inside the woman but outside the man. Semen, like menstrual blood, is polluting, albeit in a different way.[16] A man is both identified with and yet separate from his semen. As he projects it into the woman, so he can project onto her all notions of pollution. Since semen carries the essential identity of a man, it is bound to leave an indelible imprint inside the woman, one that no amount of washing can erase. "Foreign seed . . . that is seed from any other than a woman's husband contaminates the field forever making the woman permanently defiled. Since a man does not receive any substance from the woman with whom he copulates, he does not become defiled by having intercourse with a defiled woman" (Engelbrektsson 1978: 137). I would qualify this statement somewhat to read that a man becomes temporarily defiled: that is, he is defiled only until he performs an *aptes* (ritual ablution). The mixture of sexual fluids during inter-

16. Meeker confirmed this from his notes (personal communication). See also Delaney 1988; Eilberg-Schwartz 1990; Marcus 1984; Reinhart 1990.

course is considered *bulaşık,* which means soiled, tainted, and contagious and is the local gloss for "pollution." Intercourse within marriage is not sinful, but it is polluting.

Analogously, social intercourse between unrelated men and women is almost equivalent to sexual intercourse, which is why town and city (as well as Europe and America) are considered *bulaşık,* unlike the village, which is *temiz* (clean, pure) because it is *kapalı* (covered), as are its women. In the town and city, women and men mix more openly; they can hardly avoid it. This inability to control the times and places of such mixing is unsettling for villagers. It is almost certainly the reason that those who move to town keep their women at home and under much stricter surveillance than in the village.[17]

If a girl engages in conversation or receives glances from any man outside the immediate family, she can be defiled and her reputation tarnished. As the evil eye of an envious person can bring misfortune to the one at whom it is directed, so too can the eye of desire, if not deflected, penetrate the woman and bring about her defilement.[18] It is as if something physical, some extension of the man, passes with the glance. She will be blamed for having received and accepted it. In order to preserve her reputation, a girl participates in her own enclosure: she averts her eyes when unrelated men are around, wears the headscarf and other voluminous coverings such as *şalvar* (baggy pants), and stays at home. By these activities she demonstrates that she is *kapalı* (covered, closed) as opposed to *açık* (open, uncovered), that she is *temiz* (clean, pure) as opposed to *pis* (dirty, defiled). She is preserved[19] in this state until marriage, when her husband has the right to open her and thereafter control the times and places of her opening.

In the next section we examine the ways the theory of procreation affects and is exhibited by that most intimate of activities, sex. Thereafter we shall follow the process of coming-into-being from conception through puberty, when gendered persons are able to repeat the process.

17. This is even truer among immigrant families in Europe. Such constriction has been visually expressed in two films by Tevfik Başer, "40 Meters Square in Germany" (1987) and "Farewell to Paradise" (1989).

18. These ideas may ultimately derive from Aristotle. In *Generation of Animals* (1979: 247), he talks of the eyes as being the most seminal organs of the head.

19. Villagers also think in these terms. When they asked what I was waiting for to marry off my 16-year-old daughter, they said: "What, are you planning to preserve her as pickle?"

Sexual Activity

Sexual activity always exists in a context of meaning. Whatever else it may be, it is also symbolic activity. Who does what with whom, where, when, and how are matters that not only vary but carry different meanings in different societies or in different contexts in one society. Generally taken for granted as a direct expression of "natural" desires or urges, sexual behavior is beginning to be analyzed as a culturally constructed phenomenon (e.g. Butler 1990; Coward 1983; Foucault 1980; Ortner and Whitehead 1981; Vance 1984). In the process, however, "sexuality" is reified and seems to circumscribe an almost autonomous domain of human experience. Concomitantly, the same process is going on with regard to "spirituality," with the result that both terms, in my opinion, perpetuate the age-old spirit-body split that many of these theorists wish to overcome. In contrast, because sex can have a spiritual dimension and spiritual matters are often intertwined with sexual ones, I would prefer to speak of sexual activity and sexual response, spiritual activity and spiritual response, that is to examine different responses of the person, not separate and distinct domains of experience.

Ethnographically, sexual activity, whether inside or outside of marriage, is one of the most difficult things to gain accurate information about (though in Turkey accurate information about land holdings is just about as difficult). Women spoke freely with me about sexual matters, especially at the weekly tea parties in my house, but still I found it extremely difficult to know exactly what they meant and what kinds of activities were and are engaged in. Sometimes it was because I could not find equivalent terms to express what I wanted; sometimes I could not tell if we meant the same thing even when we used terms that seemed equivalent; at other times they did not seem to have any idea what I was referring to. Among the men, it was often difficult to know when they were bragging or trying to conceal actual practices. The attempt has made me somewhat skeptical of accounts that assert such information with assurance. I would want to know how the writers got their information and on what basis they assume it is reliable or representative. What follows is the result of many discussions, many observations, and a certain amount of conjecture.

It is my impression that premarital sex in the village is quite rare,

A weekly tea party at my house

given the extreme penalties it could incur, but no doubt it exists. A girl who engages in it, or about whom there are rumors, makes her chances for marriage precarious at best. Second, it is difficult for an unmarried girl, or even a married woman, to go anywhere unaccompanied. People live physically very close to each other and are always under surveillance by neighbors. Finally, most people keep fierce watchdogs who announce the arrival of any outsiders, meaning anyone not a member of the household. Nevertheless, it was rumored that one girl of eighteen entertained boys at night. Her house was on the periphery of the village, making it more difficult to keep her under surveillance; but whether it was only this difficulty that gave rise to the rumor or some basis in fact was impossible to ascertain. In any case, she soon married a neighbor's son who had an administrative job in town, a situation that was exactly what she wanted. There was also speculation that a young woman who had left her husband and returned to her father's house with her small child might be disposed to engage in an extramarital affair. Since she was a close neighbor and one of my most intimate friends, I am confident that the rumors were groundless.

The rural doctor in Yoldakent, the closest town, who had the responsibility of providing health care to about twenty villages in the area, told me that occasionally girls are pregnant before marriage. However, in our village, during the time I was there, no unmarried girl became pregnant; nor, to my knowledge, did a baby ever appear too soon. Premarital sex that does occur most likely happens during the period of engagement. Some of the older men related stories about their courtships. Mehmet, on a visit to Buçukköy (the nearest village), had caught a glimpse of Ayşe and learned that she was not married. He had his father negotiate the marriage; and when they were *nişanlı* (engaged), he used to walk seven miles over the mountain late at night to Buçukköy to try to visit her. This involved not only danger from wolves but also the danger of being caught, since his approach to the village would have been announced by the barking of dogs. In a show of bravado, he claimed he visited her often.

Sexual activity in marriage most often occurs at home and at night. Newly married women may wear a nightgown to bed now that manufactured, store-bought lingerie is becoming part of the trousseau. However, most women said they normally sleep fully clothed, that is, with a blouse or sweater and pajama bottoms, which are worn under the *şalvar* (baggy trousers) during the day. They also keep their *yemeni* (a small headscarf) on at night; otherwise "Allah's angels will not enter the house." I was told that only men can sleep "naked," keeping on shorts that cover their genitals.

Some women complained that their husbands wanted sex every day; others said less often. But in any case a woman does not have the right to refuse. In perhaps an ironically titled article, "Traditional Affirmations Concerning the Role of Women," Haddad cites Al-Bayhani: "The greatest thing in which obedience is imperative is intercourse, which is the goal of marriage. It is the most important thing the man asks of his wife. It is not permissible for her to refuse it except for a legal purpose such as menstruation, sickness and child-birth. For if she does, she commits sin, and her right of clothing, housing, and upkeep from her husband becomes invalidated and God's curse will be upon her" (1980: 70).

That it is man's right to demand sex and woman's duty to obey not only is an expression of male power, but also may affect the pleasure a woman will experience. On this issue I found no consensus. Some women said they enjoyed sex and found it sweet (*tatlı*); others evinced disgust and regarded it as a duty to be gotten through as quickly as possible. An older man who was a close neighbor told me that if the woman "came" before the man and produced much sexual fluid, the child would resemble her,[20] and vice versa. This would seem to indicate that, in his experience at least, women had orgasms. However, most of the women I spoke with did not seem to understand what I was referring to when I asked about this, and I could elicit no word that might refer to it. (I would prefer to think it was because of my inability to explain myself properly.) Women also professed ignorance about masturbation. This became evident to me from their expression of surprise and disbelief when it was a topic of discussion in my house after several women found a description in an article on sex in a popular women's magazine that I had brought to the village.

Although sex usually takes place at night, it can occur during the daytime if other members of the household are absent. At one of our weekly tea parties one woman told another that she knew the latter had had intercourse the previous day because she had overheard her husband ask her to prepare water for the *aptes* (ritual ablution). An ablution after sexual intercourse is mandatory in Islam because it is believed that the sexual fluids are *cünüb* (ritually unclean) and the mixing of them is felt to be particularly *bulaşık* (polluting) and *pis* (dirty). An *aptes* is also mandatory after menstruation, after childbirth, after emissions of sexual fluids other than at intercourse, before entering the mosque, and at death. A minor *aptes* is also performed after elimination, and only with the left hand.[21] It must be noted that women have several ablutions in addition to those required of men, which further reinforces the association of women with dirt and pollution.

Both men and women are said to produce sexual fluids, and this is well documented in literature on Muslim purification rituals (cf.

20. This should not be taken as evidence that villagers accepted the notion of a genetic contribution from women. Ideas about resemblance and heredity vary widely historically and culturally and need not presuppose ideas about genetic contributions. Lamarck, for instance, talked of the inheritance of "acquired characteristics." Illuminating anthropological discussions can be found in Malinowski 1929 and Ashley-Montagu 1937: 325f.

21. For widespread association of the left hand with dirt and evil, see Needham 1973.

Bouhdiba 1985; Reinhart 1990; Marcus 1984; Farah 1984; Sabbah 1984). All villagers I spoke with on this topic—including both men and women—agreed that women produce sexual fluids, and that they could emit these fluids spontaneously, in sleep for example. These secretions, like the male's nocturnal emission, require an *aptes*. A few people referred to women's secretions not as *cünüb*, the usual term, but as *meni*, a term normally reserved for men and occasionally used in place of *tohum*. The dictionary definition of *meni* is semen or sperm. Here, I thought, was a suggestion of a "duogenetic" theory of procreation, one in which both men and women produced and contributed "seed."

What I learned from pursuing this discussion may help to clarify some of the murky issues in contemporary debates. Villagers were quick to point out that woman's *meni* does not contain seed (*tohum* or *döl*), and that it is the *tohum* or *döl* that carries the *can* (soul or life). In other words, the few who used the word *meni* were referring to sexual fluids that both men and women produce, but made it clear that women's fluids were not generative.

As proof, they pointed out that not all women produce sexual fluids and that women can conceive without producing them. Therefore such fluids are irrelevant with regard to generation, though they may be an accompaniment to pleasure. This empirically sound and sophisticated observation recapitulates a major point, if not the intricacy, of the impassioned debate on this topic not only in the medieval Muslim world but also in the medieval Christian world (cf. Hewson 1975; Noonan 1986 [1965]), debates that harked back to similar debates in ancient Greece and may have been sparked by the resurrection of the Greek texts. The major issue of these debates was whether the male seed was the formal but immaterial cause (Aristotle) that provided the form and soul to fetal material, or whether the male seed also contributed some material substance (Galen). Galen argued that the male seed was substance, but that this did not make it like female matter. He perpetuated Aristotle's belief that the male seed, whatever its composition, was *the* generative component.

Part of the problem of obtaining any simple answer to my questions about women's contribution to procreation is that the old arguments on which village beliefs were formed were structured around different questions and erected on different premises from those employed today. My fieldwork experience, combined with my reading on these issues, makes me very skeptical of assertions that Islam promoted a "duo-genetic" view.[22]

Just because the term "female seed" occurs in some texts, it is not necessarily accorded the same status as male "seed." One problem has to do with *what* is being identified as female seed: is it lubricating fluid, a distillation of menstrual blood, or something else? Another problem stems from equating necessity with generativity: the female contribution to conception may be necessary, as the villagers consider it, but that does not imply that it is generative, let alone that the contributions are equal in kind or in value. Ibn Sina (Avicenna) uses the word "seed" for the female contribution, but had in mind something very close to the villagers' view: "It is clear that the seed of woman is fit to be matter, but not fit to be the principle of movement. The seed of men is the principle of movement, for there is no doubt that the female semen is like menstrual blood, and menstrual blood is fit to be matter and not the principle of movement" (Musallam 1983: 48). "Movement" is another of those words that could take us deep into ancient and medieval philosophy,[23] but it seems very close to what villagers meant when they talked about the male seed as *canlı*—as being alive, as having soul or life in it.

Let us return to the issue of washing. A man can signal his wife that he wants to have intercourse by telling her to get the water ready. To speak of intercourse is to speak of washing, and the latter can serve as a euphemism for the former.[24] However, behind the functional expla-

22. E.g. L. Ahmed (1989) and Musallam (1983). Musallam has presented one of the first discussions of these issues in English, but does not to my mind persuasively document his conclusion that *the* "Islamic attitude towards sexual generation . . . [is] that father and mother are equal contributors to the form and matter of the offspring" (p. 52). Clearly it is not the only or the most widespread attitude. He bases some of his argument on the supposedly "duogenetic" views of Ibn Qayyim, who comes later onto the scene than either Ibn Sina, Ibn Rushd, or al-Ghazali. Even if it is true of Ibn Qayyim, one jurist's view does not constitute *the* Islamic view.

Although Galen sometimes speaks of two "seeds," he also clearly saw the female contribution as inferior and not generative. Nowhere have I seen any ancient, medieval, or early modern argument that would qualify as saying that both men and women contribute *equally and the same kind of thing.*

23. A. L. Peck, the translator of Aristotle's *Generation of Animals*, has a good discussion in the appendix. See also Sissa 1989.

24. Bouhdiba corroborates this with regard to the Arab peoples and literature he is familiar with. Going to the *hamam* (bathhouse), he said, was synonymous with sexual activity, and he likened the physical structure of the *hamam* to the female anatomy (1985: 172). For a Turkish account see Orga (1950), who recalls his boyhood visits to a *hamam* in Istanbul at the beginning of this century.

nation lies another. In intercourse the man is watering his field as God's rain waters the earth and quickens it (Sura 50: 9–10). Once when the soil of my pot of flowers was dry, a woman said, "It is in need of water, like a woman's cunt." Rain is God's *bereket* (blessing, abundance, increase) as semen is the man's; both help to increase and multiply the fruits of the fields.[25] Sex is forbidden during menstruation for reasons to be taken up below, but immediately afterward is felt to be an auspicious time for conception because the womb is fresh and clean. Both the menstrual blood and the ritual ablution after menstruation cleanse the woman's body of accumulated impurities and leave the *dölyatağı* (seedbed-womb) an immaculate ground or virgin soil for the reception of seed.

Among the women with whom I could speak intimately about sexual matters, I learned that the most common position during intercourse is with the man on top and the woman on the bottom, most commonly *bacak omuza* (legs to shoulders, in which the woman's legs are raised and placed on the man's shoulders) rather than what is called in our society the missionary position. If it is true that women sleep fully clothed, this makes sense, for she need only pull down her pajama bottoms without removing them. On the other hand, I believe this position has more than functional significance. The traditional plow is composed of two long handles attached to an iron instrument. The woman's legs, then, are like the two handles the man leans against as he pushes the plow through the soil to prepare the furrow for seed. (The analogy of sex with plowing and the female orifice with a furrow is ancient; cf. duBois 1988.) In this sexual position it is believed that the seed-semen is deposited in such a way that it does not easily spill out, making it more likely the woman would become pregnant. This position also

25. This interpretation contrasts with Abu-Lughod's (1986: 126), which claims that Bedouin women and girls rather than men are associated with rain because in rain-making rituals they dress dolls in red (the color of fertility) and attach bread-making implements and a weaving shuttle. I suggest instead that they are symbolizing fertility and soil and that in these rituals rain is seen as something like semen, a substance that will cause the earth to become fruitful. Roper's eyewitness account of a rain-making ceremony in central Turkey (1974: 39–40) appears to confirm this interpretation. Rahman (1980: 118) discusses Sura 50 in connection with God's ability to resurrect the dead, which is likened to a "new creation": God quickens the dead as his rain quickens the earth in the spring. Boddy (personal communication) reports that in the Sudan women are associated with water—not with rain (because it hardly ever rains) but with the water that overflows the river banks, a very different image.

makes it more difficult to distinguish the vaginal from the anal orifice, even though it seems an unlikely position for anal intercourse. I was told that anal intercourse is not normal but does occur. One woman actually left her husband because he practiced anal intercourse regularly with her, damaging her anus badly. Although the practice can be understood as an expression of desire or rationalized as a simple form of birth control, we cannot discount the possibility that it may be an expression of cultural meanings about gender and the place of women.

In an interesting article about verbal dueling rhymes practiced by Turkish adolescent males, Dundes, Leach, and Özkök conclude that the idea of "an active penis attacking a passive anus has been a critical psychological configuration in Turkish culture for some time" (1972: 160). In this verbal game, one of the rules is that the retort must rhyme with the initial provocative insult and encompass it; it must fit and incorporate the former. Although that seems to give the power to the "female" position, what is intended is the power to circumscribe women:

One of the most important goals is to force one's opponent into a female, passive role. This may be done by defining the opponent or his mother or sister as a wanton sexual receptacle. If the male opponent is thus defined, it is usually by means of casting him as a submissive anus, an anus which must accept the brunt of the verbal duelist's attacking phallus. . . . Much of the skill in the dueling process consists of parrying phallic thrusts such that the would-be attacking penis is frustrated and the would-be attacker is accused of receiving a penis instead. According to this code, a young boy defends and asserts his virile standing in his peer group by seeing to it that his phallus threatens the anus of any rival who may challenge him. *It is important to play the active role in a homosexual relationship, it is shameful and demeaning to be forced to take the passive role.* (1972: 135, italics in original)

In these rhymes, regardless of whether the sexual object is male or female, the subject is the active, aggressive male, and this is the culturally valued role.[26] The devalued role not only is female but is symbolized by the anus. "Sexual submission in the rhymes serves as a

26. The importance of fulfilling one gender role or the other and of having gender correspond to sexual characteristics has been taken to its logical conclusion in Turkey, where a great number of passive homosexuals have had sex change operations. According to a television documentary, more such operations have been performed on Turkish men than on any other population in the world. When I was in Turkey the sexual transformation of a popular singer (Bülent Ersoy) was detailed in the news almost every day. Interestingly, Ersoy's sex change was not legalized, and following a law that forbids homosexuals to perform (sing, act, etc.) an act of Parliament barred the singer from continuing his/her career.

symbol of interactional inferiority" (ibid.: 130). Thus the act of anal intercourse with a woman is a most forceful statement of power relations; it tells her what she is and what her place is. Here the association soil-earth is closely drawn, for human feces are used as fertilizer on the fields.

Anal intercourse with animals figures in innuendo and appears to be a feature of a kind of folk mythology. Because I am a woman and because there is a strict taboo on speaking of sexual matters especially in mixed company, it was difficult to obtain any information about actual practices and incidence.

The doctor at the health center mentioned above indicated that it certainly exists, but that he too could not be sure about incidence. He told me of a recent case in which a 13-year-old boy came to the clinic terrified that he might have contracted rabies. The boy first said he had fought with a dog; the doctor informed him that if the dog did not bite him, he was all right. The boy went off, only to return later saying he had poked the dog in the anus; that too was no reason to treat him for rabies. Finally it came out that he had been having anal intercourse with the dog, and he was treated for rabies. Sheep would seem to be the most likely candidates for sexual activity, since boys are often alone with them and they are docile. But the informants of Dundes et al. said it was only possible with animals one does not eat. It would be interesting to know if this prohibition is widespread, but such knowledge must await a male investigator.[27]

When I approached the topic of oral sex with my informants, they expressed surprise and shock. Only one woman in the group knew of fellatio, thanks to photographs in a book her husband had bought in Ankara. It was in a foreign language, and he had it in mind to bring it to me to translate. (That never came to pass.) Given the extreme emphasis on the penis, I found it hard to believe that fellatio was not more common, yet the response by this group of women leads me to believe that it is rare; still, I hesitate to generalize about such an intimate subject. Instead, oral sex, or the possibility of it, does seem to be symbolically displaced—in time with regard to fellatio and by object with regard to cunnilingus. The former will be noted when we speak of

27. I have since been told informally (and not by a villager) that sheep are not used for intercourse, but that donkeys and dogs are.

mother-infant son relations, and the latter in the discussion of religious symbolism in the last chapter. Interestingly, they are projected to the beginning and end of life; this makes sense, however, for sex is primarily for the purpose of procreation and therefore genital, heterosexual intercourse is the normal and normative practice.

Conception-Contraception

One can learn much about theories of conception from ideas about and practices relating to contraception;[28] in fact, ideas about conception have been taken for granted and so have rarely been a focus of attention. In Turkey attitudes to contraception are ambivalent, since a woman's primary function in life is to bear children, especially sons. In any case, contraception will not be used in any form until after the first child, and normally not until after the birth of several children, including at least one son.

Today about one-quarter of the women who have borne several children, including a son, use an IUD; only one woman was taking birth control pills. A few men were using condoms, which, however, were not easy to obtain, were thought to be of low quality, and I believe were often used more than once, making their overall effectiveness minimal. The most common method of birth control is *geri çekme* (literally pulling back), that is, withdrawal.

Regardless of contraceptive practices, it is clear that conception does not follow each act of intercourse. The theory of procreation implies that the inability to conceive (or conceive a son) would be considered the man's fault. But that is not the case. Instead it is believed that there is something the matter with the woman, that her body is rejecting the seed (or the seed that would produce a male). Villagers give several reasons for this: (1) the ablution may not have been complete and impurities remaining in the womb may inhibit conception; (2) the woman may be anemic, the relevance of this to be taken up shortly; and (3) she may be barren. Her barrenness, like that of certain fields, is intrinsic; there is something wrong with her. Her insides are *bozulmuş* (tainted, ruined) or *berbat* (rotten, putrid), and barrenness is taken as a sign of

---

28. See Noonan 1986. Ashley-Montagu 1974 [1937] and Malinowski 1982 [1929] both state that in the groups they report on no contraception was practiced. Both came to the conclusion that this was a corollary to the natives' theory about procreation.

divine punishment. If a child is not produced within a reasonable amount of time, the man is free to divorce or take a second wife. Although polygyny is forbidden in modern Turkish law, it sometimes occurs in villages where traditions of the Şeriat (Islamic law) still operate. The system of beliefs implies that the marriage bond is less important than physiological paternity.[29]

Because of the meaning of paternity, a woman contemplating divorce or a widow contemplating remarriage must face leaving her children behind. If she is divorced, they are, according to village custom, the man's by right; if she is widowed, the children will stay with their dead father's parents or relatives. All these practices reinforce the belief that the child comes from the man, that he is the one who with God's help creates it. Any man capable of producing semen is believed capable of producing a child. However, with the gradual infiltration of modern Western medical beliefs, some people are beginning to learn that this is not always the case. One couple in the village, unable to have children, sought outside medical help and were told that the man was sterile. Their understanding of this, however, was filtered through the net of their own beliefs, for they told me he was unable to produce *canlı tohum* (live seed). At the same time, for obvious social reasons, this knowledge was not broadcast. The couple remained married and looked after the children of his dead brother, whose widow had married outside the village. Although the knowledge of male sterility is not widespread in the village, the notion of *canlı* vs. *ölü* (dead) seed has been integrated by some and is occasionally given as an additional reason that conception does not follow every act of intercourse; in other words, sometimes the seed is alive and sometimes it is not, just as not all wheat seed sprouts.

Let us assume that conception took place and the woman is pregnant. *Gebe kalmak* is usually translated as "to be pregnant," but this translation misses the flavor of the Turkish. *Kalmak* means "to stay or remain,

29. That physiological paternity is the important factor is also attested by the fact that to adopt a child legally, a man must be at least 40 and without a child of his own. The rationale for the late age is partly to give him time to produce a child, but also because it is a widespread belief that no man can care for another man's child. Villagers are not constrained by the legal codes of the city and people do care for other people's children; however, it is more like foster care than adoption. One woman gave a daughter to a childless sister; girls are basically interchangeable and in any case soon leave their natal home for marriage. Occasionally a female foster child is intended as the bride of a couple's son. I don't believe anyone would give away a son, for a son is a sign of virility, a token of God's favor, and a continuator of the line.

or to be left"; the verb "to be" (*olmak*) is rarely used in this context. *Gebe* is related to a root that implies "to swell." Thus *gebe kalmak* means to be left pregnant; that is, the seed remained and will swell up.

The discovery that women contribute essentially, and not just physical substance, to the formation of a child is related, I believe, to women's demands to control their own bodies in marriage, sexual activity, and pregnancy. In the village, on the contrary, a woman quickly learns that her body is at the disposal of others; she has little control over her marriage, sexual activity, or pregnancy. This was poignantly illustrated to me when I talked to a bride who was pregnant. I asked her if she was pleased. I expected an affirmative answer, especially since everyone had been concerned when she was still not pregnant after six months had passed. Instead she was listless and uninvolved. "It is *mecbur* [obligatory]; my husband and *kaynana* [mother-in-law] want it; I would have preferred to wait." She was a spectator to the event taking place inside of her; it had nothing to do with her or her desires. She was merely the ground upon which the desires of others took shape, the medium through which they were achieved. The woman's role in procreation is secondary; it begins only after the male has fulfilled the primary role of putting the seed in. The woman's role consists in nurturing the seed-child and bringing it forth.

Pregnancy

As the soil provides the medium in which a seed can grow but itself is not the seed, so by analogy does the rich, luxuriant (*gümrah*), and moist (*gönen, nemli*) climate of the womb provide the ground for the seed-child to grow. The word *gebe* is related etymologically to *gebermek*— which means to die, but actually refers to the swelling of an animal's body in death. The function of the woman is to swell up the fetus, and in so doing her body swells. As the soil passes nutrients to the plant, so the womb passes blood and other nutrients to the fetus by means of *meme* (breasts) in the womb (cf. Aristotle 1979: 241). This blood is not to be confused with menstrual blood; nor, from what I could gather, are the *meme* to be confused with either the placenta or the umbilical cord. All women were insistent that nutrient blood is clean, whereas menstrual blood is dirty; the source is the same, but it has two quite different valences and destinations. This contrasts with the ideas of certain Iranian women who believe, according to Good, that "the dirty blood of the menses is consumed by the fetus thus ridding the mother of her natural pollutants" (Good 1980: 150).[30] Women in the Turkish village were shocked by such a notion.

Pregnancy is known by the cessation of menses, but sometimes even this is not definitive. One woman of about 35 had not menstruated for more than five years, but she was not pregnant nor was she considered menopausal. On the other hand, an obviously pregnant woman was having blood drawn from her finger by the midwife to check for anemia. When the midwife could get no blood, one of the women present said to the pregnant woman, "You must be having your period!" When several other women laughed, she realized her mistake: that normally menstruation and pregnancy are mutually exclusive. (She also implied a belief that menstruation draws blood from the rest of the body.) Anemia is felt to be the cause of the inability to "conceive" as well as the cause of miscarriage; in village terms, anemia is referred to as kansız (without blood). Since an anemic woman, a woman without blood, clearly cannot nurture a child, the seed-fetus falls out. Düşük means aborted or miscarried and derives from the verb düşmek (to fall).

A woman who is labeled kansız or who has a miscarriage is not fulfilling her role, which is to nurture the fetus and to fill out its being. Such a state also reflects adversely on her husband. It is his job to provide her with food that in turn replenishes her blood; the fact that she is kansız implies that he is not feeding her enough.

Because of the severe health problems caused by inadequate diet and prenatal and neonatal care, the government has instituted a nationwide health system with a primary emphasis on mothers and children. Theoretically this project has been implemented in a majority of the provinces, but the actual care varies significantly, as I learned when I visited a number of such projects in several provinces.[31] In our village there was a midwife (ebe) trained and appointed by the government. Her function was to deliver babies and to educate villagers about health matters, especially in the area of procreation and child care. Nevertheless, her

30. This point was also confirmed by Erika Friedl in a presentation for the Colloquium on Conception and Birth, University of Chicago, April 2, 1984.

31. A new law passed after the military took control of the government may ameliorate this situation. The law requires that medical students, whose education is paid for by the government, must contribute three years of service in rural areas upon completion of their training.

scientific training seemed to be little more than a veneer, which quickly peeled away under the impact of more pervasive cultural notions. In her training she had heard the words for ova and ovaries (*yumurta* and *yumurtalık*), but she confused these with the vulva and the womb. The function of the ovaries, their relation to menstruation and to the scientific theory of conception, was unknown to her. She suggested that women eat foods rich in iron, for example *pekmez*, a kind of molasses made from cooked grapes. Because it is sweet, she assumed that jam (*recel*) would be a suitable substitute, yet jams are mostly sugar mixed with fruit and not all fruits contain iron. She also warned pregnant women to eat less salt and butter, both of which are used in great quantity in Turkish village cooking. Her advice was rarely followed. Most younger women who are pregnant live with the husband's family. Everyone eats together and the food is prepared for all. *Ne yapıyım?* (What can I do?), they say. On the other hand, if a woman craved a particular food, everything was done to give it to her, because it is the baby who is thought to crave it. The baby is not part of the woman but has an identity all its own; however, in this small way women can get treats like baklava or candy that they could not demand in their own right.[32]

Except among family members and close neighbors pregnancy passes unnoticed for a long time, not only because of the loose, baggy clothes women wear, which makes most women look pregnant all the time, but also because the ideal of health and beauty in women is fat. A round *göbek* (belly) is a desired quality in a woman; in belly dancing (*göbek atmak*, literally to throw the belly), it is a plump, not a flat, belly that is aesthetically pleasing. A plump woman also shows that she is well taken care of; the husband of a thin woman is accused of being stingy and ungenerous. A woman is a vessel that can be filled by a man's wealth, and the primary signs of wealth in village terms are food and children. Both are essential "to increase and multiply" the household; they are signs of prosperity and God's favor. A plump woman, especially a pregnant woman, is an emblem on which signs of male status, wealth, and generosity are emblazoned. In our own society a thin, well-groomed

32. There are, however, no zar cults, as attested in Egypt and North Africa (e.g. Boddy 1986, 1989), in which a similar dynamic is at work. These appear to be more institutionalized and are explained as a legitimate way for women to gain personal benefits; they need only claim they are possessed by someone or something else.

woman with a fur coat symbolizes the same thing; the signs are different but the message is identical (cf. Collier 1986). In this communication between men, the woman remains mute.

No more eloquent statement of woman's position could be made than
that of a young bride who remained speechless throughout her entire
pregnancy. This extreme and unusual case epitomized the cultural
norms. Her body had been taken over by someone else, and she had lost
the power to speak for it; perhaps she suddenly realized that she had
never had this power. Others speak for women. A woman does not announce her pregnancy or draw attention to it, for doing so would draw
attention to her genitals, which are shameful and unmentionable. Pregnancy bespeaks sexual activity, which is the prerogative of men to
initiate, as are words. Men control the times and places for both conversation and sexuality (social and sexual intercourse) in recognition
of their power to call things into being, to give form to substance. Because of this power, men are enjoined to "Eline, diline, beline sahıp
ol"—be master of your hand, your word, and your sperm.

Although men have been given the power to procreate, they cannot
know whether the child will be a boy or girl, and this becomes a matter
of speculation and some anxiety. The sex of a child is one of the things
that supposedly only God knows, along with the Hour (Day of Judgment), the times it will rain, what a man will earn, and the place of
one's death (Sura 31: 34). Since sex is divinely ordained, it would not
be surprising to find divinatory rites to learn the sex of an unborn child;
and indeed many such rites have been recorded from all parts of Turkey
and are part of a body of folklore tradition (cf. Acıpayamlı 1974; Örnek
1979). In our village, however, they seem to have all but died out in
recent times. The only generally held belief was that if the child was
positioned on the right side it would be male; if on the left side, female.
Sağ (right) also means healthy, as in the phrase *sağ olsun* (may you be
healthy), which is used as we use "thank you." *Sağ* is the side of *sevap*
(good works); *sol* (left) is the side of *günah* (sin).

When I was first in Ankara, a pamphlet peddled door-to-door by
some private organization proposed that certain foods eaten by the
pregnant woman might influence the baby's sex: white, bland, and
sweet foods such as milk, yoghurt, white cheese, chicken, and rice
would help produce a girl, but red and hearty foods such as meat, *salça*
(tomato paste), and *kızartma* (fried foods) would help produce a boy.

Although I did not hear villagers indicate that certain foods would influence the sex of a child, the gender-related classification of foods is the same.

The first stirrings in the womb are felt to mark the infusion of soul. In colloquial use soul is referred to by the same word as "life" (*can*) rather than "spirit" (*ruh*). The soul is believed to come from God, but there was divergent opinion about how. A few felt that souls pre-exist in *Cennet* (Paradise) and are sent down by an angel during pregnancy; others imply that God activates the soul dormant in seed. In either case, the soul of a boy comes/opens at 40 days,[33] that of a girl at 80 days. This notion of ensoulment has implications for policy relating to abortions.

The physical development of the two sexes in the womb is thought to proceed differentially, and this is proved by the evidence of miscarriage or abortion. If the aborted/miscarried material is well defined and has evidence of its parts, it is presumed to be male; if it is just a mass of stuff, like a piece of meat, it is presumed to be female. This, too, follows the gender logic we have been discussing.

There are a great number of miscarriages and abortions in the village, but it is very difficult to determine exactly how many of each. Even the midwife's records do not distinguish between miscarriage and abortion; her forms use the same word (*düşük*) for both. Since there is great emphasis on production of children, it seems surprising that women may wish to abort. However, among women who have had several children, or have been told that another pregnancy would be dangerous, or when an unmarried girl becomes pregnant, abortion is "normal." Women described some methods of abortion to me: *nişadır* (ammonium nitrate), a substance used by the *kalaycı* for tinning copper pots; aspirin taken on an empty stomach; knitting needles or bundles of burnt matches injected into the womb. This last method caused the death of a girl in a nearby village, but no woman in our village died from either abortion or birth while I was there.

During the time I was in Turkey, abortion was becoming a matter of official concern and policy (cf. Tezcan, Carpenter-Yaman, and Fişek 1980). According to Balcı (1980), abortion caused five times as many deaths as traffic accidents, and Turkey has one of the highest traffic fa-

---

33. This notion may also derive from Aristotle; however, Bourdieu (1977: 28) notes that it is the time that shoots from seed sown in the autumn first emerge from the soil.

tality rates in the world. Deaths due to abortion were also ten times as many as deaths from all other kinds of accidents; in sum, 25,000 women a year was considered a low estimate.

The rate of infant mortality is also high, exceeding that of women who die because of abortion; and although high infant mortality may correlate with lack of education (Timur 1978), lack of access to medical care is also a significant factor.[34] Most women during their childbearing years have experienced either a miscarriage or the death of a child in the first few years of life. Women of the older generation, namely those over 40, described their pregnancies in the following terms: "on tane oldu, beş tane dünya geldi, bes tane öbür dünya"—I had ten children, five came into the world, five are in the other world.

Birth

Birth must be understood in relation to the concept of *dünya* (world). Although we in the West also speak of birth as coming into the world, it is not consciously juxtaposed to the other world. For us this world is reality par excellence; for villagers the other world is not only a conscious and ever-present reality, but the more valued of the two. *Dünya* (this world) is conceptualized in terms of the female body—as seductress, seedbed, old hag, depending on what aspect it shows. The world is symbolically female, and females are identified with the physical world. To speak of one evokes images of the other; worldliness and bodiliness are symbolically associated and female. The beauty and fertility of either will wither, for physical, material qualities are prone to decay and corruption. Life in this world is brief, like life in the womb, and perishable, like the world itself.

Birth, then, is highly ambivalent. On the one hand, children are greatly desired and having children is the purpose of life, what woman was created for and her primary function; on the other hand, coming into the world is a kind of exile. In addition, since the means of coming into the world are the woman's genitals, birth is somewhat shameful.

34. *Hürriyet,* 6/28/81, claimed that of 1.5 million babies born, 150,000 died. See also *Briefing Paper for the UNFPA Basic Needs Mission in Turkey,* 1979. Rates of infant mortality in the area where I worked (95 per 1,000 in 1974; 93 per 1,000 in 1980; 99 per 1,000 in 1981), although high, were lower than the national average, perhaps because this area had been served by a rural medical program for about ten years. Despite these statistics, Turkey continues to have one of the highest rates of population increase in the world.

Both of these reasons are no doubt involved in the fact that birth is not marked and birthdays are forgotten. Instead, death days are remembered and commemorated. Death rather than Baptism, as in Christianity, is the means of the second and higher birth. Since the practices and beliefs surrounding death are intimately related to those of procreation and birth, any discussion of birth must be situated and understood in relation to death and the other world.

Doğum means birth and *doğurmak* means to give birth. *Doğmak* (to be born) is also used for the rising of the sun, and *doğu* is East. Expressed in all of these is a sense of origins—where do you issue from, where did you arise, where did you become manifest? The new Turkish word for nature (*doğa*) is meant to convey this, but it irritates some villagers and confounds some cherished categories. The word they use for nature is *tabiat*, which is derived from Arabic. According to Massignon, the word derives from something meaning "to imprint upon a thing, a seal. In the Koran it is used in a rather pejorative sense, a mark of God the Creator's contempt for His Creation, which He imprints with a seal of separation, a shadow . . . and the names which He gives to things are like a veil that both protects nature from His radiance and conceals Him" (1968: 315).

Nature is veiled, yet it is also a sign pointing to its Author and those who have faith are given the means to read it. Despite the incommensurability between God and His Creation, God has given man a soul and the ability to distinguish right from wrong; thus humans are not totally of nature. What villagers mean to convey by *tabiat*, I believe, is that the possibility of procreation emanates from God; it does not arise from nature. Although the physical, material aspects of life and bodiliness are identified with *dünya*, the essence of life came from elsewhere and is identified with the other world. Life is embodied spirit. Spirit comes from God but is passed by men via "seed," whereas women, by the nurture they give, give body to others and are thus more associated with bodiliness. They are the means through which essential spiritual being enters the physical world.

Coming into this world, the actual birth, is accomplished quietly and with little fuss (cf. Roper 1974: 56). Villagers do not generally anticipate difficulties with birth. "Bebek girdiği gibi kolay çıkar"—The baby will come out as easily as it went in! This expression also, of course, reinforces the notion that the baby has originally come from outside the women, namely from the man, from his seed.

Although Ipek, the government-appointed midwife, was required to visit all pregnant women to provide prenatal care, the kind of care she provided depended to a great extent on her personal likes and dislikes. If she felt there was a likelihood of difficulties from high blood pressure, anemia, a narrow pelvis, or a poorly positioned fetus, or if there was a history of difficult births, she might recommend that a woman go to the hospital; but her advice was not necessarily followed. Village women had three options for birth: to use Ipek, to go to the hospital, or to use the local village midwife, about whose activities Ipek was unaware even though both of them lived in the village. *Ebe* means midwife but is also the term for grandmother. It is an inappropriate term for the government-trained midwives, who are all young, often unmarried girls; it is, however, appropriate for the local village midwife, who is an older woman and a grandmother. She has a good record of delivering babies and claims never to have lost one. The government midwife keeps the official records of births and the method (or place) chosen. Her records, however, conceal the actual state of affairs, for those listed as having given birth by themselves were in fact assisted by the older village *ebe*. The statistics were relatively stable for the few years for which I could obtain information:

Date	Births	Method[35]
1979	16	8 DSP, 2 *ebe*, 6 kk
1980	19	7 DSP, 8 *ebe*, 4 kk
1981	18	6 DSP, 6 *ebe*, 6 kk
1982 (to June)	6	2 DSP, 2 *ebe*, 2 kk

If problems are anticipated, a woman may go to the hospital: either to the small rural hospital in Söğüt that serves the entire area or to the Büyük Doğum Evi in Ankara. Both of these options were used by village women, though most women considered hospital births undesirable because the genitals are opened to strange men. For some younger women, however, the longing to be modern overcame fears of defile-

35. DSP = dispensary/hospital; *ebe* = government midwife; kk = *kendi kendine*, which literally means "by herself" but in fact meant that the woman was assisted by the local village midwife. During 1979–80 there were several changes of government midwives and short periods in which there was no official midwife.

ment. If a woman can gain the support of her husband and *kaynana* (mother-in-law), she may go to the hospital.

As pregnancy can be used to obtain special attention and treats, so too, in theory, can a hospital birth be used in this way. It is a dramatic event that begins with the journey down the mountain to the capital city, a trip that takes over an hour. A close friend who did not get along with Ipek and hoped someday to move to the city with her husband decided to go to the hospital in Ankara for the birth of her first child. What began as an exciting journey into modernity ended with bitter disappointment. She had expected that educated doctors would treat women with more respect than they generally receive in the village, but her illusions were shattered. "We are all human, but they treated me as if I was not." She planned to write a letter of complaint to the director of the hospital, but after thinking about it finally gave up. "Who will listen to a village woman?"

During my first winter in Turkey, before I lived in the village, I did some participant observation at the Doğum Evi, the major maternity hospital in Ankara. I was appalled by the treatment village women received. Doctors and nurses seemed to consider them almost subhuman, like animals, unable to speak or think. Village women walked to the delivery table by themselves; they kept their upper clothes on and removed only their *şalvar.* Delivery tables were lined up in a row, and each woman could see and hear the others. It was humiliating, for their genitals were exposed to whoever came in. The women talked to each other, but the doctors and nurses communicated as little as possible with them; instead they talked and joked among themselves. An episeotomy was routine but anesthesia was not, not even for the stitching process. It was a gruesome sight to watch, with all the women screaming and thinking they were about to die or wanting to. Afterward they said the stitching-up was the most painful part of the entire birth. The hospital is often crowded, but even when there were empty rooms village women were placed in wards. Often two women shared a cot and two infants a crib.

In the village, birth occurs in the privacy of the woman's house—that is, in the home of her husband and his parents—and usually in the room where she lives and sleeps. Even if the couple is not living with the husband's parents, the woman may go to his parents' home for the birth. The son of one of my neighbors and his wife had moved to town;

but when he was called up for military service, his pregnant wife returned to his parents' home for the duration of the pregnancy and birth instead of staying in town with her own parents. She used the local village *ebe*, not the government one.

Birth is an affair of women; only the midwife and the mother-in-law are present. When labor is well under way, someone is discreetly dispatched to summon the *ebe*. Secrecy is due in part to shame, but is also a way to preserve some privacy. One day I was casually chatting with a group of women, one of whom was quite pregnant, and learned only a few hours later that she had given birth. She had simply excused herself, saying she felt ill (*hasta*).

One room is set aside for the birth. If it is winter, it will be the room with the *soba* (heater). Water is put on to boil, and other items are collected: a *leğen* (a large, low, round washtub, used normally for doing laundry), made of tinned copper or plastic; an *oturak* (a low stool), and some clean cloths. The stool is placed inside the *leğen*, and the woman sits on it with her legs extended so that she can press against the sides for support and grip the edges with her hands. If the woman is very large, a plastic sheet is spread on the floor with a *çarsaf* (sheet) on top and a few pillows to raise her.

The woman is allowed to walk around and to drink water. Ipek, the government midwife, advised the women to eat heartily at the onset of labor. Time is spent gossiping and joking in order to relax the woman. When it becomes necessary for her to push, she sits on the stool and uses the sides of the *leğen* to push against. She is supported in back by her mother-in-law while the midwife kneels in front. The talking and joking continue, and the midwife massages the abdomen and manipulates the fetus from the outside. She is not permitted to "go in" to manipulate the fetus or to perform an episeotomy, and thus there is no stitching. Ipek's kit, a gift from UNICEF, includes a plastic apron, a mask, a cloth in which plastic gloves are wrapped, powder to put inside the gloves, scissors, a clamp for the umbilical cord, drops for the eyes, a purifier for the water, and an injection to help detach the placenta if this does not happen within half an hour. The kit was filthy, and the apron and gloves were torn; nothing was sterile.

The older woman's methods were no different except that she had no kit. Perhaps that was a blessing! Since Ipek had had no eyedrops for months, and since the water is boiled for a long time, making the purifier superfluous, the only difference was the injection to expel the placenta. But drugs and needles are easily obtainable, and I suspect that the local *ebe* also used them on occasion.

If the baby was born covered in *yağ* (oil-like substance), the government midwife assumed the couple had been having intercourse late in pregnancy. In other words, she assumed that the *yağ* was stale semen, which is *cünüb* (ritually unclean) and *pis* (dirty). She expressed disgust about such births.

When the baby is out, it is normal for the woman to say "Kurtuldum" ("I am saved," also, "I have delivered"). This could be taken at face value: that is, as saying that she is saved from death, a possibility not to be taken lightly given the high rate of maternal mortality in the near past and in some areas in the present. Yet according to villagers, the most dangerous period is just beginning. Perhaps "Kurtuldum" also implies that she has validated herself in her husband's family by fulfilling the function for which she was created. If the child is a son, she has also saved the lineage, and in this way also she has saved herself because a woman who has borne a son is far less likely to be repudiated.

Afterbirth—Loğusalık

The placenta (*eş*) is supposed to be buried in the courtyard, i.e. within the house precincts; it is *günah* (sin) to feed it to the dogs, though this happens. The placenta is not a focus of ritual, and there is little concern about its destination. Nevertheless, the term *eş* is significant. Not only does it mean placenta, but it is also used to refer to spouse or sibling; basically it means partner. Singleness is abhorred and creates anxiety; ideally every person must be part of a pair as well as a partner. Once again we see the tension between likeness and difference. By duplication of similarity (pair) and by combination of difference (partner) the social order is created. The child in the womb has its *eş*; an only child must have its *eş*; if there are two girls and one boy, the boy must have an *eş*; and finally, when one is married, the spouse is *eş*.

My own singular position in the village was thus even more singular. Not only was I alone without a husband, but also I had only one child, and a daughter at that. I was continually entreated to marry in order to have a son. When I said I might consider marrying again but that I would not have another child, this made no sense. There is not much of a reason to marry except to have a child, and a child is the sign of being married.

A baby, whether a son or a daughter, whether a first child or the *eş* of one already living, is still a valuable object. All objects of value and beauty, that is of desirability, are covered in order not to arouse envy or attract the evil eye. In the case of food or inanimate objects, the action of the evil eye is indirect and rebounds on the person who possesses the object but does not share it; whereas in the case of women and babies, the action is direct and can cause harm to their persons. Several interesting points about the polysemy of "covering" come to light. The most striking point is that men are not covered, which indicates not only that they are self-contained and invulnerable, but also that they are the source of desire and generators of value, not objects of desire or value. Men can be harmed only through their women and children. The covering of babies and women points not only to their value/beauty, but also to the fact that their social exterior is somewhat inadequate, their personal boundaries more fluid and permeable. They are not self-contained and must be contained by covering.[36] Before a baby can be presented socially to the world it must be wrapped.

After a brief washing, the baby is completely swaddled (*kundak*). The baby's legs are held straight[37] and cloth is bound round them, then a sheet of plastic, then more cloth to keep the arms straight, up over the shoulder and head, and finally tied in front. The baby has become a neat portable bundle, but immobile. Mauss (1973), who first suggested a relationship between "techniques of the body" and culture, might make a connection between this swaddling and the ability of adult Turks to remain immobile for long periods of time. On top of the *kundak* a blue bead, sometimes accompanied by a gold piece, is attached to ward off the evil eye. Everyone was shocked at my description of how American babies are dressed, especially in the summertime, for villagers believe that a baby must be kept warm and well-wrapped. Because it is believed that most illnesses come from drafts, babies are totally covered and kept in an overheated room. As a result, many are often feverish. The remedy is not to remove clothes but to add more.

36. Antoun (1968: 674–75) suggests that covering is specifically meant to cover the child's genitals.

37. Mansur (1972: 119) says that *kundak* is for the purpose of making the legs straight. Sadly enough, many people develop dislocated hips because of the tight swaddling.

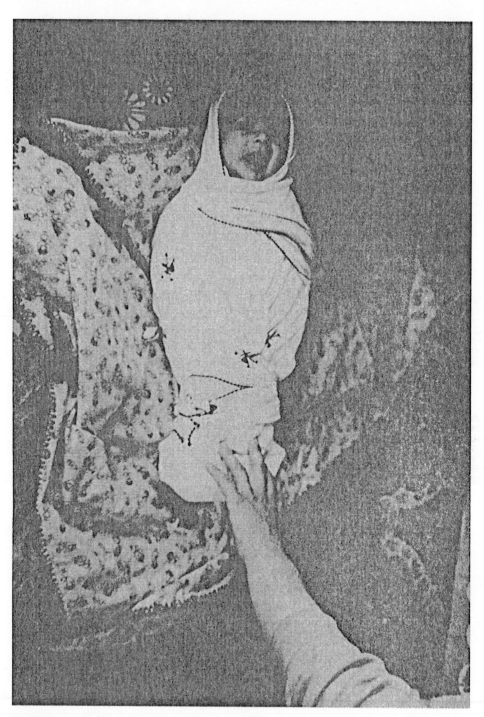

Swaddling

Covering thus has many meanings, but can perhaps best be understood as a kind of protective social membrane that keeps a person's own
substance from leaking away. At the same time, it keeps harmful if invisible forces (for example, the evil eye or drafts) from penetrating its
substance. Since babies, women, and dead people are covered, it implies
that they are neither self-contained nor invulnerable to outside influences. The covering of a baby's nakedness, openness, and vulnerability
by *kundak* also shows that it is spoken for, covered by the care of its
parents. This is reciprocated at death when children cover, speak for,
and protect the openness and vulnerability of their dead parents, when
their substance is flowing away. After death, the corpse is also washed
and wrapped just like *kundak*, with yards of white cloth (*kefen*), before
it is delivered into the other world.

This normal order of events may get confused if the child dies, but
the symbolic relation is illuminated. In this case, the *kundak* becomes
its *kefen* (shroud). An aborted or miscarried fetus has no *kefen* and is
buried in the courtyard (like the placenta); but if the child dies after
birth, even if it has not breathed, it is wrapped in *kefen-kundak* and buried in the *mezar* (cemetery).

If the child dies, it goes straight to heaven with no questions asked.
It is sinless, since sin does not begin to accumulate until puberty. A child
who dies can intercede on behalf of its parents upon their death. The
logic of the system would imply that it was a good thing to have at least
one dead child (cf. Farah 1984: 58), but when I suggested such a thing,
people pretended not to understand. This sentiment may not be conscious but may contribute to the nonchalance with which parents speak
of the death of a baby.

A woman who dies in childbirth or shortly after is also said to go
straight to heaven with no questions asked. Her sins are pardoned. This
might imply that giving birth is a sacred task, but this interpretation
has no echo in daily life. Giving birth is *mecbur* (obligatory); it is woman's role and function. Rather, I believe that the pardoning implies a
notion of sacrifice—the woman has made the supreme sacrifice in giving
her life. This interpretation is supported by the fact that the only other
adult who goes straight to heaven at death is the man who dies in battle.
However, an important difference must be noted. *Fedakar* (self-sacrifice)
is the esteemed virtue of motherhood and wifeliness. Women give their
lives for other specific physical people, whereas men give theirs for an

abstract ideal, whether nation or God. A man's sacrifice is called *kurban*, a concept Atatürk utilized to inspire his soldiers during the battle at Gallipoli. *Kurban* invariably evokes the story of Abraham (Ibrahim) and the almost-sacrifice of his son, to be discussed in Chapter Five, which is commemorated each year on the most holy day of the Muslim calendar, Kurban Bayramı. In that story, Abraham did not sacrifice himself for either his son or his God, but was willing to sacrifice his son. The message of the story has been that the proper object of love for a man is God, but the implication is that men must be willing to sacrifice others for their beliefs, principles, and ideals. In war, the "fathers" are willing to sacrifice their "sons" for their ideals and beliefs.[38] Although women should also love God, it is believed that they cannot fully abstract themselves from their immersion in and attachment to physical life, and therefore that their love of God is expressed through their devotion to their husbands and children.

In giving birth a woman faces death, not only during the birth itself but for 40 days after, a period known as *loğusalık*. "Loğusanın mezarı kirk gün açıktır"—the tomb of the *loğusa* (postpartum woman) is open for 40 days. The tomb is said to be open because the woman is more likely to die during this period; but also the womb is open and therefore open to evil influences and infections. The womb is the way to the tomb, and the tomb is the womb preceding the second birth into eternal life.

Intercourse is forbidden during *loğusalık*. Not only is the woman in danger, but she is a danger to her husband. The blood of childbirth and the blood that continues to flow afterward is comparable to menstrual blood, but its power to pollute is intensified. When a woman is most open (at childbirth and marriage), she must be most enclosed (cf. Hirschon 1978). Theoretically she should be in quarantine, and in both cases she is kept indoors for a certain period of time. Today most women generally do stay at home during this period, but friends are able to visit

---

38. This story, as in the case of Atatürk, is often evoked in times of war. During World War I it was the subject of many sermons and a poem by Wilfred Owen. Bob Dylan wrote a song on the same theme during the Vietnam War, and a statue commissioned for the Kent State incident depicted Abraham with his knife ready to kill his son. It was also explicitly the theme of the novel and film *Fail-Safe* (Burdick and Wheeler, 1962); the last chapter of the novel is entitled "The Sacrifice of Abraham." In order for the President of the United States to prove to the Russians that a U.S. bombing of Moscow was a mistake, that is, to show that he is upholding a gentleman's agreement, he decided to annihilate New York. When he is about to give the signal, he turns to his aide and recalls the story of Abraham.

shortly after the birth. If it is a first birth, the husband may be in the military, and so intercourse is generally out of the question. Indeed, it is thought good for a man to marry before his military service (at age 20), both as an anchor to keep him from straying and so that his wife can present him with a child on his return. One young man, the son of close neighbors, was away in the military when his wife gave birth to their first child, a son. A week or so after the birth, his mother and sister were at my house having tea with a group of women from the neighborhood. In the midst of our discussion about birth and babies, he suddenly appeared; the army had given him *izin* (permission) to return home for a brief visit. Such permission was apparently unusual and was cause for comment and amusement. Everyone joked that he was too impatient, not only to see the baby but also to have intercourse with his wife. His mother laughed and replied that the *kirkiçik* (40-day period) had passed, and rushed off with him. We knew that much less time had passed, but knew also that this was her way of legitimating what was bound to occur.

A violation of the 40-day period was far less shocking than that a husband should witness[39] and assist the birth, as many men in America are now doing, for no man should see a woman's genital area so exposed. And yet fathers in Turkey have much more involvement, if by that one means physical contact and time spent, with their babies and children than their American counterparts. Men in Turkey need and want children as much as women do; it is a sign that they are fully adult and is a matter of pride—at least in relation to the outside. Inside the house, their pride does not distance them from babies. Although I never saw a man change a baby's diaper, men were extremely affectionate and tender with babies, holding, kissing, and playing with them. Even teenage boys—siblings or not—affected no disdain for babies; they were obviously interested in them and cared about them, and babies were often left in their care for short periods. Grandfathers, perhaps even

39. For us "to witness" means "to see," pointing to the emphasis we place on empirical knowledge verified by sight. The villagers, by contrast, have a notion much more like the Biblical meaning whereby to witness is an affirmation of faith. In ancient Judaic practice men swore oaths by holding their testicles, which were thought to be, as for the villagers, the seat of procreative power, an idea that was itself a matter of belief or faith. The notion of witnessing is, in origin, intimately connected to ideas about male procreative power, that is, paternity. The words testicle, testimony, and testament are etymologically related, and thus it is not surprising that the testimony of women was discounted.

Roles get revised when grand parents die

Men stay in women's world

more than grandmothers, served routinely as babysitters, taking babies out to the street while they talked with friends or playing with them and watching them in the house while the women went about their chores. To a certain extent, older women become more like men in that they are freer to go about the village, and older men become more like women, staying about the house and performing female tasks of child care and even food preparation. Often during our women's lunch parties, which rotated from house to house in the neighborhood during the spring and fall periods when the men were off in the fields, the old man of the house would join the party and gossip with very little self-consciousness.

Traditionally in Islam the grandfather or father would whisper a prayer into the baby's ear immediately after birth and give it a name.[40] This seems to give symbolic expression to the notion that men have the power to call things into being; in addition, by naming a child, he recognizes it and allocates to it a place in the social world. Nevertheless, I must confess that I never saw or heard that this was done in our village. During pregnancy names are discussed, and sometimes there is no question. For example, a young couple living with the husband's mother and his other siblings had decided early on to name the child, if male, after the husband's dead father. They had not decided on a name for a girl, and fortunately it was a boy. Several other babies I knew went without names for a number of days or weeks while the parents vacillated, argued, and asked for everyone's opinion, including mine. Although it is considered customary to name a child after a relative (especially a grandparent, living or dead), this was not always done, and Başgöz[41] suggests that this practice is decreasing.

Babies must wait a few days for the breast, during which time they are fed warm sugar water. For the same period, the mother drinks nothing but soup or *hoşaf* (a sugary syrup in which dried fruit has been cooked), not tea. It is said these measures help the cord to fall off. The midriff is cleaned several times a day with lemon cologne, the normal antiseptic, and is wrapped in a clean cloth. On the third day the baby is given the breast and thereafter whenever it cries. Usually it is given

40. This recalls the story that the Virgin Mary conceived by means of the seminal word spoken in her ear. I do not know if there are Muslim versions of this story.
41. Ilhan Başgöz presented a talk on this topic, "The Name and Society: A Case Study of Personal Names in Turkey," at the University of Chicago in March 1983.

only one breast at each nursing, and it nurses only for a few minutes. When the baby does not suck properly it is jiggled. Nursing is not a quiet time for the communion between mother and child, as it is characterized in America by health manuals and practitioners. It is a feeding time; either the child must eat or, if it loses interest, the breast will be withdrawn. Babies are not burped after nursing, but are put down to sleep on their backs. Since babies are wrapped in *kundak* with their legs and arms straight, it would be dangerous for them to sleep on their stomachs. As a result of this practice, many people have heads that are flat in the back.

The baby sleeps in a *sallangaç* (a cradle made of cloth or of *kilim*, a kind of woven rug), which is suspended from the ceiling on ropes. A scarf is laid across to keep off flies, and a string is attached so that the woman can swing the cradle while she is sitting elsewhere.

The *loğusalık* period ends after 40 days. "Kirkiçik geçti" means that the 40 days have passed. Since this liminal period is considered the most dangerous for both mother and child, those who survive can then be reintegrated into society in what Van Gennep (1909) would describe as a ritual of reaggregation. This passage is effected by a ritual bath, a kind of baptism, in which the pollutions of profane birth are washed away, leaving them clean and transformed. After the bath, mother and child are free to go out. In practice, of course, they have bathed before that and may even have visited within the neighborhood.

At this bath, the woman will normally be accompanied by friends. If her mother can afford it, she may choose this time to bring the *beşik* (crib) to replace the *sallangaç*. Then the women will gather and dance and make a little *düğün*. *Düğün* is the word that ordinarily refers to wedding and is also used for circumcision (*sünnet*); it means basically festivity. At this festivity women dance as they do during a wedding. The *loğusalık* period ends after this celebration, and the mother resumes her normal tasks.

In the past, *loğusalık* was a luxury. Many women of the older generation said they had to get up and work both in the fields and at home soon after the birth, and gave this as a reason women age so quickly. My youthfulness for my age was always commented upon, and the interpretation was that I did not have to work so hard. Surely work is a contributing factor, but just as surely poor nutrition and too many pregnancies are more important causes.

People were also curious that at my age I was still in school. When I explained that I had first had a child and then went back to school, one man commented in tragicomic mode: "Here women just have children and then go to the cemetery." Although his wife was several years younger than I, she appeared to be twenty years older. When I left the village, I learned that she was pregnant with her ninth child. Age in the village seems to have more to do with the stage of life one is in than with chronology, and there are certain activities that are specific to each stage.

Women continue to have babies until their own children begin to marry and reproduce, and sometimes after. Although it is considered *ayıp* (shameful) and crude if a mother has a child at the same time as her daughter—or especially her daughter-in-law, who will be living in the house—some women do have children until well into their forties; and it was reported that one woman, now dead, had her last child at age 55. In other words, it may be true that some women "just have children and then go to the cemetery."

Child Care

Babies are nursed anywhere from one to three years. Women say girls are nursed for 18 months and boys for two years. Although boys are thought to develop more quickly in the womb, they take longer to mature once they are outside. The extra nursing is also intended to give them the strength they will need to endure military service. If a woman is unable to nurse, it is said that a curse (*nazar*) has been placed on her; the fault is not hers but is projected outward onto others.[42] In the recent past, if a woman was unable to nurse an infant, another woman would take over. She would become the baby's *süt anne* (milk mother), and by so doing she would establish kinship not only between herself and the child but between that child and her own children. This practice is still common if there is another woman in the same household who is nursing. With the introduction of formula and bottles a few women have

42. In commenting on folk healing practices, a Turkish psychologist says that "the general tendency is to project all that is internally undesirable and all responsibility onto the institutionalized external forces, there is little or no awareness of guilt associated with one's own impulses or responsibility as long as one complies with the rules and rituals of these forces. Certain atonement devices are also provided in daily religious ritual—daily prayers and worship and annual fasting and sacrifice" (Öztürk 1964: 361).

adopted this method. Bottle feeding is promoted in advertisements in magazines and on television as the "modern" method, yet its use in the village entails serious health risks owing to the water, the lack of sterilization, and careless thinning of the formula.

A few women lost their ability to nurse during the fast of Ramazan (see Chapter Five), which lasts from before the first light until after sunset every day for an entire month. Since Ramazan fell in August and July, respectively, while I was in the village, this meant that these women did not eat or drink anything on fast days from approximately 2:30 A.M. to 8:00 P.M., or about 18 hours. Although pregnant and nursing women are exempt from the fast, most of them kept it anyway; they claimed that their husbands had not given them *izin* (permission) to stop. To keep the fast is a Muslim duty and is thought to bring *sevap* (reward for good works); to abstain from eating and drinking even when one does not have to is thought to be even more valuable in the eyes of God. I tried to suggest that having a healthy baby is also *sevap*, but this idea made little progress.

Most women are able to nurse, and all desire to do so, since not only is breast milk considered the baby's most important food but nursing is an important aspect of woman's role and the primary symbol of femininity. Inside the womb the baby suckles blood; once outside it suckles milk. Woman's body is the continuous source of sustenance for the child. By depleting their own substance to substantiate a child, women establish *süt hakkı* (milk rights) to be supported and sustained by their grown children. It is a reciprocal feeding arrangement, a kind of old age security. Milk represents the closest physical tie, surpassing even that of blood since it constitutes siblingship even between children born of different mothers. The milk and blood bond can be characterized as primarily substantive, in the sense that milk and blood are nurturant, physical material. This bond characterizes relationships that are lateral (siblings) and present (nonreproductive), whereas the seed bond is essential, spiritual, lineal, and over time.

Nevertheless, life is lived in the present. Everyone said that the children are closer to the mother, not only because mother and child are together much of the time but also because children have been made from the physical substance of their mother's body. But because something is physically closer does not necessarily imply that it is the more valued. Physical closeness is applicable to *this* world. Thus we begin to discern some of the conflicts inherent in the ideology of procreation. These conflicts are played out on a grand scale, for a tension is created between commitments and orientations—that is, shall one be more attached to and committed to the physical world and earthly life or to the other world and eternal life? An orientation to this world, characterized by attachment to the physical and to women, is seen by many as Western and therefore associated with "modern" life; an orientation to the other world and things of the spirit is considered more Islamic and "traditional." This way of perceiving the issues (often identified with modernization theory) may be true, but it is important to realize that the symbols and meanings for the interpretation of this duality are internal to the system of beliefs. In any case, the tension is not easily resolved and the choice affects economic and political activities.

In this world, procreation is what life is all about; a child fulfills and encapsulates the meaning of life. Government efforts to reduce the rate of population growth and to encourage birth control have not been very successful despite the passage in 1965 of the Family Planning Law, which made access to information and devices more available. Efforts to discover the reasons for this have generally focused on the status of women, making correlations between their educational level, participation in the labor force, and fertility. But the results have been disappointing. Kandiyoti's conclusion that "the labor productivity of women has little direct impact on their status" (1977: 72) was negatively confirmed by Özbay: "women's participation in the labor force is associated with low status" (1982: 147). And although low educational level did correlate with high fertility, Timur concluded that the expansion of female education (a desirable goal) would "probably result solely in decreasing the explanatory power of this variable" (1978: 75).

Another study, part of a nine-country cross-cultural comparison, sought to assess the value of children to parents in terms of perceived benefits less perceived costs (Kağıtçıbaşı 1982: 152). To me this approach suffers from an excessively utilitarian view of humanity, one which, as Geertz says, "sees men as impelled by rational calculation of their consciously recognized advantage" (1973: 202). Kağıtçıbaşı herself notes: "an implicit decision-making model is used . . . and there is an underlying assumption that advantages and disadvantages of having children are weighed against each other" (ibid.). Those who follow this logic believe that the solution is to be found in shifting the balance between advantages and disadvantages and in finding alternatives for the values that children satisfy. That is a tall order.

Something continues to elude these researchers; I suggest it has to do with the way the problem is construed in the first place. Rather than turn away from reproduction in a search for solutions, the source of the problem may contain the solution. In these studies, "reproduction" is assumed to be a self-evident, natural, and biological process that is universal, and it is assumed to be primarily a problem of women. Such theoretical assumptions are not only ethnocentric but reductive; they efface all that is culturally distinctive. Instead, we must begin to investigate particular theories of coming-into-being, and what the roles of men and women (and perhaps others) are in the process of human coming-into-being.

In the correlation studies, "fertility" is another term that excludes the culturally salient meanings. In Turkey, the emphasis is not so much on nonspecific fertility as on producing a son; and the importance of sons has been noted both as one of the most tenacious cultural values impeding the growth of a more egalitarian society and as an obstacle to lowering fertility. This emphasis is expressed in a number of ways. The word çocuk, for example, means both child and boy. When asked how many children they have, people in the village generally gave the number of boys. Girls in some important sense do not count; they are concealed linguistically as their bodies are concealed beneath their baggy clothes, behind their veils, and within the house. Çocuk functions like the English "man"; it is both generic and gender-specific, and it is often very difficult to determine which meaning is implied, a problem that confounds those who deal with historical or census documents.

Although the production of a child is synonymous with marriage, child is synonymous with son; therefore, women must continue to produce children until a son is born. Villagers say you must have a son; otherwise "Who will take care of you in your old age?" Although young men are increasingly leaving the village to find work and a life in the city, returning to the village only on holidays, the cultural norm persists. Another reason given is that sons are important for helping with the farm work, yet this too seems like a rationalization. Not only does it take a long time to raise a child (and a fair number die), but also there are more efficient means of obtaining labor at peak periods. In addition, girls and women have always done a great deal of the agricultural work in rural Turkey. There is nothing that physically prevents women from doing certain kinds of work; rather the division of labor is itself part of the symbolic logic involved in the cultural construction of gender.

The focus in the cross-cultural study on the consciously expressed value of sons, whether in the form of providing labor and social security or raising woman's status in her husband's home, is myopic. Not only does it miss the forest for the trees, but it ignores the invisible but all-important root of the matter, the importance of seed. Since it is only men who are thought capable of transmitting the inextinguishable life in seed, it is necessary to produce a son in order that the line continue.

Although a son is absolutely necessary to continue the family, children in general are a source of delight and the family's primary amusement. When asked what was necessary for a happy life, everyone answered "children." One woman told the following story to illustrate her view:

There were two couples, one with a child and one childless. The couple with a child were always laughing. The other couple could not understand what made them so happy, and asked for their secret. "We have a golden ball, and whenever we play with it we are happy." The childless couple went out and bought a golden ball and tossed it back and forth. But it did not make them laugh and after a while they grew weary. They returned to the other couple to learn what they were doing wrong. "Our child is our golden ball. It is the *tat* [flavor, taste] of life like *meyva* [fruit]."

Children are both distracting and a distraction; without a child life is considered dull and tasteless. Although everyone would like to have more land, more goods, and so on, such things are not considered essential in the way that children are. They are essential not only for a complete life, but also to complete the socialization of their parents. A person without a child has not fulfilled the purpose for which he or she was created, and thus is still unfinished. Such a person is considered neither responsible nor fully adult.[43]

Babies are the most immature persons. They are like toys; they are picked up, fondled, and transferred from person to person throughout the day. When a child fusses, rarely do people assume it might be tired

43. After the military intervention on September 12, 1980, a portrait of each of the generals was presented on television and the first things noted of each man were their marital status and how many children they had. In Pakistan, before Benazir Bhutto became prime minister, she got married and had a child; otherwise, I do not think she would have been acceptable in that position.

and in need of sleep. Instead, it is picked up, jiggled, and fussed over. When exhausted, children just fall asleep wherever they are. One feverish and fussy child was dragged off to a wedding and fell asleep amidst the crowd of women, the dancing, and the noise. Children are expected to conform to the mother's activities and not vice versa.

Children, it is said, do not yet have reason and therefore cannot be reasoned with. Adults rarely tried to offer children rational arguments for or against certain behaviors. Undesirable behaviors were called *ayıp* (shameful), but the child was not really held responsible; in fact, what is undesirable seemed to depend not on the actions themselves but on the context. Sometimes and in some places certain actions were more annoying than at others. Discipline was relatively arbitrary, as were rewards. When children did something that annoyed their parents, they were yelled at or given a light slap but were rarely beaten. Sometimes they were threatened by the midwife's needle (injection), with which they were all familiar (cf. Mansur 1972: 122).

Children were indulged and spoiled. They were given anything they saw and asked for, not just in order to pacify them but because it was believed to be sinful and greedy to withhold something from a child. Children cannot be held responsible for making unreasonable demands; things they should not have ought to be hidden, "covered." Thus people delivering food or other items to a neighbor covered them so that all the children in the street would not ask for a share.

Girls are spoiled even more than boys, not because they are seen as more valuable than boys but precisely because they are seen as less valuable. Girls are merely guests for a brief time in their parents' home; they are *el* (foreign, outsiders), as they will also be in their husband's house. It is by way of compensation for their status that they are spoiled more when they are small. The differences between small girls and boys were quite pronounced when they came to visit me. The girls scrambled all over and got into everything, investigating all the contents of my house, demanding this and that, shrieking and laughing and tumbling over each other. Their behavior, of course, exhibits and reproduces the notions that women are not self-contained and lack control. Boys were much more composed and sedate. They came shyly, often bearing gifts of flowers, stones, and fossils, and sat quietly, asking questions, drawing pictures, and doing very little fighting. At first I thought that the girls might feel more comfortable around me because I am a woman, but

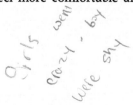

the same behavior was observable in village homes. As children, boys are much more constrained by the notions of respect and deference to elders; at the same time, this demeanor is an expression of their worth.

One day a group of neighbors gathered near the log that serves as the meeting, sitting, and gossiping place for the neighborhood as well as the place where everyone waits in the evening for the cows to return. On this occasion, the son of one neighbor and the daughter of another were playing together. Fatma, my closest neighbor, was charmed by the boy and jokingly asked the father if she could buy him. "I'll give you 100,000 TL" (about $1,000), she said. "You don't buy boys," said the father; "they are more valuable." The words for taking and giving girls in marriage are those normally used for buying (*almak*) and selling (*satmak*). Fatma's jest inverted the normal usage, for the terms are applicable only to daughters, never to sons. Although villagers insist that the marriage arrangement is not buying and selling as in the market, girls are valuables transacted by others in a process they do not control. This example merely illustrates that a son's value is inestimable.

Boys learn this very early. A boy is constantly told he is *erkek* (male), and his penis is the focus of much attention. Often when boys' diapers were changed their penises were kissed and stroked. And when boys were fully clothed grandparents and parents fondled their genitals and repeated: "You are male, you are male." A baby boy's sister once put a scarf over his head and said "Kız oldu" (you've become a girl). Their mother got very angry and shouted "Erkek, erkek!" (he is male).

At another house when I was visiting, a small boy was running around the house nude. The grandfather poked his head in the window, pointed to the child's penis, and asked: "What can men do that women can't?" "Go to the mosque" was the right answer. In other words, the connection between maleness, concentrated in the penis, and Islam was made quite explicit, as if the penis is the ticket of admission to the Islamic brotherhood. The implication is that girls' lack of a penis is reason for their exclusion, that they can never be full members.

Female genitals are ignored. Even when small girls touched themselves in what appeared to be masturbatory gestures, they were not told to stop; such behavior was simply ignored. To talk of it would make it exist, would call attention to it. As noted earlier, most women appeared not to know that girls or women could masturbate.

Blowing on the penis is also the way a boy is encouraged to urinate, as I learned when I saw Gül take her 8-month-old son to the doorway, pull down his pants, blow on his penis, and tell him to urinate. He complied immediately. Her method of toilet training also consisted of holding the child over the toilet each morning and evening until he defecated and urinated. Her daughter had apparently been able to sleep through the night without wetting by the time she was his age; but boys are believed to be slower than girls to mature. Most people do not follow such a regime; instead, they wait until the child is old enough to indicate when it is ready to go. Mothers try to encourage this by showing disgust and saying *pis* (dirty) whenever the child defecates in its pants. The smell is referred to and the child is shamed in front of others.

Smell plays an important part in Turkish social life. Smells can be characterized along two axes, foul-pleasant and impersonal-personal. In general, foul smells seem to be organic, that is, the result of some kind of organic transformation. Impersonal foul odors are those arising from the putrefaction of garbage, from animal wastes, and from cooking, especially fish and garlic, whereas personal foul odors are the result of metabolic processes—feces, urine, sweat, and menstrual blood. All foul odors seem to point to the susceptibility of physical matter to corruption and decay, which is a primary attribute of this world (*dünya*). The other world (*öbür dünya*) not surprisingly is a complete reversal of this one; it is characterized as clean and sweet-smelling, and by the absence of both foul smells and metabolic processes. In the other world there is food and drink of an ambrosial sort, but as more than one villager said, "There is no shit, no piss, and no sweat." There is sex but no issue, no child. Sex in the other world is recreational; sex in this world is for the purpose of procreation, which is ultimately what this world is all about.

All foul odors are considered *pis* (dirty), and the notion of "dirt as matter out of place" (Douglas 1966: 35) is apposite here. Bodily exudates should be removed from the body as quickly as possible, and in the case of feces and urine deposited in the proper place. But personal odors in general are an intimate part of the self, and like glances appear to be an aspect of the person that extends beyond his or her bodily boundaries: an invisible but personal substance that moves and can permeate others. They should be perceived only by members of the family; the act of smelling another person is an intimate act and should be performed only by intimates. Smells in social space should be fresh, pleasing, and impersonal. No doubt this is the reason that lemon cologne is the first thing offered to guests and fellow travelers, for example on a bus. It is a sign of hospitality, but at the same time disguises offensive odors and neutralizes personal ones. We shall have occasion to speak of the significance of smell in other contexts; here I wish to comment on the lesson the child is supposed to learn.

By defecating in his diaper he confused the boundary between inside and outside his body, for what should have either remained inside the body or been deposited away from it has been retained with it. At the same time, by intruding the foul smell into the sitting room, he confused the boundary between personal and social space and transgressed against the guest. Breathing in foul odors is *günah* (sinful), and he, as the cause of it, is *ayıp* (shameful).

Substances that transgress bodily boundaries are marked either by sanctions or by ritual celebration. When the first tooth comes in, another boundary is broken and this is sometimes a cause for celebration. Women gather in the home of the baby, dance, and have a party, for which a special dish, *diş bulguru* (tooth bulgur), composed of cooked chopped wheat kernels and chick-peas, is prepared. No one was able to tell me what the dish represented, only that it was customary. They made an association between cooked food (which is soft) and the wish that the child's teeth might come in softly, easily. Yet although this bulgur is cooked, it is not very soft; there are many softer foods that one could substitute. Its significance rests, I suggest, not on its consistency but on its content. It resembles *aşure*, a dish made of grains, nuts, and dried fruits that commemorates the month of Muharrem but also, according to And (1981: 9), symbolizes the food taken aboard Noah's Ark to sustain people during the Flood. Other informants told me *aşure* might be related to *asermek*, a compound of *as* (cooked food) and *ermek* (to ripen or to mature) that refers to the cravings women have during pregnancy and also has the meaning of spiritual awakening. The connection made was that the child was maturing in the womb, that the life had stirred (the soul opened) and was craving potent food. I do not know what the addition of chick-peas (*nohut*) may signify, but wheat as seed is the quintessential symbol of male fertility and potency[44] and

44. My own connection was to the teeth sown like wheat in Greek legend; the Myrmidons sprouted as men and were warriors.

wheat as bread is the quintessential food, the staff of life. Both sons and bread are needed to sustain life and to continue the family. The cutting of the first tooth is another stage in the process of maturing, and perhaps the dish is offered with the wish that the child will have food and children to sustain him. At this stage of life, the wish is offered with wheat that is chopped and cooked; at weddings, the same wish is offered but the wheat is thrown whole and dry.

Sometimes the *diş bulguru* is merely distributed to the neighbors; sometimes there is a party, as there was when the imam's wife celebrated the first tooth of her second baby, a boy. I went with my neighbor, Nuriye, who took a porcelain plate and a headscarf as gifts for the baby and mother. When we arrived, there were already a number of women assembled and dancing to tape music. The *diş bulguru* was served, and after a time we were served tea and two types of cakes. The first child, a daughter, was noticeably jealous, not only because of the gifts and the party in her brother's honor, but also because he still got the breast. The coming of teeth does not put an end to nursing.

During the time when a child is nursed, it is also learning to walk and talk. In one case the breast was used as an incentive to walk: "Kalk, em" (get up and nurse), the mother called from across the room, baring her breast. A child who is walking follows its mother around, pulls at her *şalvar* demanding the breast (*meme*), and climbs all over her to get it. Watching this reminded me of Çatal Hüyük, a prehistoric site in central Turkey where figures of huge women often with a child perched at the breast have been taken as evidence of a female fertility cult that existed 8,000 years ago.[45] Witnessing such a scene I felt it had never died out.

Toward the end of the second year, a mother may decide that she has had enough and that it is time to wean the child. This happens abruptly. People say the child is separated from the mother, using the same word as for divorce (*ayırmak*). Weaning is as sudden and as much of a shock. The child demanding the breast will find to its surprise that the breast has changed. One woman put *salça* (salty red tomato paste) on her nipple; another, paint. In each case the child was furious, screamed, and hit the mother, but she did not relent. The child who confronted *salça*

45. For discussions of the theories and the evidence, see Mellaart (1965) and Gimbutas (1982).

in place of milk refused for several weeks to eat any white foods—no milk, cheese, yoghurt, or white soup.

Boys and girls are dressed similarly in pants or pajamas, jerseys and sweaters, and they are allowed to play together. They have the run of the house and of the *mahalle* (neighborhood); indeed, they are the only ones allowed to run. Exuberantly they run into all the nooks and crannies of the village. Their unrestrained movement contrasts sharply with that of adults, in whom any sign of hurrying is considered unseemly and arouses curiosity. In order to avoid questions and preserve privacy, people go about their daily life at a measured pace. A man's evenness of pace and composed exterior is a sign of his self-containment; a woman's movement reflects on her husband or father. Ideally women should be sedentary and enclosed in the house, but in practice this is not always possible. A woman may be forced to hurry at her husband's command.

The forms of movement are important in the village and can be interpreted in relation to conceptions of different personal/social boundaries. Men, for example, are thought to be self-contained and self-motivated. Women are neither, but are socially contained and motivated. Children are not contained or motivated in any way; their personal and social boundaries are diffuse. As they accompany either their mother or father, siblings, or neighbors about their respective activities, they learn the boundaries of the known world; the social geography is imprinted. In this apprenticeship, children embody the structures of the world (Bourdieu 1977: 89). Indeed, "the 'book' from which the children learn their vision of the world is read with the body" (ibid.: 90).

The village itself is situated within a cosmological geography, since everyone knows the direction to Mecca. Mecca, like an invisible sun, seems to create a kind of psychological tropism, a turning toward the source of their identity. These orientations connect villagers, almost unconsciously, to the other world, yet they are also part of the lived, taken-for-granted world, as are more mundane orientations and boundaries.

Physical space becomes social space; children become socialized by walking the paces and going through the motions. And yet the space is more than merely social, since its meanings extend beyond the known physical and social world. Some areas are out of bounds, as I discovered when I accompanied several small children and two 11-year-old boys outside the village. We had intended to go only to the steep, shaly hill that they used for sliding down (on buttocks or feet) and where they had found some fossils and figurines. From there, however, we saw a fountain and went there to refresh ourselves. In the distance far below, we could see an orchard that was reputed to have superior apples. I had been longing for a walk, and the two boys assured me they knew what to do if we should meet the fierce dogs that guard the flocks and are taught to attack intruders. In my innocence, before I was attacked by one, I believed them. So we set off. The apples were the best; there was a stream nearby in which the children played. About 3:30 P.M. I began to get nervous about the shepherds returning with the flocks and the dogs, so we left. The parents of the children were very angry with me, not only because of the dogs, but chiefly because we might have met a *yabancı* (an outsider), who, finding me "unprotected," would have taken advantage of me. Because we had entered the *yaban* (wild, outside) area we, and especially I, had overstepped the proper boundaries, and in so doing had exposed ourselves to danger.

It was not just that we were in the wrong place, but also that wandering (*gezmek*) itself is frowned upon. Women and children do go outside the village to their gardens, or to gather wood or fruit, but only on organized, socially approved expeditions with a specific purpose. Women are not allowed to wander about. Children can wander around the village, but men are the only legitimate wanderers outside the village.[46]

By the time school starts, at age seven, children know the village area. Parents do not accompany children to school on the first day; they consider it off limits to them. Instead, children accompany older brothers or sisters or neighbors. They must wear school uniforms, which consist of black smocks with white collars; the collars are often made of plastic and detachable. Uniforms can be interpreted as a symbol of democratization, so that in school, at least, all children are equal; or they could be interpreted as an effort on the part of the government to in-

46. It is not only in the village that such a classification of movement exists. I encountered similar attitudes to wandering even among highly educated middle-class urban Turks. Women ideally should be at home or, if they must go out, should be accompanied. The doorman (*kapıcı*) in a modern apartment building does many small errands, and often husbands will do the shopping. In Ankara, the capital city, as in the village, I was told "çok geziyorsun"—you are wandering around too much! Such an attitude was more common toward grown women than toward certain groups of teen-agers, namely those of the urban, educated middle class.

culcate a uniform identity, to cast all children into the same mold. Whatever they may symbolize, the requirement of uniforms imposes a hardship on many village families, especially those with many children; and the resulting inequality shows very obviously. Some children have new and well-fitting uniforms; others are in patched, faded, ill-fitting castoffs.

The teachers have yet another view of school uniforms. They seem to think of them as a symbol of elitism, the badge of an educated class. Once after school, the children had removed their uniforms and were helping transfer a load of coal into the storage room bucket by bucket. It was a cheerful scene and one of the few cooperative efforts I witnessed. When I started to take a photograph, the teachers became very angry. "It would be very bad for Americans to see the children without their uniforms." When I explained that most American children do not wear uniforms to school, they were incredulous. The fact that the children were working was also considered *ayıp* (shameful). Children do, of course, learn simple tasks by watching and helping, but they are rarely given any responsibilities.

Before and during elementary school children are freer than they ever will be again. Neither classes nor play are segregated by sex; school provides the only place and time that girls and boys get to know each other. This mingling is permitted because children are morally neutral, if not quite socially neuter. The almost asexual existence of early childhood begins to change during the elementary school years. Children do not become sexual persons until puberty, but before that they are initiated into a gendered world.

Transition to Gender

Sometime between the ages of seven and twelve, that is during primary school and before the production of semen, boys must be circumcised. Whether boys perceive circumcision as a prerequisite for the production of semen I do not know, but it seems highly likely. Villagers say *sünnet* (circumcision) is performed for reasons of cleanliness, that is, before *pislik* (dirtiness, but here meaning seminal discharge) occurs. Cleanliness is not meant only in the hygienic sense, for *pis* (dirty) and *temiz* (clean) imply moral qualities as well. *Temizlik Islam dininin temellidir*—cleanliness is the foundation of Islam. Male sexual fluids, like women's blood, are polluting not only to members of the other sex but also to the self. If semen accumulates under the foreskin, it is polluting for the man because he has retained what should be gotten rid of. In addition, it is thought to cause an offensive odor. The excision of the foreskin renders a man invulnerable and removes this vestige of weakness.

If cleanliness were the only reason for *sünnet,* there is nothing to prevent its being performed in infancy, but it is not. A friend told me of a baby who was born with a narrow sheath covering his penis, which caused difficulty in urination. The parents were advised to have *sünnet* done immediately, but preferred to have the urethral passage painfully enlarged. The relatively late age for circumcision would seem to indicate a desire to have boys consciously experience this ordeal; it is the first test of manliness (Erdentuğ 1959: 40) and a matter of pride. Pride and masculinity are focused on the penis.

A high percentage of the drawings boys made at my house included some reference to *sünnet* or the *sünnetçi* (the man who performs it). In the discussions that followed, it was clear that *sünnet* had left an indelible impression. Research on this subject (Cansever 1965; Öztürk 1963, 1973) suggests that a boy experiences *sünnet* as an act of aggression in which he is the submissive victim. Öztürk (1964) thinks this experience forms one of the psychological poles, perhaps the most basic, of the character of Turkish men, who, as adults, must combine the seemingly contradictory tendencies of passivity/dependence and aggression/independence (cf. also Kağıtçıbaşı 1977; Dundes, Leach, Özkök 1972). At this age, however, submissiveness is mandated. The boy has come under the knife, not of the father, but of a father substitute. Several of the boys made a reference to the story of Abraham, a story that is also associated with circumcision in the Bible. Circumcision is a sign engraved on the flesh of the covenant between God and Abraham and from him to all *men*[47] who believe and submit. Submission to the cutting of the foreskin may be seen as submission to the power of God and therefore analogous to the sacrifice story. In Islam, *sünnet* is also the prerequisite for membership in the Muslim brotherhood (cf. Mansur 1972: 124); thus the relationship between power, religion, and sexuality is poignantly incised in the mind.

47. For a similar analysis of the meanings of circumcision in rabbinic Judaism, see Eilberg-Schwartz 1990.

Sünnet is an affair of men; women are not present. The *sünnetçi* is brought from outside and is normally a barber. Girls and women are not allowed to have their hair cut after puberty, and certainly not by a barber. Villagers were shocked to learn that women in the city go to beauty salons where men see, as well as cut, their hair. Although the relationship between hair and sexuality is not established by the *sünnet* ritual, the ritual does sustain it.

In some villages and in the city *sünnet* is an occasion for a big celebration called a *düğün*; the same word is used for a wedding, and the two events are comparable in the Turkish worldview, evoking a phrase used only on these occasions, *mürüvvet görmek*—to see the good day of the child. *Mürüvvet* means munificence or generosity, but in this case seems to imply something like reproductive wealth.[48] The good day portends the fulfillment of what children were created for, namely to continue the procreation of the family. Both days celebrate a socially defined potential. Boys are dressed up in white clothes with red ribbons, like a bride. Like a bride, but unveiled and openly exposed, they are paraded around on the backs of donkeys or in cars decorated with red and white flowers and ribbons.

In both events, circumcision and weddings, a part of the self is relinquished or sacrificed—the foreskin and the hymen—and blood is shed. But here the similarity ends. After circumcision the red ribbons are removed, as is the last vestige of weakness or "femininity." The boys are placed on large beds, lavishly decorated, where they receive guests and gifts. The bed on which their manhood is displayed is also, in marriage, the arena in which it will be tested and acknowledged. The excision of the foreskin makes a boy invulnerable to pollution either from his own semen or from women. Self-containment and invulnerability are the pride of men, and the ideal of the person is expressed in imagery such as a rock or a fortress. A well-educated city Turk at the breakup of a serious romantic involvement confided, "I am not hurt, nothing can hurt me, I'm invulnerable." Would anyone be able to break through such defenses? A woman, by her nature, is not self-contained and cannot attain the ideal. A woman's bodily boundaries are broken by the ex-

---

48. I have also been told that it literally means manliness, but I have yet to find that meaning in any dictionary. Meeker (personal communication) tells me that the villagers seem to have preserved the classical meaning of the Arabic word *muruwwa*, manly. For further discussion see Meeker 1976: 252–53.

periences of budding breasts, menstruation, first coitus, childbirth, lactation, all of which contravene the ideal of self-containment. It is, however, the genital area that is the means of her pollution, not only because of menstruation, to which we shall turn shortly, but also because of sexual intercourse, which is redeemed only by marriage. Her transformation into a woman and simultaneous initiation into sexuality are, however, dependent on a man, her husband. Boys' transformation occurs with the aid of and in the company of men. Above the duality of sex stands the generative, unpolluted community of men. The *sünnet* ritual makes the man symbolically invulnerable; the woman's initiation demonstrates her vulnerability.

As *sünnet* marks the transition of a boy into a gendered world, of which marriage is the fulfillment, so I believe there is an event that marks the transition to a gendered world for a girl, namely "covering." The headscarf is forbidden in school, but many girls begin to wear it outside of school; and in any case it is mandatory in village custom at the end of primary school, when girls are about twelve. "Covering" does not coincide with menarche, but is the social recognition (Van Gennep 1960: 65ff) of its imminence.

The two events, *sünnet* and "covering," are differentially marked, and their contrast points up more clearly the differences between the sexes. *Sünnet* is a special day that is celebrated and remembered, whereas no girl can remember when she first donned the scarf; her covering is a gradual process. No doubt this is a strong reason it has been ignored in this context. More importantly, male sexuality is revealed by the removal of a covering, whereas female sexuality is hidden by covering![49] It is also said that God "covers" sins, and this may further reinforce a feeling of shame. A girl learns that "the female body is an obscenity that must be carefully hidden" (Saadawi 1980: 46). A female's genitals, unlike the male's, are not a source of pride, but a reminder of her shame and as such unmentionable. Because of this, the focus of attention on female sexuality is displaced from the genitals to the hair,[50] the displacement made more obvious by the fact that pubic hair is removed.

---

49. This is reminiscent of Christian beliefs: "A man ought not to cover his head for he is the image and glory of God; but woman is the glory of man. For man was not made from woman but woman from man. Neither was man created for woman, but woman for man." Corinthians 11:7–9.

50. Leach (1958), following Berg (1951), argued that hair represented phallic sexuality, that its symbolic manipulation was related to psychosexual development, and that

Like flowers of the field, a young girl's hair grows freely, representing the rampant fecundity, beauty, and seductiveness of the world as well as the entanglements by which men are ensnared. Around the time of menarche, when a girl's sexuality ripens, it must be enclosed; it is not free for the plucking. The hair and the girl must be domesticated. The headscarf binds and covers her hair and symbolically binds her sexuality, which is henceforth under the mantle of her father and brothers until conveyed to her husband at marriage.

The meanings of the scarf become more apparent in considering the contradictions involved if a girl wants to continue school. Our village is very unusual because it has a middle school, and so a girl seeking further schooling need not even leave the village; however, few girls are enrolled. Since the headscarf is forbidden in school,[51] a girl in middle school flouts village ideas about what is proper female behavior. In this case, being *açık* (open, uncovered) has a double meaning: her head will be uncovered, and thus open to the eyes of boys; it will also be open to knowledge. She is supposed to be occupied with handwork, not headwork. The following example, discussed in greater detail elsewhere (Delaney 1987, 1989), may be instructive.

The daughter of my next door neighbor was the brightest student in her class throughout primary school, but she was not going to be sent to middle school. Her father, Ahmet, had only completed third grade and was one of the poorest men in the village. He had two children still in primary school and felt he could not sustain the additional expense, which includes not just books, supplies, and uniforms but also, in primary school, coal money for heating. He had not been informed that in middle school the coal money, which is the largest expense, is paid by the government.

Ayşe's work at home was not really necessary, since one of her older sisters was still at home. It was distressing to contemplate such a waste of talent and curiosity, and I decided against conventional anthropo-

---

uality, that its symbolic manipulation was related to psychosexual development, and that it was often deployed for religious purposes (cf. Obeyesekere 1981). Hallpike (1969) criticized the psychosexual interpretation and suggested that hair practices represented a person's relation to society. Taking something from both, I suggest that in the Turkish case, at least, hair has sexual (not only phallic), social, and religious significance.

51. This is a result of the modernizing, Westernizing policies initiated by Atatürk after the declaration of the Republic in 1923. Today the headscarf is a highly charged political issue, with a growing number of urban women demanding the right to wear it. (Cf. Olson 1985 and Mandel 1989 for a discussion of this practice among Turks in Europe.)

Primary school children

logical practice to interfere. A friend of Ahmet's who worked as the *hademe* (custodian) of the school had already tried to convince him to send Ayşe without success. Practical arguments that she could become a teacher or midwife, and therefore be a support in his old age, had not worked. He was not going to barter her future.

Ahmet, though poor and uneducated, was one of the most intelligent, thoughtful, and open-minded men in the village. He felt that poverty and hard work had improved his ability to think; and he had plenty of time to think, since he worked as a *çoban* (shepherd), wandering the mountains each day with a flock of sheep. He recognized the arbitrariness of fate. Since one can count on nothing, the practical reasons were not sufficient for him to transgress custom. I argued in reply that a good mind is a gift from God, and that perhaps it would be sinful to squander God's gifts even if we do not understand why they were given. He agreed, and had appreciated the level of the discussion. That afternoon,

Middle school class

three weeks after school had started, Ayşe was sent off and received even without a uniform. She had two friends there who were delighted to have another girl. The class was composed of the three girls and seven boys. At the end of the first semester, Ayşe was at the top of her class and received an honor certificate.

The comments of some neighbors are instructive. "She is such a huge girl and her breasts are already showing." "She is *açık* [open] now and it will bring trouble." The other two girls had not yet matured as much as Ayşe, but all three were in violation of village norms. Their fathers were accused by some of being Communists, a charge that puzzled me at first because there was nothing Communist about them. But I soon came to see the charge as a clear example of sexual politics. The designation "Communist" had, in this instance, little to do with what the girls were being taught. It had to do with the headscarf!

Villagers think that Communists hold both land and women in common. (The Communist is assumed to be male!) This state of affairs is anathema to villagers because it would confuse both the source of the produce—whether seed or seed-child—and the right to it. Removing the headscarf is symbolically equivalent to removing the boundaries that separate women; they become like common land. Or, in a metaphor more appropriate to the sexual politics involved here, they become like prostitutes. Fathers who willfully permitted their teen-age daughters to be bareheaded (açık) therefore not only were thought to be Communists, but were considered to be sending their daughters into prostitution. Not everyone agreed and a few people were pleased that the girls were going to school, but no others were sent that year.

Ironically, the girls in middle school, whose heads were filled with history, literature, and math, had little time to be thinking of boys and sex; rather, it was those sitting at home working on their çeyiz (trousseau) whose thoughts and conversations gravitated to that topic. Dr. Gengis of the rural health station was of the opinion that the strict segregation of the sexes during this period intensified rather than diffused the preoccupation with sex. "Paradoxically, sexual segregation heightens the sexual dimension of any heterosexual interaction" (Mernissi 1975: 83). If so, it is clearly here that the system contradicts itself, for the consequence of segregation produces results exactly the opposite of those intended.

Sex is politics as well as education and religion. To make a statement, such as sending a girl to school, implies certain attitudes and orientations with regard to the others. Analytically these institutions can be separated, but in the village and in everyday life they are inextricably interwoven.

Whether Ayşe would be able to continue to the *lise* (lycée or high school) was at that time impossible to predict.[52] More importantly, even

---

52. By the time she was ready to go to high school, a married sister had moved to Ambarlı. She and her husband, who was the çaycı (tea maker) in a municipal office, had two small children and were already pressed for space, but were willing to take Ayşe in. Ayşe finished high school but was unable to go on to college. She returned to the village, married in the fall of 1988, and a year later gave birth to a daughter.

if she decided to become a teacher or an *ebe*, it is government policy not to assign teachers or midwives to their own villages for fear they will be subjected to the traditional authority structures. This is another reason villagers see no point in educating daughters. They cannot imagine sending them off into the world unprotected and without cover; it would mean willfully consigning them to *gurbet* (exile), and no parents would willingly do that to their child. Daughters sometimes do leave the village to marry; but the husband is invariably another villager living in the city, and thus the vital connection and protective cover are maintained.

Puberty

The covering of girls and the *sünnet* of boys signify the entrance into a gendered world; however, they are not fully sexual beings until puberty, nor are they sinful. Sin begins to accumulate with the onset of puberty, described as the production of semen (white) in boys and menstruation (red) in girls. After puberty, one is held accountable for one's sins. The attainment of reason—that is, the ability to distinguish right from wrong—coincides with the attainment of puberty and thus is intimately related to the attainment of adult sexuality. Consequently, sin lies in the improper use of sexuality and the lack of understanding about the function and meaning of these substances.

The actual event of physical puberty is not ritually remarked. From what I could gather, menarche occurs somewhere between the ages of twelve and sixteen, though in some cases as late as eighteen. The most common terms for menstruation are *adet* (custom or habit), which stresses its habitual character, and *aybaşı* (literally the beginning or head of the moon-month); but the meaning of these terms is not specific, and they are used in a variety of contexts having nothing to do with menstruation.

Since menstruation is unmentionable,[53] many girls do not know about it until it happens. Although I cannot say with certainty that this is true throughout Turkey or more generally in the Muslim world, the

---

53. It is not unmentionable only in the village. When I applied for my research permit, I had to submit a brief summary of the topics of my research and included menstruation. A male professor friend in Ankara advised that I omit that because some of the unmarried men processing the application might not even know what I was referring to! That, of course, may have been a way of saying that the topic was taboo.

few published sources appear to confirm that it is. For example, Saadawi, an Egyptian physician, laments that the "ignorance about the
body and its functions in girls and women is considered a sign of honor
and purity" (1980: 45). She related her shock at menarche; thinking
there was something terribly wrong with her, she took to her bed for
several days before confiding in her mother. The response of Saadawi's
mother led her "to understand that in me there was something degrad-
ing which appeared regularly in the form of this impure blood, and that
it was something to be ashamed of, to hide from others" (ibid.). Especially is it to be hidden from men, including one's father and brothers,
but older sisters do not necessarily share information with their younger
sisters. It is not a topic of conversation in mixed-sex groups; whether
men speak about it among themselves I do not know. My knowledge of
men's attitudes about menstruation come from a few private conversations, but more generally from elliptical remarks. Women, however,
once the threshold to womanhood has been crossed, talk quite openly
about "blood and babies" (see Good 1980 for an account of Iranian
women's beliefs).

Village women believe, and men confirm, that menstruation was
given to women because of Eve's act of disobedience in *Cennet* (Garden/
Paradise). The susceptibility to the persuasions of Satan that led her to
eat the forbidden fruit is a sign of her moral weakness, and this is why
women must be under the cover of men. But there were more serious
consequences.

Her transgression against the command of God is responsible for
bringing *pislik* (dirtiness) into the world, notably the creaturely functions of defecation, urination, and sweating, and in the case of women,
menstruation, which signals their closer identification with carnal existence. Blood, almost a universal symbol of life, becomes in this worldview also a symbol of mortality; for the primary opposition is not
between life and death, but between earthly existence and that in the
other world.

As earthly life is bounded by birth and death; the possibility of this
life is bounded by menarche and menopause. In other words, earthly
existence is intimately associated with women's bodiliness. Menstruation as an index of fertility opens the way for life, but at the same time
represents the messy flux or mortal flow (Delaney 1988) that is its inherent characteristic. Menstruation, by means of menstrual taboos, be-

comes the focus for the expression of the incommensurability between this world and the other world. An examination of these taboos also deepens our understanding of the differences between men and women.

Most easily comprehended are those directly related to the practice of Islam. During the menstrual period a woman may not touch the Qur'an, enter the mosque, or keep the fast of Ramazan. To touch the sacred Book or to enter the sacred precinct while menstruating would introduce an element of the profane where it does not belong; it would besmirch the spiritual domain, especially during the sacred month of Ramazan, when one's mind and body should be devoted to God and concentrated on the other world. Although menstruation is listed along with other exemptions from keeping the fast, there is a great difference that is often overlooked. Menstruation by itself makes the fast *bozulmuş* (ruined), and thus fasting would bring no spiritual reward. During Ramazan, menstruating women did eat and drink, but did so secretly. Occasionally my house became a kind of "menstrual hut" comparable to such institutions known to exist in some societies; since I was not keeping the fast, menstruating women could come and eat or have tea with me. The belief that a menstruating woman can ruin a sacred ritual applies also to the Hajj (Pilgrimage) to Mecca, where a menstruating woman may not enter the sacred precinct or perform any of the rituals.

There are other taboos that do not relate specifically to religious ritual but highlight the notion of creativity/generativity, which is a primary attribute of God. Intercourse, considered to be the act of procreating, is forbidden during menstruation. "They question thee (O Muhammed) concerning menstruation. Say: It is an illness, so let women alone at such times and go not unto them till they are cleansed" (Sura 2: 222). This is a directive given to men and tells them how to view women. Menstruation is an illness, a reminder of woman's constitutional infirmity. Menstrual blood, like other bodily exudates, is unclean, as the colloquial terms for menstruation illustrate: *kirli* (soiled, blemished, canonically unclean) or *lekeli* (spotted, stained, dishonored). It is unclean because it is believed to be saturated with impurities accumulated during the course of the month. Since the seed carries the spiritual, generative essence relating men to God, and since the act of procreation is the earthly/human equivalent of Creation, clearly intercourse during menstruation would constitute a most flagrant mixing of the two domains. Menstrual blood, in its negative aspect symbolizing corruption and decay, would impede the creative and essentially spiritual process of conception. This creative act must be performed in a clean and pure environment made so by a ritual ablution. An *aptes* must be performed after menstruation in order "cemi bedeni bütünce pak yapmak"—to make one's earthly body totally clean and holy.

The period of incubation of seed (pregnancy) is a precarious time when the new seed of life is taking root. A woman who is menstruating should not approach one who is pregnant. That menstrual blood is impregnated with impurities is evidenced by its noxious odor, which, when released into the air, has the power to penetrate bodily boundaries and bring about a miscarriage or deform the fetus. The first 40 days of gestation are analogous to the first 40 days after birth; precautions against the deleterious effects of menstrual blood are taken at both times.

This logic, never entirely explicit, is transferred to breadmaking, which, in the village imagination, is analogous to the process of procreation. Unlike cooking, which is a daily repetition, bread is reproduced. In order for the bread to "increase and multiply," *maya* (yeast, leaven, but also essence, root, origin) from the previous batch must be introjected into the inert mixture of flour and water, whence it incubates overnight. The *maya* is the live germ transmitted from batch to batch as seed from generation to generation; thus is bread self-perpetuated. Although breadmaking is not a sacred activity, the creative, engendering process is.[54] The rising of dough is a mysterious and creative process similar to pregnancy, and it is feared that the powerful impurities in menstrual blood may inhibit the process. Menstruating women are thus not permitted to make bread.[55]

Although menstruation signals a woman's fertility and thus is a precondition for procreation, it is not prerequisite for marriage. A number of women told me that they had been married before menarche. The custom of *beşik kertme* (cradle engagement) also occasionally obtains. Thus, it is not true in our village that menarche "represents the earliest point in the life cycle at which bargaining over rights to a girl's fertility

54. The analogy between breadmaking and the divine creative process is also contained in the Bible in the parables about leaven; see Luke 13:18–21; Matthew 13:31–33.

55. For an interesting parallel see Lawrence 1988. Ott (1979) makes an analogy between cheese-making and procreation among the Basques, but does not discuss the relation of menstruation to the process.

becomes critical" (Paige and Paige 1981: 79). The meanings of gender and marriage strategies are constructed not from universal physiological facts, but from the ways these facts are construed within a particular theory of procreation. Unfortunately notions of procreation are rarely the focus of investigation, but a few sources confirm that this particular theory is fairly widespread in the Muslim circum-Mediterranean area (cf. Boddy 1986; Bouhdiba 1985; Mernissi 1975; Saadawi 1980).

Physical puberty for boys is attained with the first seminal emission. This is said to be caused by dreams of women who at the moment of intercourse run away and the boys ejaculate. These dreams are referred to as *şeytan kaçırdı* (the devil made it leak out), but the devil in this case is a woman. They are also known as *kayadan atlamak*—to jump from a rock. This may adequately describe the sensation, but also encodes the notion of something going out from a rock, which, as noted, is a symbol of male containment and permanence. In any case, these occurrences are felt to be brought about by external agency; they are not by nature uncontrollable, like women's menstrual periods. It is the essence of manhood to be able to control the times and places when ejaculation occurs, and the purpose of adolescence is to bring sexual substance under control.[56] Adolescence for boys is recognized as a time of turmoil; they are referred to as *delikanlı* (crazybloods); the blood boiling in them is clearly an allusion to the welling up of sexual energy. At the same time, sexual activity of any kind is forbidden. Pubescent girls and boys before marriage are kept strictly apart; this applies even to brothers and sisters outside the home. Masturbation is forbidden and is *günah* (sinful). Boys are told their brains and spinal cords will dry up, implying that semen comes from the head, as in ancient Greek belief.[57] Some may resort to animals or homosexuality, and a few of the older boys may experience the forbidden pleasures of the *genelev* (general house, brothel). Although I have no supporting evidence, I do not believe any of these practices are common. But the consequence of the sanctions is

56. Antoun says that men are able to control their sexuality because of reason; they are intermediate beings of Creation, that is, between the angels and animals. Although "man" was used in the generic sense, Antoun noted that "it must be clear from all that has been said in this essay . . . that women are closer to the animalistic end of the continuum than men and as such are less capable of exerting reason and belief to overcome lust" (1968: 691). See also Eilberg-Schwartz 1990.

57. Meeker confirms this belief for the Turkish group he studied (notes, personal communication). See also Onians 1988 [1951], Bouhdiba 1985, and Eliade 1971.

that sex is perceived as something dirty and forbidden, and that women come to be thought of as sexual objects.[58] As with many objects, a woman has more value when she is new and unused, a virgin whom no other man has touched (cf. Saadawi 1980: 77).

Although boys say they would like to have social relationships and intimacy with girls, they also say they would not respect such a girl and would not have her as a wife. For if a girl is willing to talk or be intimate with one boy, clearly she would be willing to do so with other boys (cf. Mansur 1972: 154). The very act of participating in such a relationship proves she is indiscriminate and untrustworthy. It is a system in contradiction with itself; for boys by their beliefs prevent themselves from having what they say they want, and girls by accepting the customary constraints help to perpetuate their own inferior status. Yet the penalties are very high for girls who challenge the system: such a girl may forfeit her chances for marriage, or even her life. Thus most women comply with and enforce rules of seclusion.

The difference between the sexes is most marked at this time. Boys spend a great deal of time and thought on their appearance, strutting about in open shirts and tight-fitting pants in what seemed to me an exaggerated attempt to attract girls' attention. I also wondered if the pants were not cut too tight in the crotch, for one often sees men and boys walking down the street with their hands on their genitals. They walk about exhibiting their sexuality; their bodies are a matter of pride. Girls, by contrast, are covered in layers of baggy clothes and several headscarves, and enclosed in the "stone veil" (Bouhdiba 1985: 36) of the house. They are not permitted to be concerned with or pay any attention to their bodies; any attempt to do so is punished and ridiculed. The use of makeup is frequently associated with prostitution, at least on the surface. City women, or foreigners, who wear short-sleeved and open-necked blouses, are considered çiplak (naked).

Because there are few mirrors in the village, people do not spend time looking at themselves; indeed, many could not at first recognize themselves in the photographs I took of them. They could recognize

58. Mernissi says something similar about Moroccan society: "The rural Moroccan male is brought, because of the restrictions on heterosexual encounters, to perceive women solely in terms of sexual need; both inside and outside of marriage, the woman is merely a more suitable way to satisfy sexual needs than animals or other males" (1975: 33). She also recognizes that men would prefer women; nevertheless, the point that women are viewed primarily as sexual objects is, I believe, accurate.

others but not themselves. My experience in the village gave me a new perspective on all the time, energy, and money that adolescent girls (and women) in the United States spend on their appearance, an expenditure that seems to increase rather than ease their feelings of insecurity about their looks and their bodies. At the same time, it made me aware that regardless of whether women conceal or reveal their bodies, they are being defined by them in a way that men are not.

Boys gather in groups and play ball in the cleared space in the center of the village. Girls also get together, but usually inside someone's house for tea and handwork. A few girls in the lower *mahalle* (neighborhood) got together to play volleyball, but their games were hidden and their clothes a hindrance. Occasionally, they have a tea party outdoors. Girls are continually employed; boys are allowed much free time. Although they occasionally help their fathers in the fields or with machinery, more often they are idle.

Nevertheless, in order to marry, a boy must work. Weddings are expensive, and he is expected to contribute to the expenses. A boy is considered ready to marry once he has experienced sexual dreams and ejaculation, not before; physical puberty is in his case a necessary though not sufficient condition for marriage. Yet, given the entire discussion about procreation, can seminal production really be considered merely physical? Or is it more that the creative spark has leapt into flame, the dormant seed sprung to life?

Knowledge of the body is always culturally mediated; indeed what the body is and what it means are not self-evident. The corpus of knowledge about procreation has created gendered beings. From seed to seed and field to field, these beings are now capable of reproducing themselves. The next chapter will discuss the ways the theory of procreation enters into strategies of marriage and is symbolized in the wedding ritual.

TWO

Marriage Practices and Wedding Ritual

> Only Allah is one, all else was created in pairs so as to receive instruction.

Singleness is an attribute of God, not of creatures. A single lifestyle is not viable in the village, and marriage is all but obligatory.[1] In most anthropological analyses of marriage, it is simply assumed that one of its major functions is the legitimate reproduction of persons. Little attempt has been made to understand how a particular theory of procreation is related to particular marriage practices. The biological (universal) function of marriage is assumed, and the focus is directed to its social functions, the implication being that these are separate and separable. By contrast, my effort in this chapter will be to integrate the two functions. I shall follow a cue given by Devisch: "The nature of bodiliness or more precisely the cultural symbolic shaping of bodiliness in a given culture is at the heart of an internal understanding of the socio-cultural patterning of the life cycle events" (1981: 53). I would qualify his statement and speak not of bodiliness in general, but of how the cultural understanding of both male and female bodies illuminates the life cycle event of marriage.

In the first part of this chapter I show how the seed-field (*tohum-tarla*) theory of procreation also provides implicitly a theory of marriage strategies. In the second part I shall describe the wedding ceremony, which,

---

1. There were two people (a man and a woman) in the village beyond the normal age of marriage who were not married and had never been married. They were considered to be a little bit strange in the head. The man lived in a separate room attached to his parents' house, and used this room as an informal gathering place for some of the younger men. The woman also lived at home, but like all other unmarried women was socially mute and invisible. I have already noted the singularity of my own position in the village.

as the most important social event in the life of the village as well as of the families and individuals involved, expresses the meaning of marriage and utilizes the symbols of procreation.

Marriage Strategy and Implementation

Middle Eastern–Mediterranean marriage tends to be characterized by endogamy, a preference for marrying within the group. This preference seems to confound the notions of alliance, exchange, and reciprocity that have informed anthropological reasoning about marriage and what it is supposed to accomplish. These ideas derive from the belief that "in the course of history savage people have clearly and constantly been faced with the simple and brutal choice powerfully expressed by Tylor, 'between marrying-out and being killed out'" (Lévi-Strauss 1969: 43). Besides the presumption of a Hobbesian state of nature, Lévi-Strauss, and Tylor before him, ignored the fact that Middle Eastern peoples not only marry in, but are most often killed within the group.

The introverted character of Middle Eastern–Mediterranean marriage, exuding as it does a scent of incest, may partly explain the relative reluctance of anthropologists to stick their noses into it. Those who have ventured into this area have typically relied on the received tradition of anthropological explanations, with results that are far from satisfactory. The focus of the discussion has centered almost entirely on patrilateral parallel cousin marriage, that is, on marriage between the children of two brothers, conventionally referred to as father's brother's daughter marriage (FBD).[2] The bias reflected in this ascription excludes not only women's point of view but even the point of view of men with daughters, and in so doing misplaces the emphasis, or at least seriously distorts the picture. Father's brother's son marriage (FBS) would more accurately reflect the desire, expressed by all villagers, of keeping daughters within the group. Since excluding either side of the equation may lead to ignoring certain kinds of information that might contribute to a more satisfactory explanation of this practice in particular and of endogamy in general, I shall use "FBS-FBD" henceforth.

Conventional anthropological explanations have been utilitarian in

2. Throughout this text the following conventional abbreviations will be used to indicate kin relations: M = mother; F = father; B = brother; Z = sister; S = son; D = daughter; H = husband; W = wife.

character, that is, in terms of economic or political advantages thought to accrue from such marriages. Although FBS-FBD marriage may be the most striking type to an outsider, it is statistically the least common among a wide range of marriages that could be considered endogamous, including those with fellow villagers. Nevertheless, it may provide an important clue to explaining the general preference for endogamy.

Strictly speaking, "endogamy" refers to a marriage system in which there is a rule forbidding marriage outside the group (Pitt-Rivers 1977: 162). In the Middle East, however, there is no such rule. Instead there is a preference that "inclines them to choose those who are closest and best known and who already share the collective honour of the patriline" (ibid.: 165). Antoun has said something similar: "Marriage within the patrilineal group is not only marriage to the closest in blood and therefore the 'best' (Gulick 1955: 127), it is also the guarantee of loyalty, ethical behavior, of modesty and thereby of the honor of the group" (1968: 693).

Although the focus of both of these theorists remains on the patrilineal relations, it is important to note the emphasis given to honor. In other words, regardless of, or in addition to, whatever economic or political gains might be obtained from such marriages, honor is seen to be a crucial factor in marriage strategy. "From the moment that the notion of honour is attached to female purity, kinship loses its basis of reciprocity and becomes political . . . a competition in which the winners are those who keep their daughters and take the women of other groups in addition" (Pitt-Rivers 1977: 166). Male honor is threatened by women. Specifically, a man's honor is a function of the purity of the women in his family: his mother, his sister, his daughter. Since he cannot marry these women, "it follows that the best, or least bad of women is the one who is sprung from the men of the lineage, the patrilateral parallel cousin" (Bourdieu 1977: 44).[3] Clearly the honor code or the

3. Meeker (1976: 406ff) suggests that Arab men prefer to marry the FBD so that a man's father and uncle can help in the control of his wife. Turkish men, he says, prefer to marry a more distant woman so as to avoid such interference, and he correlates this with different patterns of the defense of honor. An Arab woman's brother is the one who would defend or avenge her transgressions against honor, whereas in Turkey it would be the woman's husband and his father. The difference may have something to do with the salience of the patrilineage and whether women continue to belong to it after marriage, a topic to be addressed in Chapter Three. In the area where I worked, the *sülale* (patriline) had very little social significance and woman's membership in it was very ambiguous. Since our village practiced village endogamy, all marriages were "close" and about a

honor/shame complex is one expression of the extreme concern for paternity; in other words, it is a social code of values and behavior that is derived from the specific theory of procreation I have been discussing. I shall argue, therefore, that the preference for endogamous marriage is intimately related to the seed-field theory of procreation.

The popular view that Middle Eastern–Mediterranean marriage represents a desire to keep land in the family may have been nearer the mark than the other explanations. The mistake has been to interpret this explanation too literally. It is not that women inherit land,[4] but rather that women *are* land—not earthly fields, but human fields. Both are sources of sustenance for the perpetuation of the family group. To give a daughter to a stranger or an outsider would be equivalent to giving away a field; it would diminish the livelihood and honor of the group. Both fields and daughters are tended, and the fruits of this labor are to be kept within the group. Endogamy ensures this outcome, and patrilateral parallel cousin marriage is the most perfect kind of endogamy.

The theory of procreation in which the man gives the seed-child and the woman is the field that nurtures it helps us to understand Middle Eastern marriage practices. A marriage between patrilateral parallel cousins is an attempt neither to alienate the female land nor to have an alien (*el*) as a mother of children. The seed and the field have both come from the same source. In Bourdieu's terms, "it is a marriage most per-

---

quarter were between first cousins, matrilateral as well as patrilateral. My experience also suggests that marriage preferences may have quite a lot to do with whom one speaks to: to fathers of sons or fathers of daughters, as well as to husbands or wives. Regardless of the differences between Turks and Arabs, the primary concern is the purity of the woman and consequently her ability to guarantee that the children are from the man's seed.

4. In most Islamic countries, despite the Qur'anic rule and secular legal reforms, women in rural areas did not and do not inherit land. Even if a woman should inherit land, her share is half that of her brother and she can usually be persuaded to sell it to him. If she did take the land, her brother would normally work it and give her a share. But if all women inherited land, a boy's family could demand a bride who stood to inherit the same amount as his sister would or as his cousin would. Land doesn't usually "fall" until the death of the father, and that is generally long after the young couple is married, by which time the fortunes of all could have changed dramatically. Even if brothers divide the patrimony with their sisters, the brother giving a daughter will stand to lose some of his land to his brother's side at the expense of his own sons. Finally, as Keyser points out, "retention of the patrimony is an economic argument. It assures the advantage of maximizing economic gain on the part of the interacting parties. If this were true, then presumably anyone who met the desired economic criteria would do, not only the FBD" (1974: 294). For information about women's legal status in Turkey, see Toprak 1981: 52–54 and Erder 1985, Part Two.

fectly consistent with the mythico-ritual representation of the sexual division of labor" (1977: 44).

As Pitt-Rivers, Antoun, and others have noted, men (but surely women also) prefer to keep daughters as close as possible, since sons typically stay with the father and within the family group. Partners who are *haram* (forbidden) in marriage are listed in the Qur'an and include grandparents, parents, parents' siblings, and *süt* (milk) siblings. The Qur'an does not specify whether intercourse with those who are *haram* is also forbidden, except that illicit sex (*zina*), namely intercourse outside of marriage, is a sin, but this makes the notion of incest very ambiguous. The Turkish dictionaries are unhelpful: the newly coined phrase *akrabayla zina* (adultery or fornication with a relative) leaves it unclear whether the sinful act is the transgression against the marriage bond or the choice of sex partner. Similarly, the definition of "incest" in the new English-Turkish dictionary, *yakın akraba arasında cinsi münasebet* (sexual relations between relatives), makes no sense in a village where relatives marry.

The importance of keeping a daughter within the patrilineage is perhaps more important in nomadic societies, for then the girl would move with the group (cf. Abu-Lughod 1986). And within the patriline it need not be marriage with the patrilateral parallel cousin, but could also be with FBSS, FFBS, or the grandfather's brothers or the male offspring of the grandfather, that is, a father's brother by a different wife. In village society, however, the goal of keeping a daughter close can be attained by a number of other endogamous choices. Marriage with any of the first cousins is marriage within the first circle of closest relatives, but marriage with more distant kin as well as with fellow villagers satisfies, albeit in varying degrees, the same practical as well as symbolic demands, namely to keep the seeds and fields of the group circulating within and for the group.

Although patrilateral parallel cousin marriages may be ideal, the difference between this form and any of the others noted above is one of degree, not kind; for all can be considered endogamous, and all follow the same logic in an ever-widening circle of inclusion. Thus I cannot agree with Bourdieu, who makes an extreme division between patrilateral parallel cousin marriage and all others, relegating these last "to the class of ordinary marriages, generally arranged by women, within the area of practical kinship or practical relationships, . . . which have no other function, apart from biological reproduction, than the re-production of those social relationships which make them possible" (1977: 53).

Bourdieu's strict division between "ideal" patrilateral parallel cousin marriages and "ordinary" marriages makes sense for societies in which patrilineages have more social salience. In the village where I worked, however, the *sülale* (patriline) is simply a conceptual model for constru-ing relationship; it does not constitute a circumscribed group of people on the ground. In this context, patrilateral parallel cousin marriage is the epitome of a more general tendency toward endogamy, a tendency that Bourdieu's theory does not explain. In addition, the marital rela-tion is always formally arranged by men, even though women make the informal negotiations and maintain the relations thereafter. The fathers of the couple may or may not have much to do with each other after the marriage, an observation that undermines theories that explain mar-riage strategies primarily in terms of economic or political motivations.

At the village level in Turkey economic and political considerations surely enter into marriage strategies, but I do not think these motiva-tions are primary. Admittedly, Turkey was under martial law during the time I was there, and thus there was very little opportunity to observe conventional political activity. The economic picture is clearer. Except for the brideprice, which is standardized in the village, and the girl's trousseau, also fairly standard, no property is transferred at marriage. The boy's side cannot expect any economic benefit from the marriage other than the girl's labor, which any healthy girl can provide. The girl's father wants his daughter to be well provided for, and would not give her to a family that was more economically disadvantaged than his own, but this is not a consideration from the boy's point of view; in fact, on several occasions a boy from one of the wealthier families married a girl from one of the poorest. However, no matter how well off the groom's father may be, the couple's fortune will change dramatically upon his death. There are no wills; he cannot leave his property to the person of his choice, nor does it fall solely to the widow. The division of property is traditional and based on Muslim law; the specific proportions are known to all. A widow receives a share along with the sons (and pos-sibly daughters), one of whom will take care of her. The pattern of in-heritance hinders the development of large hereditary fortunes (cf. Stirling 1963).

Similarly, there is no basis for the development of hereditary leadership. There are no corporate groups who control certain resources such as water and land for grazing; these are owned by the village as a whole.[5] There are only families with more or less land, and influence or power is not necessarily correlated with land ownership or wealth (cf. Stirling 1957, 1965). Official leadership is confined to the *muhtar* (headman), who is elected by the men of the village and paid a minimal salary by the central government. A *muhtar's* power varies according to village; in our village the job was reduced to bureaucratic tasks, and most men did not regard it highly. People today usually take major grievances or disputes to the court in the administrative center about 20 kilometers away, rather than resolving them at the village level.[6]

Other men, however, gain a reputation for sound judgment and are listened to at times of crisis or if a village project is to be undertaken; their leadership has to do with personal qualities and the ability to understand public opinion and organize public support. These are characteristics that each man must develop for himself. "A father's importance is less relevant to the importance of descendants than their own hard work, health, fertility and luck" (Stirling 1963: 208).

With regard to men, at least, the village is fairly democratic; aside from differences of prestige and status based on age, that was how the villagers themselves saw it. This does not mean the village is harmonious or homogeneous; rather it is an arena, albeit quite limited, for vigorous assertions of individual freedom. Cooperation is not a social virtue among Turkish men; during the time I was there, any cooperative venture was labeled "Communist." As one man told me, "Today everyone wants to be his own *komutan* [military commander]"; in the past the term would have been *ağa* (lord, master) or *sultan* (ruler, lord). What he meant was that each *ev reisi* (house head, chief) wants to be his own boss, that no one wants to tell his fellow villagers what to do or especially to be told by another villager what to do. "They pine for an autocrat to lead them, but they insist on democracy" (Hotham 1972: 124).

---

5. The situation appears to have been quite different in the Black Sea area, where the presence of *ağas* (overlords) and clans with differential prestige worked against village solidarity and created a political arena for marriage (cf. Meeker 1976). In our village there were neither *ağas* nor prestigious clans. Meeker's point about honor having more to do with access to "significances," to illustrious history, than access to resources should be kept in mind by analysts with a predominantly sociological orientation.

6. For an exception to this trend, see Chapter 3; see also Starr 1978, 1989.

What this meant in our village was a lack of leadership and an absence of any structure of authority. As might be imagined, this atmosphere fostered divisions within families instead of leading to the consolidation of their fortunes and power.

Although social ranking takes into account wealth and rhetorical skills, any particular ranking seemed primarily to depend on the political and religious tendencies of the person doing the ranking. Parents of a daughter would not give her to a family they do not like, no matter how high its objective ranking; thus marriage cannot be viewed primarily as a strategy to win allegiance or consolidate political power. A marriage creates the social pathways needed for women to visit, and it might also reinforce a friendship that was already in existence.

With only one exception all marriages during my stay in the village were endogamous; that is, villagers married either kin or other villagers whether they lived in the village, in a town, or in Ankara. A daughter may be given to a relative or villager no longer living in the village; similarly, daughters of relatives and villagers living outside the village could be married back into the village.

Of 41 marriages that took place from February 1980 to June 1982, 19 were between *akraba* (relatives) and 8 of those were between first cousins. These were fairly evenly distributed: 2 girls married MBS (for boy FZD), 2 married their FZS (MBD), 1 married her MZS (MZD), and 3 married patrilaterally (FBS-FBD). In two of the last three cases the fathers lived next door to each other. In the other years for which I was able to obtain records, 1973–74, 22 marriages were made, 9 of them between *akraba*, of which 6 were between first cousins. This time 4 girls married their FZS (MBD), 1 married her MZS (MZD), and only 1 married patrilaterally (FBS-FBD). Thus, marriages between *akraba* seem stable at about one-half, with first cousins composing about one-half of these. The remainder in both periods were, with one or two exceptions, contracted between other villagers.

The one exception that I know personally merits some attention. First, it must be noted that in no case was a girl given to an outsider. In the exception referred to, a girl from outside (living in a small town) was brought in as a bride for Mehmet. He had wanted a girl who was a close neighbor and a relative on his mother's side, but her mother (father dead) refused him. A friend of his father had relatives living in the town, and a girl was found. After their marriage, a relative of hers living in Ankara married a relative of his, also in Ankara, after which they proudly announced, "Now we are relatives."

Akraba marriage and village endogamy can both be seen as an expression of the same thing: a distrust of outsiders and a concomitant desire to keep as close(d) as possible. "Hep akrabayız" (we are all relatives), and indeed they are. Village endogamy practiced for generations has produced a community that is *ekli* (patched together, intertwined), *akıntı* (flowed together), *girintili* (intermeshed). In the villagers' minds, at least, the village is a close-knit, closed, self-sufficient community. They give and take daughters from each other as they do food and help. *Akraba* marriage and village endogamy represent a denial of separation. We are all one family, we all derive from the same source and the same soil, we are insiders as compared to all those out there.

The inside-outside dichotomy is pervasive but not fixed to any particular thing. Its meaning is relative and depends on where one is in relation to home. In the Turkish village inside-outside can be invoked at the boundaries of any number of concentric circles that demarcate areas of inclusion and exclusion.[7] At its most exclusive, the line is drawn with reference to the body, then the *ev* (house), the family, the *sülale* (patriline), the *mahalle* (neighborhood), the *köy* (village), the *memleket* (provincial area), and the *millet* (nation). According to Dubetsky, the importance of inside-outside in Turkish culture is ultimately based on the differentiation of men "who share the protection of honor of a group of women from those who don't" (1973: 17). Although true, this is superficial, for one must ask why it is that certain men must guard certain women. The outsiders are only other men, but they are viewed with suspicion because they can tarnish the reputation of the women. What is at stake here is the honor of the men, and this in turn depends on the women's value as potential guarantors of seed.

At its most basic, the inside-outside dichotomy is rooted in notions of sexuality and procreation, specifically the seed-child in the womb. The female body is a resource for the symbolic construction of relations between inside-outside, open-closed, and near-far. Those women who are insiders, who are protected by kin and fellow villagers, are those

7. Compare the Nuer concept of *cieng*, which could mean house, hamlet, village, or tribal section depending on where one was and with whom one was speaking (Evans-Pritchard 1940). See also Geertz's comments with regard to Morocco (1976: 232–33).

who a man can be sure will guarantee his seed. Thus the search for a bride begins as close as possible.

The search for a bride, initiated by the boy's family, follows a pattern of concentric circles emanating from ego and proceeding from inside to outside. The first circle is among close kin, but the possibilities there are already known. The next circle of perusal is other kin, neighbors, and fellow villagers, both in the village and living in town. Only when all these possibilities are exhausted would parents seek elsewhere by means of friends as in the case of Mehmet. The search for a bride also begins early. Unattached youth are a source of anxiety among elders. It is as if they were an unstable element giving off a kind of dangerous psychosocial radioactivity until a stabilizing complement can be found to bind and channel it productively. Singleness is not prized; the sooner the unattached are paired, the better. Mothers of sons use every op-portunity to survey the available girls—at the *çamaşırhane* (laundry house), when visiting, and especially at weddings, when all the women and girls of the village, as well as friends and relatives from outside, are gathered. Marriages make marriages.

Of course, the parents of the girl can refuse any offer they feel is unsuitable. A girl's preference might become known, and today she is usually consulted about any offer. In most cases a girl's refusal will stand; although I knew of one very unhappy young wife who had been sent out of the village against her will to marry a much older relative, a widower with four children. In the next village a young girl went crazy after marriage, allegedly owing to a *büyü* (spell), and one young man from our village is said to have killed himself because he could not have the girl he wanted. Although a number of people, especially the older generation, admitted they had wanted to marry someone else, most sub-mitted to the desires of their parents (who supposedly know best) or to the luck of the draw, both of which they see as God's will (*Allahın emri*). Any marriage that is made has clearly been written by God; *Allah yazmış* (Allah has written it so).

Every year there were a certain number of unmarried girls and boys of marriageable age; the distribution by sex was not always even. Some-times I felt as if it was a game of musical chairs, the question being who would end up with whom by the time fall came. The pairings seemed to be fairly arbitrary, at least with regard to the fates of the married couple themselves, but this simply reinforced the notion that any particular marriage was God's will.

Marriage is something that should occur at a specific time in one's life. Life seems to be a series of stages marked externally; a door to one opens while another closes. The passage is signified by the fulfillment of certain actions rather than by a sense of development or continual unfolding. Boys marry later than girls, some before they enter military service, which is compulsory at 20, some on their return at 22. If a man marries before his military service, he expects to be presented with a child upon return; if not married before his service, he expects to marry on his return. A woman is the prize or reward for having endured the hardships of military service. Also he feels it is his due to marry, and his parents feel it is their duty to find him a bride. Marriage is obligatory, but it is the parents' obligation to see that it happens.

Marriage does not depend on emotional readiness, except insofar as the boy should have experienced ejaculation and sexual dreams, or on finding someone compatible. Compatibility is expected after marriage. Young men, when asked about the qualities they wanted in a potential spouse, said they wanted one who is modest (i.e., one who is covered, whose purity is above suspicion), a good worker, and someone their mother liked and could get along with. Only a few mentioned beauty, commonly in terms of skin color. A beautiful woman should have white skin; women with olive or dark skin were not prized, and only men could be *kızılderi*—red-skinned, meaning tanned. No one mentioned intelligence (cf. Mansur 1972: 157). A girl wanted a husband who could provide for her, who had a house (usually a room in his parents' house), who knew what his source of livelihood would be, and who did not drink, swear, or play cards.

Individual preference on the basis of romantic love is not an overriding issue, especially since there is very little opportunity for young people to get to know each other well. Preferences, therefore, are stated in more general terms. Stirling's observations in 1950 are still appropriate: "Women do not look to their husbands for companionship, still less do men look to their wives. It is taken for granted that there is no common ground for conversation. The relationship is limited to economic cooperation and to sexual intimacy" (1965: 113). He goes on to say that the "notion of a successful marriage in terms of personal relations does not exist in the village. The main criterion of success is the existence of healthy sons" (1965: 114). The personal compatibility that matters most is between the bride and her *kaynana*. *Kaynana* is usually translated as "mother-in-law," but "husband's mother" is perhaps more appropriate. The notion of "in-law" not only contrasts law with custom, a distinction not so clearly drawn in the village, but contrasts relations of affinity with those of consanguinity, a blurred distinction where consanguineal relations marry each other.

Parents of daughters often say they prefer to give a daughter to the son of a female relative on either side because it is this woman with whom their daughter will work and spend most of her time, and with whom she must get along. The *kaynana*, if she is not already so, becomes a close relative and is referred to as *anne* (mother).

The closest female relative is felt to be the *teyze*, the sister of the girl's mother (MZ). She is expected to be like a second mother to the girl, since it is assumed that sisters are similar. Underpinning this belief are specific notions of kinship that are addressed more fully in the next chapter; here I wish to point out only the notion of a shared and amorphous substance that signifies physical and therefore emotional closeness. Brothers, of course, also share substance, but their personal boundaries are conceptually more defined. Although brothers may wish for their children to marry each other in order to keep the offspring within the *sülale* (patriline), that is, to continue the line of seed and expand the *sülale*, women are more concerned with ongoing and immediate relationships that are physically and materially substantive. In general, women would prefer to give a daughter to their sister's son (MZS). The next choice is the son of the *hala* (FZS), since she and the girl will certainly know each other, and she too is expected to treat the girl well, at least in theory. If a girl marries her MBS or FBS, the *kaynana* is *el* (an outsider) and the girl's mother may be less sure of how well her daughter will be treated. In practice, however, even in this case the *kaynana* will also often be a relative. Thus the preferences of men and women are not necessarily antagonistic or mutually exclusive; they dovetail with regard to patrilateral parallel cousin marriage, but they are also accommodated to some extent by any of the other kinds of marriage as long as the line demarcating the village group is not crossed.

Before a choice can actually be made, the boy and his parents must have accumulated enough money to begin the negotiations. Marriage is an expensive proposition, and most expenses occur before the wedding. If the parents' house has no room for the new couple, an addition must be built, more rarely an entire house. Money is also needed for the brideprice, for gold jewelry, and for certain items of clothing and furniture, as well as for the entertainment expenses of the wedding itself. The cost can easily exceed a family's entire annual income. As we have seen, a boy is expected to contribute to the expenses of his marriage; thus, if he wishes to marry, he must first find a job.

In the village the possibilities were limited, primarily to being a shepherd (*çoban*) for a man with a large flock. Often this means that the young man will have to live outside the village for much of the year in a private *ahır* (corral). For example, Isa, son of Ibrahim, lived for part of the year in such an *ahır* as *çoban* for 600 *davar* (goats and sheep); in the summer he lived in a cave on top of the mountain. It was a hard life, but he stood to earn about 200,000 TL (about $2,000), which would be a considerable help toward wedding expenses. It was rumored that he wanted to marry the daughter of his employer, but the father would not consider such a marriage until after the work was finished. He said it would be *ayıp* (shameful) to pay Isa for his labor and also give him his daughter, for the payment would ultimately be used for the brideprice; thus the father would be paying for his own daughter, a transaction that not only would be dishonorable but carried a hint of incest.

The only other possibility in the village was to work in the fields at harvest time, harvesting melons, sugar beets, and vegetables for 500 TL ($5) a day. Not everyone plants these crops, and among those who do there is not always sufficient labor within the family at the peak period. But since money earned in this manner was clearly insufficient to meet wedding expenses, this type of work was frowned upon by older adolescents, being generally performed mostly by girls, women, and younger boys.

Most older boys go to the town or city in search of work, where they may find jobs in factories or hospitals or with the government. Most will live with a relative: an older married sibling or an uncle or aunt. Mehmet, however, rented a room and had to eat all his meals out; he was able to save very little, and returned to the village. Mustafa worked for four years in a sweater factory before he returned to the village to marry. Nuriye's son worked at the blood bank in a hospital in Ankara and then received additional training while in the military; he will not return to the village to live. Nor will one of the *muhtar*'s sons, who finished *lise* (lycée) in Milas and works for the Ministry of Public Works in Ankara, commuting from Ambarlı, where he lives with relatives. For some this period of work is the beginning of a transition to the city; others seek only to make enough money to return to the village and marry.

For the young people themselves, marriage signifies the entrance into social adulthood. Before marriage, both boys and girls are socially mute. The unmarried boys, *delikanlılar* (crazybloods), gather for sports, talk, mischief, and political discussions, but their opinions have little weight in village affairs. They are under the authority of their fathers, and although this continues after marriage, marriage does give them some say in the administration of the household. Single girls, who share with their mothers the internal management of the household, have a very practical effect on this domain. Girls get together to do handwork, play games, and drink tea, but if older women, and especially men, are present, they are required to be demure and quiet, to speak only when spoken to, and to affect a servile demeanor.

After puberty, but before marriage, a girl cannot go anywhere un-accompanied; after marriage she is freer to visit and invite guests, and freer to voice opinions and initiate conversation. Her openness (open-ings) has been closed, covered by her husband, and thus she is no longer perceived as provocative by others. Marriage is thus the instrument that transforms her into a stable, bounded, social adult. At the same time, her social activity is conducted in the close(d) world of the house.

A house (*ev*) is the precondition for marriage. Marriage (*evlilik*) is literally the state of being with a house; to marry (*evlenmek*) is to become enhoused. The house traditionally has been made of *kerpiç* (mud-brick); in other words, it is constructed from village soil, indeed soil taken from the man's own fields (see Dittemore 1983 for an excellent description of house construction). The *ev* is the physical structure that encloses and protects the *aile* within. *Aile* is generally translated as "family," but as a number of ethnographers (e.g. Stirling 1965, Özertuğ 1973, Duben 1985) have noted, that translation is inexact. I soon learned that *aile* meant different things to men and women. *Aile* most often refers to wife or wife and children; therefore only a man has an *aile*.[8] When I asked

8. Yet Engels (1972 [1884]: 68) reminded us that the English word "family" derives

Making mud-brick

a woman about her *aile*, there would be a moment of confusion and hesitation and then she would begin to speak about her mother and siblings, that is, the *aile* of her father. *Aile* for a woman is her natal family, her family of origin, which she regards with a backward glance and a feeling of nostalgia. A man often continues to live with his natal family, which incorporates his *aile*, his family of procreation. His orientation is forward-looking; his family is a matter of pride as well as honor. A woman is part of a family; a man has one. Women are always under the mantle of a man, be he father, husband, brother, or son. Translating *aile* as "family" glosses over this important distinction.

Neither the *ev* nor the *aile* is a social unit. After the village itself, *hane* is the major social unit. The meaning of *hane*, to be further discussed in Chapters Three and Four, can vary according to context, and this may explain the confusion that exists in the literature. Here it is important to stress that in order to become a full social being, one must be married.

from the Latin "famulus," which meant all those dependent on the male head; that is slaves, women, and children. Perhaps the notion of family and *aile* are not as far apart as first thought.

The term *hane* includes both *ev* and *aile*; in other words, there must be an *ev* and an *aile* for there to be a *hane*. But *hane* means more than married couple; it is a social unit constituted both of persons (a man and his *aile*) and of the physical dwelling space, *ev*. In the village it is most often used as a kind of counting word. Village population is given in terms of *hane*, not people, making it difficult to calculate the number of persons in the village from the number of *hane*.

Although marriage is necessary for both men and women to be considered adult, it does, and means, different things for them. For a man, marriage is the prerequisite for establishing a *hane*, and thus for becoming a social presence in the village. He represents the *hane* to the outside world. For a woman, marriage is the only channel by which to fulfill her destiny, namely to bear children to continue the man's line. "On beşinde kiz çocuğu ya erde ya yerde gerek"—a girl of fifteen must go either to a man or into the ground, i.e., die. Sometimes this is shortened to "ya ele ya yere"—either to a stranger or into the ground. The term *el* means stranger, alien, outsider. A girl is often referred to within her own family as *el kızı* (stranger girl), implying that she is a stranger in her own house, for she will have to leave it to go to a stranger. In this village, to be sure, the "stranger" often is a relative. Nevertheless, whether or not she marries a relative and whether or not she stays within the village, the house she goes to, and will henceforth be identified with and confined within, *is* a strange house. The sense of emotional dislocation is also captured in the concept of *gurbet* (see below, p. 117).

The house, as the material earth structure that encloses and protects its members, is analogous to the female body. Ideally, it should be *kapalı* (closed) to the outside world, an inner sanctuary. The boundary between inside and outside is well marked, with entrances and exits controlled. It is represented or "covered" by the man, who defends its purity vis-à-vis other comparable units in the same way that men represent, cover, and defend women. The *ev* is owned by the man, yet the woman who comes to reside at its center is *el* (an outsider). The boy's house encloses her; in relation to the house she is like the seed introjected into the womb. Symbolically, this poses a major contradiction, for at the sexual level it is the woman's womb which incorporates and safeguards the man's seed, which comes from outside herself. This contradiction is minimized by the practice of endogamy—marriage within the same group of origin, marriage of those who are the product of native seeds and native soil.

As there is a time to marry, so are there specific times for weddings. The year, like all else, is divided in two, a pairing of opposites: summer and winter. "In winter we sleep, in summer we work." In the summer, villagers work and burn in the hot sun; to them it is a premonition of Hell. Villagers must work, but they do not like to; work in any form is looked down upon.[9] It is not seen as a way of learning about life, or as an affirmation or fulfillment of the self. Certainly, the meaning of life is not conceived in terms of work.[10] The exemplary human activity is sitting. To live is to sit; the verb *oturmak* has both meanings. In winter villagers visit, and to visit is to sit and talk. Winter is the time when human existence is at its best and is almost the closest thing to Heaven.

Engagements and weddings occur on the borders of these seasons. Partly this has to do with economics; there is more money available after the harvest or the sale of spring lambs. But this is not all. Although it would be difficult to have a wedding in the summer, at the time of the heaviest work, there is no practical reason not to marry in winter— certainly a wedding would liven things up. The timing also has to do with the fields, after the planting has been done. Most weddings take place after the harvest and when fields are being prepared for fall seeding. Over the winter both seedbeds are expected to germinate new life.

The timing of weddings implicitly reinforces the suggestion that figurative language is no mere decoration but is integral to a particular perception of reality. Human fertility is mimetically tied to that of the fields, even in its timing. From seed to seed, field to field, the tension between these two modes of existence ramifies throughout village life. Though bound together, they are not united.

---

9. Women shoulder the major portion of the physical work. I had hoped in vain to hire a few of the young men to help me fix my house and chop my wood; although they would help me with "head" work, they would not condescend to do manual labor. When I told them that many American teen-agers work after school and during the summer, they did not believe me, clinging instead to their curious conviction that all American teens spend their time sitting around in a hashish haze.

10. Criticizing a number of theories of work, Moore (1988: 43) states that "Work is not just a matter of what people do because any definition must also include the conditions under which that work is performed, and its perceived social value or worth within a given cultural context." That is still very much a *social* definition and does not touch upon the *meaning* of work in a particular culture.

We tend to think of marriage as a union, no doubt because of our Christian heritage, which views marriage as a mystical union in which two become one flesh. This notion has entered the cultural mainstream; even those without any religious training or connection to the Church consider marriage to be a union of individuals, at least in the sense of a merging of interests for a common project. In the village, by contrast, neither conception nor marriage is considered a union; significantly, the notion of union is also a problem in Islamic mystical theology. In Islam, mystics can only speak of striving toward union with the godhead without ever achieving it. To entertain such an idea is heretical because "God has no equal and because of this incommensurability can unite with nothing and no one" (Meier 1964 [1954]: 41). Because of the symbolism of gender, something of this is transferred to marriage. Marriage is not a union, but the coexistence of opposites, the coming together of the two complementary spheres of activity that are necessary to produce and continue a household, that is, the *hane,* the male line. "There is no rite symbolizing the union of the young pair during the marriage" (Erdentuğ 1959: 34). The entire wedding is celebrated by each side separately. Marriage appears to be another stage in a series of social dualisms of incorporators and incorporated.

The incorporation of the girl into the boy's family is symbolized by where they take up residence. The young couple do not, as is typical in America, set up their own household. Instead, they are allotted a separate room in the boy's father's house and eat communally with all other members of the household.

In such a small community it would be impossible for the girl not to continue to have relations with her family, but after the wedding she must remain in the boy's house for a specified period of time—ideally forty days, but often in practice much less, depending on the discretion of the in-laws. This is a period of transition, a time both dangerous and auspicious. Like a parturient woman a new bride is open. "Although there is no doubt about the auspicious nature of 'opening' in marriage and in creating new life . . . for the woman the value of 'open' is dependent on context, and its auspicious aspect exists only if contained within the family headed by her husband" (Hirschon 1978: 81, a discussion of similar customs among Greeks).

After this period of seclusion, which is designed to help incorporate the girl into her husband's household, her "in-laws" allow her to visit her former house, but only under the mantle of her husband. The inclusion of a woman into her husband's family extends even to death, when she is buried with her husband and his kin, not her own. Especially in the case of a girl who marries outside the village (even if to a fellow villager), this means she is in permanent and eternal *gurbet* (exile).

Gurbet is a very important concept in Turkish life. In its ultimate sense, as used by certain religious Muslims, it refers to our sojourn on earth, seen as an exile from the heavenly home. It is also used, however, in a number of more this-worldly contexts: for example, to describe the condition of Turkish laborers in Europe (Delaney 1990), of men during their military service, and of women in marriage.

To Americans, who are used to being far from our parental homes and often so by choice, it may be hard to imagine the emotions of *hasret* (longing, nostalgia, pining) felt by village girls whose parental home may be only a few lanes away. Nevertheless, *hasret* is a pervasive quality or tone of their emotional lives. One of the songs sung at weddings expresses this vividly. Although the song refers to a girl who has married outside the village, one can substitute "parental home" for "village" with very little change in the sentiment expressed:

It's been six years since I left my village
The bitter words of my father have become honey to me
The thorns of my village have become roses to me
I miss my village, both my mother and father, I miss my village.
If my father had a horse, he would mount it and come to me
If my mother had a boat, she would sail to me
If my siblings knew the way, they would come to me.

The following standardized poem was included in several letters sent home by young men who were away doing military service. It too describes the sentiments of *gurbet*:

Without a mother or father can *gurbet* end?
Can a nightingale sing on a branch without leaves?
Can these days be ended just by counting?

Similar feelings are experienced when young men must go to the city to find work, but since recently married boys normally remain with or nearby their natal families, they never experience the utter dislocation that marriage entails for girls. Because boys and men are free to wander about the village and visit whenever and whomever they please, it may be difficult for them to understand the intensity of *gurbet* for girls and women, who are enclosed in the house and cut off from their familiar social environment.

The newly married girl is referred to as "our *gelin*" (our bride) by all members of her husband's *sülale*, not just his immediate family. The fruits of her body—that is her children, but especially sons—will increase and bring honor to the entire *sülale*. The reverse is not true. The boy is not claimed as "our *damat*" (our bridegroom) except by his wife's immediate relatives. He owes her parents his respect and certain kinds of help if requested, but his obligations do not extend beyond her immediate family.

Negotiations

Once the boy's family selects a prospective bride, his mother or other female relatives visit the girl's mother to assess whether a proposal will be welcomed. In some areas the girl is asked to make coffee. If she makes it sweet (also the normal way of drinking it), the implication is that she is pleased by the offer. If, on the other hand, she "forgets" to add sugar and makes it bitter, it is an indication of her personal disfavor. (During the time I was in Turkey there was no coffee because the money the government could spare for imports was used to import fuel. The press ran stories about the havoc the absence of coffee was wreaking with respect to marriage.) Regardless of the girl's response, no definite answer will be given at this time. The offer will be discussed later with the girl's father (and today usually with the girl). After a decision has been reached, the girl's mother will make a return visit to the boy's mother to tell her informally. If the offer is refused, the honor of neither of the fathers is touched. This kind of negotiation also has the virtue of saving embarrassment for both the girl and the boy.

Although marriage is generally held to be imminent by boys and girls after a certain age, the actual deal is struck suddenly. One day a young person has no idea or intimation that he or she will soon be married; the next day it is all settled.

If the offer is accepted, the fathers meet to *söz kesmek* (to cut the words), that is, to make a promise. To cut something is to make it irrevocable, such as cutting a sheep at sacrifice. In addition, they negotiate the *başlık* (literally, head-thing), meaning the brideprice, and other items of the "contract." The translation of *başlık* as "bridewealth" conflates several elements that ought to be kept separate and has confused the discussion of this topic. The *başlık* is paid in money to the father of the girl. Magnarella asserted that "the value of the bridewealth is not standard, even within the same village" (1969: 144–45), and suggested that it varied according to the prestige and wealth of the families involved. By contrast, in our village the *başlık* was standardized at a relatively low figure (approximately 10,000 TL or $100), and did not depend on the family's standing in the village. The *başlık* could be slightly higher if the groom's family wanted the "tray to be shown," that is, if he wanted gifts from the bride to the groom's family to be publicly carried from her house to his and displayed. Indeed, several people said the *başlık* is essentially to pay for the *zini* (tray).

There was no correlation between brideprice and the girl's *çeyiz* (trousseau), again in contrast with Magnarella's findings, for the *çeyiz*, too, was fairly standard throughout the village. Perhaps this is a further indication that, although differences in wealth exist, villagers consider each other basically equals. Significantly, brideprice may be dispensed with altogether between two brothers, that is, in the case of a patrilateral parallel cousin marriage (FBD-FBS), and this offers an interesting clue to the meaning of the brideprice. Brideprice has been interpreted as compensation for the loss of a worker (Erdentuğ 1959: 31), as a way of maintaining prestige (Magnarella 1969: 146), as compensation for the trousseau (Stirling 1965: 186), and as a way of covering wedding expenses (Magnarella 1969: 145; Stirling 1965: 187). All of these may be part of the answer, but I believe that brideprice may also be seen as a symbolic payment to the bride's father for *his* labor in bringing her up. It is in recognition that the fruits of her body, which her father has cultivated, are now to be reaped by the boy's family. In the case of patrilateral parallel cousin marriage, the fruits of the girl's body, in the form of both labor and children, will be kept within the family; thus no brideprice is necessary.

Magnarella also claims that a "large bridewealth is accompanied by a large celebration" (1969: 145), and this is confirmed by Stirling (1965: 187). In our village the scale of the wedding celebration correlated positively with the wealth of the families, but had no correlation with the brideprice.

Between brothers there is generally little or no *başlık*, yet the three patrilateral parallel cousin weddings during my time were among the largest and most lavishly celebrated. In any case, despite regional variations it would seem that the brideprice does not represent the "transfer of rights" over a woman, for a bride is a bride whether or not any *başlık* has been paid.

In addition to the *başlık*, a number of items of gold[11]—bracelets, coins, earrings, pendants, and chains—are felt to be mandatory, with the specific amount decided between the fathers. In our village five bracelets were standard and minimum, and a sixth was often given by the bride's mother. At a cost of $250–400 each, this represents a considerable expense. If a *başlık* is agreed upon, it must be paid before the wedding, and this is usually true of the gold as well. In one case, a girl was to be married to a boy in another village; the words had been cut, the *başlık* paid, and the gold given, and then she eloped with a neighbor boy. The gold and the money were returned.

In most discussions of brideprice in Turkey, it has been unclear whether what was being talked about was the *başlık* or the gold, or both together. It is, however, important to distinguish the two. Whereas the *başlık* goes to the girl's father, the gold is a gift to the bride; it is her personal property, at least in theory, meant to be used as insurance against divorce, death, or financial crisis. In practice, however, it is often only an adornment for a brief period of time, after which the bride is pressured or persuaded to convert it into cash to help finance an economic venture of her husband's, such as buying a share in a tractor. Women do not have to give it up, but there is often no alternative. Many of the older women no longer even had their wedding bands. As one woman said: "Ali ate my gold."

In addition to the *başlık* and the gold, certain items of clothing and household equipment must also be provided. The boy's side must provide a number of "city" clothes (clothes for outside the village) such as a dress, skirts, sweaters or blouses, a raincoat, a purse, and shoes. His side also normally buys the wedding dress, and sometimes also a separate *nişan* (engagement) dress. Both are of modern Western style— taffeta, tulle, and lace. The wedding dress is usually white, but occa-

11. Gold, incorruptible, shining, a symbol of wealth and beneficence, is often associated with divinity. Although the notion is pure speculation on my part, this association may be what makes it particularly suitable as a contribution from the boy's family, as against the girl's.

sionally the *nişan* dress, which is similar but of pastel color, serves for both occasions.

Today the boy's side must also provide a *takım* (set) of furniture. The *takım*'s largest item will probably be a *bufe*, a cabinet for the display and storage of glassware, china, and other bric-a-brac and with a special niche for a television set. This niche is often equipped with a blue plastic door, which, although ostensibly to decrease glare, was also cited as protection against the evil eye. The *takım* may also include a table and a *sandık* (hope chest) for storage of the *çeyiz* (trousseau). Many girls now demand a sewing machine. More affluent families, or those in which the son has worked in a furniture factory, may give a *koltuk* (armchair). Several rugs are also requested, though often the father of the bride contributes one. The boy must provide the bed and the external (outside) fittings as well as additional pieces for guests and future children; generally this means five *döşek* (wool-stuffed mattresses), five *yorgan* (heavy wool-stuffed quilts), and five *yastık* (pillows). The girl's *çeyiz* will be taken up below.

Once these items have been decided upon, a shopping trip to the largest nearby town, or in many cases to Ankara, will be made at the groom's expense. Sometimes the bride and her mother accompany the groom, in which case it may be one of the first times the young couple are together. On one of my trips to Ankara, I happened to witness the beginnings of one such outing. Several of us had already gathered early in the morning in the village *meydan* (square) to wait for the village *dolmuş*. *Dolmuş* means "filled," and in the city is used to refer to a shared taxi. In the village it meant a Ford or Chevy van used to transport people back and forth to town. When the driver arrived, he told us that the van would go all the way to Ankara rather than terminating as usual in Ambarlı.

A thin young man in a pale new suit, strangely out of place among the rest of us in our rumpled, dusty clothes, waited with a preoccupied and slightly embarrassed air. Only after we went to pick up a crowd waiting at the house of the bride-to-be did I realize what was going on. A great fluster was caused by trying to decide who should sit where, and we all had to get out again and rearrange ourselves. The driver and several other men unrelated to the event sat in front. In the next seat were the bride-to-be, her sister, and her mother, a few others sat on tiny stools in the empty space, and in the back seat I sat with the groom and a couple of other people. Halfway down the mountain, the bride calmly removed her *şalvar,* under which she had on "city" clothes, a skirt and sweater, nylons and pumps. Her mother pretended to ignore this quick-change act, as did the groom, who affected a detached air throughout the trip. Shortly afterward the bride got a bloody nose and turned to me, knowing I was the only one to carry Kleenex; and thus, in strained but charged silence, did we proceed all the way to Ankara. Normally a girl is not involved in choosing her clothes; she is simply presented with them.[12] This outing was permitted by the girl's father, known in the village for his "progressive, modern" outlook.

During the initial marriage negotiations the fathers will also have decided whether there is to be a separate public ceremony for attaching the rings (*yüzük takma*) and a *nişan* (engagement) ceremony in addition to the *düğün* (wedding). There can be three separate occasions, or the *yüzük* and *nişan* can be held together; sometimes the *nişan* and *düğün* are collapsed into one, and sometimes there is just a *düğün*. With more affluence there appears to be a tendency to increase the number of ceremonies.

The *yüzük takma* is held at the girl's house. Relatives and friends of both sides gather, but men and women are kept separate, either in different rooms or one group inside and the other outside. At one *yüzük takma* I attended, which seemed fairly typical, the rings were tied together with a red ribbon and brought out on a tray. An older man read a brief prayer, attached the rings to both boy and girl, then cut the ribbon. Although the joining of the rings may symbolize the joining of the couple, the emphasis is on the cutting, which symbolizes the irrevocability of the act. After the ribbon was cut, the couple went around to kiss everyone's hand. Male relatives stuffed 100 and 500 TL ($1 and $5) notes in the girl's hand as she passed; female relatives gave small gifts (scarves, towels, cloth). There may or may not be dancing. At Mehmet's *yüzük takma* many of us went by *dolmuş* to the town where the girl lived. In this case, the men danced in pairs in the courtyard while the women sat indoors. The men's dancing was similar to the women's, to

12. This was brought home to me when I returned in the summer of 1986 for a visit. I took Ayşe (the girl I had encouraged to go to high school) to town to buy her some supplies and clothes for school. She found it very difficult and embarrassing to express her preferences, but even more so to try on the clothes to see if they fit.

be described below, except that they used wooden spoons as castanets and their footwork was more elaborate and energetic.

Often the ring ceremony is performed privately or at the time of the *nişan*, a gala party, primarily for women, that usually, but not always, takes place in the late afternoon. At every *nişan* I attended, the girls wore special *nişan* dresses and were heavily veiled. When a large crowd has assembled, the girl is brought out, her veil is lifted, and the shower of gifts begins. One woman is delegated as the caller. As each gift is given, she calls out the name of the donor and says what the gift is. The first gifts are those of gold, which are donated by close kin on both sides. The girl is bedecked with earrings, gold chains, pendants, bracelets, and special coins. After these come gifts of clothes (dresses, sweaters, skirts, a purse, a raincoat, shoes and slippers), lengths of cloth, towels and table sets, and money. This is not only a ritual but a public display and a kind of public record. Today some people are beginning to keep a written list of the gifts, but in a predominantly illiterate society, such public witness performed a vital function, especially in the event of disputes. Because of my training and tendency to make lists, I found it difficult to remember who gave what, but I quickly learned that villagers are trained differently and their memories are generally excellent. After the gifts have been given, peanuts and *leblebi* (roasted and salted chickpeas) are handed around, after which some of the guests depart and others stay to dance.

During the period of engagement (sometimes only a few weeks, usually between spring and fall, more rarely a year) the couple may be permitted to meet a few times to get to know each other. Meetings take place at the girl's house, where they are well chaperoned. Ayşe and Durmuş, for example, were allowed a private talk of about an hour, during which time they discussed such things as whether they would remove body hair, especially in the pubic area. While the parents negotiated the financial arrangements, the couple negotiated the physical one. The discussion of such intimate topics without the basis of an intimate relationship struck me, but not the participants, as odd; our difference in this respect reflects the very different views about the nature and function of marriage in the two societies. In the customary American view, marriage is an expression of romantic love, which is believed to dissolve all practical problems; in the Turkish view, marriage is a contractual agreement of a particular kind, specifically sexual cohabitation for the purpose of procreation, and must be grounded in practical supports if it is to survive and thrive. These beliefs are given expression in the wedding rituals.

Wedding

Marriage is the focal point in the life of a person and his or her family. Really, there are only two phases in life: the short period of childhood before marriage and the longer period of marriage. Years of preparation and great expenditures of time, energy, and money are involved in a marriage. The wedding (*düğün*) is at once the culmination of this preparation, the overt expression of it, and the major ceremonial event in village life.

A marriage affects everyone; new kinship relations are forged, old ones need to be restructured, and roles must be worked out anew. More simply, two people who have been almost invisible will now become visible as a unit that must be acknowledged. Although marriage is such an important event, it is very difficult to say when a wedding begins or ends. Fifteen days before, notice of the impending marriage is hung in the mosque; if anyone has cause to believe it should not take place— for example, if someone knew that the bride and groom had been nursed by the same woman—that person should speak up.

Although the main events of a wedding occur between Friday and Sunday, guests may arrive earlier, especially if the wedding coincides with a *bayram* (holiday). During the first fall that I was in the village, several weddings coincided with one of the two important religious holidays—Şeker (Sugar) and Kurban (Sacrifice). While holding a wedding between these two holidays is considered highly improper, there was not much that could be done: because the Islamic calendar is lunar, every year holidays occur ten days earlier than the previous year, and in 1980 the entire period between these two holidays coincided with the normal timing of weddings. In consequence, the religious injunction (not really a rule) was ignored. Since many relatives living outside the village would normally visit the village on one or another of these holidays, a wedding at the same time saved them an extra trip; it also enabled the households to save on entertainment expenses by combining both celebrations. In addition, of course, the festive aura of each was enhanced by the other.

Some families ordered printed wedding invitations that specified Friday through Sunday, but at the time these functioned more as status symbols and keepsakes than as a means for excluding some people. Everyone in the village (though men and women separately) can partake of the dancing and the festivities, if not of the food. There follows a detailed account of activities on each of the three primary days of a wedding.

Friday

Early Friday morning people from the girl's side take a flag to the boy's house and collect *başlık* (not to be confused with brideprice—here it means small number of coins per head) or *bahşiş* (tips). Nowadays the flag is usually the national flag, but on one occasion it was a family heirloom. The important thing is that there be some red in it. The flag will fly from the rooftop, indicating that this is a house to which a bride will come. Meanwhile, the morning at the bride's house is spent preparing food and the *çeyiz*. Last-minute sewing, ironing, and stitching of the headscarves to a sheet (so they can be displayed) must be finished before the entire *çeyiz* can be viewed. The viewing of the *çeyiz* is very important, for it is a public validation of the girl's worth, in terms not only of the number and kind of items, but also of the quality of her own handiwork. In some areas, but not in this village, the exact estimation of the worth of the articles is tallied and recorded. Here the value is recorded primarily in the minds and eyes of the beholders. In an unusual case in which a girl left her husband, her *çeyiz* was not returned. Since she had eloped with him, the *çeyiz* had never been publicly viewed; no one except her own family knew what was in it.

Notice (*ilan*) that the wedding has officially begun is announced from the minaret around noontime on Friday to invite the *kınacılar* (girls who will participate in the henna party, known as *kına gecesi*, the following evening) to proceed to the bride's house to view the *çeyiz*. At the same time, the men are invited to the tearoom for a tea provided by the boy's family after the noontime *namaz* (prayer) in the mosque.

On Friday, people say ''Kına konacak''—the henna will alight and perch. A powder of ground henna leaves mixed with water is a major ingredient in the *kına gecesi*, a party for all the women at which the bride's hands and feet are stained with henna. The meaning of henna

Display of trousseau

is discussed below. On Friday the *kına* just sits, and like all valuable things is covered (with a *kına örtüsü* or henna covering). It will remain covered until the following night.

Girls and women begin to show up in the afternoon with small gifts. They will view the *çeyiz*, comment, and criticize. The occasion is an opportunity to show off their own handwork, and they wear their fanciest *yemeni* (scarves). In fact, the party is a viewing of different types of covers! One whole room is taken up with a display of the *çeyiz*, which includes *yemeni*, often as many as a hundred, that the girl has spent years decorating with lace, *mekek* (tatting), and beads. The *çeyiz* also includes 8–10 lace-edged and embroidered sets of sheets and pillowcases, bed skirts, two square pillows and covers, hand-knitted socks, sweaters, and *yelek* (vests), and covers for everything: runners like antimacassars for along the tops of divans, for the tops of bureaus, for the television set, for the *tüp* (gas container), for the iron—everything must have a cover. Also displayed are underwear, colored short slips, and nightgowns, gifts of cloth for *şalvar* and pajamas, towels, cooking utensils, copper trays, pots and *güğüm* (specially shaped jugs for heating water), glasses, a tea set, clothes given by the groom (raincoat, city dresses and skirts, bought sweaters, a purse, and shoes), and sometimes a rug from the bride's father.

A wedding is a break in routine and an escape from housework; everyone is joking and in good spirits. Girls sometimes dance indoors to taped music. At the same time, winter food preparation continues alongside. I often left the hot, overcrowded rooms to sit outside and help women cut and string beans to be spread for drying.

Friday evening women return for more dancing—this time generally outdoors in the courtyard. The bride wears one of the store-bought dresses given by the groom, her *nişan* dress, or even her wedding dress. There seems to be no rule, just something pretty. Occasionally a *nişan* will take place on this night, but usually it has preceded the wedding by weeks or months.

The men gather in a tearoom to dance. They are accompanied by a *saz* (a lute-like guitar) or, in times of plenty, by the music of imported *davul* (drum) and *zurna* (reed flute) players. Musicians are brought in from outside because it is considered *ayıp* (shameful) for local men to play anything but the *saz*—and even that should be played only by younger men. One man was an accomplished tin whistle player, but considered it improper for a grown man with children to indulge in such frivolity. He played privately in his house, but when I suggested a musical evening it was quickly vetoed. Yet this same man was willing to go to the nearby town to dance when the Prime Minister was passing through. In any case, professional musicians for weddings are hired at great expense (40,000 TL, or about $400, for three days) and are put up in a tearoom and taken care of by the boy's family. Their presence makes a tremendous difference in the wedding celebrations. The music is very loud and piercing, and villagers find it very exciting. When the musicians first arrive (late Friday afternoon), they play a kind of presentation piece that everyone rushes to hear. After that they are not expected to play again until the next day.

Saturday

Saturday is the day of biggest celebration, lasting from early morning until the early hours of Sunday morning and often all night. To use a term of Victor Turner (1967), it is a "liminal" period; it is the day of transition, the transformation of a girl into a wife. Once crossed, this threshold is forever behind. The bride begins her transformation with a bath. Water is a polysemous symbol. In the form of rain it transforms the dry earth into a fertile field. Its use for ablutions not only cleanses a person of impurities, but also, according to Reinhart (1990), creates a kind of seal. Both meanings are quite appropriate here.

Since there are no bathtubs and no running water, a bath requires an assistant. Mothers assist their children, including grown sons; daughters assist mothers, wives assist husbands, and mothers-in-law assist daughters-in-law. No one except me took a bath alone. A bath can take place at several locations: in the house, in the *ocak* (hearth), which is a separate room or building in the house compound, or in the *çamaşırhane* (laundry house). In a corner of most rooms there is an area bounded by a raised ridge of cement to keep water from flowing onto the floor and carpet (see house plans, pp. 234 and 235, "washing up place"). Within this area there is a hole in the wall to the outside for the water to drain off. The person taking the bath squats in the area while the attendant pours the water. A bath in the *ocak* normally took place only in summer. Wedding baths usually took place in the *çamaşırhane*. There are three such buildings in the village, one in each *mahalle* (neighborhood), all located next to a *çeşme* (fountain) so as to ensure a steady supply of cold running water. The building I knew best was made of mud-brick and was about the size of a large room. Inside along one wall was a high trough of cold water from the fountain, along another side was a low bench used for soaping clothes, and on the third side were several niches in which fires were built and water boiled in huge copper cauldrons.

At one wedding I was the *sağdıç* (helper, attendant to the bride), and was the first to bathe at the laundry house. Several women had gathered to do laundry, but really to watch the proceedings. Ayşe, the bride, suggested that I bathe before most of the girls and women arrived because she thought it would be embarrassing for me, or awkward for them, to see me *keçi gibi* (like a goat), because of my pubic hair. They consider pubic hair *pis* (dirty); adult women remove theirs by plucking or shaving, or with a depilatory made of sugar and water. When bathing, a woman either squats or sits on a low stool (*oturak*) and often retains her underpants. As we have seen, the *am*[13] (female genitals) are *ayıp* (shameful) and women are ashamed to expose them.

For my bath, I sat on the *oturak* in the corner. My throat hurt because of the heavy, acrid smoke from the *tezek* (dried dung) fire. On my left was the trough of cold water, on my right the cauldron of hot water. Ayşe mixed both in a container and poured it over me. She washed my hair with soap several times and rinsed it. Then she scrubbed me with a rough glove as in a *hamam* (Turkish steam bath). The bath is like any other except more attention is given to the hair. After I had finished and dressed, I performed the same service for Ayşe.

She crouched in a dark corner and lathered herself with soap. I stood by and assisted by pouring water at appropriate moments. Still crouching and hiding in the shadows, she got dressed and covered her hair. Hair dries very slowly because it is kept damp beneath the head coverings. Only once was I able to persuade a girl to remove her scarf and let her hair dry in the sun that was filling my house.

Dressed in new Western clothes, the bride donned a fancy lace-edged *yemeni* and returned home to kiss everyone's hand, but mainly to show respect to her mother. When her hair was almost dry, she went to a nearby house of a relative for the ceremonial braiding of hair (*tel örmek*). The word *tel* refers both to the thin silver strands, like tinsel, that will be woven into the hair, and to the braids themselves. At this ceremony a crowd of girls gather to help braid and to dance. Nothing is hurried, for the occasion offers an excuse for them to see each other and enjoy themselves. While the hair is being braided, some dance in an adjoining room. First, lengths of *tel* and black yarn (to attach to the end of the bride's hair) are cut to reach the floor. Several women working at once begin the braiding. There are usually at least 20 braids, often more. They are braided with four parts (two parts of hair and two of *tel*). Brides should be solemn on such occasions, and sometimes they cry—as well they might, if only from the pain of having their hair untangled, combed, and pulled. All in all, the braiding ceremony is an excruciating ordeal. The girl must sit for hours in an overheated room, not allowed to joke and barely to speak while everyone else is bantering back and

13. The word itself is hardly ever mentioned. Americans (and Europeans) often say something like "am" or "um" as a filler in speech, which can create problems of which they are unaware.

forth and joking at her expense. The process of transformation from a girl to a woman is something enacted upon her; she is a mute spectator, and not even a true spectator since she cannot really view what is being done to her.

It is not surprising that the bride's hair receives special attention at the wedding. It will be remembered that at puberty, or at least by way of social recognition of it, a girl's hair is covered; since loose hair is felt to be erotic, it is *günah* (sinful) to let even one strand show. Never cut, a girl's hair is allowed to grow long and luxuriant, but its luxuriance is hardly ever experienced. At puberty it is bound and covered, and at marriage it is further tamed and domesticated by braiding. The connection of women's hair with sexuality is made explicit by the fact that their pubic hair is removed. Although ostensibly this is done for hygienic reasons, I believe the notion of being entangled in dank sensuality is also operating. The hair at the nape of the neck that is wild and disorderly and cannot be controlled is called *cingene saçı* (gypsy hair), and gypsy women are thought to have an unbridled sexuality. What is being effected by means of work on the bride's hair is a transformation from tangle to order, from unfocused sensuality to the focused sexuality of procreation in marriage.

The liminal period of the transformation begins with the braiding and ends "forty" days later when the braids are cut;[14] by that time the binding of the girl into her new home and role should have been accomplished. Each friend takes part in braiding her hair. The multi-stranded, playful friendships of youth are woven into an orderly, sedate form as the bride's sexuality is being channeled into marriage. Left over *tel* is cut into smaller lengths and distributed as keepsakes to unmarried girls, who attach it to a button or pin it on their sweaters. Upon completion of the braiding, a blue bead is attached to one of the braids to ward off the evil eye (*nazar*); such a bead is attached to a newborn baby for the same reason, a gesture that reinforces the symbolic equivalence of marriage and childbirth.

By the end of the braiding, the bride is often crying quite hard. She

---

14. Hair cutting in anthropological literature has often been interpreted as symbolizing the renunciation of sexuality for religious purposes, sometimes even as symbolic castration (cf. Berg 1951; Leach 1958; Obeyesekere 1981), suggesting the male bias of the ethnographers. Here hair cutting indicates not the renunciation of sexuality but a girl's initiation into sexuality and disciplined use of it.

gets up, solemnly kisses everyone's hand, embraces her closest friends, and then goes home to kiss the hands of those there and to be with her mother. This is a very sad day for mothers; they are losing their closest confidant. "Who will I lean on, who will I confide in?" my neighbor Fatma moaned as she writhed on the floor sobbing and singing sad songs because her daughter was leaving (cf. Roper 1974: 67). The daughter was moving only two lanes away and Fatma still had three girls at home, but she was still inconsolable. At the same time, the crying symbolizes love; if a mother didn't cry, one would suspect she didn't care for the girl. Similarly women moan, wail, and cry at funerals. Women's tears spill freely and seem to express the fluidity of their personal boundaries and their emotions. They are "naturally" unrestrained, lacking as they do men's capacity to contain and restrain themselves. Men frown on crying and consider it shameful, for it expresses women's undue attachment to the physical nature of persons.

Şenlik (cheerfulness, gaiety) takes over in the afternoon. If there are musicians, they play for an hour or so in an open place in the vicinity of the boy's house. The drummer(s) wear short, white şalvar (baggy pants) that end above the knee and droop in back. I remarked to a neighbor that they resembled yerli koyun (Anatolian fat-tailed sheep), and this became the big joke of the day. A woven cummerbund is wound round their göbek (belly) and is stuffed in front with a decorated scarf of the bride. On their chest they wear a small, tight vest rather like a bra, though brightly colored. The drum, carried on a strap over the shoulder and held in front, is beaten with a wooden mallet on one side and a thin drumstick on the other. Slow and ceremonious movements accompany the playing. The deep drumbeats seem to make the heart stand still, while the high-pitched tune of the zurna simulates its fluttering. Exciting as the music is, I also found it somewhat somber and melancholy, for it seemed to express in sound the feeling of the inexorable march of fate (drum) soon to take over the capricious yearning of the soul (flute). The villagers enjoyed it and were moved by it, but did not offer interpretations of their feelings.

More typically there were no musicians, but other forms of şenlik took place. At one house a sister of the bride made up very funny impromptu skits to teach the bride what each new utensil was for, how to use it, and how to serve a proper meal: "This is for dolma [stuffed vegetables], this for çorba [soup]," etc. They made me play the guest, which I was

Musicians from outside

anyway, and pretend to eat and comment. The sister offered me *sütlü kahve* (coffee with milk), which I don't like, so I told her to make it again *sütsüz* (without milk). They made a joke that I am "without": not only *sütsüz* (without milk), *tuzsuz* (without salt), and *şekersiz* (without sugar), since I use very little of these ingredients, but also that I was *yastıksız* (without a pillow). They had observed that I do indeed sleep without a pillow, but their real meaning was that I was without a husband.

Saturday both sides prepare food for the two family feasts, which are celebrated separately, spatially as well as temporally. The girl's side (family, relatives, and guests) has its wedding feast on Saturday night, the groom's side on Sunday afternoon, after the bride has come to the groom's house. The menu can vary a great deal, depending on the number of guests and the affluence of the family. *Düğün pilavı* (wedding rice), a special food replacing *bulgur* (wheat), the more common staple, is usually provided at weddings. Yet one meager wedding feast, at which a male friend of the girl's father and I were the only guests, consisted only of soup, eggplant (which I'd donated), cheese, olives, and melon. A more normal wedding feast would include, in addition to *düğün pilavı,* yoghurt soup (white), meat, *turşu* (pickles), a vegetable dish (green beans, eggplant), stuffed peppers, fruit, and baklava. A token meal (enough for one to three persons) is sent over to the tearoom where the boys and men affiliated with the boy's side are gathered for tea. Although physically excluded from the Saturday night feast, these men thereby are ritually included; by partaking of common substance, a group of friends is substantiated.

At the bride's house, guests will eat together if there are few; when there are many, the men eat first. At one wedding where I was an intimate guest, the men (about twenty in number) sat upstairs at two *sofras* (large trays). Women on the ground level dished out the food, and girls or young boys served; as soon as utensils were used, women began to wash them. The men were very demanding—"bring this, bring more of that." The men's group was solemn and orderly; of course, they were the ones being served and waited on. The women, after waiting so long, dived in with gusto and helped themselves.

While we were eating, the bride, not exactly secretly but unobtrusively, left with her father and uncle to go to the imam and the *muhtar* for the *nikâh,* which is the formal, official marriage protocol. She was not permitted to go in her Western clothes, but had to change into her *şalvar* and be heavily covered. The groom, his father, and two witnesses would also be present. Formerly, the girl was not present but was represented by her father and another male relative; today her presence is required by law. The *muhtar* has a ledger in which he records all marriages. The bride and groom must sign the ledger, supply a photograph (another excuse to go to town), and give birth dates as accurately as possible. Because there is a resident government midwife in the village, birth dates are recorded and birth certificates (*nüfüs kâğıdı*) are registered. These are required both for marriage and to determine the date at which a boy must begin military service. In the past, before there were any government midwives, many births were not reported or were inaccurately reported. Often people knew only the year of their birth, which gave them some leeway with regard to both marriage and military service. Since many villages even today do not have an official *ebe,* some babies have no birth certificates and many of them are registered long after their birth. Every few years the government passes a law to legitimate all such children.

Today *nikâh* is the term used to refer to the legal, civil ceremony of marriage. Formerly only the imam's recognition, known as *imam nikâhı*, was necessary to make a marriage legal; today the *nikâh* is generally required as well. Sometimes, however, it is not possible to have a civil marriage. Because the mother of one bride was not "legally" married, the bride had no birth certificate; without a birth certificate she could not have a civil *nikâh*, but only the religious one. In village eyes, she was quite definitely married.[15] To villagers, *nikâh* implies much more than a civil contract; it is the bond that ties them together until death. "Kefenli kurtulmuş, eşinden nikâhlı kurtulamamış"—the married person [*nikâhlı*] cannot be set free from his or her spouse until released by the shroud [*kefen*]. In any case, it is generally held that "nikâhlı ölmek sevap"—to die still married is a great blessing.

When the bride returned from signing the legal contract, she changed into her wedding dress. At another quite lavish wedding the bride had arranged to borrow a dress. When it came, she saw it was dirty; she then turned to another friend, who supplied one that was clean, if a little small. On this occasion of so much conspicuous consumption, what struck me as odd was not so much that she should borrow a dress, but that this seemingly important detail should be left until the last moment. Clearly it was rather low on her list of priorities. Of course, in a village community one knows the other girls who have dresses one could borrow. In return, some of the bride's closest friends and sisters wear her new clothes, some of which are gifts from the groom. She shares her wealth and pleasure and in this way removes envy. The mother of the bride had no special clothes. The following account is derived from my attendance at a number of weddings.

Guests, all women, begin to arrive after dark and take up places on canvases spread on the ground. I received quite a shock once seeing what I took to be a man at the women's festivity; dressed in jeans and with a cap over his long black hair, he also had a mustache and was smoking. Presaging the pranks to follow at the *kına gecesi* (see below), a friend of the bride had dressed as a man to entertain and titillate the guests. She was very effective.

15. Their children will not be further cursed by illegitimacy if they can secure a birth certificate from the local midwife, or if the woman goes to the hospital for the birth.

The dancing takes place in the courtyard, which is often shared with cows, dogs, cats, and chickens. Although there is barely any light except stars, the moon, and an occasional dim light bulb, the dancing is a colorful sight. Women are dressed in a kaleidoscope of colors and prints. Their prettiest *yemeni* (scarves) are saved for just such occasions. Some wear *şalvar* of velvet with metallic threads; others remove their *şalvar* and reveal city clothes. If there are any engaged girls, they may come in their *nişanlı* dresses. A few will arrive in *bindal* (antique wedding dresses), which are a kind of caftan made of velvet in deep rich colors, embroidered with gold and silver threads, and secured with silver belts. Then there will be special dances for the *nişanlı, bindallı,* etc.

Dancing is a very important activity for women; it represents not only a release from inactivity and a chance to move and express oneself, but the only occasion on which one's movements are not constrained by others. Any girl or woman who wants to dance can; all she needs to do is ask someone (it is considered rude to refuse). Most girls and women, young or old, fat or thin, seem to enjoy dancing. Music for dancing is today provided by tapes, or, if there is no electricity, by tambourines and singing. The dancing follows a very definite pattern and requires two at minimum, though any number can join. Usually it is done in sets of six or eight. The women form two lines, each "couple" facing each other. The music is very repetitive and rhythmic; the steps involve coming together and parting, then at specific intervals a circling around each other. If there is a large group, they form a circle at this point and then, when the music changes, revert back to the two lines. The body is held straight and the dance partners never touch, but the dancing can be quite erotic, especially when those who know how begin to undulate their shoulders and shake their breasts.

According to Roper (1974: 68), women consider the dancing to be *the* binding part of a wedding. Dancing is also important, I suggest, because it brings together the community of women. It is the only occasion on which so many women—often several hundred; the entire female population of the village, plus guests—get together at one time. Although men also dance, their dancing rarely involves the entire male community. The women's celebration is comparable to the community of men gathered at the mosque. The comparison seems to highlight the gender differences: men's community is formed spiritually, women's expressed physically.

Dancing at a wedding (note boys on rooftop)

One late October wedding I shall never forget. Emine, Samiye, and Sevin called for me and we went hand in hand to the other side of the village. There are no street lamps. We had no flashlight, and the lanes were rutted, uneven, and full of rocks, holes, and puddles. As we crossed the open field in pitch dark, the stars seemed to splinter the cold, clear air. It was an unearthly quiet except for the soft tread of our feet and the distant barking of dogs. The dancing was being held in a three-sided mud-brick shed. Women in *bindal* and gauzy scarves shot with gold were leaning against the wall nibbling dried fruits and nuts. Others were dancing, and there was a small open fire in the middle. I felt I was stepping into a medieval pageant.

After a large crowd had gathered and the dancing had gone on for some time, the bride was brought out, danced one dance, and then went around to kiss or shake each guest's hand and thank her for coming. This is quite a task if there are many guests. The dancing continued, and nuts and *leblebi* (roasted and salted chick-peas) were handed round the room from a large sack until the crowd thinned about 11:00 P.M. The bride, secreted away from her family, changed into a *gecelik* (nightgown) and was hidden.

Except when there are outside musicians, the men's celebration is far more subdued than the women's and there is rarely such a crowd. During my first year in the village, there were no musicians; during my second year, thanks to increasing affluence, several families could afford them. If there are musicians, the men, usually only the young, gather in a neighborhood tearoom and dance to taped music and the *saz*. When there were musicians, things were much livelier. Once a huge bonfire made from old tractor tires was lit in the *harman* (literally threshing floor, but here meaning an open space). Everyone went to watch. Men gathered around the fire; women sat farther back in the shadows before they went to the bride's house. On this occasion, the men danced the *sinsin*, which seems to be a form of tag. One man at a time hopped around on one foot with his arm behind his back and tried to incite others to push him out of the dancing area. Several jesters made up as gypsies with blackened faces used long rods to prod the crowd and tried to shoo away a few men dressed up as women. Occasionally, it is said, people get hurt in this horseplay. Formerly there were skits enacting a mock struggle to catch the bride, but these are now rare.

Although some of the older men participate in the *sinsin*, it is more a spectator show. About 11:00 P.M., some of the men go to the tearoom to continue to dance, often all night. It must be noted that whereas the women's celebration takes place inside the enclosed space of the home, the men gather together first in the public open space and later in the tearoom. Although the tearoom is not truly a public place, being more like a private men's club, in either case men are not tied to the house in the same way as women.

Kına Gecesi. From what I have seen, the structure of this celebration is also fairly uniform. While the bride is being hidden, some guests leave and those remaining go inside the house. Women from the boy's side go to find the bride; when they do, she is led into the house and onto the bed. Meanwhile, others have made the *kına* (henna) into a paste and put it in a large round cake pan with candles stuck into it. If there is a lamp burning, it is turned off, and those carrying the lit-up *kına* march in singing. *Kına* is considered auspicious; it is the sacred soil of *Cennet* (Heaven, Paradise), which is envisioned as a garden, and it exudes the smell of Heaven as opposed to earthly soil. The woman (human soil) is anointed with sacred soil, and the flame, a symbol of male (but divine) procreative power, transforms her into a bride of Heaven. The songs that are sung while it is being brought in confirm this interpretation:

> She wore a slipper of divine light on her feet
> She comes swaying swaying
> She's the bride [gelin] of Muhammed
> Woman, let your kına [henna] be auspicious
> Where is this girl's mother
> May candles burn in her hand
> May her place be Paradise
> May her words be sweet there.
> Girl [kız], did your father reach the pazar
> Did he buy kına for your hand
> Woman [kadın], let your kına be auspicious
> May your words be sweet there.
> He struck [çalmak] the lining [astar] with his hand
> A saw cut her hand
> May your Lord make you look delicious
> May your words be sweet there.

There is a great deal of sexual allusion in this song, though it is somewhat obscure. Clearly a sacred marriage is taking place, not only because of reference to Cennet but also because the girl is referred to as the bride of Muhammed. Paradise could, of course, be an allusion to sexual intercourse itself. In Paradise (or during intercourse) let your kına be fortunate; that is, let your sacred soil be fecund. In the song there are three words for woman, indicating her transformation: kız (girl), gelin (bride), kadın (woman). It is important to note that the word kadın is used when she is in Cennet, whereas kız (girl) is used only in connection with her parents, who are absent when the divine candles are joined with the sacred soil (kına).

The hands (el) I believe represent genital organs, as we shall see by the way kına is applied to both the girl's hands and the boy's. Astar, an obscure word, can mean lining or undercoat (of paint) but is also a gypsy slang word for sexual intercourse. Çalmak means to strike or blow, and thus the fourth and third from last lines could be rendered: "He struck his organ to her lining / A saw cut her organ." In other words, his penis pierced her hymen. "May your Lord make you look delicious" could allude to the analogy between eating and intercourse, as the last line, "May your words be sweet there," appears to confirm. It might mean "Whatever issues from that nether mouth (vagina), let it be sweet." Women's sexual fluids are likened to honey.

The second song conveys a similar theme:

Mother Fatma[16] is sitting and crushing her henna
My dearest son's wedding is in heaven, in heaven, the throne of God.
There are three minarets there, one of them is short
From there the prophet Moses calls the *ezan* [call to prayer]
My dearest son's wedding is in heaven . . .
Wearing slippers of light on her feet
She comes swaying in the garden of paradise
My dearest son's wedding is in heaven . . .
There are three windows facing the *kible*
Mother Fatma is sitting and watching the throne of God.

The imagery once again bespeaks a hierosgamos (sacred wedding) taking place in the Garden, which, in Islam, is the place of the most exquisite voluptuous pleasures for men. The imagery, though somewhat more obscure, is still sexually suggestive. There must be one minaret; in addition there may be several more, but normally there would be four, not three. This could be an allusion to the male genitalia, the penis and testicles; or it could refer to God, Muhammed, and the human male, the short one being the human male. In either event the prophet Moses calls the prayer from that place, indicating the sacred patriline, the transmission of the sacred spark (seed) through men.

The *kible* is the pulpit toward which everyone turns in prayer, toward Mecca the sacred city, the earthly equivalent of *Cennet*. Facing it is something with three windows or openings. I believe this refers to the woman, who turns toward her husband as her lord, her earthly equivalent of God, and opens to him. She is not the originator of the life-giving message, but the receiver (transformer) through which it is passed and by means of three openings (breasts and womb) given substance.[17] The tie between mother and son is strong, but at a wedding

16. Fatma was really Muhammed's daughter, although she is referred to as the mother of faith. She is also known as "the Shining One" and is associated with divine light. One legend has it that God created the light of Fatma and lodged this in Muhammed's loins (perpetuating the connection between seed and light), from which he deposited it in his wife, who gave body and birth to the girl. Others speculate that there were connections between the cults of the Virgin Mary and Fatma. See *Encyclopaedia of Islam*, vol. 2 (1965), pp. 841–50.

17. Sabbah (1984: 52) quotes from an erotic Muslim text to the effect that the three holes are *within* the female genitalia.

(and during intercourse) the mother must take a back seat; the main action takes place on the throne (woman's body?) on which the son will sit. The relationship between religion and sexuality is made quite explicit. The minaret is both a phallic and a religious symbol. The divine call may be a reference to the power of God to call things into being, a power that is passed through men.

After the *kına* has been brought in, a struggle ensues between the bride and a couple of women related to the boy. They try to open her right hand in order to place a coin in it. Her final acceptance of the coin symbolizes her acceptance of the man. The coin remains in her palm as she dips her hand in the *kına* and her attendants spread and smooth it over her hands. These are then wrapped in lambswool and covered with a *yemeni* (headscarf), or in one case pink satin mitts. In the morning, her hands are unwrapped and then, except for the white place left by the coin, are stained red from the *kına*. Red is the color of fertility, and in this case she is imbued with the auspiciousness of the sacred soil of heaven.

Next her legs are extended and a piece of string is wound between two middle toes, up and crossed over the instep, and around the ankle and tied in front. Village women did not know the significance of this pattern, but a few noted that it resembles the *mest* (thin leather shoes) that men wear to the mosque. *Kına* is spread over the feet and up to the ankle, but not on the soles, for it would be *günah* (sinful) to walk on *kına*, or rather for *kına* to touch the profane earth. The feet are also wrapped in lambswool and covered with scarves or booties. Now the bride is immobile, her hands and feet are bound, she cannot escape her destiny.

All the while the women have been singing *mani* (short poems) and collecting money for the *kına*, which is stuffed into a purse and given to the bride as "pin money" for the first few months of marriage. The use of money on this occasion may have other meanings, however. Money may signify the *mürüvvet* (munificence, abundance, reproductive wealth) and thus symbolize their wishes that she help to increase and multiply the group with children. Young friends begin to beat on the bride to make her sleep and sing her a lullaby (*ninne, ninne*). At this point most of the guests depart, taking small packets of *kına* as they leave. They too will smear it on their hands. Thus the common substance of women is reinforced; a community of women is formed by sharing *kına*, the sacred soil.

Several close friends stay behind to entertain the bride in her immobile condition. There is more dancing, sitting, and talking, and occasionally a prank. During my first week in the village, I witnessed one that was quite bawdy and sacrilegious. The bride's sister, who was a great comic, and a friend dressed up as men, that is, with jackets, pants, caps, and mustaches. One pretended to be the groom, who, in the skit, had not been circumcised. The other, dressed as a barber, came bearing a basket full of knives, a cleaver, and a sharpener. "How can you marry if you've not been circumcised?" "Why have you waited so long?" The barber first sharpened the knife and the cleaver, and then with ribald laughter and lecherous gestures rummaged in the groom's pants and pulled out his penis—a large cucumber. With a great flourish he chopped off the end and examined it very closely. "Now you can go to the mosque." For the next episode, in the mosque, the barber changed into the imam, but with clothes awry and unkempt. The *namaz* (prayer) was done backwards, not only facing in the wrong direction but with the order reversed.

The relation between religion and male sexuality is clearly drawn here, especially that of *sünnet* (circumcision) as an initiation into the sacred brotherhood. On this night the penis looms large in the imagination of the bride and the assembled company. The skit seems to say: "Why all the fuss? Let's lop it off and be done with it." The penis, which women lack, and institutional religion, from which they are excluded, are explicit emblems of power, toward which these women's ridicule seems to express their latent hostility. But it was only older women, secure in themselves and their marriages, who could get away with such a prank. Several of the younger girls, perhaps attending their first *kına gecesi*, seemed to be both shocked and offended.

That evening, long after midnight, a group of us started out for the groom's house. Passing the tearoom, we got a glimpse of the men's celebration. Unlike the irreverent and ebullient women's party, the men's was quiet, somber, and serious, even though a few men were dancing to a melancholy *saz*. The groom had already departed, and was at home alone with his family. The object of our visit was to place some *kına* in the groom's palm to match the empty space on the bride's; the relationship between the hand and sexual organ was thereby made explicit. The red circle of *kına* on his hand will match the white empty space on hers; that is, he will provide the missing part that will fit into her empty space. We left him alone to contemplate this and returned to the bride. Those who planned to stay the night to keep her company were served a light meal before trying to catch a few hours of sleep.

Sunday

The men who have been dancing all night waken the village at dawn just as the sun is rising and the moon is setting. First they go to the groom's house to try to steal the flag that was put there by the girl's side. Perhaps that is a last desperate gesture to prevent the marriage, to keep the girl in circulation. If the father is awake, he will try to buy them off with a few coins (*başlık*). If they succeed in taking the flag, they carry it around the village as a standard while they dance the *zeybek*—a mournful, melancholy tune punctuated with the staccato of wooden spoons. Some return to the tearoom; others go to the groom's house, where a tractor and wagon are being made ready to go to fetch the bride's *çeyiz*. After that has been done, they career around the village honking the horn in triumph, leaving in their wake a tearful household. When there are musicians they play for the last time at this point, reiterating in their music both the exuberance and the sadness of the occasion.

The sleepy and anxious bride again wears her wedding dress, this time tied with a red sash or ribbon or veil that has been given to her by her brother or another male relative. Red, the traditional color for brides in Turkey (cf. Roper 1974: 64), is said to symbolize *kızlık* (virginity). Red (*kızıl*) is also used to symbolize valuable objects (Laude-Cirtautas 1961), and the word *kız* (girl) can also mean a scarce object, though this usage is uncommon. Whether there is any etymological connection between *kız* and *kızıl* I do not know. The similar sound may be partly responsible for the strong cultural association between red and femininity. Many words that incorporate the root *kız* express the color and feeling of redness and heat, among them *kızan* (an animal in heat), *kızmak* (to be angry or hot-tempered, to get sexually excited), *kızarmak* (to blush or get rosy; also used in cooking—to be roasted, toasted, sautéed), and *kızartmak* (to roast).

The sash or ribbon may function as a sign of the agnate's protection of the girl, a message that upon his honor she goes as a virgin. It may also represent fertility and be a sign of ripeness; for example, wheat when ripe is considered red. *Kına*, the sacred soil, is also red, and the woman's womb (her fertile field) is red, as evidenced by menstrual blood; thus the sash may also represent a transfer of her fertility (ripeness) from her father's house to the groom's.[18] Of course, it could be simply a sign of blood relationship, a small reminder of her continuing, albeit much curtailed, tie to her family. Although none of these meanings is consciously articulated, some combination of them seems to evoke a meaningful complex for the participants.

As the girl prepares to leave her family for the liminal journey between her house and the groom's, she is completely covered. A veil covers her face, a raincoat covers her body, and a large woolen shawl (*atkı*) covers her head and torso. A car decorated with red and white flowers and ribbons, and sometimes a baby doll on the hood, comes to fetch her. In the car are the father of the groom, other male relatives, and one or two women attendants (*hakçı*); the groom is not present, and she will not see him until nightfall. The men solemnly get out and come to take her. A mock struggle takes place between them and the men of her family, who must be conciliated by further payment of *başlık* (coins). As the bride leaves, seeds of various kinds (wheat, lentils, rice) are thrown to wish her fruitfulness and prosperity. Further down the lane the car is stopped by a large crowd of men who try to prevent its passing. (Are they trying to hold on to the women of the *mahalle*? Is this yet another indication of the desire to keep the women within their small group?) A prayer is read by the imam, more *başlık* is paid, and the car is released. Although shooting off guns at weddings is forbidden by law, gunshots are occasionally heard at this point. As the bride enters the groom's house, a lambskin might be laid for her to walk on to ensure her docility. She spends the day sitting on display so that friends of the husband's family may come to take a look.

Meanwhile the groom is absent. Forced out of his house, he seeks friends to visit and spend the day with. I was at Emine's once when a

---

18. Abu-Lughod says (1986: 135) of the Bedouin she studied: "The red belt that every married woman wears symbolizes her fertility and association with the creation of life." If by "association with the creation of life" she means the contribution women make to the physical constitution of persons, this would be very close to the Turkish meaning.

young friend of her husband who was being married that day came to visit. He was dressed in a suit, seemed very nervous, and smoked a lot. He did not remove his shoes when he entered the house, as is customary, because there is also a custom that on such a day the host might hide the groom's shoes to prevent him from leaving. He stayed awhile and then went to visit other friends; and so he passed the time until evening.

His house, meanwhile, is aflurry with preparation for the wedding meal. The bride's feasting on Saturday is private and within the confines of the household; the groom's family and guests will also eat inside the house, but the feasting can become more public. Occasionally the entire village will partake. At one wedding, for instance, five sheep were killed, 35 kilos of rice cooked, buckets of *hoşaf* (a watery conserve of fruit) were prepared, and all the food was ladled from huge cauldrons set up on a *ramuk* (open wagon) in the open space of the *harman* (threshing floor).

In the afternoon, girls from the bride's side will sometimes visit the groom's house on the pretext that some of the *çeyiz* was left behind, but also to help the bride set up the display in her new home and to take a tray of baklava for the nuptial feast. The bride's new home is generally one room in her father-in-law's house, and all the couple's belongings will be crammed into it. The groom's side has contributed the large furniture, including the bed.

The bed must have about eight layers when it is finally made up. Starting at the bottom is the mattress, then a cover, next a sheet and a bed skirt. The bed skirt is white and hangs down over the side; it is embroidered and has a deep lace border, all examples of the bride's handwork. An old sheet (to be used for the display of hymeneal blood) is the final bottom layer. The top layer begins from the inside out with another sheet, also embroidered and laced to match the skirt; it is not loose, but is sewn to the *yorgan* (a quilt filled with wool and covered with intricately stitched satin). The top part of the sheet is folded over to reveal the embroidery and lace. On top of all this is an embroidered bedspread and two pillows (*yastık*) with covers to match the skirt and sheet set. Several other pillows are scattered about. When faced with such an imposing piece of furniture, one wonders what the couple will do—just to get into it will take some effort. Is opening the bed meant to be homologous to opening the woman?

On one wall is hung a sheet decked with all the scarves the girl has decorated. Drapes are hung and then covers are put over everything. Everything of value has a cover; everything that is covered is valuable. At the same time one could also say that the physical nature of the objects is concealed, as if there is something obscene about the naked instrumentality of the objects. They must be covered, bound, and kept in place.

Extra quilts (*yorgan*) piled in a corner will be covered, as will be the top of the *bufe* (cabinet), the sewing machine, and of course, the divan and the pillows that form the back of it—rather like antimacassars. Everything is new, yet nothing matches. There is a great profusion of fabric, design, and color. Each item is considered by itself without regard to harmony with every other thing. Finally, the rug is laid and the guests take their leave.

I once visited a bride late in the afternoon to find her fully clothed in bed with a girlfriend who is now her *elti* (HBW). She was exhausted and trying to sleep, but the girl was giving her some sexual instruction.

After the last *namaz*, called *yatsı*, which is about an hour after sunset, the groom is finally allowed to go to his bride. Gunshots can again be heard as he enters the nuptial chamber. They celebrate the *gerdek gecesi* (nuptial night) by eating a special meal of saltless chicken and baklava. Since Turks consume vast quantities of salt, the absence of it here is significant. When one asks why this meal is *tuzsuz* (without salt), the answer is invariably, "That is the custom; it brings *sevap* [blessings]." Since the first bites of nuptial food are thought to remain in the stomach as food in the other world, one man hypothesized that salt, symbolizing *acı* (grief and sorrow), would be inappropriate. However, it also seems likely there is a sexual meaning, for salty foods are associated with men and sweet with women.[19] A *mani* recited in another context confirmed this:

Can the moon that passed be caught?
Can salt be mixed with honey?
In these long nights
Can one sleep alone?

---

19. Because of the power and influence of these meanings, a Turkish male friend confided that he does not eat sweet foods and prefers salty ones.

Salt and honey refer to sexual fluids of men and women, respectively. The absence of salt in the food may point to the presence of it in intercourse, the place where honey and salt do mix; but why, then, is honey permitted in the wedding food? The logic of beliefs about men and women and procreation would suggest something like the following: Honey is a kind of ambrosial food, something to sustain one in the other world, as women sustain life but do not generate it. Indeed, women are a kind of food, something that is consumed in the process of procreation. Salt is not food, but gives it its spark and is also used for preservation of food. Semen is for preservation of life (that is, perpetuation) in this world. In the other world sex, at least for men, is for recreation; in this world it is specifically for procreation. The woman's body provides the first food in this world; so, too, something representing the substantive nature of woman becomes the food in the next world.

The baklava is cut into many sections, often in a star design, and is referred to as *yüz görümlü* (with a hundred looks). The baklava is distributed to the neighbors who watch and wait to see the bloody sheet as proof that the bride was a virgin. *Yüz görümlü* may be a corruption or variant of *yüz görümlüğü* (the face worth seeing), which in other areas refers to the present the groom gives the bride to lift her veil.

The morning after the nuptial night, the bride must rise early. She must light the *soba* (something like a Franklin stove), make tea, and sweep the floor before anyone else is up. This is more than a token gesture, for that is what is expected of her during the early weeks and months of marriage. The contractual, rather than the romantic, nature of marriage is what is stressed and expressed. Part of that contract, albeit unwritten, is the production of a child within the first year of marriage. A child, especially a son, ratifies and legitimates the marriage and substantiates the new unit in the eyes of the community.

As fall ends, a new crop of brides have been tucked in and the fields have been seeded. Both are expected to germinate new life over the winter. In the next chapter we take up the constellation of relationships engendered by the coming together of man and woman.

THREE 🌢 Relatives and Relations

When a child is born, it is born into an already constituted social world. In order for it to be integrated into that world, its identity and relationship to other people must be established. Who one is is related to notions of where one comes from; a person's identity involves notions of origin that are simultaneously physical, social, and cosmological.

If, as I have argued, procreation concerns beliefs about where, from what, and how a person comes into being, then implicitly, at least, it concerns beliefs about how persons are related to each other. On the basis of these beliefs certain people are distinguished from all others; they are "our kind." Anthropologists have designated this area of human society "kinship." Following Morgan, the nineteenth-century theorist who first studied kinship systematically and whose study helped to make it a central focus in anthropology, most have assumed that "all kinship systems were based on a recognition of a community of blood through procreation" (Ashley-Montagu 1937: 310).

But is procreation always and everywhere considered a "natural" process? Hasn't the notion of the natural developed within a culture that has distinguished between natural and supernatural, that is, within a particular worldview that, however widespread, is not universal? Is blood universally the essential element in people's notions of relatedness? Does blood constitute these relationships or symbolize them? Contrary to conventional approaches, Schneider has forcefully argued that when biophysical elements such as blood are used to differentiate between groups of people, they are used symbolically, not scientifically. But if kinship is not a fact of nature, why should procreation be? If beliefs about procreation form and are informed by major categories through which people perceive and order their world, then

147

the classification of and the relationships between persons are part of that order. Rather than assuming "kinship" to be the social elaboration of natural facts, I view notions of relationship as part of the more embracing generative logic of coming-into-being, which includes both physical and cosmological dimensions.

In this chapter I explore the way the theory of procreation illuminates villagers' views of relatedness. In Turkey the people one is related to are one's *akraba* (relatives). In Turkish, the suffix *-lik* (or *-lık, -luk, -lük,* depending on the preceding vowel) can be attached to certain words to make them abstract nouns: for example, *güzel* means beautiful, *güzellik* beauty; *dost* means friend, *dostluk* friendship; *akraba* means relative, *akrabalık* relationship or relatedness. *Akraba* and *akrabalık* do not function like the English "relative" or "relation" and "kinship," which have other meanings in other contexts. In Turkish, these words are used only in the context of kinship; but, as we shall see, they are not quite the equivalents of "relative" and "kinship" when these terms are defined primarily by consanguinity.

Kökler in Gökler

The title for this section was coined when the American television series "Roots" was first shown on Turkish television.[1] In Turkish, *kök* means root, base, or origin; *kökler,* therefore, would be "roots." The book on which the television series was based was an attempt by a black historian to answer the question "Where did we come from?" as a part of an effort to understand who American blacks are. This is an appropriate way to introduce ideas about kinship in the village because a similar question is in the minds and on the lips of villagers.

The first question asked of a stranger is "Where do you come from?"—where were you born, where is your *memleket* (native soil). This is followed in quick succession by "Who is your father?"[2] "Are you

1. I would like to thank Philip Remler for this suggestion.
2. That this is a very old practice among the Turks is attested in the Diwan Luyat al Turk (c. 1075). "The Turks, like the Arabs, traced their descent back to eponymous ancestors, and had to know the genealogies of their immediate tribal groupings" (Dankoff 1972: 331, n. 25). Dankoff also cites Vambery, who, when traveling in Central Asia in 1864, made the following observation: "When two Kirgiz meet, the first question is 'Who are thy seven father-ancestors?'—the person addressed . . . always has his answer ready, for otherwise *it would be considered as very ill bred*" (ibid.; emphasis in original).

married?'' and ''How many children do you have?'' These questions are
not as simple as they first appear. They involve complex notions not only
of origins and destinations, but of proper orientation in life, which in
Turkey is largely a matter of birth—not in the aristocratic sense, but in
the sense of origins and identities.

Gökler is the name chosen for the village because villagers believe
they have descended from the Göktürkler, who they say were the original, true Turks. *Gök* means sky, heaven, and a shade of blue; *Gökler*
therefore means ''the heavens,'' a suitable name for a village on a mountain near the sky. Since in Turkish K and G sounds are often interchangeable, one can also find references to the Köktürkler, the very
same original Turks, who are believed to have descended from the sky[3]
to Central Asia, whence they dispersed to Turkey and elsewhere. Villagers thus attribute their roots, *kök*, to these ''bluebloods''!

Ethnically they imagine their roots are with the heavenly ancestors,
a belief in line with the Muslim notion that our original home was
Heaven and that at death we will return there. Villagers believe they
have come from Heaven and will return there; at the same time, they
paradoxically believe they have come from the soil and will return there.
They see their village as buffeted by tensions and conflicts, delicately
poised as it is between Heaven and Earth, between this world and the
other world. Since these tensions and conflicts remain unresolved, a
decision for one world or the other entails certain orientations and
commitments.

As the physical location of the village gives a majestic view of the
plain below and cannot help but give a sense of lofty superiority to its
inhabitants, so too does their self-identification with the ''blueblood''
Turks reinforce feelings of ethnic superiority. This may also contribute
to their desire to remain one inside, closed group, untainted and unpolluted by mixture with outsiders.

To make matters more confusing, or perhaps to illuminate the inextricable relation between ethnic identity and kinship, *kök* is also the
primary term used to discuss descent. The study of relations of descent
is one of the two primary approaches to the study of kinship that have
been developed by anthropologists. The other is the study of ego-based

3. We used to make a joke that I too descended from the sky (by airplane). ''Gökten
Göklere dustum''—I fell from the sky to Gökler—also implies that I came to Gökler ''out
of the blue.''

relations with relatives on the ground, that is, with the network of living kin; this will be addressed in the next section. In both kinds of study anthropologists have generally relied on genealogies based on a biological model of origin. Here I try to outline the notions of descent as they are discussed by villagers.

Kök as root or origin in this context refers to the *ata* (father-ancestor) or *dede* (grandfather) from whom one traces one's descent. As one woman put it, "Sülale bir kökten [kocadan] tam çakılır"—from one root [man] the patriline is completely "established." Literally, *çakmak* means to drive in with a nail, to tether to a pin or pole, to strike a fire or flash like lightning. The word evokes images of a nomadic past in which a man was likened to the central pole from which the tent was spread.[4] It also gives a sense of the generative spark passed through males, and thus gives a richer meaning than "established" can possibly convey. When we recall that the term *sülale* encodes a notion of reproductive semen, it becomes clear that there can only be one *kök* and that is male. Both men and women are included in the *sülale*, but descent is through males. Women are like the leaves of the tree; when they die, that is the end. They are the end of the house, the terminus of the line. Neither descent nor the *sülale* continues through them.

Who is considered to be a *kök* and who are descendants depends to a great extent on who is doing the reckoning. Looking back, people in the present trace descent to and from a patrilineal ancestor; for example, the *kök* of one's mother is traced through her father and his father, but one's own *kök* is traced through one's own father and his father. However, a man as *kök* looking forward counts all his children, male and female, as *filiz* (shoots, buds) from the same *kök*, root. He would certainly include his son's children as descending from the same *kök*; and some men, especially on the occasion of a large family gathering to which a daughter and her children came, might include them as well. However, these children would consider themselves to be not from his *kök*, but from their father's.

Casson and Özertuğ maintain that "*kök* refers to a cognatic construct by way of which relationships of descent are traced through both males and females. . . . Irrespective of patrilineal ties, any two people who

---

4. I was not surprised to learn that the notion of "tent-pole man" is well known in Muslim erotic literature. According to Sabbah (1984: 44), such a man has a penis in a constant state of erection and it holds out his robe as a tent pole holds up a tent!

share a common ancestor are kinsmen because they are descended from a common *kök* or root" (1974: 351). I would agree that people who share a common ancestor are *akraba* (relatives), but I would disagree that it is because they are descended from the same *kök*. Although ego and the mother's brother have ancestors in common, they are not from the same *kök*, even though they would surely be *akraba*. When reckoning descent those "dişardan sayılmaz" (those from outside) are not counted. For example, "Dayı [mother's brother] bulaşmıyor, ama amca bulaşıyor, ayrı kökten meydana geliyor"—"The mother's brother is not counted but the father's brother is; they came into existence from separate *köks*." The use of the term *bulaşmak* is curious, for it means to taint, to pass by contagion, and in the form of *bulaşık* means something like pollution. Here contagion means that the mother's brother does not pass the lineage "germ" or seed to his sister's child; the children are from different *kök*. *Karışmak* (to mingle, mix in) is also used in this context; but, as we have noted, the mixing and mingling of different substances is considered polluting. The use of *bulaşmak* seems to mean that nothing can pass between those constituted by different *kök* (or seed), that the boundaries of *kök* are distinct and pure. It should also be clear that a man's wife's brother, the daughter's husband, and the son's wife would not be considered derived from the same *kök*; yet they are *akraba*.

There has been some question whether a married woman is counted in only one *sülale* or in two. Casson and Özertuğ claim that "although a woman may leave her father's *sülale* and live all her life many miles away, she is always counted in her father's *sülale* and never in her husband's" (1974: 351). Stirling does not use the word *sülale*, but he states that "the lineage is an affair of men. Women . . . except that is, for those who marry within the lineage, belong to at least two lineages" (1965: 161). In Gökler a married woman may continue to count herself in her father's *sülale*; her father may or may not continue to count her. Several men said that a woman cuts her tie with her *sülale* upon marriage.[5] At the same time, although she is incorporated or subsumed into her husband's *sülale* she is not counted in the same sense he is. In some im-

5. Engelbrektsson has suggested that "lack of agreement as to the 'proper' counting of *sülale* membership among the villagers may be partially due to recent changes in the inheritance laws. Earlier it was taken for granted that a woman left all rights of inheritance behind when she left her father's home" (1978: 54). In practice this may be true, but in theory women in Islam are allotted a share.

portant sense, she is socially invisible; her identity is fluid and passes between two men, her father and her husband.

In any case, "whether or not a woman can be counted as belonging to more than one *sülale* . . . it would be an affiliation counted through a male link, either through that of her husband and/or that of her father" (Engelbrektsson 1978: 54). And that is the main point. There is no term or concept of matrilineal descent; though women can trace descent, it is always through men. It is similar to the practice in the West whereby a woman receives her father's surname; although it is theoretically possible to trace descent through one's mother, not only is her maiden name her father's, but in time these names are lost.[6] Women are clearly relatives and do have relationships, but these are of a different kind. This causes no problem in daily life, since *kök* and *sülale* are not corporate lineage groups but simply conceptual principles by which people trace and reckon descent. The *sülale* or line of reproductive seed inscribes identity that unites past with future and gives definition to material substance. Women are the ever renewable ground upon which descent is delineated and inscribed.

Soyadı—from *soy* (family, race, lineage, ancestors) and *adı* (name)—means roughly "last name." Before the *soyadı* law of 1935 was passed in Turkey, all families in the village had *lakap* (nicknames) that may or may not have had some relation to the older *sülale* names. *Lakap* of the near past are still used occasionally for some people in the village: among them Sellektorgil, the family of a man who was noted for being able to manage the water depot; Çıtakgil, from *çıtak* (boorish, country bumpkin); Hatipgil, the family of a man who was skilled in Islamic ritual; Terzigil, the family of the former village tailor; and Paşagil, the family of a rich man or general. Among friends, the nickname can be a kind of secret code to refer to someone, as in the case of a man referred to behind his back as Khomeini because he sympathized with and behaved like the Ayatollah Khomeini. His family would be referred to as Khomeinigil. In a lighter vein, the *muhtar* (headman) was referred to as Colombo because, like the American television character of that name, he always looked disorganized and had his pockets stuffed with scraps of paper and letters. (For example, a letter addressed to me was

---

6. That there is something important about the notion of descent as given in a name is clear from the desire of many women today to keep their names and give them or hyphenated names to their children.

given to me six weeks late.) In daily conversation, the suffix -*gil* (family of, or those affiliated with) can be attached to practically anyone, male or female. Thus to convey that Ali and his family came to visit, one might say "Aligil geldi," or to say that we are going to Fatma's house, "Fatmagile gidiyoruz."

Some of the *lakap* are held to derive from named *sülale*, which in turn were considered to be branches of the original two, three, or ten *kabile* (tribes), depending on whose version one accepts, who founded the village. These carried names such as Emiroğulları (sons of Emir), Kadiroğulları (sons of Kadir), and Hafızoğulları (sons of Hafız). These names have all but been forgotten, and no one is concerned to trace his or her descent back to them. They exist more as folk ancestors, and confirm that the village was properly established by *ata* (ancestor, father). As we shall see in Chapter Four, this is important at the national level as well. Mustafa Kemal, whose efforts at the end of World War I led to the establishment of the Republic of Turkey in 1923, was given the name Atatürk, father of the Turks.

The notion of descent has to do with personal, ethnic, national, and religious identity. But deeply embedded in this concept are ideological premises that have to do with power and gender. At its root it is male, for only males are considered generative in this way. The ancestors, except for one's father or grandfather, may be absent, but they are an ethereal construct, present to the mind or imagination, their presence felt in the structure and perception of the empirical world.

The symbol of a plant or tree rooted in the ground has been turned upside down. Its rootedness in heaven will become more apparent when we discuss the notion of *Cennet* (Paradise), from which humanity originally came and to which the chosen will return.

Nevertheless, it is with the *filiz* (the shoots and buds), the living embodiments of the ancestors, that one is in daily contact and conversation, and it is they with whom relationships are defined, maintained, and worked out on the ground.

Circle of Kin

The principle of descent is temporal and linear, establishing a unity of identity over time. By contrast, relationships with those on the ground are seen as spatial. People who are related are either *yakın ak-*

raba (close, near relatives) or *uzaktan akraba*—alternatively, *hısım*—(more distant relatives).[7]

Akraba in its most embracing sense means relatives and includes those conventionally understood in anthropology as related by blood and marriage. However, *yakın akraba* (close relatives) has been glossed in studies of Turkish kinship as consanguines and is opposed to the term *hısım*, which is glossed as affines. This may be true for some groups in certain areas, but these meanings were not attributed to these terms in Gökler, or by anyone I talked to in Ankara.

Villagers say that *akraba* and *hısım* mean the same thing, that *hısım* is an old term that is not used much today. Others, when pressed, said *hısım* referred to more distant kin, but in neither case could this be construed as a distinction between consanguinity and affinity. Often those considered *hısım* were relatives of one's grandfather or grandmother, whereas those considered *akraba* included relatives of one's spouse. *Hısım*, if used at all, referred to distant relations either by blood or by marriage.

Blood is an ambiguous concept, and ideas about it are confusing and contradictory. When I asked whose blood a baby has, most people replied "the mother's." But some said that it had the blood of both parents, that it "must be able to mix"; and a few older men said that a child has its father's blood. All agreed, however, that the baby suckles the mother's blood in the womb. Villagers are surely not alone in holding contradictory views; yet at another level the seeming contradiction can be resolved if one realizes that the essential blood is contained in the seed. A bit of Aristotle and Galen seems to linger on; according to them, semen or seed is a finer concoction of blood, and semen is the medium through which the divine, eternal element (soul) is transmitted. In the village, women's blood seems to be something additive, thought of more as food; it is one of the means by which people are consubstantiated, that is, by which they share physical substance. In any case, since the identity of the person comes from seed, not blood, villagers are relatively unconcerned about blood. The notion that the bloods must mix (*uyaşmak*), implying that the bloods must be different (pairing of op-

7. This also is attested to as early as c. 1075 in the Diwan Luyat al Turk. "Among terms referring to the individual, the basic contrast is between *yoq*—near one, relative, and *yat*—stranger, foreigner" (Dankoff 1972).

posites), is being reinforced and reinterpreted owing to government pressure for blood tests before marriage.

The government has also launched a campaign to discourage marriages between close kin, arguing that marriages between blood kin (*kan akraba*, a term not in use in the village) produce *sakat* (deformed, disabled, crippled) children. Short television programs described the lives of deaf, blind, and crippled people alleged to be products of such marriages, and just before I left Turkey there were headline stories in the press about one village in which a number of hermaphrodite children had apparently been born. As might be expected, this message was shocking to villagers, since it called into question their most fundamental ideas about inherent differences between the sexes, ideas that are basic to their beliefs about the nature of the universe and the social order.

With regard to *sakat* offspring, villagers said: "The doctors don't understand. We've been trying to tell them for years, but they don't listen. Blood has nothing to do with it. We always marry relatives and nothing happens. It is only when we inadvertently marry *süt kardeş* [milk siblings] that *sakat* children develop." A woman who gives suck to an infant builds up the *material* substance of that person; it is a continuation of what she provided in the womb. Thus a "substantive" relationship is created between her own child and any other whom she nurses. They call each other *kardeş* (sibling), and this relationship is an impediment to marriage. It applies to all children in a given family born after the initial *süt kardeş*, but not to those before, and it does not continue down the generations. It is not generative, but is a bond arising from and applicable to the present. The separate, abiding identities of the children are in no way confused, for that comes from the father. What seems to be at issue is an idea that in order for substances to mix they must be different. In fact, it seems that to generate something requires two different orders of things, for example seed and field; two things of the same order would be sterile.

Although the logic used by the government is the same, the referent, blood, is not the critical issue to villagers. For clearly close relatives who marry, like any other couple, will have been nurtured by the blood of different wombs. If, however, they were suckled by the same woman, then at least part of the substance of the children would be the same.

Within their own system of beliefs, the villagers' views make perfect sense.

Blood, of course, is also not the critical issue in the theory of Western medicine that the government has espoused. It is nothing more than a "cover" term representing genetic relationship, and as such it obscures the central point that the scientific theory of procreation is duogenetic rather than monogenetic. The message of genetic theory is that both parents contribute to the genetic makeup of a child, that a child is related in the same way to both parents.

As we have seen, this is not the case in the village. A child is the product of both mother and father; but their contributions are different and carry different meanings, and these differences very much affect the way kinship is construed. The essential identity of a child is derived from the father's seed. The mother's role is simply to provide the "material" to swell its substance.

This theory of procreation lends itself to a distinction between spiritual/essential and material/supportive, the first male and the second female. However, it is perhaps more accurate to characterize the differences as between a generative principle definitive of God and men, and a nurturant principle exhibited by the earth and women. The distinction is not between nature and culture, and especially not between nature and nurture. Here nature and nurture are on one side, creativity and spirit on the other. This plausible contrast raises the question of why nature and nurture are so often seen as opposite, and whether anthropologists' distinction between nature and culture is just a residue left by the evaporation of the hegemony of the religious worldview.

The Turkish distinctions are not strict dualisms or binary oppositions; rather, they are relative and hierarchically related, encompassed and encompassing. On the one hand, men have bodies and thus have physical, material existence; on the other, women partake of the "spiritual," since they are of their father's seed.

Villagers say that humans are "Allahın tarafından" (from the side of God, not from the side of nature): that is, humans have not arisen from nature alone. Not only is the physical natural world created by and dependent upon God, but ultimately it is embraced and enclosed within the spiritual. From the perspective of earthly existence, however, the spiritual is enclosed and embodied in the physical. These two relative but interlocking categories affect the way kinship/relationship is construed. We have discussed the generative aspect in terms of descent, a concept by which individuals are related across time. But during one's time in this world, in one's physical embodiment, the aspects of sustenance and nurture displayed by the earth and women come to symbolize the closest physical relationships. The female body provides a model not only for the structuring of relations of inside-outside, but also for those of close-distant. The model is of a series of concentric circles proceeding outward from ego, the person to whom notions of closeness and distance are relevant. A woman in the village traced such a diagram in the dirt. In the city I came across several Turkish kinship charts that used the tree as a model; but it was the rings of the tree trunk that were salient, rather than the tree's branches, as in typical Western genealogical trees.

At the innermost core is the *aile* (a woman and children). This is a uterine unit in that the woman's womb serves as the matrix for the creation of the closest physical ties, those thought to exist between siblings. *Kardeş*, the word for sibling, is related to the word for womb (*karın*). The suffix *-daş* gives the notion of "fellow" (G. Lewis 1975 [1967]: 64); thus *kardeş* (from *karın daş*) literally means womb mate. In similar fashion, one can get the flavor of *adaş* (from *ad daş*, person with the same name), *arkadaş* (literally fellow of the back, friend), *yoldaş* (fellow traveler, fellow of the road) and *vatandaş* (compatriot, fellow citizen). Since *vatan* (also *anavatan*) means native country or motherland, fellow citizens are those who have been nurtured by the same soil.

Similarly, *kardeş* are those whose substance has been built up by the same womb and milk. They are of the same substance; that is why it is said there is no *akraba* (relation) in the *aile*. As we have seen, those nursed by the same woman, regardless of any "blood" connection, are considered *süt kardeş* (milk siblings). Milk is considered the first food, and thus is important for contributing to the substance of a person. The importance of milk does not, however, deny that of the womb, since children are generally nurtured by the womb and milk of the same woman; rather it emphasizes the importance of substance or nurture for understanding the nature of physical, earthly ties. Sharing the substance of womb and milk, or even milk alone, creates *kardeş* (siblings), not *akraba* (relatives). People cannot marry *kardeş*, those of the same substance, whereas people can, and often do, marry *akraba*.

The tie between *kardeş* is closest; after this, the relationship between mother and child is felt to be closer than that between father and child. Why? Proximity is one consideration, because children spend a lot of time in the company of their mothers; but a more important consideration is that the mother has nourished the child from the resources of her body.

Akraba (relatives) are one remove from the *aile*. In general, villagers say *yakın akraba* (close relatives) include the *kardeş* of one's mother and father *and* those who marry them: one's aunts and uncles and their spouses. This relationship is described not in terms of blood (consanguinity), but in terms of *kardeş*: it is a relation between uterine units characterized by physical substance (blood and milk). Those who marry the *kardeş* of one's mother and father are also *yakın akraba* because by their marriage a new *aile* will be established. Their children are the most closely related persons of the same generation without being of the same *aile*.[8] These are not *kardeş*, but *yakın akraba*, and the closest relatives one can marry. At the same time it is said that the *akraba* on the mother's side are closer than those on the father's side. Again this points to physical and substantive closeness rather than merely proximity, for people do not live with their mother's relatives but often live with their father's.

In short, villagers understand their relationship to their mother and father differently, and the theory of procreation helps to illuminate and clarify these differences. The father's side can be called *sulb tarafı* (*sulb* means loins, descendants, seed; spinal column; hard, rigid, firm), the mother's side *süt tarafı* or the milk side (Erdentuğ 1956: 31). In Erdentuğ's English translation (1959: 9), *süt* (milk) is rendered "fostering," which is very close to what I have characterized as "nurturing."

These two sides or notions of relationship are not, however, mutually exclusive, nor can they be treated separately, since relations on the ground are specified by relations of descent. Superimposed upon and giving definition to relationships of physical nature are those of descent and identity. They meet in the concept of the *ocak* (hearth), which is an appropriate place to begin the discussion of ego-based kinship. In order to do that, let us return to where we left off at the end of the last chapter.

A child is expected within the first year of marriage. The birth of a

---

8. In other words, *yakın akraba* includes both consanguines and affines, in contrast to conventional anthropological understandings. The villagers' category accords well with their belief that a child makes a marriage: thus the spouses of one's *kardeş* or one's parents' *kardeş* are *yakın akraba*, not so much because of their marriage as because of their children.

child is the real consummation of the marriage, for a childless marriage is not really considered a marriage. After the fall weddings during my first year in the village, all the brides produced sons. Thus each woman redeemed herself in her husband's household, for the continuation of his *ocak* (hearth) was thereby assured. It is said of a man without sons, "ocaği sonmuş"—his hearth is extinguished, his patriline has died out.

The *ocak* is another way of talking about the house, that physical embodiment of the male line, and the spark that keeps it going. It is the place where the woman (wife-mother) transforms the wheat seed into bread, the mainstay of the village diet, in the same way that she transforms the man's seed into a child, the continuator of the line.

Those who eat from the same *ocak* are a man and his *aile* (wife and children). When his son marries, his *aile* will also be included. In order to describe the terms in use, let us begin with this nuclear group. There is a father (*baba*), a mother (*anne*), and their children (*çocuklar*). *Çocuk* can mean either child or boy. Parents distinguish in daily conversation between sons and daughters; *oğlum* (my son), *kızım* (my daughter). Since *kızım* is also the normal word for girl, girls and daughters are interchangeable linguistically.

The children are *kardeş* (siblings) to each other. Among siblings distinctions are made to indicate both sex and age. An older brother is *ağabey* (or simply *abi*); an older sister is *abla*, occasionally *bacı*. A younger sibling would not call an older one by his or her first name alone, but would instead either use or append *abi* or *abla*: thus Fatma *abla* or Murat *abi*, or simply *abla* or *abi*. Older siblings do call younger ones by name.

There are differences with respect to the way the various terms are used, classically discussed in anthropology as terms of address (used in talking *to* someone) and reference (used in talking *about* someone). In practice, however, not only can they overlap but they can also be used for other than true kinship relations. For example, the term "sister" in English can be used all three ways: I may speak about my sister to someone else, or I can say "Hey, sis" to get her attention, or I can address a nun as "Sister." Where applicable, I shall try to indicate the difference in the Turkish terms.

Let us assume that the older brother has just married and his bride is incorporated into the household. She will be called *gelin*, or *kız*, by his parents and *yenge* by his siblings. She will also be referred to as "our *gelin*" by both his parents and his siblings. She will call her husband's parents *anne* and *baba* (mother and father), though she may refer to them as *kaynana* and *kaynata* (mother-in-law and father-in-law). Her husband's brother, strictly speaking, is her *kayın* or *kayınbirader.* She will call him whatever her husband calls him: that is, *abi* if older and by name if younger. In practice, *kayın* is relevant only for men; that is, a man uses it to refer to his wife's relatives, and indeed it seems likely that this was the original meaning.[9] The husband's sister is *görümce*, but will be called *abla* if older; his sister's husband is *enişte.* In other words, a wife calls her husband's relatives by the same terms that he does, reinforcing the notion that she has been fully incorporated into his household. This extends as well to his uncles and aunts; thus she would call his FB *amca* as he would, and his MB *dayı*, and so on. He would refer to her parents as *kaynana* and *kaynata*, but if the relationship is close would probably call them *anne* and *baba.* He would refer to her brother as *kayınbirader,* her sister as *baldız.* In addition, men married to sisters are *bacanak* to each other; women married to brothers, and thus often living in the same household, are *elti* to each other, but will call each other *yenge.*

Once a child is born, other terms come into play. The child's FF will be its *dede*, but will be called merely *baba*; FM is its *ebe* or *nine*, but will be called *babaanne* or merely *anne*. The child's FB is *amca*, its FZ is *hala*, and (as indicated above) its own siblings are distinguished by sex and age. FBW, who might also be living in the same house, will be *yenge*, thus collapsing two generations into one.

These are the people whom one grows up with and who are considered close; yet those on the mother's side, although not members of the *ev* or gathered around the *ocak*, are felt to be even closer than those on the father's. The mother's *kardeş* are *dayı* (MB) and *teyze* (MZ). Anything to do with the mother implies closeness.

The mother's parents are referred to as *dede* for MF, *nine* or *anneanne* for MM, but are probably called just *anne* or *baba*, sometimes with *büyük* (big) prefixed. Grandparents on both sides refer to grandchildren as *torun*. The *dayı*'s wife is called *yenge*, especially if there is not much of an

---

9. It is felt to be related linguistically to the old Turkish root *ka* (receptacle, womb), from which *karın* (womb) is derived. At least as early as c. 1075 the woman's relatives were referred to by the man as *qadın* (related to *kayın*), whereas the man's were referred to by the woman as *dünür* (Dankoff 1972: 41). Today *dünür* is reciprocal between the parents of the couple. The distinction between in-laws may also be related to what Erdentuğ calls the "fostering side" versus the "loin side."

age difference, or perhaps *abla* or even *teyze*; the *teyze*'s husband will be *enişte*. Finally, one's nieces and nephews are *yeğen* regardless of side. The term *yeğen* has been described as relevant only to those related through women, for example one's sister's or MB's children (Pierce 1964: 80); but my Turkish informants say this is incorrect.

A terminology system is clearly part of any study of kinship, but it is less clear whether such a system is a direct reflection of a society's knowledge of the "facts" of reproduction, as Morgan and others since have argued; a reflection of its social structure, which itself is often presumed to be rooted in biophysical relationships established through marriage and reproduction; or something autonomous. Although the Turkish terminology system has equivalent terms for men and women, villagers do not believe that men and women contribute equally to biophysical relationships, nor do they think about relationships to and through men and women in similar ways. That being so, we must wonder what the terms do reflect, if anything. Casson and Özertuğ assert that their analysis "supports the position that kinship terminologies reflect social structure, i.e., that social structure is primary and prior and that semantic structure is secondary and reflective" (1974: 348). But they give no rationale for the privileging of the terminology system to the exclusion of all other factors in trying to understand what either kinship or social structure is all about. Instead, I suggest that the terminology system is only one part, and perhaps a very small part, of a "kinship system" if by this term we mean all the ways in which relationships are understood and affect daily life.

Ocak

The *ocak* is the place where concepts of descent and substantive relationships are integrated and defined. It represents the continuity of the line; the flame passed from father to son, as is seed. "A boy is the flame of the line, a girl the ashes of a house." In other words, a boy continues the *ocak*; a girl extinguishes it. The *ocak* is also the place where substance is transformed for the purpose of perpetuating the line (in terms of both bread and sons). Women, as wives, are brought in to feed the fire; they are the fuel that is consumed in the process. Not surprisingly, it is the task of women to make the fuel (*tezek*—dried dung), to feed the fire, and to dispose of the ashes, which are used as fertilizer on the fields to make them more productive. One nickname for wife is *küldöken*, the one who dumps the ashes.

The *ocak* is the living eternal flame of the line and is the psychological center of the house.[10] It is contained by the house as seed is contained in the womb for a brief period. The house, as the physical structure through which the flame is passed, is analogous to the female body, through which the seed is passed. As a woman must be protected, covered, and represented by a man, so also is a house; as a woman is passed between two men (father to husband), so also is a house (father to son).

There has been much discussion of how the "extended" household functions in Turkey. *Hane* is usually translated as "household"; like "family" for *aile*, this translation is not exactly wrong, but it obscures aspects of the *hane* that are culturally specific. In Western social science and statistical practice, "household" generally designates the people, usually a family, and the dwelling space. Turkish officials such as census takers, health personnel, and tax collectors use *hane* in this sense. Casson and Özertuğ argue that "the primary criterion used in defining a household is the payment of *salma*, the village tax . . . a tax collected within the village to support employees of the village—the village headman (*muhtar*), the watchman (*bekçi*), and the religious leader (*imam*)" (1974: 353). In our village, these were government employees and received their pay from the state. The *muhtar*'s small salary was indeed supplemented by *salma*, but according to villagers this was a very minor matter; I hardly ever heard it mentioned, and it was certainly not the salient feature in discussing the meaning of *hane*. Villagers assert that there can be several *hane* in one dwelling space. *Hane* refers to a social unit defined by a married man (a man and his *aile*) and his *ev* (house). But since *ev* can mean merely a room in his father's house, both he and his father (and his married brother or brothers) can be defined individually as *hane*. Thus there can be one, two, three, or more *hane* in one dwelling compound.

For villagers, an extended household represents an ideal model of what a household should be. What they mean by "extended" differs somewhat from the anthropologists' model, and thus we get conflicting reports about whether the ideal accords with reality (cf. Yanagisako 1979). If an extended household must by definition be composed of an

10. See Fustel de Coulanges 1956 [1864] for an early discussion of this idea.

older couple with their sons, at least one of whom is married with children, and unmarried daughters, then Özertuğ (1973), who assumes this definition, is probably correct that such a configuration does not account statistically for the majority of households. However, if the term can be stretched to include a household composed of two married generations, whether or not both partners are alive and whether or not all married sons are living within the same complex, the number of extended households would change dramatically. In this enlarged definition, most village households would be "extended" for certain periods of time during the domestic cycle, particularly but not only at the time of a son's marriage. How long a household will continue in this form depends on a number of factors, notably space, personality, and the way relationships unfold; thus time is a critical factor in any account of an extended household. The fission of an extended household need not await the death of the patriarch, as Stirling (1963, 1965) believed, but can and does occur earlier, as Özertuğ has pointed out.

An even broader definition of "extended" may be desirable to accommodate the enormous flexibility, and indeed the generosity, of households in Turkish village society. A household can extend, for example, when a daughter and child(ren) return home or a married niece takes refuge in her uncle's house, both of which happened while I was in the village. A married son who has previously moved to town may send his wife and child(ren) back to his parents' house while he is in the military or if he goes abroad to work. Occasionally a young man returns home after trying to work in the city; he may remain in the village thereafter, or he may try the city again. In addition, many households also extend for varying periods of time during the year. The wife's mother or father, especially if widowed, may come for extended visits; sisters and sisters-in-law with their children may also come, and the children of a brother or sister may come to spend the summer months and often years at a time. Some households absorb widows who are living alone, even if they are not related; they become a kind of expected presence and return to their own house only to sleep. Finally, some households accepted a schoolteacher.[11] This is to stress that village

11. And some can even accept an anthropologist! Although I was able to have my own house, initially I lived with a family for some weeks. Another anthropologist conducting fieldwork in another area lived with a family for more than a year. When I returned to visit the village in the summer of 1986, my house had collapsed and I stayed

households are extremely flexible and extend and contract periodically. A few examples that represent different but typical configurations may prove helpful, and may also help to clarify the use of the term *hane*.

Yazan. Osman Yazan has four sons, two of whom went to Ankara to work and have remained there. The two oldest, Ibrahim and Ali, who, when I knew them, were 50 and 44, respectively, remained in the village and live close by. At first, Osman and his family lived in one house. After the marriages of Ibrahim and Ali and the growth of their families, an addition was built. Later, Ali built a separate house next door for his family of six children. An unrelated widow who lives across the street spends a great deal of time in this house. Osman continues to live in the original house with his second wife and their teen-age son. Ibrahim and Ali work the farm for their father and share the produce. Their wives work primarily for their own households, but help each other and share work. They provide for the old couple, though Osman's wife usually does her own cooking. All these families normally, but not always, eat separately. This household complex was considered 3 *hane*, though there are only two house complexes.

Yerden. Ibrahim Yerden, an eldest son 40 years old, lived with his parents, his wife, and their four children. His wife's mother was occasionally absorbed into the household for long visits. His other siblings have left for the city; he remains and works the land, giving them all a share. The old couple eat and live with Ibrahim, whose father often acts as a babysitter. This household is considered 2 *hane*, two married men living in one house; in this case also, house and *hane* are not isomorphic.

Kiymetli. Nazim, the middle son (age 35), lives with his wife, their four children, his younger brother Hasan, and his old father Ali, a widower. His older brother Ahmet quarreled with their father and separated from the household. Hasan has just returned from the military, will soon be married, and plans to remain in the household. Nazim and his father used to work the farm together; after his father became ill, he worked it alone. Now he has the help of Hasan. The produce is shared only with members of that household. When Ali dies, however, the land will be divided between Nazim, Hasan, and Ahmet, at which time Na-

with the family who had been my closest neighbors and best friends. By their own account a person is considered a guest for only three days, after which he or she is a member of the household and is expected to do his or her share of the work, which I did.

zim's fortune will diminish. This is considered 2 *hane*; but when Hasan marries it will be 3 *hane*, all living in the same household.

Kiymetli. Ahmet, the son mentioned above who left his father's household, lived for over 20 years with his wife and their seven children in a small two-room house. They were very poor and had a difficult time, for they could not share in the produce of his father's land. One daughter recently married; another daughter left her husband (see next paragraph) and returned home with her two-year-old daughter. Ahmet's son Isa just returned from the military, will soon be married, and wants to remain in the village. In order to accommodate all of them, Ahmet, with the help of his son and his earnings as a *çoban* (shepherd), built a large new house. This is 1 *hane*, soon to be 2 *hane*, living in the same household; the daughter with child is not considered a *hane*.

Şaşkin. Murat Şaşkin is his parents' only remaining son. Out of eight pregnancies, his mother had two miscarriages and four of the children she bore died. The other living child, a daughter, is married and lives in the village. Murat's mother and his wife fought continuously, so Murat, his wife, and his infant daughter moved out into a tiny, old, dark one-room house. Although Murat stands to inherit a rather large house and considerable land, he can have the use of neither until the death of his father. By their action, Murat and his *aile* cut themselves off from their source of livelihood; with no income and no land, they had a very difficult time. Worse yet, now that he no longer had a mother to watch over his wife, he became insanely suspicious of his wife and locked her in the house. She finally left him and returned to her father's house. Murat first returned to his parents' house and several months later entered the military. When Murat and his *aile* were living in the tiny house, they were 1 *hane*; had they remained in his parents' house, there would have been 2 *hane* in the same house complex.

Karaoğlu. Mustafa Karaoğlu lives with his widowed mother, his wife, their three children, and his younger brother Veli, who recently married. Mustafa is notoriously lazy, and Veli does most of the work. All live and eat together. What will happen in this case depends on how long Veli and Mustafa can get along, and also how well the new *gelin*, from town, can adjust to village life. This is considered 2 *hane* in one household. Mustafa's mother, though of a different generation, is not considered a *hane* because she is female.

Küvet. Suleyman and Emine Küvet, an elderly couple, lived together separately from their children, several of whom had moved to town. Their son's widow, Fatma, lives down the lane, along with her married son, his wife, and their new baby and four of Fatma's younger children. A 16-year-old daughter, soon to be married to her FZS (i.e., a son of the old couple's daughter), looked after Suleyman and Emine even though she did not live with them. Suleyman died shortly before I left, leaving Emine alone. She plans to remain in the house until her death. There are no plans to move her to Fatma's house, partly because there are too many stairs and she is quite ill.

Except for Emine Küvet, Ali Yazan, and Murat Şaşkin's parents, all of the households discussed are currently extended (or in Murat's case no longer extant), and all the people mentioned have been part of an extended household for certain periods of the domestic cycle. When a widower lives with a married son, they are counted as two *hane*; when a widow lives with a married son, they are counted as one *hane*. Not all old people live with their children, but no man can live by himself; because of the strict division of labor a man cannot be expected to do household chores, and one widower without children living in the village was quickly remarried. Widows, however, can live alone, and there were a number of such widows in the village. Because I had been married and had a child, I was put in the category of widow (*dul kadın*). Although each of us occupied a separate house, none of us was counted as a *hane*.

Although a widow can remain in the house of her deceased husband, she cannot dispose of it because it is not her property. She is entitled to support and to a share of the inheritance, but the house itself belongs to the man and is passed to his sons. If the sons have left the village, the house and any decisions concerning it are still theirs. If there are no sons, it will pass to the deceased husband's brother. The devolution of inheritance and the specific shares are specified in Muslim law. But why are things arranged this way? The woman, who is symbolically identified with the house, would seem to be its "natural" owner and inheritor; similarly, since women are symbolically identified with land, they might just as easily have been owners of land, with men moving in at the time of marriage. However, that is generally not the case. Why not? At this point some writers, particularly those influenced by Marxist thought, simply assert that men *naturally* want to pass down *their* property to *their* sons (e.g. Bourdieu 1977; Engels 1972 [1884]; Goody

1976; Meillassoux 1981). But why wouldn't women want to pass down *their* property to *their* daughters? Much is assumed in these assertions that needs to be demonstrated. Male inheritance may be natural not because of the naturalness of reproduction, but because of the naturalization of a specific theory of procreation. Theories of male inheritance implicitly incorporate a view close to that of the villagers, a view that imagines men as "creators" and "owners" of children, who partake of their essence and are indeed part of themselves.

The one exception to the above norms of inheritance would appear to conform with the "natural" symbolic logic. This is the unusual case of an *iç güvey* (an "inside" bridegroom or son-in-law), a man who comes to live with his wife's parents. Sometimes this arrangement is resorted to by a man who has no son and may not have a brother, or whose only son has left the village. The man is generally fairly wealthy and wants a younger man to help with the work. Generally also the man who comes into the house is poor and might not be able to marry otherwise. In exchange, the house will pass to the *iç güvey*'s sons at the older man's death, though if there are absent sons or brothers, they will claim their share. Neither the land nor the house passes to or through women; it is more that the man has adopted a son. The fact that the house does not pass to the daughter is also a clear indication that there is no "equivalence of spouses" (Casson and Özertuğ 1974) in the composition of the household.

The situation of the *iç güvey* is rare because most men, regardless of the economic benefits, find it dishonorable. It is also a delicate task to arrange. A fairly rich neighbor, Riza, had two daughters. The son of another neighbor, hired as a shepherd, became fond of one of the daughters and made an offer to marry her. Riza responded by proposing that he become an *iç güvey*. Even though the young man wanted the girl, and even though they would have been quite well off, he refused. He is now married to someone else.

Life in a village is far too complicated to arrive at rules that will perfectly predict action. Rather, it has seemed useful to describe some of the variables and the range of possibilities. The terminology system may be bilateral, but except in a purely technical sense the system of relations by which social life is structured and lived is patrilineal. Those who ignore this, and they are few, cut the tie that binds and supports them.

Rather than trying to pull Turkish notions of relatedness through the consanguinity/affinity grid, it has made more sense to think in terms of a series of concentric circles representing degrees of "substantive" closeness that are transected by the line of descent that is generative and passes down the generations. This generative principle that symbolically allies men with God not only creates "physical substance," for men engender girls as well as boys, but embraces it (see diagram on p. 199). It is this principle that relates different uterine (substantive) units to each other, as it is the man who encloses the *hane*, represents it, and differentiates it from all others. At the center of these circles is the *aile*. Next come *akraba*—the closest being one's parents and siblings and their spouses and those who marry one's own siblings. In other words, *yakın akraba* are those for whom there is a kinship term. The exception is cousins, for whom no single term exists but who, as we have seen, are the only *akraba* one can marry.

The outer circle of those more distantly related are referred to as *uzaktan akraba*, occasionally as *hısım*. They are not affines but "blood" relatives, some of whom might even be considered part of one's *sülale* (lineage group) if that concept had more social relevance. They are at several removes from ego, representing such relationships as FZSS and FZDD. There are no kinship terms for them, strictly speaking, but such terms may be used when generation differences are purposely ignored for one reason or another. For instance, one man called his MMZ *teyze* (MZ); another addressed as *enişte* (ZH or aunt's husband) a man who was in fact his MBSDH! Similarly, a man called his cousin (MBS) *dayı* (MB), probably because the difference in age made *dayı* seem more appropriate. One woman referred to the grown children of her BS as her *yeğen*, a term usually reserved for the children of one's *kardeş*.

Old Ali, one of my best sources of kinship information, explained the differences between *akraba* and *hısım* by personal illustration. Nazim (his son) and Nuriye are married. Before marriage, Nazim's in-laws were *hısım*, somewhat distantly related—Ali's WZ was Nuriye's MM; thus Nazim married his MZDD. After marriage, they became *akraba*. I asked: "You mean Nuriye's parents are Nazim's *akraba*?" "Evet, kaynana var, kaynata var, değil mi?"—"Yes, there is a mother-in-law, a father-in-law, isn't there?"

The rationale seems to be the existence of a kinship term; since there is a kinship term, they must be *akraba*. For Ali himself, the "in-laws" were not only *akraba* but also *dünür*—that is, both sets of parents of the couple are *dünür* to each other. Moreover, Ahmet and Nazim are brothers (*kardeş*); Ahmet's wife's brother Sedat is Ahmet's *kayın*. Sedat and his family are *akraba* for Ahmet, *hısım* for Ali, but no relation to Nazim (BWB). Others in the village, however, might have included these as *akraba*. Who is and who is not included in the circle of *akraba* depends on the quality of a relationship as well as its proximity. In other words, notions of relationship are used both to define who is a relative in proximity terms and to incorporate borderline cases in pragmatic terms.

All villagers recognize the use of kinship terms to refer to people other than *öz* (real, true) *akraba*. For a time I would get very confused at hearing a man called Hüseyn *amca* when I knew he could not possibly be the speaker's FB. I would give a puzzled look; the speaker would laugh and say "öz amca değil"—not a true *amca*. But again it must be stressed that *öz akraba* means not just blood relatives, but anyone in the circle of *akrabalık*.

In daily conversation everyone is referred to by a kinship term. Unless one is of the same age and sex, or an older sibling of either sex, one never calls another person by his or her first name alone: a kinship term is always suffixed. I could not be called simply Carol, for example; that would have been *ayıp* (improper, shameful) and disrespectful. Instead, I was Carol *abla* (older sister), Carol *teyze* (MZ), or Carol *yenge* (BW), or more often simply *abla*, *teyze*, or *yenge*. Last names are not generally used; indeed, many villagers do not even know each other's last names. Chosen from a list supplied by the government in 1936 after the passage of the Last Name Law, last names are used for government record keeping but very little else.

Degrees of closeness and distance can be expressed by the choice of term. Closeness is indicated by using a term expressing relationship through the mother (*teyze* or *dayı*), distance or respect by a term expressing relationship through the father (*amca* or *hala*). Women will generally call men *amca* to express the distance felt appropriate between men and women. If the relation is close, they might use *abi* (older brother). Men will often refer to women as *teyze* (MZ), which indicates a feeling of closeness but also means that the woman need not fear the man, who is expressing protectiveness toward her in this way. If a woman is older or demands more respect, she will be called *hala*, though I rarely heard this.

Women who wish to commemorate their close friendship declare they are *ahret kardeş* (sisters in the next world); whoever precedes can intercede for the other. Similarly, men who have been best friends from childhood declare *kardeşlik* (brotherhood) to exist between them. They will refer to each other as *kardeş*, which can make matters very confusing when one is trying to figure out the *öz* (real, true) kinship relations. Also men often call other men *kardeş* as a term of address to indicate equality, *abi* for respect and closeness, and *amca* for respect and authority.

Relations

The foregoing discussion has focused on whom Turkish villagers specify as relatives; this section will look at how relations are conducted, that is, the quality of the relationships. The father is the *ev reisi* and *ev sahıbı* (house chief and house owner). Ethnographies of Turkey generally discuss patriarchal authority in terms of the patriarch's control of economic resources, but rarely ask how this control comes about. Thus, whereas Meillassoux is surely right that the very nature of agricultural production creates relations of dependence, since "the workers of one cycle are indebted for seeds and food to the workers of the previous one" (1972: 99), nothing in nature requires that "one man . . . the elder is logically appointed to receive and manage the product of his junior partners to whom he will advance seed and food until the next crop" (ibid.). Why is it logical that the elder male is appointed as manager? Indeed, why are seeds and their control assumed to be naturally in the hands of men? They might just as easily be in the hands of middle-aged women, who could just as easily watch over their use and distribution. Meillassoux does not entertain the possibility that the activities are organized symbolically rather than naturally, that their organization may result from a particular theory of procreation rather than from the "facts" of reproduction. Behind his theory are assumptions about power and authority, and these assumptions are never questioned. What is needed is a much more nuanced analysis of the basis of authority, an analysis that would take more seriously the symbolic logic of gender by which work is allocated.[12]

12. Although a number of feminists have criticized Meillassoux (e.g. Moore 1988;

In the village, the elder male is *ev sahıbı* because of his potential as *çocuk sahıbı* (child possessor): that is, because of his *tohum* (seed). In other words, authority and power reside in a man's procreative ability. Because he has the power to give life, it is his also to control and to mete out punishment.[13] As the world is muslim (in submission) to God, so too are women and children muslim to men.

Children owe their life to their fathers, and thus owe them obedience and respect. This relationship is particularly severe for sons, who depend on their fathers to raise the money for the brideprice and for their future livelihood. A grown boy should not talk back to his father, speak in public without his father's permission, or smoke in his father's presence (Stirling 1965: 101). One quite violent argument erupted in the village square because an adolescent had smoked in front of his father and this was interpreted as an act of defiance. Other men gathered around to contribute their thoughts, but also to keep the fight from escalating. Even a grown man, married and living in his father's house, will not usually smoke in front of him. In adulthood, men must learn to combine the seemingly contradictory characteristics of authority and submission.

My closest neighbor and friend, Ahmet, complained that his father had made him leave school after the third grade and during his early manhood had made him work very hard. Ahmet did not respect his father because he apparently used to drink, play cards, dance, and go to women. Soon after Ahmet's marriage, he and his father quarreled and Ahmet and his wife moved out. It was midwinter; they could not even take the bed, which is part of the paternal endowment of a marriage. Because he moved out, he no longer could share in the produce of his father's land; as a result, he and his wife nearly starved that first year. Happily they were helped out by a few friends and allotted some United States government surplus food (flour, cheese, butter, and powdered milk) by the village headman, with whom Ahmet was on good

---

Edholm, Harris, Young 1977; Harris and Young 1981; Mackinnon 1983; Mackintosh 1977), they have not really challenged the meanings of "reproduction" in the sense that I have been suggesting. But see Yanagisako and Collier 1987.

13. Some even assume the right of power over life, especially when a man's honor is sullied, which can happen through the sexual misconduct of his mother, wife, or daughter, more rarely his sister. As Meeker (1976) points out, this is quite different from the prevailing view in the Arab world. Although no crimes of "honor" occurred in our village, a number of such cases were reported in the newspapers. Cf. also Antoun 1968.

terms. Meanwhile, his younger brother remained at home and helped with the farm. With the passage of years he had become the manager of the farm, and during the time I was there he was becoming rich. Deprived of land, Ahmet first worked as a laborer in a neighboring village, and for many years now he has worked as a shepherd. In compensation, of course, Ahmet is no longer under the authority of his father. He can make the decisions that affect his own family.[14]

The father's authority, besides representing the house and making decisions about its management, manifests itself in the concept of *izin* (leave, permission). Although the idea of *izin* is not confined to the domestic sphere but is characteristic of a wide range of authority relations, the home is where the idea and attitudes are instilled. Authority, except for the elder male (and even that is relative), is always outside the self. Nevertheless, its range affects people differentially. Young men need their father's *izin* to leave the village, but girls and women need it to go anywhere outside the home.[15] A young man can look forward to a progressively greater authority, whereas a woman can only look forward to a relative relaxation of it, such as when she is older and has a married son and a *gelin* (bride) to whom she can delegate work.

Izin is thus permission to cross boundaries between inside and outside, however these are construed. Having *izin* means that one is "sent," that one's leave from one's place of duty is authorized. One does not control one's mobility in space and time; ultimately, in fact, all people need God's *izin* to leave the earth, that is, to die (Qur'an 3:145). In a sense, then, *izin* is the source or cause of movement.

The importance of this concept was made clear by villagers' questions to me about my presence in the village. They wanted to know if I had *izin* from my father to be there, then whether I had *izin* from my university, and finally from my government. Did they "send" me? The no-

14. For example, he decided to send his daughter to the *orta okul* (middle school), whereas his brother could not have done so, though he also did not want to (cf. Delaney 1989). Ahmet also decided to build a new house (discussed in Chapter Four), a feat no one thought possible under the circumstances.

15. The daughter of a neighbor was not given *izin* to go on the fifth-grade trip to Ankara. She was disappointed, but was cheerful and never yelled or sulked. At the last minute her father changed his mind. On another occasion a daughter was not given *izin* to go with her mother and sister to an engagement party in the next village. She showed no sign of resentment, rebellion, or anger; she accepted her fate smilingly. "If my father doesn't give *izin*, I can't go. Besides, who will look after him and cook for him?" (This for a visit of a few hours!)

tion of autonomy, the fact that I had chosen my work and the village myself, was extremely difficult, perhaps impossible, for them to understand. And it became critical for me in the village. I was a woman living alone and a resident of one small quarter, but in order to become acquainted with other villagers and to learn how the village functioned, it was necessary for me to walk around. This behavior of mine was never forbidden, nor was it approved: "Çok geziyorsun"—you're wandering about too much. Since the streets are the province of men, a woman strolling about too much is provocative—she is seen as opening herself to advances from men. Since a woman's proper place is sitting or working in the home, a wandering woman transgresses the boundaries; she is not enclosed securely where she ought to be.

In order to leave one's place or duty one needs *izin*. Whenever I decided to go to town, people asked if I had *izin*; they knew that the teachers and the midwife, when they wanted to leave the village, needed *izin* from their superiors (who lived outside the village) to leave their place of duty. My free movement was unsettling and disorienting for them. Since men control, or like to think they control, such matters, I was also seen as resisting men's authority and setting a bad example. In order to continue under the "protection" of the *muhtar* (headman), who in fact had given me *izin* to stay in the village and who could terminate it at his discretion, I tried whenever possible to let him know when I was leaving the village and when I planned to return. It was also a matter of courtesy, so that he would not be shamed by learning from others of my movement in and out of the village.

At the beginning of my stay, a young widow with several children who lived in my quarter used to come to visit me quite often. The brother of her dead husband, under whose "protection" she lived (but not in his house), learned of this and threatened her with a beating. She sent a note with one of her children on the way to school saying "Sedat won't give me *izin* to visit you; I'll let you know when you can visit." As this suggests, women and children learn to maneuver around the *izin* problem, keeping secrets as necessary and concealing some of their activities from men. In this case, as soon as Sedat left his house, especially if she knew he would be gone for some time, she would come to visit me or send a child to tell me I could visit her.

Similarly, most men would not give *izin* for "their" women to have their photographs taken, since a public viewing of women, even in a photograph, would dishonor the men. A few suspicious types thought I was a spy and would use the photographs against them in some way. Eventually, I made a joke of it and said they were right: as soon as I returned home I would have a huge exhibit in the White House! Once when the man nicknamed Khomeini was out of the village, the women of his house invited me there to take photographs because a married daughter was visiting with her new baby. The daughter confided that she had gotten married to escape her father's bad temper, only to learn that her father-in-law's temper was worse. I went to the house with some trepidation, but they assured me that Khomeini would never see the photos. Other men were more relaxed about what went on within the confines of the house, as long as no gossip escaped its boundaries.

Children also owe respect to their mothers because of her *süt hakkı* (milk rights). Because the mother nursed the child and nourished it in other ways, the child in turn owes love and respect to the mother. However, the relationship between mother and child is generally closer and more confidential than that between father and child. The mother-son relationship is warm and close; not only is it through a son that the mother's place in the husband's household is secured, but she looks to a son for support in her old age. That this does not always happen does not seem to diminish this prospect as a rationale for having sons. From earliest childhood a son is indulged. Ideally and normally, he will stay with his mother and bring in a bride to help her. The relation between mother and son is not only loyal but physically affectionate: often one will see a mother leaning against a son, putting her head in his lap, or embracing him. "The close link between mother and son is probably the key factor in the dynamics of Muslim marriage" (Mernissi 1975: 69). Mernissi's comments about Moroccan society are applicable, on this subject, to Turkish society. She continues:

marriage, which in most societies is invested with a kind of initiation ritual function allowing the adult son to free himself from his mother, is in Moroccan Muslim society a ritual by which the mother's claim on the son is strengthened. Marriage institutionalizes the Oedipal split between love and sex in a man's life. He is encouraged to love a woman he can't engage in sexual intercourse with, his mother. He is discouraged from lavishing his affection on the woman he does engage in sexual intercourse with, his wife (1975: 69–70).

There can be no resolution of the Oedipus complex in this society. According to Freud, a man must relinquish his attachment to his mother and identify with his father; but in this society not only is a man's attachment to the mother prolonged, but a son remains in a submissive relation to his father and thus cannot identify with him. Since the son also normally remains in the parental home, he remains in some sense in an infantile position as long as the father is alive.

In this society, it is clearly the daughter who must relinquish her ties, differentiate herself from her mother, and develop a strong enough personal character to cope with her mother-in-law's demands and her husband's lack of support. Mernissi believes that the institutional arrangement of Muslim marriage is a prophylactic against "the growth of the involvement between a man and a woman into an all-encompassing love, satisfying the sexual, emotional and intellectual needs of both partners. . . . Such an involvement constitutes a direct threat to the man's allegiance to Allah, which should be the unconditional investment of all the man's energies, thoughts and feelings in his God" (1975: viii).

Although I knew of one case in which an older woman was hardly speaking to her married daughter, relations between mother and daughter are generally warm and confidential, though the ever-present knowledge that the daughter will leave places a kind of limit on their relationship. Except when the daughter is small there is not as much physical involvement as between mother and son. Mothers are more demanding of daughters, for there is really nothing they can demand of sons. They actively indulge sons, whereas their affection for daughters more often takes the form of leniency. A mother who came to my house and found her daughter smoking never said anything except that it smelled bad, and she never mentioned it to her husband.

Although the child's relationship with the mother should be one of love and respect, the father takes precedence in anything public. For example, when Isa returned on leave from the army, having been away for eighteen months, his first duties were to kiss the hand of his father, my friend Ahmet, and then to greet the guests who had assembled; only later, when the guests had left, was he able to greet and embrace his mother. It was also on this occasion that Ali (Ahmet's father, Isa's grandfather) first came to Ahmet's house, to greet his grandson. Only during the second year of my stay did Ahmet pay a return visit and thus barışmak (make peace). In order to do this after many years of being küs (not speaking), Ahmet had first to go and kiss his father's hand.

Not all relations between parents and children are so reserved and constrained. Men are very fond of, and affectionate toward, children. I shall never forget one occasion when the *muhtar* was left to mind his granddaughter and the bread being warmed on the *soba*. Very gently he combed her hair and fixed it, and at the same time kept the bread from burning.

Although Turkish men have far more physical contact with their children than their American counterparts, the relation between child and father tends to grow more distant as the child grows older. This is thought to be one way of maintaining the proper respect due to a father. Much depends, however, on the particular personalities of the men as they have developed in particular life circumstances. One woman related that her father used to be very irritable and beat her. Now she says he is very democratic and like a friend, and prefers to stay at home in the evenings.

Many other men regularly left home after dinner to visit friends or to meet in one or another of the three men's tearooms. In other households men, women, and children engaged in conversation or watched television together; if there was a visitor, everyone's behavior was more formal and women were more reserved, but they were not excluded. In other villages, perhaps most, the custom is to have a special guest room in which men receive their visitors, but in our village this was not the case. When a visitor came, he was received by the entire family and expected to sit among them. I say "he" because a single visitor is necessarily male; women did not visit at night except when accompanied by their husbands. If men needed to discuss a matter privately, they would do so outside.

During the day the spheres of activity of men and women are separate. In many villages, including the nearest one, this separation is continued even at meals: men and boys eat first in the sitting room, and only after they have finished do women and girls eat the leftovers in the kitchen. But in Gökler all members of the household eat together, and this has to some extent mitigated the strict reserve normally exhibited between husband and wife.

In some households, during and especially immediately after dinner, there is quite a lot of conviviality. If there is a television in the house, it is turned on for all to watch. When I was in Turkey, the lone television channel began broadcasting at 7:00 P.M. with the news. The television was turned on as a matter of course, but often it functioned as a background to whatever else was going on. A few men refused to let their families watch certain American programs, such as "Dallas," but others knew more about such programs than I did. Rarely, however, did I see people as glued to the set as many Americans were when television was first introduced; in the village, and in Turkey generally, relations between people take precedence.

Relations between husband and wife ranged from reserve, distance, and tolerance to companionship, joking, and even some displays of affection. Such displays are considered inappropriate in the presence of others, but some people, mostly young, newly married couples, did not seem to care. Soon after their marriage, Ayşe and Durmuş came to visit me. They were easy and affectionate with each other; Ayşe leaned against his leg and draped her arm around him. Even more surprising was that they discussed aspects of their wedding night with me.

In another household, Satılmış teased his wife that she was becoming like foreign women because the outline of her nipples was showing through her sweater. This couple joked, teased, and played with each other; yet this relaxed atmosphere was possible only because Satılmış's father had died, leaving him the senior male of the household. He and his *aile* lived with his mother and his other siblings, but his mother was an invalid and had basically turned the management of the house over to Satılmış and his wife.

Teasing can furnish invaluable insight into gender meanings. By learning what is inappropriate behavior, one learns what is appropriate or, alternatively, what the consequences of inappropriate behavior could be. Mehmet, for example, used to complain that Semiha could do nothing a woman was supposed to do—"See? She can't even light the soba," which he then proceeded to do with feigned difficulty. "She is dead," meaning worn out; "I need another wife." Obviously used to such banter, she laughingly agreed: "Then I won't have to work so hard."

Younger people are often less rigid than their elders about gender-related behavior. I was visiting Ayşe's mother when Ayşe appeared with her husband. Ayşe was going to cut and sew a pair of *şalvar* for herself. Durmuş sat around with us talking and joking, and he even helped to thread elastic around the waist. He tried the *şalvar* on, commented on how voluminous and cumbersome they were, and then jokingly wondered how one could possibly walk in them!

Another man permitted his wife to smoke in his presence. He was the only one to work outside the village and was gone for considerable periods of time. I went once with him and his wife to work in their fields, and he brought a few bottles of beer along for us to drink. This would have led to a severe reprimand had any of the elders learned of it.

Nevertheless, men should exhibit qualities of *erkeklik* (manliness) and not be *cıvık* or *kılıbık* (soft and henpecked). The way men demonstrated this manliness varied. One young husband did not seem bothered by the fact that his wife did not always obey him; for example, when she ignored an order to shut the door or get him water, he just got up and did it himself. He was bothered only when his mother said "See what a good *gelin* [bride] we have," meaning him. Murat, by contrast, was insecure in his role as a provider of bread and went to extremes. He locked his wife, Sevinç, in the house when he went out, refused to give her *izin* to visit friends or family, demanded to be waited on, and beat her. Moreover, he constantly emphasized that since he was *erkek* (male) and therefore *yüksek* (higher), she must take orders from him. She finally left him and returned to her father's house. Although the house was overcrowded, her father graciously received her and her small daughter. This case, because it is unusual, deserves some attention.

Sevinç was supposed to have married a man from another village, but she did not want to marry him and did not want to leave the village. She wanted Murat, and one night arranged to elope with him. They escaped to the *yayla* down the mountain and the next morning appeared at his parents' home, *fait accompli*. Her father was furious and did not speak to her for months, but eventually accepted the marriage. Sevinç and Murat's mother quarreled constantly; the *kaynana* was known to be *huylu* (bad-tempered) and was socially ostracized. Sevinç and Murat left his parents' house and moved into a small one-room place. Since he had no means of supporting her, their situation gradually worsened and he took it out on her. She attempted to leave several times, but was encouraged to return. When she finally left for good and her father received her, he told her that the time had come to make up her mind once and for all: stay with him or stay with Murat. Her father's views on marriage were somewhat more open than most—he believed that in quarrels someone must give in, sometimes the wife, sometimes the husband; otherwise the fighting will continue and they must separate.

I first became aware that something had happened when I was awakened early one morning by loud knocks on their door. I got up and saw that it was Hüseyn, the father-in-law of Ahmet's other daughter. Soon the *muhtar* came and both called for the *bekçi* (watchman), who lives next door. I went over on the pretext of borrowing some butter, and learned that they were planning to go to Murat to get Sevinç's things. By this time, a group of women had gathered outside Murat's house. Inside were the *muhtar*, the *bekçi*, Murat, his sister, his MZ, and Anakadın (Hüseyn's wife). Sevinç listened on the outside, squatting under the window. Neither her mother nor her father was there. Children were hanging around outside, to my surprise; at one point the *bekçi* came out and shooed them away, but they returned. Sevinç went in with her aunt Nuriye. Murat refused to give her her *çeyiz* (trousseau). Since they had had no proper wedding and the *çeyiz* was not properly displayed, no one really knew what it contained—except of course Sevinç and her mother. Items of the *çeyiz* were nowhere in sight. Murat didn't want a divorce; he wanted Sevinç to remain until he returned from the military in two years. He had their daughter, Filiz, with him, and he planned to keep her there. Fatma (Sevinç's mother) listened outside; she was very angry that he refused to return the *çeyiz*, but she did not interfere. I was surprised that the whole affair was conducted so quietly; I expected more yelling and shouting. Murat was told that the *jandarmas* (a type of rural police) in the nearest town would be called if he did not return Sevinç's things.

Sevinç left him and went home, where her mother was crying and moaning. Sevinç stated that the court would give her custody of the child because she is so young. In village custom the child belongs to the father, being his by virtue of his seed; but a court, operating under the Swiss civil code instituted under Atatürk, may decide differently. Sevinç said she hadn't eaten in two days and that Murat beat her because there was no bread. I made tea and took it over to the crowd assembled at Fatma's. They had decided to wait to call the *jandarmas* in the hope that Murat would return the things on his own initiative. Some neighbors opined that Murat was *kötü* (bad) not to return the things, but also that Sevinç was *kötü* to have left. They thought she would eventually go back to Murat, and hoped for a reconciliation.

Later a group of women came to sit in the lane between their house and mine, with a view of Murat's across the way. The child had returned to Sevinç; when the *bekçi* came to take her back to her father, she started to cry and he put her down. The women made a chorus, truly like one in a Greek tragedy, saying "tasa, tasa" (pain, affliction) and "Sevinç ile yanıyoruz"—"We are burning with Sevinç," meaning that they were burned out with waiting and that they were on her side. By nightfall, the things had still not been returned.

The separation was made public, unlike an earlier separation I learned of, in which Emine walked out from her husband's house after a beating. They had no child, and Emine went to live with her *amca* (FB). Everyone thought what she did was *ayıp* (shameful), for a beating is not a reasonable excuse to leave a husband. Most thought she would return to her husband after his military service was finished; indeed she did, and soon afterward they had a baby. But Sevinç's case is different. Although many felt that she should or would return to Murat after he had done his military service, she was adamant that she would not return.

The most common explanation for their separation was *geçimsizlik*, which means both incompatibility and lack of livelihood. What troubled people was not that Murat beat her, but that he beat her because there was no food—an *ayıp* thing to do since providing food was his responsibility, not hers. Although most men and some women felt that she was wrong to leave because "yuva yıkıldı" (the nest is destroyed), they also blame Murat because he did not provide for his *aile*. She should have married the man from Buçukköy. Since all men are the same, better to choose a rich one.

The *bekçi* thought she would not go back: "How could she survive waiting for him for two years, when there is no bread?" A neighbor woman told me, "We can give her food, just as we give it to you." It is true that I never paid for any food I received in the village. I tried once to buy some cheese that I particularly liked, but was sharply reprimanded: I was their guest, and paying them money would have contravened the conventions of hospitality and shamed the village. (I did not, of course, get all my food from villagers; I brought much of it from Ankara or sent a shopping list and money with someone going to the *pazar* in town, as other villagers often did.) But I was an honored guest,[16]

16. Even the natural world was expected to acknowledge this status. When I got a rather nasty bee sting, Osman ran in and reassured me. Although a man in the next village had died from a bee sting, I was not to worry—because I was a guest!

whereas Sevinç was one of them; our treatment could never have been the same. Neighbors had been generous to Sevinç, but their help was not enough and would not have been enough to sustain her; it was primarily offered in the hope of persuading her to stay with Murat.

If he had told her to leave, they would be considered divorced in village eyes because, according to Islam and traditionally in Turkey, a man has only to repeat three times "I divorce you" and the divorce is final. By contrast, a woman who wants a divorce must go to court. In order to do that, Sevinç would need *izin* from her father, with whom she took refuge, and money for the trip. By the time of my departure, she had not yet gone to court. She was persuaded instead to complete the waiting period (*muflet*). Normally this refers to the time between divorce and remarriage: twelve months for a woman, because she might be pregnant, but only three days for a man.

Sevinç's major concern was the child; the problem would become serious if she wanted to remarry. If she did divorce and was granted custody of the child, a new husband would be unlikely to accept Filiz as his own, for "how can one man care for another man's child?" Filiz was accordingly referred to as an orphan (*yetim, öksüz*) even though she had a mother. What is implied is that she has no father to "cover" and protect her, and eventually to provide her trousseau and make proper marriage arrangements.

As we have seen, Sevinç and her daughter moved back to her father's house. He was in the midst of building a new house in anticipation of his son Isa's marriage. When it was finished, there was plenty of room for Sevinç and her daughter and they all lived together very comfortably. Sevinç's movements were restricted because of gossip, but she seemed happier and more relaxed, and her daughter's health and demeanor also improved. As an assertion of her independence Sevinç renamed her daughter; no longer Filiz, a name given by the *kaynana*, she is now Özlem, a "modern" Turkish name meaning wish, desire.[17]

Before moving on to other relationships, one last aspect of marital relations must be mentioned, namely extramarital relationships. One of my close neighbors was known for going to Ankara to see women. His wife, Emine, one of the prettiest women in the quarter, continually

17. When I returned in the summer of 1986, Sevinç had reconciled with Murat but their daughter kept her new name. They had moved to town, where he had a job working for the municipality, and they had a new baby.

complained about his going to the city to drink and see women at the *pavyon* (pavilion, bar with prostitutes). She was jealous and angry and resented the money he spent on these adventures, but "ne yapayı-yım?"—what can I do? Sometimes she thought she would like a divorce, but she was afraid of losing the children. At the same time, she believed him when he told her that he loved her. He did provide for her and they did make love; she even confided that she enjoyed sex. Then why did he persist in these excursions?

Because village life bores him, he told me; he gets *sinirli* (nervous) and *sıkıntılı* (bored, annoyed, from the verb *sıkmak*, to squeeze, press, wring out). He liked to drink, but that is not acceptable in the village; the few who drink do so in the city. At one point he was seen with a woman at the *yayla* and it was rumored that he was going to bring a second wife (*kuma*) to the village; but he never brought a *kuma*, and Emine became pregnant again.

Other men were said to be carrying on affairs in the village itself. One neighbor was said to have had a long affair with an attractive woman who had been widowed for about fifteen years. Another man, Halil, was observed late one night sneaking out from his neighbor's *samanlık* (a kind of barn)—surprising behavior for a man known as *hatip* (preacher) who often took the place of the imam in the mosque when the latter was away and replaced him when he was removed from office, an event to be described in the next chapter. News of this escapade was soon all over the *mahalle*, and people remembered other occasions that in retrospect looked suspicious. For example, Halil and his neighbor's wife had been seen talking together that week at the *harman* (an open area) above the *mahalle*. On another occasion, the woman's son returned from school while Halil was there; she ordered her son to run after some escaped chickens, and meanwhile Halil slipped out. Another man was rumored to "go into" the wife of his dead son. She was still living in the household and was soon to be married to the man's younger son, her brother-in-law.

Although I believe that such activity exists in the village, I do not believe there is a great deal of it. First, it is potentially dangerous for a woman to engage in because her husband or, if he is dead, his relatives could punish her. Second, given the structure of the village, it is difficult to keep such behavior secret. People are constantly on the watch; houses are so close that one can hear what is going on in the next house;

there are hardly any separate rooms or private places where such behavior can go on unobserved. As a woman living alone, and as a foreign
woman who is thought to be *serbest* (free, but meaning promiscuous),
I was a likely candidate for extramarital attentions. When I was first in
the village, people were obviously concerned that I would experience
such "trouble" and also afraid that I would invite it; but soon a close
friend told me that I need not fear any "trouble" unless I wanted it.
Rape, in a village, is very rare; and despite newspaper reports of rapes
in the city or of foreign women, I believe the incidence in Turkey is
relatively low. On only one or two occasions did I ever feel anxious about
such a possibility, and never in a village. Since my house was in the
middle of the village and observable from all sections, all comings and
goings to my house were witnessed.

On a few occasions in the beginning, men did try to visit me at night,
but it was observed that I did not open my door to them. The day after
one such event, everyone commented that they had seen what happened
and were glad I had not let the man in. After a while people relaxed and
I was allowed to have male neighbors and friends visit during the day
and even occasionally at night. Once, however, I gave a dinner party for
several of the women teachers and the school *memur* (official secretary),
an unmarried village man. The next day I was severely reprimanded;
not only was it not proper for single men and women to be together, but
the *memur* was a *yabancı* (an outsider)—that is, he came from another
quarter of the village! The neighbors said they would forgive me this
time, but if it happened again, I would be blamed and they would remove their protection. Since their protection was essential to my remaining in the village, I was not tempted to offend again.

To be alone is to be vulnerable—not only to spirits, but also to outsiders (*yabancı*), who would come to plunder, rob, and rape. It is difficult
to understand how an outsider (except one from the other side of the
village) could find the village at night, let alone my house. Except for
the disappearance of a bride's gold, thought to have been taken by a
close relative, theft was unknown in the village. I never had the slightest
fear that anything of mine would be taken, yet I was constantly told to
lock my door and that of the *ahır* (stable) where I kept my wood, coal,
and *tezek*. I did latch the gate at night so wolves and stray dogs would
not come in; and later, when a whole section of the building collapsed
and the gate became useless, I took to keeping a lamp burning outside

so that my comings and goings could be seen openly by the neighbors. Only my closest neighbor knew the reason and found it very clever. During the period when the village was in much turmoil he would warn me to make sure it was turned on.[18]

Within the family, the other relations that need to be discussed are those between *kaynana* (mother-in-law) and *gelin* (bride), and between siblings. The *gelin-kaynana* relation is at once the most critical and potentially the most troublesome. In order for the household to continue, to provide for those living, and to produce sons for its future, it is essential that the *gelin* and the *kaynana* get along. But because of the strong bond between mother and son, the arrival of a young bride who to some extent replaces the mother as a focus of affection can be a source of jealousy (*kıskançlık*) and conflict. At the same time, the bride's arrival heralds the role to which the *kaynana* has been looking forward; her workload will be lightened and she will have more time for visiting and sitting, the rewards of old age.

Menopause, according to several doctors with whom I spoke, can be a traumatic time for village women. It is not because of the physical discomforts, or because they are afraid of losing their sexual appeal or desire, but rather because the rationale for their existence no longer exists. It is likely to be less traumatic if the woman's home life is happy, if her marriage is comfortable, and, most importantly, if she has a married son at home. To move into this next stage of life without bitterness, a mother needs a *gelin* (son's wife) around to whom she can delegate some of the work and whose children she can be involved with. To be denied fulfillment of the *kaynana* role exacerbates the anxieties of this period. The attention that a *gelin* can give her and her own attention to the grandchildren are the objective manifestations and legitimation of her role and status. More importantly, she continues to be embedded in and necessary to the family group.

The word *gelin* is thought to derive from the verb *gelmek* (to come); the form *gelin* would be the personal imperative "Come!" Regardless of etymology, a new bride is at the beck and call of her *kaynana*. Some

18. I never knew how severe the dangers were. Although I heard of several plots to do away with me, ostensibly in retaliation for the murders of several Turkish diplomats in the United States and Europe, I tried to treat the plots lightly and at the same time went out of my way to win over these silent adversaries. Villagers were continually astonished that I was not afraid to live alone and assumed that I must have a gun.

kaynanas are able to handle things more delicately than others, as is shown by the old saying "Kızım sana söylüyorum, gelinim sen anla"— "Daughter, I'm telling this to you, but *gelin*, it is actually meant for you to understand." Nevertheless, the *gelin's* workload, at least in the beginning, will be considerably heavier than at home; she may even have to do the entire family's washing as well as all the other routine chores. Although a *gelin's* complaints are usually phrased in terms of work, that is not the whole picture or the main problem of adjustment in the early part of her marriage.

A far more important factor is that she is alone, an outsider in a new environment where everyone else has been living together for a long time; she feels this way even though she is in the same village and close to her parents' home. Of course her husband's family must adjust to her as well as she to them, but she is the one who must accommodate and change, for it is not her house. She has no recourse; even her husband will not necessarily side with her in disputes. She no longer has the emotional support of her own mother. This is a situation that could be stressful and difficult for anyone, let alone a teen-age girl. Is it any wonder that some brides get depressed and begin to have nervous disorders?

One sixteen-year-old bride of several months bit the hand of her *kaynana*, took to her room, and did not talk or eat for three days. Her husband was concerned that she would not get accustomed to village life (she had come from town) and was afraid she would leave. He had to keep a delicate balance between his mother and his wife in a situation that was anything but delicate. If relations continued to be bad, the couple would have to leave the parental home, as in the case of Murat and Sevinç; and in that event survival would become precarious. The bride said she was upset because of the work and because she did not get along with the *kaynana*; but a major factor was surely the extraordinary changes she had had to make. She had come from outside the village, missed her friends, and as yet had had no opportunity to make any in the village. On top of that, she had just become pregnant.[19]

Other girls, especially if they have known the *kaynana* prior to marriage, seem to adjust fairly well. Although marriage offers a kind of

19. This couple later separated. The wife left the village in 1986 and returned to her paternal home in town; her husband has remarried. Since they had had only an *imam nikahı* or religious wedding, they probably did not go to court to dissolve the marriage legally.

social mobility that single people cannot enjoy, it does not come immediately. The groom is still under the authority of his father and the bride under that of the *kaynana*. During the early months of marriage a *gelin* should be unobtrusive, demure, quiet. and quick to anticipate the needs of the *kaynana* and the rest of the family.

After the birth of a child, especially a son, things become more relaxed. The bride has justified herself, and the child becomes a source of pleasure as well as a focus for the *kaynana*'s attention. As the family grows, especially if there is another married son with children in the same household, one *aile* will have to set up a separate household, even if it means just an addition. In one household two sons lived with their parents, their wives, and their children. Since the two *gelins* were good friends, this household was large and happy, if crowded. The two brothers planned to continue in this way, and had bought a tractor together.

Relations between brothers ideally are supposed to be cooperative and supportive in this way, but often are not. Some of the most bitter fights are between brothers, as a well-known expression suggests:

> *Do you have any enemies?*
> No.
> *Do you have any brothers?*
> Yes.
> *Then you have enemies.*

If relations between brothers are cordial, they must share; and that is difficult. "It is better to have separate chickens than to own a camel together" (Engelbrektsson 1978: 51). During my stay a man stabbed his brother in a land dispute, the only case of bloodshed in years. Some other brothers, though living next door to each other, barely spoke because of political-religious differences. More commonly, relations between brothers appeared cordial, if not especially warm.

With their sisters, brothers are usually shy and protective (cf. Fallers and Fallers 1976: 258). Once a sister is married, the relationship provides an excuse for visits. Especially if a sister has moved to town, this is a convenient excuse to get away from the village. A man may leave his children with his married sister occasionally; he will then reciprocate at another time. However, not all brothers and sisters get along so well. Fatma did not speak to her brother Sedat because of a dispute over her inheritance. He tried to disinherit her totally after their father died. She went to court and was awarded a claim, but it was several years before Sedat fully complied with the court's order. Because he was angry that she pressed her claim and took him to court, he did not go to the wedding of Fatma's daughter (his *yeğen*). She said "He is not a brother to me." After their mother's death, she said "Now I am really alone."

Notions of age and respect are exhibited in sibling relations also. As noted earlier, older siblings are called by the respectful terms *abla* and *abi*. In a general way the older ones can tell the younger ones what to do, but the sexual hierarchy overrides that of age, for younger brothers can order their older sisters around. One particular example stands out in my mind. I was having dinner with Kudret (who worked as the custodian for the middle school), his wife, and their three children. Tea was served after dinner, and young Kadir ordered his older sister Afife, who was busy with her schoolwork, to bring him some more. I teased him and said, "If you want some more, get it yourself." "Olmaz, kızlar iş tutuyor"—"Impossible! Girls do the work!"

Relations between sisters are generally warm and close, for these are a girl's constant companions throughout her early life. Though sisters separate when they marry, in general the supportive and friendly relations continue. I did not know of any sisters who were not speaking to each other.

Akraba, that is, kin outside the immediate family, are those with whom much of social life is conducted. "Kin visit each other's houses, spend their leisure time together, cooperate in work, help each other in small crises, such as temporary shortages or the arrival of the unexpected guest, and in major crises such as sickness, food shortages, sickness of animals, and the ceremonies of birth, circumcision, marriage and death. The degree of intimacy of relationships of this kind must obviously vary greatly" (Stirling 1965: 148). Stirling goes on to say that except for agnates different kinship roles do not carry specific and distinct rights and duties, but a general duty of affection, help, and support. Agnates' duties, by contrast, are to defend each other and avenge insults to each other's honor. Although theoretically this is true, it was not true in our village, where agnates were often on opposite sides of a dispute. It might be agnates who came to one's defense, but just as often it was matrilateral relations or neighbors. Indeed, Stirling notes, the line that distinguishes *akraba* from *komşu* (neighbors) is very vague. In a village such as Gökler, one's neighbors are also often *akraba*; but the concept of *komşuluk* (neighborliness) is at least as important in daily life as *akrabalık*.

Outside the immediate family the most intimate social intercourse is carried on among neighbors. It is with neighbors that most daily communication takes place, and from neighbors that one seeks companionship and help in all the trivial matters that constitute daily life. As the street is men's legitimate province, the house is women's. Women neighbors may freely enter one another's houses, but a male visitor must announce himself and inquire whether he may enter. *Komşuluk* (neighborliness) is primarily created and maintained by reciprocity and exchanges between women. "Gidip geliyor mu?"—does she come and go? This is the way one asks if a neighbor is a "real" neighbor, one showing traits of *komşuluk*. Does she dart in and out at any time to borrow sugar, tea, or bread, or just to say hello, or to sit and chat? Close neighbors just call out and walk in; they rarely knock. Conversely, one must be open to one's neighbor. One need not stop what one is doing; she can join in or watch as she wishes. The boundaries between women who are close neighbors are fluid; the gates, doors, thresholds are open. There is no formality involved in these visits; her house is yours and yours hers. Close neighbors are enclosed in an open world by proximity.

Neighborliness is maintained not only by constant interaction but also by small, easily repayable gifts. If a woman has made *börek* (pastry pie with cheese) or gathered some fruit, she will take some to her neighbor. Women share their bounty as they do their lives, and it is this generosity and sharing that constitutes neighborliness. Neighbors are the people one counts on at times of stress, such as having to provide food for a large number of unexpected guests, at weddings, and at times of illness and death. *Akraba* may pay a formal visit, but it is the neighbors who help, sustain, and nourish their stricken neighbors.

For a few weeks each fall and spring, when the men were gone for much of the day working in the fields, the women in my *mahalle* used to have daily lunch or tea parties in rotation. Each would take a turn at making a special lunch, or we would gather to make a cake and spend the rest of the afternoon eating it. If there was an elderly man at home, he would not stand on his dignity but would join in unembarrassed.

Still, if the husbands of these women quarreled, they would be forbidden to visit each other. Women's relations, though normally free within the *mahalle*, are subject to the discretion of their husbands. During the period of political-religious turmoil to be discussed below and the subsequent division of the village, women had to follow the lines drawn by their husbands regardless of their feelings for each other. Toward the end of my stay, when normal *komşuluk* had all but broken down, I invited women to one of my usual weekly tea parties. But Nuriye said she could not come if Emine was there, Emine said she could not come if Ayşe was there, and so on, so that in the end there was no party. Everyone was *küs* at someone. *Küs* means sulking, but as Stirling notes (1965: 248) it is more equivalent to Achilles withdrawing into his tent; it means breaking off all social relations.

Küs may last for a short time or may continue for weeks, months, or even years. "No recognized machinery exists in the village for settlement of such quarrels" (ibid.). When quarrels escalate, there seems to be no means of solution except outside intervention. This is a characteristic not only of the village, but seemingly of Turkey itself.

If a dispute is minor, however, one or the other party can resolve it by making a visit and taking a small gift. I was personally involved in such a dispute and resolution. After becoming angry with Nuriye for pestering me to move the two tons of coal sitting outside my house, I shouted at her and slammed the window. I was immediately ashamed of myself; this was no way for a good anthropologist to behave. On the other hand, anthropologists also are human and have feelings, and to pretend otherwise seems dishonest not only to the profession but also to the people with whom one lives. I also discovered that one learns a great deal from such encounters.[20]

After my outburst—which was, of course, discussed all over the village—Nuriye and I did not speak for a week. She had been making fun of me primarily because I had no male at home who could move the coal for me. I was not about to do it myself and had been unable to persuade any of the young men to do it, not even with the offer of payment; that kind of work was beneath them unless ordered by their fathers. Finally, all of the neighbor women and children helped, and we moved the coal inside in time for Kurban Bayramı. That *bayram* (holiday) is the traditional day for making visits and for making peace. Nuriye came at *bayram* bearing a gift of olives and cheese. We never

20. Cf. Malinowski 1961 [1922]. I have discussed some of these issues in Delaney 1989.

mentioned the incident; neither of us apologized, and relations were simply resumed.

For years Ahmet had not spoken with his father Ali, who lived across the street with Ahmet's brother Nazim. Finally, after Ahmet had built a new house further away, and on an evening when he knew I would be at Ali's house, he came and kissed his father's hand. If I had anything to do with their reconciliation, it was simply that I was on good speaking terms with both of them; but this may have been just enough outside intervention to do the job. Ahmet invited his father to visit him in his new house. Although the father and son and the two brothers had not spoken for years, the children of both brothers freely visited back and forth, and the two wives often met, mainly in the street or at my house.

Mehmet and Ayşe, however, have had long-standing *küs* with Sedat (brother of Fatma, wife of Ahmet), who lives in the house adjoining theirs. During the time I was in the village, Mehmet built a new house a few yards away. He also built a stone wall to separate his property from Sedat's.

Sometimes neighbors ostracize one family. This happened during the celebrations of Turgut's wedding. His brother, Mustafa, and his soon-to-be *kaynata* (father-in-law) drank during the celebrations, and the father of the bride also danced with his daughter. This was unheard of in the village and considered to be totally *ayıp* (shameful) behavior. After this, most of the neighbors were *küs* with them. Mustafa's wife Gülise was also socially ostracized, though she had nothing to do with his behavior at the wedding. For a few days the neighbors cut them off. During this difficult and stressful time, I was the only person she could visit.

At the other extreme, one finds remarkable acts of charity by which those on the boundaries (i.e., disadvantaged) are reincorporated into the village. Old Hasan and his wife Hatice had been living for seven years in Küçükler, the *yayla* halfway down the mountain. Terribly poor, they had no house in the village and no money to build one. One daughter lived in the village with her husband and five children and could do little to help. Their son, who lived in Ankara with his wife and several children, was very ill and could not work. The elderly couple had managed to live in Küçükler by keeping a few sheep and tending a small garden, and by the charity of villagers who visited there on occasion. Often a bag of groceries was left there on the way back from shopping at the *pazar* in town. Their situation was, however, a blot on the village conscience, and ideas of bringing them back had circulated from time to time.

Finally, it was decided to take up a collection to build them a new house. All villagers in the village were approached, as well as those living in town or city. Some 80,000 TL was collected from within the village and an additional 35,000 TL from villagers living outside, over $1,000 in all. With this amount, cement blocks and roof tiles were bought and an *usta* (master craftsman) and workmen were hired in the village to plan and execute the construction. The *muhtar* donated the land, a small plot directly across from my house on which a little-used shed stood; this was torn down and reusable materials recycled. Friends and neighbors pitched in to help by donating their labor, provisions for the workers, tractors to haul materials, etc. Within a few weeks the house was essentially completed. It still needed plaster on its inside and outside walls, it lacked window frames and glass, and its floors were of mud; over the summer the necessary finishing touches were slowly added. Meanwhile the elderly couple were brought back and installed in the partly finished structure and incorporated back into the social life of the village.

A similar group action was organized about eight years earlier for Nazife, a widow with five children. After a particularly bad storm, her house had caved in; no one was hurt, but the house was damaged beyond repair. Villagers collected money and volunteered help to build her a new house. It was large and spacious and one of the homes I liked to frequent when I was *bıktım* (bored or fed up) with the formality or reserve in some of the others.

This kind of charity is extended only to those perceived as "insiders." In the 1950s a large number of immigrants (*göçmen*) from Bulgaria were resettled throughout Turkey, and three such families were placed in Gökler. Within a few months, however, it was clear that these foreign bodies could not be incorporated into the village, and they were ejected. The government responded by appropriating some of Gökler's land and forming a separate village, Şekerköy, about fifteen kilometers away, where they gathered together all the *göçmen* in the vicinity. Needless to say, this action created even more hostility between the groups. During the past thirty years this has diminished and there is now some traffic between the two villages.

A few categories of outsiders, in addition to the teachers, the government-appointed midwife, and the imam (who will be discussed in the following chapter), are tolerated for brief periods.

Gypsies. Every year the village is visited by small groups of *çingene* (gypsies). Usually arriving at the time of Kurban Bayramı (Festival of Sacrifice), when there is a distribution of meat to poor people, they camp for a few days in the *harman* in the lower *mahalle* or outside the village and peddle their wares. They are not invited inside the houses. When they are spoken of, *afferdersiniz* (please excuse me) is always suffixed, as it is when one must refer to a donkey (*eşek*). *Çingene* are considered subhuman, because they have no Book (Qur'an or Bible) and are thought to be promiscuous, like animals, sharing women in common.

Other Itinerant Vendors. Individual vendors of fish, olives, nuts, salt, and soap, and of baby chicks in the spring, come to the village at irregular intervals. Other vendors called *dökücü* (literally one who spills or empties) empty their wares onto the ground to display them. These items consisted of kitchen utensils (plates, tea seats, trays) and materials for sewing (needles, scissors, beads to decorate scarves). Still other vendors sold only cloth.

Kalaycı. A *kalaycı* is a person who tins the inside of copper utensils. Two of these came during my time, were put up in one of the tearooms, and were provided for by the neighbors for their stay of ten days. During this time they relined most of the copper pots in the village.

Officials. A variety of government officials visit occasionally. These include the doctor, health inspectors, and the *jandarma* if there is trouble.

Outsiders may add a bit of variety to the gossip, as they do color to the homes and spice to the diet, but they do not really affect the body of the village. They are ingested briefly, and then evacuated; whatever is of use is absorbed.

To most visitors, including "outsiders" but excepting *çingene*, villagers are very hospitable despite personal feelings. For example, a German filmmaker, a woman I had never met or heard of, learned of my presence in the village and came in search of me. I was not there at the time, but learned later that she had arrived "uncovered" and wearing a sweater with short sleeves and a low neck, a form of dress considered by villagers to be that of a loose and immoral woman. Although she was described as *çıplak* (naked), they entertained her hospitably. Such visits impose not only on villagers' time and resources but also on their sensitivities,

Itinerant vendor

Lining copper pots with tin

something they are rarely given credit for. In this case the boorishness was all on the side of the "civilized" intruder, and I continued to hear about her visit for the remainder of my time in the village.

Hospitality (*misafirperverlik*) is the supreme virtue in Turkish society. The word is formed from *misafir*, which means guest, and *perver*, a suffix that means nourish or care for. It is a severe condemnation of a person or a village to be thought inhospitable. *Misafirperverlik* is more formal than *komşuluk* (neighborliness), in which the openness of the house is assumed; but the line between *komşu* and *misafir* is a fine one, as I learned one night when a group of small boys came to visit. I was delighted, greeted them as guests, and said how happy and honored I was by their visit. They replied, "but we're not *misafir* (guests), we're *komşu*!"

When a guest drops in for more than a brief chat, the hostess must drop what she is doing in order to make the guest welcome. Tea must be made, food brought, the fire stoked, and beds provided if necessary. Sometimes visits have been previously arranged, but more often they are unannounced. Although there is a telephone in the village, so that outsider visitors can notify those whom they plan to visit, its use has not yet become customary.[21] Word of mouth is still the major channel of communication. Americans are used to making plans and schedules, to being notified of visits, and to making and keeping appointments. In Turkey, by contrast, an unannounced visit is not thought of as an intrusion, but is an expected and desired part of domestic activity. One's own plans are dispensable, and those of others take precedence; particularly is this true for women. If the housewife is at another home, she will be sent for; if guests are present, she may not leave. Yet this hospitality is not as altruistic as it may sound, for having guests and being known as a hospitable person or household is also self-serving.

---

21. There are actually two telephones in the village, one in the *bekçi*'s office and the other, run by batteries, in the *muhtar*'s house. This is a party line used also by another village. The *bekçi* doubles as the official telephone operator, but its use depends on his being in the office. When one wants to place a call *from* the village, one must first find the *bekçi* to ask him to go to the office and place the call. Some twenty-six village homes have telephones, but these are in effect extensions: they connect to the office phone, not to separate lines. Theoretically, villagers with phones could call each other, but only if the *bekçi* is in his office. At present, the phones function more as status symbols. They are also introducing modern stress into village life with the noise they make and the frustrations of trying to conduct a conversation when the connection is poor. I frequently saw people hang up enraged by the "contraption."

A visit sheds honor on the host and raises his status in the eyes of other villagers.

An arriving guest is greeted by each member of the household: "hoş geldin / hoş geldiniz" (-*in* is familiar, -*iniz* is more formal)—you come pleasantly, welcome. Each family member must be greeted in return: "hoş bulduk / hoş gördük"—we find/see that it is pleasant. Children and women will take the hand of an elder male, kiss it, raise it to their foreheads. A man who had been on the hajj (T. *hac*) will not permit women to shake or kiss his hand, since this would defile his exalted and pure state. Women who are relatives or friends embrace and kiss each other on both cheeks. Men shake hands. These customs symbolically express the difference between the sexes and the homage owed by women to men, as well as respect for age; at the same time, they show the basic equality between men and the physical closeness of women.

Seating arrangements reflect the same principles. The eldest (or visiting) male has the seat of honor, away from the door and usually in the corner—*başköşe* (head corner)—near a window. Other men by age flank him, then older women or female guests; women of the house often take seats on the floor along with the children. Husbands and wives do not sit next to one another. As a guest I provided the boundary between men and women because I straddled the categories of guest and woman.

When guests are seated, the hostess usually sprinkles some lemon cologne into the hands of each guest, who smoothes it over his or her neck, forehead, and lower arms. The use of cologne in this context seems to be an attempt to create a Heaven on earth for the brief space of the visit. Heaven (*Cennet*) is visualized as a garden, a restful haven where cool breezes blow, clear water flows, sweet scents refresh the mind and body, and food and drink are plentifully provided with no effort.

The ritual of cologne draws a scented boundary between the toil and sweat of everyday life and the respite of a visit, where a guest can relax and be provided for. But on earth as it is in Heaven, it is women who wait upon men. Guests are not allowed to help. A jug and a glass are brought by a young girl or a woman, who stands and waits until the guest has drunk his or her fill and then moves on to the next. Occasionally, and always at *bayram* (holidays), hard sugar candy is passed. Meanwhile the hostess would have put water on for tea.

In Turkey one does not just drop in for a cup of tea. The process takes at least an hour; and since it would be rude to drink and leave, a visit involving tea also lasts at least two hours. The tea consists of two pots (*demli*); a smaller one containing dry tea is placed on top of a larger one containing water. When the water boils it is poured into the pot with tea; the tea is then allowed to steep on low heat for 30 to 45 minutes, or until all the tea leaves have fallen to the bottom of the pot. Only then is it considered fit to drink. Tea made in the village is the best I have ever had. Contrary to the expectation that long steeping would make it acid and bitter, it is very smooth and satiny.

Tea is served in tiny tulip-shaped glasses set on small saucers with demitasse spoons. Glasses are filled and passed on a tray with a bowl of sugar by a woman of the household. The first time guests came to my house, I started to pass the first cup to the oldest woman. Quickly I was told that this was *ayıp*—men come before women. They were as surprised by our custom as I was unaccustomed to theirs. Mistakes like this are a useful way to elicit commentary about implicit beliefs, but, as noted before, they can get one into trouble.

Turks normally take tea with lots of sugar (2–4 spoonfuls); everyone constantly commented on my strange preference for drinking it *şekersiz* (without sugar). Some thought I was concerned with gaining weight; one or two mentioned tooth decay;[22] but most concluded that I was economizing on sugar in order to use the money for something else. Villagers who are stingy with sugar are accused of profiting at the expense of their guests; it was noticed, however, that although I didn't use sugar myself, I offered my guests all they wanted. There is also a belief that tea without sugar is harmful to the stomach. In any case it was thought that tea should never be drunk on an empty stomach, which is why it is usually drunk after food has been consumed.

The making and giving of food is woman's task. Not only does it nourish the guests and give them sustenance, but the sharing of sub-

---

22. This is one of the worst health problems in the village. Children have very white teeth, which are generally straight. Men, by age 20, have dirty, stained teeth from smoking. Women, after several pregnancies, are often missing several teeth by the time they are 30, and a significant number have false teeth by age 35. Toothbrushing is not a common practice, though I did see a few toothbrushes. There is a dentist with modern equipment attached to the rural medical program in Yoldakent, yet very few people use his services. Women say their husbands or fathers will not give them *izin* (permission) to go to town to have a strange man poking around in their mouths. There may be an echo here of the symbolic connection between the genitals and the head, for husbands also do not like their wives to go to the doctor for gynecological examinations or for birth.

I enjoy a tea break with neighbors building a house

stance also creates a sense of solidarity,[23] which is ratified by the sharing of conversation. *Sohbet* ("sweet" conversation, conversation as a kind of art form) is normatively the prerogative of the man to initiate and terminate.

When guests are ready to leave, they must first obtain permission from the host. "Müsaadenizle gider miyim?"—may I go with your permission? "Müsaadeniz verir misinz?"—do you give your permission? Hosts normally try to detain guests by asking if they have found fault with their hospitality and by offering more food or tea; but when this is declined, "Müsaade sizin"—the permission is yours, i.e., it is granted.

23. Food can have ambivalent meaning. If you take food from someone, you cannot refuse requests made of you; you are in the feeder's debt. This surely adds to the ambivalence of hospitality. Sirman (1990) suggests that food can symbolize corruptibility, but she does not elaborate the gendered significance. Women are associated with the physical world, which is ultimately corruptible; they symbolize both the positive and negative aspects of existence, of life in this world.

A guest is escorted to the gate, at which the host's protection is relinquished and the guest is given over to the "wild" of the street.[24]

Symbolically recreated during the brief period of a visit is the Turkish
view of what the world is to human life. The world is like a guesthouse:
a place of succor, refreshment, and shelter during one's brief sojourn
called life. In this respect it is also an icon of *Cennet*, one's original and
eternal home. Women's role and function in life is to provide nurture,
as the world does for human life in general. The world is a guesthouse
briefly holding the eternal spark as the female body briefly carries the
seed within. Body as substance is identified with women and with the
world (*dünya*).

The ideology of descent answers the question of identity and derivation—who are you and where do you come from? The reproduction
of social life depends upon and partakes of both creative and generative
as well as nurturant and sustaining qualities. Nevertheless, in daily life
the nurturant aspects appear to take on more importance. Common-
ality of substance works to unite, whereas patrilineal principles work
to separate and divide. The generative principle symbolized by the notion of seed is the *sülale*, the patrilineal line, which unites past with
future and makes divisions in a generalized medium of nurture, which
is symbolically female.

Although kinship terminology distinguishes between male and female, the fact that the terms are used for all villagers means that the
system includes and embraces fellow villagers, just as the qualities of
akrabalık and *komşuluk* support and sustain them. *Hep akrabayız*—we are
all related. Villagers see the village as one close-knit, intertwined unit
bound together by blood and milk, the nurturant qualities that women
provide. Vis-à-vis the outside, the village is a corporate body; but since
corporeality or bodiliness is associated with the female, I suggest that
the village as a body is also symbolically female. Like a woman, it is
naturally open but socially closed; a proper village, like a proper
woman, should be *kapalı* (closed, covered). Its openings and closings
are controlled, and access to it is limited. Those who are inside are pro-

---

24. After visiting with neighbors in the evening, I used generally to be escorted only
to the gate of my hosts. After I was bitten by a dog and became afraid of dogs, I was
escorted all the way home. This was awkward because an unmarried woman should not
be out alone, especially at night, with an adult man. Normally, my escort would walk
several paces in front of me.

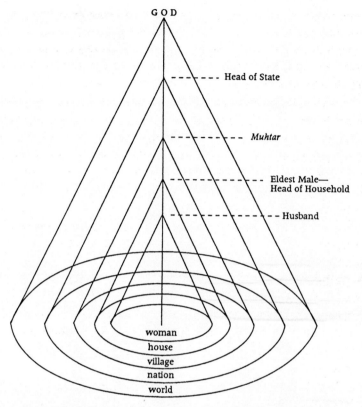

The structure of traditional authority relations as they are symbolically gendered. The female symbolizes the physical, unregenerate aspects of cultural entities—the house, the village, the nation, and the world. The male encloses, represents, and forms the generative relations between them. In this role he stands in line with the divine.

tected as if in the womb; life outside is viewed as a kind of death. *Gurbet* (exile, being away from home) is the most unenviable position. Like the succor of a woman's body, the soil of one's village is one's earthly home.

The notion of the village as a symbolic womb becomes more compelling when one realizes that its progeny lie directly outside its entrance. The *mezar* (cemetery) is the first thing one sees on entering the village and the last on leaving. In a sense the village gives birth to corpses; the dead, its nearest kin, are kept as close as possible. Their spirits hover around the entrance to the village and guard it. At the same time, the spirit that gives identity has been transferred to and renewed in the seed of the living. The creative spiritual essence is both at the center and at the circumference, providing continuity for the physical (see the diagram on p. 199).

Woman's body, meaningfully constructed within the specific theory of procreation, is generative of notions of enclosing and enclosed. It serves as a symbolic reservoir from which the related concepts of inside-outside, open-closed, and purity-pollution are brought to light and projected onto the social world. In the next chapter, we shall look at these in relation to the household, the village, and the nation.

A village is an idea, a social unit, and a physical location. The analytical distinctions may be relevant to the social scientist, but to a villager they are inseparable and form a unique combination that is his or her village. The uniqueness of each village is felt as soon as one enters—an elusive quality that invades one's senses and colors one's perceptions. It is carried by sounds of dogs or machinery, the scent of an *iğde* (oleaster) tree or a stand of graceful *kavak* (poplar), airy home to hundreds of twittering sparrows. It is evident in the structure and upkeep of the houses, in the posture of the people and the faces they turn toward you. It is all of these and more. It is nothing tangible, nothing that one can name or point to, but a sense of place that seeps through the senses and makes itself felt. This chapter discusses the way the symbols and meanings of procreation (a) help to conceptualize notions of physical space, notably the house, the village, and the nation; (b) are exemplified by the division of labor for the reproduction of the household; and (c) are utilized in the rhetoric of nationalism, an issue that became prominent during the time I was in Gökler.

Defined administratively, a village as distinct from a town is a named physical-social unit with a population of under 2,000. A population of 2,000 qualifies such a unit as a *beledeye* (municipality), which benefits from, and is required to provide, certain services. If we want to know what a village is in more general terms, Margaret Mead's definition is more helpful and is appropriate for most Anatolian villages: "Essentially I would define a village as a community in which it is possible for every resident to know every other person living there. I would also include having a name, and some awareness of the settlement as a community, continuity over time, the presence of at least three living generations and a belief in the possibility of continuity of membership in the future" (1980: 19).

Yet even this definition gives very little sense of what distinguishes a Turkish village from a French, a Greek, or an Indian one, and within Turkey what distinguishes one village from all others. "People belong to their village in a way they belong to no other social group" (Stirling 1965: 29); more than merely a place one lives, a village is an indelible part of one's being and identity. People affect their surroundings as the surroundings affect people; they are mutually conditioned and conditioning, so that a certain way of being is concretized in a landscape in very specific ways. Thus a sense of place—that inextricable combination of physical, social, and psychological factors—is indispensable for understanding what, in each case, is meant by *bizim köy* (our village).[1]

Bizim Köy

Our village is located in Orta Anadolu (Central or Middle Anatolia), the heart both physically and symbolically of Turkey. Indeed, these villagers are in the center of their world. Their orientations are not, like ours, to East and West, with Turkey in the Middle East. Instead, they are oriented in terms of Doğu Anadolu (East Anatolia), Batı Anadolu (West Anatolia), Kuzey Anadolu (North Anatolia), and Güney Anadolu (South Anatolia). Orta Anadolu is the center.

Although villagers believe their ancestors migrated to Turkey from Central Asia, the migrants did not enter an unpopulated area but mixed with descendants of the innumerable groups who traversed and settled the area throughout historic times: Hittites, Phrygians (whose capital, Gordium, is not far away), Lydians, Lycians, Persians, Greeks, Galatians, Bithynians, and Romans. The area in which the village is located was the heart of Galatia and Bithynia.[2] The ancient Pilgrim's Road is thought to have passed near Milas, the administrative center for the area, which is known to have existed in the early Byzantine period. In 1073 Milas was taken by the Selcuks, whose sovereignty was thereafter

---

1. *Bizim köy* rather than *köyümüz* (our village) is not only the phrase commonly used by villagers to refer to their own village, but also the title of a book by Mahmut Makal (1954 [1950]), who was "the first genuine villager, from the inarticulate millions of peasants all over the world, to describe the village from within" (Stirling 1965: xiii).

2. Cf. Ramsay 1890; Anderson 1897–98: 64, 1899: 63.

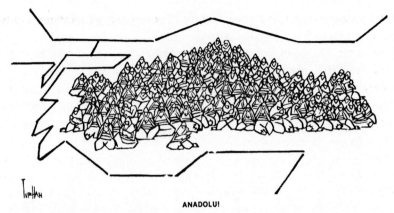

ANADOLU!

Anadolu: "filled with mothers." Cartoon by Turhan Selcuk, from *Milliyet*, April 4, 1983 (first published March 17, 1967).

intermittently challenged until 1354, when the town fell to the Ottoman Orhan Gazi, after whom a mountain near Ankara is named. Archaeological remains such as stelae, pottery, and figurines have been found in Gökler and surrounding villages.[3]

In prehistoric times the area was also inhabited, and several finds have come to light. Çatal Hüyük (farther south near Cumra, between Konya and Karaman), discovered in 1962 by James Mellaart (1962–64, 1965), is believed to have existed as early as 8000 B.C. Its discovery revolutionized archaeological theories about the Middle East, especially with respect to the beginnings of settled populations and the origin of cereal cultivation.

The wide-hipped, large-breasted female figurines found there certainly give the impression that the fecundity of women was powerful and highly valued. Their present-day counterparts in the village affirm the persistence of these values. "Anadolu" can, in folk etymology, mean "filled with mothers."[4] Perhaps the land by subterranean channels has kept some of the old religion alive.

Villagers today have little interest in history. In ancient times, it is

3. In addition children reported finding small animals and people made of clay in the soil on the lower slope of the mountain, and playing with them until they broke.

4. Etymologically, "Anadolu" is thought to derive from a Greek word that means something like "place of the dawn." This phrase was used as the title of a novel about Turkey by Gordon Taylor (1975).

said, two or perhaps three brothers and their *kabile* (tribe) came to the spot and established a village of twenty *hane* where the present mosque now stands. Villagers assert that their present customs (*görenekler*) derived from the precedents established by these settlers. The village is *görenekli* (has precedence, is properly established), and thus is unlike villages quickly set up for utilitarian purposes as Şekerköy was. The notion of being properly established is relevant also for Turkey as a whole, as we shall see below.

The present inhabitants of the village, who numbered about 850 in the early 1980s,[5] profess to be Sunni Muslims following the Hanafi teachings. They consider themselves *yerli* (native), in contrast to *göçmen* (immigrants). *Yerli* is an interesting word, composed of *yer* (earth, ground, place) and the suffix *-li* (*lı, lu, lü*), which means "belonging to" or "related to" and in this context is an identity marker. For example, *-li* is used for nationality, e.g. *Amerikalı* (American), and also in the question "Nerelisiniz?"—what place do you come from? *Yerli* thus means those who come from that particular piece of earth. The village is their place of origin as well as habitation. A village is thus composed of the soil-substance, which is symbolically female but which is delineated and defined by the *ata* (father-founder).

Göklerliler (those who come from Gökler) also consider themselves pure Anatolian Turks as opposed to ethnic minorities or mixtures, namely those who attest no founder. People who do not know their origins are thought to be *perişan* (scattered, disordered) and *pis* (dirty); their identity is unsure and sullied. Their problem is equivalent to not knowing who one's father was. Origins are important for a sense of identity but are also the source of legitimizing current practices.

A slightly different account of village history was written by a villager and published in *Köy Sesi*—"The Village Voice"!—an extraordinary, and perhaps unique, village periodical started by an ex-villager who had done well in the city and wanted to help the village get a sense of itself. Articles for *Köy Sesi* were written by villagers living either in the village or outside, and the issues were printed in Ankara. It had a brief life of about seven issues in the early 1970s.

5. Age 0–14, 121 males, 111 females; age 15–49, 236 males, 204 females; age 50 or over, 88 males, 97 females. Total population, 857.

The author of the village history claimed that Gökler had been a village, in the sense of a community of people, for about five hundred years. When the original settlement was established in 1400 by ten *kabile*, the inhabitants were dispersed around the skirt of the mountain in several encampments, whose remains are now used as rest houses for shepherds and their flocks. After a severe drought in 1880, in which many animals died and malaria was rampant, the inhabitants moved higher up the mountain to escape the mosquitoes and because they found a plentiful supply of water. By this account, the village at its present location would be about a hundred years old.

Others confirm this view because *dut* (mulberry) trees are said to split in two once every century. There are five such trees in the village. Since they would have been planted by the early settlers, the trees are proof of the village's age.

No official history could be found in the office of the *kaymakam* (mayor) in Milas, the administrative center for a number of villages in the area. He claimed that all records had been destroyed by fire some time ago; moreover, he said, he was new to his job and did not know anything about these villages.

In any case, the kind of history one might find in the *kaymakam*'s office would be an outsider's history. It would be dead and dry, a matter of records and statistics, not a living portrait inscribed in the memories of people and in the landscape (cf. Berger 1979: 9). Village history in the living sense is continually changing and being rearranged by new events and different perspectives, as is all history. Walking over the land in different moods and different weathers one finds memories like gems or buried treasures to be brought back, polished up, and re-presented. Different seasons turn over different memories as the plow turns over the soil anew each year. The people and the landscape become part of a single entity, a single identity—something that one takes with one no matter where one goes. It is this kind of village history, the insider's kind, that it is extremely important to try to convey.

Near the top of the only mountain in the area, Gökler commands a majestic view of the entire steppe below. "Gökten esinlesmiş"—it is inspired by the sky—and one is very conscious of being close to that element and its capriciousness. The village faces east toward the rising sun, and the dawns, drawn out by the *ezan* (call to prayer) from the minaret, are long and magnificent. So too is the last dance of light and shadow upon the hills below before the sun sinks behind the summit above.[6]

Electrical storms clash against the summit and sometimes lash the village with a seemingly impenetrable fence of lightning. On the other hand, after a rain the valley is spanned by double rainbows (*gökkuşağı*, literally the sky's belt) encircling the enchanted village and pointing to the pot of gold that villagers know lies hidden in the mountain.

The first soft days of spring bring the women out of doors to sit in the sun, where their very presence seems to urge forth the brilliant green shoots of wheat. The rains that follow nearly wash the village away, constructed as it is mostly of mud. In summer, fields and people are battered by hail, or obliterated by dust storms. In fall, the air is clear and at night the stars are very close. In winter, enveloped by snow and the cloying smell of *tezek* (dried dung and straw fuel), the village is isolated but also as snug as a hibernating bear. "In winter we sleep; in summer we work."

It was in February of the terrible winter of 1979–80 that I first saw the village when the road was finally opened after being impassable for nearly two months.[7] The endless steppe, covered in snow, with no evidence of habitation and barely a tree to break the desolation, could have been in Siberia. This area, I later learned, though relatively close to Ankara, is one of the most sparsely settled areas in the country.

From below, the approach to the village, by dirt road, is over thirty kilometers of barren steppe gradually rising toward the mountain in the distance, giving one the impression that one is approaching something of consequence. Conversely, people approaching the village, whether by car, by tractor, by donkey, or on foot, can be seen, and recognized or not, long before they get to the village, giving villagers the sense that they have some control over who enters. And this is exactly what they want, since all bad and threatening things are said to come from out-

---

6. Villagers, especially in summer, often eat the evening meal on their rooftops in order to watch the play of swallows while the sun makes interesting patterns over the steppe below.

7. On that occasion I traveled in a Land Rover with the rural doctor, his staff, and two other medical visitors, one of whom felt the village's isolation was a well-deserved punishment for having been built in such an inhospitable location. I felt nervous, not only because I was alone with five strange Turkish men, but also because I wondered what we would do if we got stuck. We did, and nearly froze trying to dislodge the vehicle.

side—whether it is outside the body, the family, the village, or the nation. The opposition inside-outside is the same; it is the contexts that are relative. In this chapter we will move across the various thresholds from outside to inside and back out again—a path that follows my own deepening knowledge of the structure and content of village life.

Everything outside the village in the general direction of Ankara is referred to as "Ankara" regardless of whether it is one of a number of small towns or villages along the Ankara road, an outlying *semt* (district) of the city, or the city itself. In fact, when villagers say they are going to Ankara, they rarely mean to the city itself.

When I first came to the village there were three roads: one on the right (south) leading to the next village, Buçukköy; one in the center (east) leading to another village, Şekerköy, and on to the town of Yoldakent and the main road to Ankara; and one to the left (north) that went over the back of the mountain (west) to the administrative town of Milas. Since Milas is blocked from view and the village faces east, a sweep of the hand or a glance indicates that all in front and below is "Ankara."

The village, like a proper woman, is described as *kapalı* (closed, covered); the town or city is *açık* (open). The city is *bulaşık* (tainted, soiled); the village is *temiz* (clean and pure). Villagers are proud of their clean air and water, and when visiting in town often take their own provisions. For a day trip, they prefer not to eat or drink anything but their own provisions for fear they will become ill.[8]

The idea of the village as *kapalı* and their desire to keep it that way are further illustrated by their ambivalence toward roads. During my second year in the village a new road, leading down the mountain by another route to the main road and Yoldakent, was under construction by the government. Villagers questioned its relevance—"Why do we need another road?"—and to my knowledge no one from the village worked on the construction. Roads make the services of the town more accessible, but at the same time the village becomes more accessible to polluting influences from town.

As we have seen, distinctions between village and town are more than physical; they imply social and moral qualities as well. Villagers

---

8. I experienced stomach trouble whenever I left the village for a few days; no doubt one becomes accustomed to the local food and water.

keep the precedents or traditions; townspeople have forgotten or lost them. Villagers know where they are and who they are; city people lose their way and with it their integrity.

City people, for their part, also make a strict division between city and village. A few of my acquaintances in the city evinced a sentimental nostalgia for the simple peasant life and its rich ethnic lore, but most displayed horror for the incivility, danger, and filth they believe to exist in the village. The gulf dividing peasants from the urban elite "is more than a gulf; it is an opposition. In no country that I have visited do the educated classes speak of the 'ignorance' and 'backwardness' of their own peasants so much as in Turkey. Turkish intellectuals are absolutely at sea in villages. For them they are like a foreign country, and the peasants a foreign people" (Hotham 1972: 138).[9] That Turkish villages are actually sought out by Western visitors, and that such visitors generally describe Turkish villagers as kind, honest, hospitable, and friendly, is acknowledged; but "To modern Turks, this passion of foreigners for visiting rough corners of his country seems incomprehensible. . . . The one idea of every educated Turk is to put as many miles between himself and a village as is humanly possible" (ibid.: 156).

Faced with such incomprehension on the part of those in positions to make decisions that affect them, villagers have no option but to do their best to protect what they have. For those in Gökler geography is an advantage. Separated from town by a wide and ascending expanse of land, they can keep bad influences at bay and withdraw to their mountain fastness.

From that perspective the focus shifts. No longer is the distinction between inside and outside used only to differentiate between town and village; it is also brought closer to home and used to distinguish the village proper (inside) and its lands (outside). Although the distinction between inside and outside is a major one, it is not fixed.

Viewed from outside, the village looks like one compact unit. Viewed from the village, the outside consists of the mountain summit behind and the village land spread around the remaining three sides. From the mountain flows a seemingly inexhaustible supply of water both from

---

9. The cultural dualism is vividly expressed by Yakup Kadir Karaosmanoğlu, an elite Turk marooned in a village during the Independence War, in his book *Yaban*. Villagers use the word *yaban* (wild, foreign), related to *yabancı* (outsider, stranger), to refer to everything *outside* the village!

snow melting in the winter and from underground springs, some of which are *maden suyu* (mineral water). The water is collected in a large depot above the village and channeled to four *çesme* (fountains) in the village and a number scattered outside the village proper. The water at the *çesme* is never turned off but is constantly flowing, according to Islamic custom. Since the late 1970s water has been piped to some village houses (to a spigot in the courtyard), but this water flow is controlled by the *bekçi* (watchman) and is available only for brief periods during the day. In winter the water is clean, but in summer, when the flocks are pastured on the mountain, the water can become contaminated. Nevertheless, because it comes from the mountain, people assume it to be clean,[10] and no purifiers are added. Cholera and typhoid broke out in surrounding villages during my stay, but did not appear in Gökler.

On the steep slope ascending to the rocky summit are some fruit trees—not exactly an orchard, since the trees are widely dispersed and owned individually. These include *kıraz* (cherries), *vişne* (sour cherries), *kayısı* (apricots), *erik* (plums), *şeftali* (peaches), *elma* (apples), *armut* (pears), and *dut* (mulberries). The area is known for its large succulent mulberries and for its pears. Some wild fruit trees also add variety to the diet: *muşmula* (medlar, *Mespilus germanica*), *iğde* (oleaster, *Elaeagnus angustifolia*), and my favorite, *zerdali* (wild apricot).

The mountain is also a source of legend. In very ancient times, it is said, a caravan of camels laden with gold set out to cross the mountain by means of a secret passageway. Apparently they got trapped in the passage and perished. Periodically attempts are made to try to locate the door leading to the passage. In Byzantine times a girl allegedly went into the mountains in search of the door and never came out. More recently, about twenty years ago, a woman with a map supposedly handed down over the centuries came and stayed three months but had no success. Some people thought I was yet another gold-seeker. The legend may have been the source, or perhaps the result, of a well-known ballad of the area in which a lover seeking his beloved asks, "Did a caravan go this way?"

The mountain is full of caves that can be used during the summer

---

10. The power of semantic association is reminiscent of Whorf's remarks (1956) with regard to fire. "Empty gasoline drums" suggests, he says, the absence of danger because the drums are empty; whereas in fact empty gasoline drums are probably more dangerous than full ones.

as living quarters by shepherds, who corral and tend young goats after they are separated from their mothers. The caves also provide shelter for wolves, who are a constant threat to the flocks and take numbers of animals every year, leaving only a few bones and tufts of hair.

Spread around three sides like a skirt (*etek*) is the village land. It was impossible for me to learn the exact amount of land owned by the village. The few land deeds I was able to glimpse were of individual holdings; no general plan of the village existed either in the *kaymakan*'s office or with the *muhtar.* What is important to villagers is arable land (*arazı*); they are not concerned to know the dimensions of the entire area. They claim there are about 40,000 *dönüm* of *arazı*, of which one-half in any given year are *herk* (fallow). In addition, 10,000 *dönüm* are *mera*—communal land for grazing animals. A *dönüm* is roughly 1,000 square meters or about 1/4 acre. The arable land, if formed into a single square tract, would be 6.6 kilometers on each side. The *muhtar* says the circumference of the village is about 30 kilometers, which, taking into account the unarable land and the summit, seems about right.

Most of the land is planted in *buğday* (wheat), *arpa* (barley), and *mercimek* (lentils), although one of the richer men plants some of his land in *pancar* (sugar beet), which he sells to the district sugar factory. Sometimes the fallow land is planted in *bostan* (melons; either *kavun*, honeydew, or *karpuz*, watermelon), or in vegetables for home consumption.

The *yaban* area is the legitimate province only of the *çoban*, who are generally adolescent boys and thus not yet fully social adults. Outside the village proper, but within its borders, are a number of *ahır* (or corrals), seven of which are named (e.g. Küçükler). The *çoban* and their flocks are accompanied and protected only by their sheepdogs.

These dogs, pale-colored and half-wild, bear no resemblance to the English sheepdog with hair hanging down over its eyes. They are larger than a German shepherd, and wear spiked iron collars to protect them from wolves. They are not trained, are given only dry bread to eat, are kicked and beaten, and are meant to attack anyone or anything approaching the flock. Dogs are considered unclean and are always kept out of doors.

Cats, on the other hand, are household pets and are even given morsels from the dinner tray. Ogier G. deBusbecq, a European in Süleyman's court (1554–62), attributed the affection for cats to a popular story about Muhammed, one that is still told today. It is said that rather than disturb his cat, who had fallen asleep on his arm, the Prophet cut off the sleeve of his garment (1968: 114). Yet cats are not quite pets in the American sense; they do not have names, are not spoken to, and are rarely petted. Because animals have only feelings (*hisler*) and not *akıl* (intelligence), there is a great divide separating animals and humans.[11]

Less so is that dividing the dead from the living. As we have seen, the village's dead kin are collectively located directly outside the village in the *mezar* (cemetery). When you ask people how many children they have, they may answer "three in this world, two in the *mezar,*" thus indicating that the dead children are still considered part of their world. Spirits of the dead are felt to wander about in the area of the cemetery especially on The Night of Power, three days before the end of Ramazan, when male villagers go to commune with them.

Inside the Village

The outside, the wild, and spirits of the dead are left behind as one enters the village. Once one is inside, it is as if an invisible gate had closed; one is enclosed, safe, protected, just as the womb encloses and protects the child. In relation to the outside, the village is imagined as a unified body, which in its physical aspect is, I suggest, symbolically a female body.[12] As men represent women in the sense of "covering" female bodies, so the headman or *muhtar* represents the village to the

11. This division is very old and may derive from Aristotle, who had great influence on certain traditions of Islam. In *Generation of Animals* he distinguished three kinds of soul (being): the nutritive soul distinguished between living and nonliving; the sentient soul distinguished between animals and plants; and the rational soul divided humans from animals. Since animals have feelings but not reason, they should be treated accordingly. I was at first an object of derision because of the way I spoke to and petted my kitten. But then people noticed that she would race to me whenever I returned home from another part of the village, would come when I called her name, and would let me know when she wanted to come in or go out of the house. This impressed them. Apparently I had learned the language of animals (at least of cats) like Süleyman, the Biblical Solomon.

12. This symbolism is not unique, of course; for Greece, see Hirschon 1978, 1981; DuBoulay 1974, 1986; Dubisch 1986; Friedl 1962, 1967. Michael Herzfeld's project (1985, 1986) is related but somewhat different. For Herzfeld women occupy and are associated with the interior spaces, and that is how they come to symbolize the "inside"; whereas men occupy and represent the "outside." Although Herzfeld suggests that this gender symbolism is not confined only to men and women but "may be manipulated as symbols of exterior and interior identities of other kinds" (1986: 217), the allocation of gender to different spaces and the gender associations themselves are not questioned but assumed.

outside; conversely, all outsiders who enter the village must first be taken to see the *muhtar.*

The *muhtar's* duties are primarily bureaucratic. He keeps records of marriages and transfers of property. He collects the *salma* (or head tax) used for the village budget, the tax on television (every year), and the tax on land (every four years). Since 1969, when the village was electrified, he collects the electricity bills. Since outsiders must present themselves to him, the job requires a certain amount of hospitality.

In the administration of the village he is assisted by the *bekçi* (watchman), whose main duty in our village was to turn on and off the water supply to houses, to answer the telephone, and to watch for any troublesome outsiders. In addition there are the *aza* (limb), a term that reinforces the idea of the village as a social "body"; they are a group of volunteer men who assist the *muhtar* on occasion. Every aspect of the administration of the village, down to the last pencil, is detailed by the government; there is very little room for personal initiative. Nevertheless, the *muhtar* is supposed to formulate community projects in accordance with government rules and to seek government approval for such projects. The building of Hasan's house, discussed in the previous chapter, was an internal community-based project that did not involve outside approval.

Social Geography of the Village

Before crossing the threshold of the household I would like to discuss the outside structures that are yet inside the village and their relation to the socio-spatial configurations in the village. Although these are community structures and outside the household, it does not mean they are public in the sense that anyone can use them. Most of what are usually referred to as "public" buildings are, in fact, for the use of men, reinforcing the idea that men are the only fully social beings.

By far the largest and most splendid structure in the village is the mosque. Built in 1956–62 from funds collected among villagers and of a size and material usually found only in towns, this imposing structure testifies to the wealth and faith of the villagers. It was built at the center of the village, adjacent to the older, smaller mosque on the "sacred" spot where the original inhabitants are believed to have settled. Except on the occasion of a *mevlud* (prayer commemorating a death) or the evening prayers during Ramazan, the mosque is the province of men.

Nearby is the village library. It is very unusual to find a library in a village; indeed neither the nearest town nor the administrative center for the district has a library. Established in 1958, it houses an odd assortment of books and periodicals provided by the government; many are religious, but also included are novels, historical works, and encyclopedias. In 1981 a new building was constructed with a sunny reading room and shelves on the first level, and a room on the lower level potentially for the use of women's sewing and handwork classes. We were told that a teacher from Milas would be sent once a week if there was enough interest. The government provided the money for the construction, and would choose and pay the teacher if one should be requested.

Secular education takes place in two schools, an *ilk okul* (grades 1–5) and—also unusual for a village—an *orta okul* (grades 6–8). Primary school is compulsory for all children.[13] The primary school has been in existence since 1928, but the original structure is now occupied by the middle school, which opened in 1977. The new primary school building and the lodgings for the teachers were built during the 1970s.

At one end of the village is the *sağlık evi* (health house), built in 1972, a rural out-station connected to the *sağlık ocağı* (health center) in Yoldakent, which in turn is part of a rural medical program established by the government. The government-appointed midwife lives in this house. Another building is set aside as the *muhtar's* office, but he rarely uses it except to receive outside officials. It also doubles as a telephone exchange and post office, yet, although it boasts the familiar yellow PTT sign, it neither sells stamps nor mails letters. Most people hand their letters, along with money for stamps, to anyone going to town. Incoming letters are picked up once a week from the post office in the administrative center and distributed by the *muhtar* or the *bekçi*.

Two *değirmen* (mills) are used for grinding grain. The village mill is generally used for *arpa* (rye), which is considered fodder. *Buğday* (wheat) to be ground into flour for making bread and noodles is transported to

13. Primary school attendance for the year 1981–82 was as follows: first grade, 8; second grade, 20; third grade, 13; fourth grade, 11; fifth grade, 19. The year before, however, there had been about 35 in the fifth grade, including 21 girls; I was told that 1967–68 was a big year for babies. Only three of the girls went on to the middle school and about seven boys. Another boy came from a nearby village to stay with us in order to attend the middle school. Classes in the middle school are rarely above 10.

Approaching the village

a large mill in Ambarlı, where it can be ground finer and faster than in the village.

Three *çamaşırhane* (laundry houses) are built next to the *çeşme*. The additional *çeşme* near the mosque is reputed to have the best water for drinking. Women go to the *çamaşırhane* to wash clothes and to take baths if they do not do so at home. The *çeşme* could be considered a public place for women, since they frequent it more often than men. It serves as a legitimate excuse for women to meet, although typically the time spent filling containers with water is not very long. The fountains are also visited by animals going to and from pasture and by vehicles of various kinds. Occasionally the *çamaşırhane* are taken over by men and used to cook large quantities of food, such as for the hajj meal or for weddings.

At present there are two working *bakkal* (small stores), each in a room

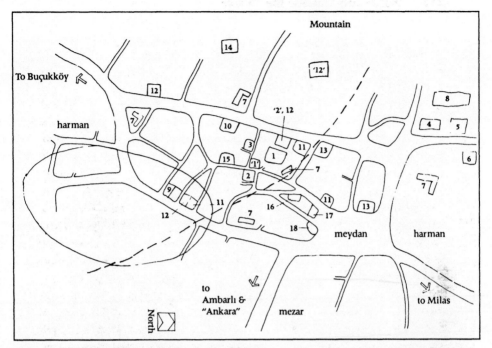

Map of the village. The dashed line divides the upper and lower sections of the village. The solid line encircles my *mahalle*. Small arrows indicate steep inclines. *Meydan*— "square." *Harman*—open space, field. *Mezar*—cemetery.

1. Mosque
2. Libraries (old '2,' new 2)
3. *Muhtar*'s house
4. Primary school
5. Middle school
6. *Sağlık evi* (health house)
7. Fountains—some with attached laundry houses
8. Teacher's quarters
9. My house

10. Machine repair shop
11. *Bakkallar* (tiny shops)
12. Tearooms ('12' semiofficial)
13. Political associations
14. Water depot
15. Telephone office
16. Imam's house
17. Building for Qur'an classes
18. Mill

Girls getting water at the fountain

of a house, stocked only with items such as sugar, tea, cigarettes, matches, thread, soap, biscuits, gum, raisins, and nuts. The future of a third such store (next door to my house) was unpredictable when I left, since its owner, who was also the village tailor, had recently died. One other man opened a *bakkal* to sell sheets, scarves, and underwear, but gave up after a few months.

No store in the village sells fresh produce or bread, nor is there a market. People produce their own staple foods, or borrow from the neighbors. Every week there is a market in Milas and another on a different day in Ambarlı. Only a few people go each week, not only because of the limited space in the village vehicles but because the trip is expensive (about $5.00 round trip). Often people will give money, an empty sack, and requests for certain vegetables or fruits to a friend or the *dolmuş* driver.

In the late 1970s, two political *dernek* (associations) were established: a *Halk odası* ("leftist") association and an *Ülküköy* ("rightist") association, the latter by a man reputed to have four wives now all living in "Ankara." On September 12, 1980, the day the military took control of the government, all political associations were disbanded; soldiers from Milas came to the village and locked the associations' doors, forbidding anyone to enter. Since that was the first night I was settled into my house, I never had the opportunity to see these rooms in use; they remained closed throughout my stay. The associations themselves continued to function, albeit in much curtailed form, in the men's tearooms.

These tearooms—three of them "official" and one semiofficial run by the only bachelor in the village, a man of about forty, for his friends— are not like town or city tearooms, which are open all day and presided over by a proprietor who makes and charges for tea. Rather, they are simply rooms maintained by people in each quarter (mahalle). The men using the tearoom themselves supply the tea and sugar, light the soba, make the tea, and clean up. Women are not allowed inside. Two have television sets, one provided by the government several years ago, the other bought from funds collected by the habitués. Although there is no strict code distinguishing one tearoom from another, those who frequent a given tearoom generally live in the neighborhood. However, the oldest tearoom, located near the mosque and above the old library, has the reputation of being the hangout of the gençler (youth). Tearooms are also used to entertain guests on occasions when there are large numbers of people from outside, such as weddings, bayrams (holidays), and funerals. In many other villages a tearoom is commandeered by the visiting doctor and used as an examining room for the sick.

A tearoom is also where an anthropologist, if male and unmarried, would have had to live. Because of the strict division of labor by sex, men are not expected to perform household tasks; thus he could not have lived alone in his own house, as I did. Nor could he have hired a village woman because of the strict segregation between the sexes, particularly when unmarried. He could not have lived with a village family for the same reasons, and his visits to families would have been much more formal. As an unmarried outside male he would most likely have been provided for, as were the kalaycı (tinsmiths), whose meals were prepared by different families in rotation. Although he might be able to gain better information about political and economic activities, at least from the male point of view, he would not have been able to observe their implicit ramifications in the home or the *mahalle,* and much ordinary social life would have been closed to him (cf. Papanek 1973; Jeffrey 1979). But he would have had access to the tearoom, which, as one arena for establishing and displaying prestige and reputation, is a valuable source of information about male gender identity.[14]

All these buildings, despite earlier remarks, testify to some kind of community consensus and cooperation, dating at least to the 1940s and 1950s, and perhaps earlier. In the 1950s, even before a proper road was built, a number of community endeavors were instituted: (1) a mosque building and maintenance society; (2) a bridge building association, which built a bridge over a ravine where several villagers had lost their lives in a tractor accident; (3) the library; (4) an association for the construction of a school and teachers' lodgings; (5) a sport club, which arranged soccer and volleyball matches with other villages; (6) a cultural exchange program. Those in charge of this last program instituted several cultural exchanges between the village and Ankara, among them folklore evenings and reciprocal visits between schoolchildren in the village and a sister school in Ankara.

Villagers recall a visit in the mid-1950s by an American professor interested in rural development who told them that their village was "like a plane ready to take off; all it needs is a pilot." Clearly there had been several energetic and imaginative people, but the village lacked coordinated planning and leadership. It later found an impressive leader in the person of Ali Aydin, *muhtar* in 1972–78, who claimed that during his term of office he was able to get fifty people to work on a project when needed. If work needed to be done, a man was sent from each household and worked free. People confirmed this and added that a community spirit went along with this community work (*imece*), a judgment reinforced by an album of photographs of communal celebrations and events of that period. To say that the villagers were a community does not mean that everyone held the same views. It means that although there were differences of opinion, these did not become polarized around political institutions—and that there was no sharp division in the village.

14. The rhetoric of male display in coffee- and teahouses in the Middle East and the Mediterranean is discussed by Abu-Lughod 1986; Brandes 1980; Campbell 1964; Dubisch 1986; DuBoulay 1974, 1976; Gilmore 1987, 1990; Herzfeld 1985; Meeker 1976; and Mernissi 1975.

Unlike the more culturally oriented 1950s projects, Aydin's tended to focus on the welfare and development of the village. The *sağlık evi* (health house) was built at the beginning of his term, for the first time bringing the village some of the benefits of modern medicine, notably the inoculation of children. The sewage system, known as *kanalızasyon*, was built in 1973. He also initiated two projects that would benefit the village economically: a village development cooperative and a production-consumption cooperative that brought in wholesale such items as coal, fertilizer, sugar, and tea. Also started was an irrigation project that would have doubled the yield of grain, but this was left half-finished and lay in ruins. It was also during this time that *Köy Sesi* (The Village Voice) was published. The Mutual Aid Society helped several poor children, including at least one girl, to continue their education beyond primary school. And in 1977 the middle school opened. Clearly Aydin's term as *muhtar* was an active one.

Since these various village associations were also officially closed after the military intervention (September 12, 1980), I was never able to witness this kind of organizing activity. Yet it was not the action of the military that actually closed them. Except for the mosque committee, all had already died sometime before. Toward the end of the 1970s some malaise settled over the village, struck at its vital core, and left it paralyzed. What happened? Since the malaise that hit the village seems to parallel that of Turkey's government shortly before the military takeover, villagers' explanations of what happened in the village may shed some light on broader issues at the national level.

Villagers have several explanations for the paralysis of the village. Nearly all relate it to the establishment of the two political *derneks*, which institutionalized as well as polarized differences of opinion, causing people to take sides and paralyzing cooperative efforts. "If you belonged to one side you would not help someone from the other side, and so nothing got done." The same kind of infighting occurred at the national level between heads of opposing parties and caused them to lose sight of the interests and security of the nation. According to Dodd (1983), differences of opinion became polarized; instead of trying to work out a compromise, each party did its best to delegitimize the other. State institutions also became polarized as different ministries came under partisan leadership. There was no recognized authority and no consensus about what direction the government should take.

In the village election of 1979, another man replaced Aydin as *muhtar*, but his election represented not so much a consensus in favor of his views as it did the line of least resistance. The change of Prime Minister in the national election was similar; he could not form a majority in Parliament, and his position was weakened by having to form coalition governments. Although our village did not experience violence on the scale of many other villages, or the nation as a whole,[15] its moral conscience was wounded.

As has been noted, the villagers believe that all bad things come from outside. The importation of national politics in the form of the two political *derneks* seems to confirm this. Similarly, the government tried to blame much of the anarchy on outside influence and interference. The military assumed that closing all the *derneks* and rounding up political activists would remove the foreign body. But it was not that simple. *Derneks* could not have been established had there not been a cultural medium in which to grow.

Since villagers tend to blame the divisiveness on outside influence, it is necessary to give an account of the outsiders living in the village. In my time there, these were the teachers, the midwife, the librarian's assistant, the imam, and myself. Except for me, all of these were appointed and paid by the government. The government policy of appointing outsiders[16] is informed by a particular view of peasants, namely that they are conservative, uninterested in change, and unintelligent. They must be led rather than being included as partners, and the trained outsider is sent in as the leader, the agent of change. Leder (1976) argues that the agent of change often becomes a catalyst of division.

What the government failed to take into account is the resentment that inevitably builds up on both sides. I cannot speak for teachers and midwives in general, but most of those I talked with resented being in the village. They scorned the village way of life and considered villagers stupid and ignorant. The villagers were of course aware of their sentiments and resented their interference.

15. Estimated deaths from political violence were as follows: 1975, 35; 1976, 90; 1977, 260; 1978, 800–1,000; 1979, 1,500; 1980, 3,500 until September 12 (Dodd 1983: 27).

16. Could this policy possibly be a different version of the older Ottoman notion of the *devşirme*, the recruitment of boys to the Janissary Corps? Cut off from their home and kin, educated at government expense, they were expected not only to carry out the government's wishes but also to be more loyal.

From everything I could gather, including an interview with an elderly former teacher who returned for a brief visit, this was not the case in the past. Not only were the teachers respected, but they seemed to be of a different type and quality. The literature about the early cadre of teachers, many of whom were trained in the Village Institutes,[17] testifies to their dedication and zeal. Excited at being in at the beginning of radical social change, they may have been overbearing at times, but most were dedicated to helping villagers to modernize. Atatürk had stressed the role of education in making Turkey a modern, "civilized" nation, and teachers carried this message into the classrooms.[18]

Yet the spirit of nation-building extended well beyond the nation's teachers. Some 113 men from our village fought in the War of Independence: 74 died, 37 returned, and two were listed as missing. In our village as elsewhere Atatürk was considered a savior; and despite his secular policies the nation was bound together by a fervent desire to make Turkey a great nation.

Although Atatürk's ultimate goal was to create a modern, democratic nation, the means he chose at the beginning of the Republic was a benign dictatorship. Despite the momentous change from an Empire to a Republic, the form of authority under Atatürk was essentially unchanged, and it was one most people understood. Whether the authority was *devlet baba* (father state) or Atatürk (father of the Turks), the person and the state became intertwined and identified with the party.

Borrowing the term "monoparty" from Harold Laski, Feroz Ahmad uses it "in preference to 'one party' or 'single party' in order to emphasize the coalescing of party and state in Turkey during the years 1924–45" (1977: 1; see also Yerasimos 1987). This is another expression of the essential feature of "monogenesis"—that authority rests with the founder-creator—a model that is consonant with monotheism and suggests that the state and power are symbolically gendered. Ata-

17. These schools, established in 1940, were located throughout Turkey. Boys who had completed primary school were examined, and the most able were chosen to attend the Institutes. During their education they were fully supported by the government for five years, after which time they owed twenty years of service teaching in villages. The Institutes have been criticized: for example, for training people with modern equipment that they would never see again. Also some of the teachers displayed feelings of superiority, which rankled at the village level. Village Institutes were disbanded soon after Menderes came to power in 1950.

18. Atatürk himself, especially at the beginning of the Republic, had gone around the nation giving lectures, often with a blackboard.

türk was the founder-creator of the Republic. Upon his death he was also declared founder and eternal chairman of the Republican People's Party, a declaration that inevitably gave that party a certain aura of sanctity. Although Atatürk was committed to democracy, which in theory allows for the expression of divergent points of view, his autocratic style extended the traditional one. The legacy of monotheism (Islam) and monoparty rule, whether by the sultan or by Atatürk, has been a political disposition suspicious of duality or plurality (Tachau 1984: 68), a disposition that makes the transition to democracy difficult. This became evident over the issue of succession.

The commitment and consensus generated by the charismatic leader deteriorated after his death on November 10, 1938. His closest associate and comrade in arms, Inönü, was declared successor; differences arose between him and other close associates of Atatürk's, and these differences became codified and institutionalized with the formation of the Democratic Party in 1946. There was no change in government until 1950, when the new party, capitalizing on the peasant's growing resentment of secularism, won the election as the champion of religion.

Thus the victory of the Democratic Party reflects not only the triumph of the democratic process, but also a reaction against laicism (*layiklik*), as conceived and established by Atatürk. *Layiklik* was one of the "six arrows" used to characterize the principles of Kemalism[19] on which the Republic was founded. It was also arguably the most important, the one on which all others turned, the "axis for defining progressive versus conservative, and revolutionary versus reactionary categories" (Toprak 1987: 218). In designating it the fifth arrow, was there a not so subtle barb aimed at the five pillars of Islam? Because Islam has much greater scope or dominion over social and political life than Christianity, the imposition of *layiklik* is far more drastic. In Sunni Islam the boundaries between religion and society are blurred, if not effaced: "There is *one* God in heaven, who gave *one* law to mankind and established *one* ruler to maintain and enforce that law in his *one* community" (B. Lewis 1988: 46, emphasis mine). Previously politics had been encompassed

---

19. Kemalism, also known as Atatürkism, is the term given to Mustafa Kemal's philosophy of government. Its six "arrows" are republicanism (Çümhürriyetçilik), nationalism (Milliyetçilik), populism (Halkçılık), reformism (Inkılapçılık), secularism (Layiklik), and etatism (Devletçilik). See Dumont 1984.

by Islam; in the new republic, religious institutions were put under the control of the state.[20]

To change the basis of law, of the state, and of the ruler's authority implied more than a rejection of God and a self-imposed exile from the Muslim community; it also meant that the state no longer rested on a secure foundation. To be properly founded, as we have noted, means to have a proper founder. In his lifetime Atatürk filled this symbolic role, but his death and the end of the "monoparty" system brought problems. Few could comprehend the notion that the legitimate basis for rule rests with the people, an idea basic to democracy. Even fewer could accept Atatürk's view that "the voice of the people is the voice of God" (speech of February 17, 1923, quoted in B. Lewis 1968 [1961]: 466).[21] For many ordinary people, this was blasphemy.

In 1950, then, using democratic means, the people paradoxically voted for the party they thought represented a restitution of the authority and principles of Islam over Kemalism. That the Democratic Party intended no such restitution soon became clear, even though one of its first moves was to permit the call to prayer in Arabic, something that had been outlawed by Atatürk. In time the new party's continuing commitment to *layiklik* led to the development of more radical, religious "rightist" organizations.

The resulting disintegration affected not only students but also teachers, who are assigned to villages by the government for terms of two years. Most of the teachers in our village were not particularly dedicated or even interested in their work. Nor were they politically of the same mind. Unlike the community studied by Leder (1976), where the teachers were all Marxists and where their conflicts were with some of the townspeople, the teachers in our village were divided among themselves. Their differences surfaced in verbal and physical fights, which further antagonized villagers and made them reluctant to entrust their children to such people.

In my view, the conflict really has to do with orientations, which in turn entail concepts of what the state is or should be. Hotham's remarks

20. For an excellent discussion of the rhetoric and process of secularism in Turkey, see Toprak 1981; also of note are Berkes 1964, Landau 1984, and Schick and Tonak 1987.

21. This statement has an echo of Durkheim. Atatürk was familiar with the works of the French theorist, and his ideas were discussed in relation to nationalism among the intellectuals with whom Atatürk associated, especially in his student days.

in 1972 are still apposite. There is, he said, "a conflict as to what the basis of the state really is. According to Kemalism, it is the principles of Atatürk, above all secularism: but according to democracy, it is the will of the people. 'Sovereignty belongs to the people,' said Atatürk. The people were represented by parliament, and in practice, by the majority in parliament. But what happens if this same majority, representing the people, acts against Kemalist principles?" (1972: 63). The change to a multiparty system, the *sine qua non* of democracy, by splitting loyalties and thus identities, also called into question the very foundation of the Republic by calling into question the legitimacy of its *ata* (father or ancestor, but meaning also founder).

Villagers also said their current problems were derived from the *ata*, meaning problems not so much of specific people as of history, origins, descent, and identity. Atatürk himself was well aware that his vision of the future of Turkey rested on his revision of the past; this was the motivation behind his energetic investigations into linguistics and history. If people were to be reoriented, they needed to be given a new sense of where they came from, a new sense of history and of identity. The fact that villagers attributed their problems to the forefathers points, I believe, to a severe identity crisis: they were confused about where they came from and where they were going. I believe it was the same problem at the national level.

Hotham saw the problem as a matter of "dual legitimacy" (1972: 63), that is, a confusion "about what body in the state represents the nation" (ibid.). This analysis, with its use of the word "body," relates very much to the argument I have been making, that the understanding and symbolization of authority is gendered and draws upon notions of coming-into-being. In the context of government, what is often not realized is that the problem of "dual legitimacy" involves a problem of dual descent. In villagers' view that is impossible. There is only one principle of descent (and legitimacy), and it is based on a theory of conception in which only the male (*ata*—father, founder) is author of the child. Dual descent would imply another principle of descent of equal value; but given the logic of their understanding of conception, that cannot be.

Regardless of which side one is on, the recognition of duality, or even more to the point, of the *legitimacy* of duality or opposition, is a threat to the symbolic system. From either side, there cannot be dual legitimacy. For a people whose heritage has been shaped to a large extent by Islam, the "question of political legitimacy . . . is primarily a theocratic question rather than a political one" (Toprak 1981: 25). Toprak goes on to say that the effort to establish a "national identity and political legitimacy based on secular as opposed to sacred appeals . . . leaves most of its members in an ideological and emotional void" (ibid.: 37). Because of the incompatibility between Islam and a secular ideology, Atatürk severed the Turkish nation from its mooring and set it adrift. It could no longer find its sense of identity in a common past, but had to become reoriented toward a vision of a common future. This is what I believe villagers are struggling with.

The polarization of the village (and the nation) is not, in my opinion, something new, but represents the latest incarnation of a very old and characteristic attitude in which the entire cosmos is divided: God-Creation, other world–this world, Dar el Islam–Dar el Harb; East-West, Islamic state–secular Republic; right-left; good-evil; upper-lower; spirit-matter; male-female. In the traditional religious worldview, however, these divisions are not really oppositions: the duality is only apparent, for the second item in each set is dependent on and encompassed by the first. From the perspective of earthly life, the spirit is encompassed in the physical as the seed-child is in the womb; but ultimately the physical world is encompassed by the spiritual as the woman is by the man.

In other words, the theory of procreation helps us to see the logic behind these dualisms and the way they are related. One could also argue that they are inherent in notions of Creation: that ideas of conception are intimately related to conceptions of the deity because they are analogues. Thus it is that women are associated with the Creation, men with the Creator; women associated with the perishable aspects of this world, men with the eternal aspects of the other world; men united by the bond of Islam, women associated with dissension; men associated with the right and good, women with the left and evil. Women, allied with the material aspects of the world, can also be associated with secularism and materialism, whether in the form of capitalism or Communism.

What men and women are, the relation between them as defined by their perceived role in procreation, expresses the nature and order of the Creation. To change this relation, to acknowledge the equal status of men and women or their equal claim to allegiance in any of the oppositions above, is to rock the foundation of the universe. Any change in the relation and value of any of the terms implies changes for all the others; a change in women's status is so difficult because it involves the entire symbolic universe. Such a change would be a sign to villagers that the end of the world is approaching, a time characterized by a capitulation not only to the physical world but to women, a time at which (they prophesy) women will begin to rule over men. They see that in the world and in their own society some women are gaining positions of authority; they see these changes with alarm, as heralding the imminent end. But even less momentous changes made them anxious, and during the two years before I came to the village there had been several significant changes. The political *derneks* had been established; cooperative ventures had collapsed; there was a change of *muhtar,* teachers, and midwife. My own arrival, coinciding as it did with the military intervention, was surely cause for suspicion. Shortly before I came, the imam of ten years was replaced[22] by a Kurd from eastern Turkey, a large, solid, belligerent-looking man with fixed opinions. Opposed to the secular government and quick to recall the glories of the Ottoman Empire, he represented the quite common conjunction of religious and ultranationalist views that seek a return to the unity of Islam and the state. After the military intervention there were no more changes, since all civil service positions were frozen. Political tensions also seemed to be on hold, only to flare up again much later.

Two events triggered the explosion. The first had already occurred in April 1980, when certain villagers reportedly did not stand up when the Istiklâl (Independence) March was played during the Children's Holiday program. Several villagers and a few of the teachers were offended and reported the matter to the court. A lengthy investigation took place, including the transportation of all schoolchildren to the court to bear witness.[23] Although this investigation kept the issue alive,

22. As we have seen, religious officials, like teachers and midwives, are appointed by and under the control of the central government. The former imam was promoted to a large mosque in Milas, the administrative center for the region.

23. I was surprised to find the same event described in many different ways. Not only did the date change (was it Children's Holiday or May Day?), but so did the march (was it the Independence March or the Internationale?), and even the participants (were the teachers behind it or certain villagers?). I was reminded of the game in which children form a circle and one child whispers something to the next, that child passes the message to the next, and so on until it returns back to the first child. Usually the end result is nothing at all like the original statement.

it was not perceived as important in itself and would surely have been forgotten but for the second event.

Almost two years later, the imam began calling certain people Communists and making anti-Atatürk remarks. He went too far one day during a sermon in the mosque, calling Atatürk a *gavur* (infidel) and a Communist. By law, among those considered guilty of high treason are people "who, by misuse of religion . . . incite the people to action prejudicial to the security of the state" (Article 163) and "religious leaders and preachers who, in the course of their functions, bring the administration, laws, or executive actions of the government into disrepute, or incite to disobedience" (from Articles 241 and 242; cf. B. Lewis 1968 [1961]: 412). It is no wonder that the imam was reported to the court.

Accusations and counteraccusations escalated, and long-buried grievances were exhumed and aired again, until almost everyone was drawn into the fray. No one was happy about the arguments and fights that divided the village, but no one knew how to stop them. Eventually the government (now military) intervened, removed the imam from the village, and forbade him to practice, a series of steps comparable to the intervention of the military at the national level.

But what exactly was the issue, and how did the village divide? A clue is found in the imam's description of Atatürk as a Communist. It is well known that Atatürk was committed to Westernization and wished to model Turkey after Western nations; in terms of our familiar distinction between Communism and capitalism, he was patently a capitalist, though his capitalism was state capitalism. But in terms of the distinction between Islam and secularism, the distinction between Communism and capitalism is trivial. What matters is that both are associated with secularism and materialism; both stand in sharp contrast to the Islamic world view. Whether secularism takes the form of capitalism or Communism is in itself of little concern; whichever form is felt to be the most imminent threat to Islam will be focused on. In this view, which identifies the "right" with Islam, secularists become a "surrogate left" (Toprak 1987: 218) regardless of their political views.

The division of the village was drawn roughly in terms of *mahalle* (neighborhoods)—"roughly" because it had more to do with the symbolic dimensions, which only roughly correlated with physical ones. If one stands in the center of the village facing the valley, Ankara, the capital of the secular republic, is on the left and Mecca is on the right.

The *aşağı mahalle* (lower section of the village) is also on the left. This part of the village had always been seen as more open to the world (*açık*), somewhat more modern, progressive, and "Western." Now it was labeled "leftist" and sometimes even Communist. The *yukarı mahalle* (upper section), which is farthest from the school and the road to town, was seen as more enclosed .(*kapalı*), somewhat more traditional, conservative, and religious. It was relabeled "rightist."

As indicated, this left-right division cannot be taken as categorical. For example, the brothers Muharrem and Ali Aydin lived next door to each other in the lower *mahalle* but were on opposite sides of the religious-political fence. Similarly, several of the most open-minded men lived in the upper *mahalle* in close proximity to the most religiously fanatical man, the one referred to as Khomeini.

Nor can the division be seen in terms of blood ties. Not only were brothers divided, but so too were parents and children. Villagers said the division had little to do with land or wealth, since not only do several men in both the upper and lower *mahalles* have considerable amounts of land but comparatively poor men were found on both sides. It might, however, have to do with land in the symbolic sense: that is, with land in terms of its meaning and purpose. For what seems to be at issue is the future orientation of the village, whether its life and allegiance will be primarily directed by and to Islam (the other world), or by and to the secular state (this world).

In "Turkish Democracy at Impasse," written after the military intervention in September 1980, Kemal Karpat noted that with respect to the form and role of government "the chief issue that seemed to underlie all discussions after 1945 was secularism" (1981: 22). I believe this to be true in the village as well. But I also believe that most sociopolitical analysts have not understood the nuances or symbolic ramifications of this issue, at least among the village population.

Since education is a major means of resocializing people, it is not surprising that one place the conflict between traditionalism and secularism erupted was in education. The secularizing elements in Turkish society have continued to emphasize *terbiye* (education) rather than the traditional concept of *maarif* (knowledge) (Winter 1984: 184). Traditional learning can be seen as a "taking in," usually through memorizing, of a set body of material, rather than as the "drawing out" signaled by the etymology of the word education (cf. Eickelman 1978, 1989).

The style as well as the method of traditional Muslim learning sets it at odds with educational practices in the West (cf. Van Nieuwenhuijze 1977: 23).

My neighbor Nazim (who lived in the upper *mahalle*) expressed the extreme "rightist" view in response to a brief announcement on television. Flashed across the screen were the words "Aydınlığa ulasmanın yolu okumaktır"—reading/studying is the road to attain enlightenment. "That is a bunch of lies," he said; "the only path is the Qur'an." Actually he did not so much object to the *path*, in this case literacy or learning to read. What he objected to was the *goal*, enlightenment, which has the connotation of opening the mind and is a very Western concept.[24]

The Qur'an is thought to have been first revealed to Muhammed in the form of a command. God said "Read!" (*Oku*) (Sura 96: 1). Tradition has it that since Muhammed was illiterate he protested that he did not know how. God said again: "Read!" This has been interpreted to mean "recite," and recitation of the Qur'an is not just a religious duty but in itself constitutes an important form of knowledge. In the village those who could recite it by heart were called *hafız* (literally keeper, protector) and were especially esteemed. All children are sent to Qur'an classes after completing fifth grade. Here they learn the Arabic alphabet, but they do not learn to *read* Arabic in the sense of understanding what the words mean. They memorize the Qur'an without knowing what it says. The Turkish translation, which they could have understood, is not used because it is considered only an interpretation, not the Qur'an. What is more important is the knowledge of the original, right words.

There is also an oral catechism, certain questions to which there are specific right answers that one must learn by heart. An emphasis on right words and answers implies a magical attitude to words and a conservative attitude toward knowledge and social reproduction. "This type of education tends to mold the child in the pattern of his ancestors and to forge for him a future which will be a living image of the past, so much so that this past is not experienced as such, that is as something left behind and situated some distance back in the temporal series, but

24. I have since learned that *Aydınlık* (meaning enlightenment) was at that time the name of a pro-Communist-Chinese publication. Whether or not the villagers knew of it I don't know; if they did, the notion of enlightenment had even more subversive connotations.

as being lived again in the eternal present of the collective memory" (Bourdieu 1962: 95).

From my observations in the village school, it was not the method that distinguished religious from secular education but the content. The method in both was catechetical and authoritarian; one must learn by rote and memorize the right answers. Nor was the opposition to secular education categorical; rather, it was situated literally on the heads of young women. It is state law that the heads of girls going to school must be *açık*—open, uncovered. This multilayered sign points to the West and symbolizes modernity, secularism, and a different type of education. Not only are girls uncovered, but they are mixing openly with boys; and any mixing of unmarried people of opposite sexes sullies a woman's purity and casts doubt upon her honor. Central to secular education, then, is the issue of sexuality. In fact, I sometimes felt that secular education was analogous to sexual education; as if learning about the world, which is symbolically female, should be a prerogative only of men.[25] "Secular" is not just a synonym for "left" but has also become almost a synonym for "sexual," as "right" has become a symbol for "spiritual."

At least since 1928, people in the lower *mahalle* have lived near and in close association with teachers, at first the only outsiders with whom they came in contact. Even today, despite the divisions among villagers and teachers, teachers' primary social contacts are with those in the lower *mahalle*. Thus people there have gotten to know the teachers, including several women who must by law be uncovered. Furthermore, it was Ali Aydın (from the lower *mahalle*) who introduced the middle school, thus bringing in more teachers with higher educational backgrounds; and the *sağlık evi* (health house), with its resident government-appointed midwife, was established under his initiative and built in the lower *mahalle*.

The differences between the upper and lower *mahalles* in the treat-

25. Previously education had meant the attainment of religious knowledge, which was also primarily for men. Nor is a sexist bias toward education restricted to Islam or Turkey; regarding ancient Judaism, see Eilberg-Schwartz 1990. Until fairly recently, women in the West were excluded from educational institutions of both kinds. Today a similar logic takes the form of the association of specific fields with men and others with women. Indeed, the fields themselves are gendered: that is, certain fields are thought to be in and of themselves more masculine or more feminine, and these associations may in turn subtly influence people's admission, performance, and advancement in those fields. The work of Keller (1985) and Lloyd (1984) is relevant.

ment and behavior of women would hardly be perceptible to an outsider visiting for a brief time, but they exist. Several lower *mahalle* girls attended the middle school; a few are currently studying for an exam to enter *lise* (high school) outside the village. A few have bobbed hair and have appeared at special occasions such as weddings not only uncovered but in Western clothes—pants or skirts. Furthermore, they visit back and forth more freely, read, and play volleyball—not in the open space at the center of the village where the boys do, but in the space behind the school. They look upon the girls in the upper *mahalle* as *geri* (backward). These may seem to be small differences, but in the village they loom large.

It would be a mistake to see the conflict as centering mainly on the school. Although a very few girls are sent to middle school, neither they nor women in general are given *izin* (permission) to use the library; one woman told me that her husband would divorce her if she went. The men say it is because other men will see their wives, but this problem could easily be solved by having special hours or days for women only. When I raised this possibility with the group of men who regularly spent time at the library, it became clear that much more was at issue. "What use have women for books?" "Women are supposed to do hand work, not head work."

Although there are many books in the library about health, child care, nutrition, and cooking that would be useful to women, what the men were really talking about was books about sex and procreation—including novels, which were considered to be sexually stimulating and which, by revealing other ways of life, might make the women become dissatisfied with their own. In addition, they were adamant that women not learn anything about evolution and genetics, two subjects that are taught in the middle school. These men were afraid that if women became familiar with such heretical ideas, they would be dissuaded from Islam. (The men, of course, were reading about them.) The men were aware, in a way that the urban elite are not, that such knowledge poses a threat to their masculine authority, which, as we have seen, rests upon a specific theory of procreation that is inherent in and supported by Islam. In order to safeguard their position, they make excuses about "protecting" women from this knowledge. Women as the "soil" or material of reproduction must embody the traditions in pure form; changes in the perceived nature of women might cause the traditions to be adulterated in the next generation of offspring. No longer would villagers have a clear sense of identity: everything would be *bulaşık* (tainted, polluted) and *karışık* (mixed up).

Because of Atatürk's emphasis on the role of education in restructuring and reorienting Turkish society, it has become the site of much conflict. As education was a vehicle for the spread of his ideas, so today it is also the vehicle for ideological purposes. The difference is that today a conflict of ideologies is apparent and embodied in the teachers. Nevertheless, education is only one aspect of the broader issue of orientations. Politics, education, and religion are tightly interwoven; a common thread is sexuality and gender, for the theory and symbols of procreation are central to the ways power and authority are represented. We shall return to this in the last section of the chapter, but first we must examine how power and authority function in the household and the division of labor.

The Household: Inside and Outside

As the village encloses inhabitants vis-à-vis outsiders, so does the house enclose its inhabitants vis-à-vis other villagers. As a village is not just a place one lives, neither is a house. Both are symbolic representations of social and cultural values that are an integral part of a person's identity (cf. Daniel 1984).

A house is constructed from mud bricks (*kerpiç*), that is, from native soil, and specifically from soil owned by the particular man whose house it will be. (See Dittemore 1983 for an excellent description of house construction.) Today some people are beginning to build houses out of cement blocks bought in town; but others note that such houses are not as well insulated as those made of mud bricks, being cold in the winter and too hot in the summer.

The house is like a fortress. As in a fortress, windows, if there are any in the outside walls, are high and generally small. Since the house complex usually consists of several buildings, their outside walls also serve as part of the exterior wall that encloses the courtyard and dwelling space. The gate or door is latched, however flimsily, partly to keep out stray dogs and other animals, including wolves at night, but also to alert those inside that someone is coming. The gate also marks the transition from the "wild, polluted" street to the sanctuary of the household. Any outsider who enters the village is usually taken at once into someone's house, not only as an act of hospitality but also as a way of disarming the visitor. For once you have passed through the gate you are a guest, under the protection of the host.

Although villagers have not been nomadic for some time, something of the nomadic seems to linger, not only in their custom of hospitality but also in their attitudes toward houses. By nomadic traditions of hospitality, travelers granted refuge in an encampment must abide by their host's rules of hospitality. In particular, they may not steal, harm, or make sexual advances to the women; otherwise they relinquish protection and their lives are in danger.

Among villagers, casual transactions and visits take place in the courtyard, but more formal visiting takes place inside the house. Houses are generally two-story affairs; the lower level is used for animals, storage, and the *ocak*, which, besides being the place where bread is baked, sometimes serves as a kitchen. The upper level is the supremely human domain used for visiting, sitting, and talking, as well as for eating and sleeping. Today much of the cooking is done upstairs either on gas burners supplied with *tüp gaz* (propane gas in steel containers) or on the *soba* (stove-heater). However, there is a kind of "seasonal migration in the house" (Dittemore 1983: 248). In summer the *soba* may be moved outdoors, or cooking may be done below in the *ocak*, where it is cool. In winter cooking is done indoors, often in the room with the *soba*.

The traditional Anatolian house plan is called *karnıyarık*, which is also the name for a traditional food dish—split eggplant stuffed with a meat mixture. Literally, *karnıyarık* means split womb; the house is traditionally divided by brothers. The house itself as symbolic womb is also divided; or perhaps it is better to say replicated, since theoretically each room is a separate house (like a tent) for each married couple. Today, however, there is some spatial specialization. The traditional *karnıyarık* has a central room, often referred to as *hayat* (life, living), which serves as an entrance hall; sometimes a corner or end of this room will be used as a kitchen. Opening off from the central "hall" are rooms on either side. Other houses were basically variations on this pattern; for example, my house was half a *karnıyarık*. Alternatively, the two rooms on either side can be divided into four, or a few basic *karnıyarık*-type houses

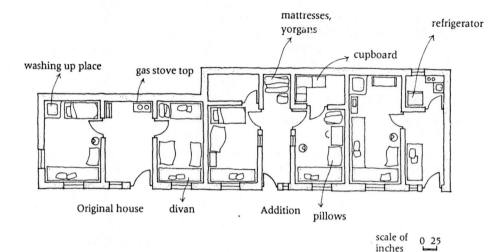

Karnıyarık: traditional house plan

can be attached in a row. Recently several newer designs have been attempted (see p. 236), but the conceptualization in terms of the *karnıyarık* is still evident.

Toilets are always separate from the bathing place[26] as well as from the main house. They are placed in the courtyard below or on the upper level but outside the house; for example, on the roof of an adjoining building. Within the house, however, and often in each room, there is a corner reserved for washing. An edge of slightly raised earth, now covered with cement, forms its boundary, and a hole in the wall channels the water to the outside.[27]

Another transition is marked as one enters the house. Outer footwear is discarded at the door, and one crosses the threshold in stocking feet. Rubbers (*cömele*, from the verb *cömelmek*—to squat down on one's heels) have become the standard village footwear; they are easy to take off and

26. Turks believe the two functions should not be carried out in the same place and consider European-American arrangements disgusting. In Europe, Turks will often build an extra room (perhaps in a hallway) for one or the other function. Europeans, for their part, assume Turks have an aversion to bathing when they see bathtubs being used for storage! Prejudice and ignorance exist on both sides.

27. Similar structures have been found in houses at Çatal Hüyük (c. 8000 B.C.) but are thought to be "altars." See Mellaart 1962–64, 1965.

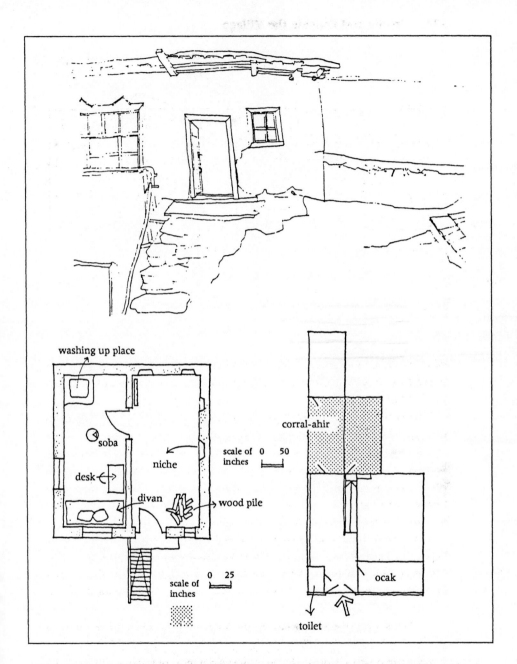

Half a *karnıyarık*: plan of my house. The sketch and all house plans were drawn by Oya Aksoy.

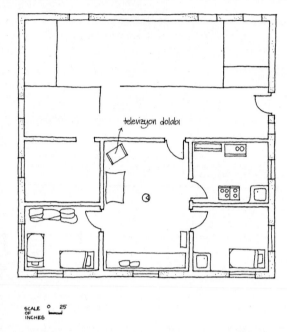

televizyon dolabı

SCALE
OF
INCHES   0   25

New house plan (half under construction)

put on, and keep the feet dry. When there are many guests, the array of identical black rubbers makes quite a sight. The pairs of rubbers are turned around by the hostess or some girl in the family, so that departing guests may step directly into their rubbers without first having to step outside. People seem to know instinctively which pairs are theirs; in any case, you can tell as soon as you step into them.

From the "hall" one enters the main room through a door that is generally kept closed to keep out flies in summer and cold drafts in winter. Even if there are several rooms, one will be designated as the main room. Traditionally, and in most villages, this was the *oda* (room), meaning the room where the male head received guests. Other rooms are private, used for additional sleeping quarters or perhaps the *ev* of a *gelin* and her husband. The main room is multifunctional (cf. Dittemore 1983). It is used primarily for sitting, sleeping, and eating, but also for sewing, carding *tiftik* (angora goat hair), and watching television. In one *oda* I saw an entire cow carcass being cut up for a variety of uses.

bed Rooms
are
Private

Floors are usually made of mud covered with cement; then linoleum is laid and finally carpets. Around several sides are built-in divans, which serve a double function as couches and beds. On top of these are large cushions, and ranged along the back are hard bolsters filled with straw. Divans, cushions, and bolsters are all covered with either *basma* (printed cloth) or narrow strips of carpeting. Along the top of the bolsters are long white runners bordered with embroidery and lace (part of the woman's *çeyiz*). All divans have skirts behind which are stored the family's possessions—clothes, equipment of various sorts, and children's school supplies. Square pillows called *minder* are scattered about and on the floor. The fabrics are all of different designs, colors, and ages, giving a very vivid and to Western tastes aesthetically discordant appearance.

Guests sit on the divan, and children may fall asleep there at any time, even when guests are present. A *yorgan* (a heavy, wool-filled quilt) may be brought and laid over a sleeping child. The parents' bed, if there is no separate room, would stand in one corner and would be more elaborately covered.

Today the *oda* of most families also includes a *bufe* (a dresser with glassed-in shelves), which displays bric-a-brac and the television. Tables, which are now considered *de rigueur* in wedding transactions, are used more as a sideboard. They cannot be used for sitting or eating at, since there are no chairs.

The inside of the house is as clean as the street is dirty. Houses are swept several times a day, in the morning and after each meal. This contrasts sharply with the "wild" and polluted outside. Garbage is dumped outside the house onto the street, where most of it is eventually eaten by passing dogs, cats, chickens, goats, sheep, and cows. In addition, broken glass, old machinery, and sometimes ash from the *soba* litter the streets.

To enter the street is to enter the wild area of the village, comparable at a different level to the wild area outside the village. As men are the only legitimate wanderers outside the village, so too are they the legitimate occupants of the street. Women's place is in the home; "men make outside relations." A woman enters the street unprotected and open to contagion through the potential mixing of the sexes. In order to signify that she is "covered" she dons another, larger, and more enveloping scarf that covers not only her head but also her breasts. Older women, following an older custom, will draw their scarves over their mouths. Women hesitate at their gates to see who is around and then move into the lanes.

This is not to say that women usually stay in the house. They often go out, but generally at times that men are not around. Women rarely leave their *mahalle* (neighborhood quarter) and never without *izin* (permission), and they rarely go unaccompanied. It is not that the women are timid, far from it; in their own world, many are strong and outspoken characters. It is rather that these rules and restrictions are hardly seen as such, hardly ever questioned; they are givens, part of the way life is lived there. When I described the situation to an American friend, he was appalled and asked, "Why don't they just leave?" The simple answer is that there is no place to go. Some younger women may long for such amenities as Western clothes, makeup, cinema, and travel, but they cannot imagine going off by themselves: the obstacles are too great. A woman could not just walk out of the village without being seen, and it is thirty kilometers to the main road. She could not walk alone to the village "square" to catch the village *dolmuş* without arousing suspicion. Where would she get the money? Where would she go? If to relatives in the city, they would return her. There are no halfway houses or cheap rooms except in the worst part of town, and women do not generally share apartments. Even in the city, many men and women remain at home until, and even after, marriage. The only way for a woman to leave the village except for visits with her family is by marrying a villager who lives elsewhere. The mobility of women is attached to and controlled by men, whereas men's mobility is relatively independent. They can move alone, inside and outside the village, and in the connections they make they perpetuate, reproduce, and enlarge the social sphere.

In this section I have sketched the idea, structure, and organization of the village. I have stressed the significance of the notion of inside-outside, which defines the physical boundaries of the village, of the house, and to a lesser extent of the *mahalle*. The source for these analogies, I suggest, is the female body, symbolically understood, and the male's relation to it. These structures and relations are gendered; the world becomes an icon of gender as constructed within a specific ideology of procreation. In the following section I look at the way that ideology encompasses the division of labor directed to the perpetuation and increase of the household. The important distinction seems to be that between male and female roles. I argue that "reproduction" and "production" are not two separate domains or spheres of activity with separate symbols, but are instead two aspects or modes of the same thing and organized by the same symbols.

The Sexual Division of Labor

The major forms of livelihood in the village are wheat and sheep. Although there has been some diversification of occupations to supplement income from these sources, all villagers, with varying degrees and varying emphases, depended on wheat and sheep. Only the imam, the teachers, the midwife, and I had other sources of support, and we too depended on the resources of the village for food. The major division of labor is by sex, and that division parallels the perceived roles of men and woman in procreation. As man and woman must come together to produce a child, so too must they cooperate in "increasing and multiplying" (reproducing) the household. Normally the working pair are husband and wife; but they also could be an unmarried pair such as a widow and her son or a widower and his daughter. Relations between men and women in both aspects of "increasing and multiplying" are distinct, complementary, and asymmetrically ordered; men and women are involved in "productive" activities related to the forms of livelihood in different ways and at different times, and their tasks are assigned, I suggest, not from some natural, ordained disposition, but according to the symbolic associations of gender. Let us see how this works out in practice in dealing with wheat and sheep.

Men are the owners of seed, in the form of both grain and children, and they control the seedbeds in which these are planted. Men provide the seed, the essential ingredient in procreation. Women transform this by the nurturing field that is their body—blood in the womb and milk at the breast. The male provides the essential ingredient; women work on the process of transformation. Men's labor is episodic or intermittent, women's continuous; women's role is important but derivative.

Wheat (*buğday*) is preeminently the field of men. They prepare the soil, seed it, and fertilize it; they harvest and thresh the wheat. Until the mid-1950s all these operations were done by hand. Plowing was done with an ox-drawn, hand-held plow, and seed was hand-scattered; grain was harvested by hand and threshed by an ox-drawn sledge weighted down by a man standing on top. Tractors were introduced in the 1950s and more recently combines. By the 1980s most families in our village had a tractor; and three or four combines were owned jointly by several families, who not only used them on their own fields but rented them to others. Yet some people continue to use the old methods, or a combination of old and new.

In the fall men prepare the soil, and in Ekim (October) they sow. The word Ekim is related to the words for grain (*ekin*), to sow (*ekmek, eker, ekecek*), and bread (*ekmek*). Seed is left over the winter to germinate, just as the new crop of brides incubate their received seed.

Nine months later, usually by mid-July, grain is *kırmızı, kızıl* (red), ripened, and ready to harvest. In our village machines facilitate the harvest, and it is primarily men who are in charge of and associated with machines. But even when the harvest was done by hand, men wielded the scythes while women followed and made the wheat into bundles. "Cutting," as we shall see, is also something associated with men. After the grain has been harvested and threshed, it is divided into portions, one to be used for reseeding in the fall, another for flour, and smaller amounts for bulghur and *tarhana*, the basis of a soup. Men take the grain to be ground into flour. Formerly this was done in the village; today it is done in the depot town. The flour is then stored in huge wooden bins in the room on the ground floor where the *ocak* (hearth) is located.

The *ocak* is used primarily for bread-making, and bread-making is women's work; there is no bakery in the village and no communal oven. Bread made in our area was round but flattened, rather like a large English muffin. Roughly every eight to ten days each woman makes a batch of sixty to a hundred "loaves."

The night before bread is to be made, the woman mixes a portion of flour, water, and salt with the leavening agent, *maya*, which is a small ball of dough kept over from the last bread-making session. This mixture is covered and left overnight in the *tekne* (a large wooden trough) in order that *hamur gelecek* ("the dough will come," will rise). In the morning, more flour, water, and salt is added to this mixture, which is then kneaded and left to rise again. By mid-morning, after breakfast is finished and the house swept, the dough will be ready for baking. With a small spatula (*eşiyan*) the woman takes out lumps of dough and forms them into balls about the size of a tennis ball. These are placed on a

Separating the wheat from the chaff

Making bread

canvas sheet until all the dough has been used. When ready to begin baking, she takes each ball of dough and flattens it somewhat on a wooden paddle (*yaslaç*) about the size of a ping-pong paddle. Four or five of these can fit on the round iron baking sheet (*saç*), which is placed over the *tandır*. The *tandır* is a deep, brick-lined pit in the floor to which air is supplied by means of a thin shaft channeled through the floor to the bottom of the pit.

The fire is fed by a mixture of straw and sheep dung previously gathered for this purpose. This kind of bread (*baslama*), made from *makarna* (macaroni) flour, keeps for about ten days if kept in a dry place; it may harden but it does not rot, and it becomes almost fresh again when heated. It is delicious. Villagers normally eat at least one round at every meal.[28] Left-over scraps are saved and fed to the dogs. Bread is almost holy; it is considered *günah* (sinful) to throw it away. If any is found on the ground, it is picked up.

Bread is the staff of life, literally and figuratively. It is estimated that the average consumption nationwide is 400 grams per day. In the village, where bread represents the major part of most people's diet, average consumption must be at least one kilo. Bread is the generic word for food. All other food is seen as an addition (*katık*). Villagers do not ask "Have you eaten?" but "Ekmek yedin mi?"—Have you eaten bread? They do not ask "Do you want something to eat?" but "Ekmek ister misin?"—Do you want some bread? It is no wonder the *ocak* is the symbol of the household, since it is the meeting place of male and female labor at which is created the source of sustenance for the reproduction of the household.

Villagers also keep animals: cows and *davar*, the collective term for sheep and goats. Traditionally only small flocks were kept—just enough animals to provide for the family's needs, that is, occasional meat, milk (from which yoghurt, cheese, and butter are made), wool for stuffing *yorgan*, and goat hair (*tiftik*) to be spun into yarn for sweaters and socks. Today, as we shall see in the next section, some people keep larger flocks and sell the surplus products.

---

28. Occasionally women will make *yufka* (thin sheets of rolled-out dough) to make baklava, *börek* (layered cheese with herbs, spinach, or ground meat), or *gözleme*, a kind of thin pancake that is spread with butter, folded over, rolled again, and sprinkled with sugar. A *tabla*, a short-legged, round wooden table-tray, is used for rolling out the dough and sometimes also as a *sofra* or dinner tray. The thin, long wooden rolling pin used to roll out the *yufka* is called an *oklaç*.

Boys herd, girls milk

Boy shearing

Men control the breeding, herding, shearing; women the milking, cooking, and spinning. As men control the sexuality and movement of women, so too they control that of their flocks, which are, except for the *koç* (ram), female. Similarly, just as hair, women's erotic adornment, is under the strict control of men, so too is the hair or fleece of animals. Men also do the slaughtering. Since men give life, only they are permitted to take it, whereas it is women's function and a part of their "nature" to sustain life by providing nurture.

In the "productive" realm women are responsible for milking and turning milk into yoghurt, cheese, and butter. The major work associated with milk occurs in the late spring and summer after the young animals have been weaned. Women milk (*sağmak*) them in the morning before they go to pasture and in the evening when they return. The milk is heated and then separated in a turbine-like, hand-turned machine composed of a number of interlocking parts and two spouts. From one flows the *yağlı* (with fat) or *tatlı* (sweet) milk, from the other the *yavan* (plain, insipid) or *ekşi* (sour, tart) milk.

Villagers claim they make three kinds of yoghurt. *Yağlı yoğurt* is full of fat and sweet. *Çalma yoğurt* is made from *yavan* milk and is usually sold, either to the itinerant yoghurt dealer who comes every week in a small truck or in the town of Ambarlı. *Torba yoğurt* is *yavan* yoghurt that has been put into a cheesecloth bag and had the water pressed out; it is thick, almost like cheese. From *torba yoğurt* they make *ayran,* a drink mixed with water and salt that is very refreshing in the summer.

Cheese is made from fresh *yağlı* milk, not from yoghurt. The milk is mixed with a special *maya* and left to set in cheesecloth in a pan over-night. By the next day the mixture has set to the consistency of pudding. It is then cut into squares, dipped in salt, and spread on a tray to dry and harden somewhat. The pieces are then stored in brine in large jars and referred to as *salamura peynir* (cheese pickled in brine). *Oğma peynir* (crumbled cheese) is made from large, pancake-shaped pieces of cheese put into a meat grinder, spread on a sheet with salt, and then packed in pottery jars. Occasionally *çörek otu* (black cumin seeds) are added. Once by accident a neighbor's *oğma peynir* turned out to taste like blue cheese. Some people became jealous when I praised this cheese, especially since they thought it was ruined.

If cheese does not mature for at least six months, it may cause brucellosis, also known as undulant fever. Nevertheless, many villagers eat it fresh (and end up with brucellosis). Although some people mentioned *sunme peynir,* which they said is like *dil* or tongue cheese, this is difficult to make and no one makes it today. Some villagers churn butter in an electric *tuhran,* which is rather like a small washing machine, but others still use a wooden churn or a pottery jar rocked back and forth.

Milk products form the second major component of the village diet. Yoghurt or cheese with bread often makes a meal. Not only do products from both male and female spheres unite to form a meal, but they are complementary and hierarchically ordered. Beyond that, it must be noted that both bread and yoghurt must be *reproduced.* Not only is the raw substance controlled and supplied by men, but each successive batch is created and increased by the addition of *maya* (yeast, leaven, but also root, origin, essence), that is, by the introjection of live germ from the previous batch. Dough cannot rise, or yoghurt take, without the addition of *maya* any more than a child can form without seed, an association not lost on villagers who make analogies between pregnancy and these processes. It is the *maya* that increases and continues the stock.

The products of male and female labor come together to form a meal for the daily reproduction of family members, thereby also perpetuating the close association between eating and sexuality. The male initiates the process and controls the outcome. In each case, he contributes the essential ingredients that the woman's labor transforms into social products—food or child. Both are necessary to increase the family. The meal, like a child, is a gift from God; and God has also made the divisions and differences necessary to produce both. In contemplation of either, one learns the order of Creation. "Sofradan uzak duran, Allaha uzak durur"—whoever strays far from the *sofra* [dinner tray] strays far from God.

In our village men, women, and children ate the evening meal together. Breakfast was also usually a family affair, lunch more flexible. Women sometimes eat at the homes of friends as men do; however, if a man returns home after the midday meal has been served, he can demand that his be made and served to him. Children come home from school at noontime; but depending on the season that might not be mealtime for the adults, in which case the children are fed separately. Adults wait until after the *öğle namazı* (midday prayer), which, because prayer times are scheduled in accordance with daylight, does not always come at the same clock time. Once again we see the conflict between nationalism and Islam in daily life. Schools, which are under the control of the state, run on standardized clock time, whereas the rhythms of village life are determined by the call to prayer (*ezan*).

Meals are taken on the floor, generally in the main room but in summer on the "terrace," i.e. the roof of the *ocak*. A cloth called a *sofra altı* (literally "under the *sofra*") is spread on the floor, and on it is placed a *kasnak*, the round wooden part of a sieve used for winnowing grain. The *sofra* (a large, round tinned-copper tray) is placed on top of this, forming a low, round table. Some people substitute the low wooden table that is used for rolling out the dough for making *börek* or *gözleme*. Warmed bread is placed around and leaning against the tray. The host or hostess says "Buyrun," inviting people to sit. Then, pulling up ends of the cloth to serve as a napkin, they crowd around the tray, one knee on the floor with the lower leg tucked under the buttocks, the other knee raised with

Evening meal on rooftop

the foot on the floor. One may not, however, place one's hands on the
floor for support, for it is believed that the devil comes up through the
floor, i.e. from the earth. When people sit outdoors on the ground, they
first put down a pillow for the same reason.

Each meal consists of a combination of male and female foods: grain
and milk, salty and sweet. There is always bread and yoghurt or cheese,
and often *tarhana* soup,[29] which is a combination of both. All other
foods must be cooked in a lot of butter (milk: sweet) and salt. People
were shocked at my cooking habits—usually without either butter or
salt—and the fact that I boiled or steamed vegetables. They also expressed disapproval when I steamed fish and then used the broth as a

29. *Tarhana* is made from a slightly fermented and then dried mixture of yoghurt,
cracked and pounded wheat kernels, tomatoes, and pepper. Soup is made by adding water
to a small piece of this mixture and heating the result. Herbs are often strewn on top.

basis for soup. Fish, in their view, should be fried. The fish, it should be noted, were small, resembling smelts; fish of any kind was a rare treat in the village, and probably fairly recently introduced. Except for those who bought fish in town, villagers were dependent on an itinerant fishmonger who arrived with a truckload of fish a few times a year.

Soup is the first course of the meal; it should consist of flour, yoghurt, salt, and *yağ* (generic for oil, but in the village usually meaning *tereyağ*, butter, rather than *zeytinyağ*, olive oil). It is served in one large dish, from which everyone eats with his or her own spoon. Bread is omnipresent; other accompaniments might include cheese, olives, or pickles. After the soup is finished, the main dish is served, also in a communal dish, sometimes accompanied by salad in the summer. The main dish is usually some sort of vegetable stew: green beans, eggplant, leeks, spinach, chick-peas, lentils, or dried beans, occasionally with an egg or ground meat mixed in.[30] Always this kind of stew is cooked for a long time with, to my taste, excessive amounts of fat and salt. Turks are very particular about the kind of *yağ* (oil or butter) they use. Most use butter from cow's milk, but some use tallow from sheep. Some use olive oil or vegetable oil; others dislike them. Villagers were very curious to know what kind of *yağ* Americans used; they feared it would be pig fat, which is not only forbidden to them but considered unfit for human consumption. Other main dishes are forms of bulghur *pilav*, a cracked wheat dish, and *makarna* with *salça*, a kind of spaghetti. In summer dessert is always fruit; at other times it might be *kabak tatlısı* (squash cooked in sugar syrup), *hoşmerim* (a doughy flour, butter, and sugar mixture), or *helva* (a somewhat similar mixture made from flour, honey, and oil). Melons can be kept through the winter by tying them to the rafters of a cold room; in the middle of January or February they are almost as fresh as in summer. (This seems to be a trick that people in the city do not know, or perhaps can no longer do because many houses and apartments in the city are centrally heated.) In addition to the foods regularly served at mealtimes, the villagers' diet may be supplemented by items found on the mountain such as salad greens or mushrooms, by honey produced in hives kept by a few villagers, and by snacks of *leblebi* (dried, roasted, and salted chick-peas) and nuts.

30. In the summer the vegetables are fresh. In the winter people use dried green beans, eggplant, and peppers as well as fresh vegetables bought from the *pazar* when these are available.

Although people eat from communal bowls, the foods are kept separate. To have different foods on the same plate, *bulaşık* (contagious, polluted) or *karışık* (mixed up, intermingled), the way Americans eat, is unthinkable. Where we would cringe at the idea of mixing germs in the communal pot, they are disturbed by the mixing of different food juices, especially oils. Because foods have gender significance, and eating and sexuality are symbolically associated, it is possible that the mixing of fluids on the plate is analogous to the mingling of sexual fluids during intercourse, for both are felt to be *bulaşık* and ritually unclean.

At the start of a meal, someone very quietly says "Bismillah" (in the name of God); this is a short form of *bismillahirrahmanirrahim* (in the name of God, the Compassionate, the Merciful). Only at a wedding did I ever hear a prayer after a meal. Meals were gotten through as quickly as possible; it was considered *ayıp* to linger. So, too, was sex apparently efficiently dispatched, and people got up immediately to wash. Lingering implies sensuality. Talk is discouraged. If you talk with your mouth full, crumbs will fall out and this is *ayıp*. Instead, as soon as you have finished, you get up and move to the divan to await tea and talk. "Sofrada el sahıbı ol, cemaata dil sahıbı ol"—at the table be master of the hand, at a gathering be master of the tongue. When everyone is finished, the woman removes the tray, starts the water for tea, shakes out the cloth, stores it with the *kasnak* under the divan, and sweeps the room. Men sit and smoke until tea is brought; women do handwork. The television may be turned on; if it is, people talk and watch at the same time. A number of villagers remarked that when television came, the art of conversation (*sohbet*) went away. Some men go to the mosque for the evening prayer and then to a tearoom.

Besides sexual activity and eating, the only other activity in which men and women spend any extended time together is working in the *bahçe* (garden). Gardens are generally located outside the village, though some people who have houses on the edge of the village are beginning to plant gardens adjoining the house.[31] A few households have tiny kitchen gardens, called *hayat* (life), in their courtyards.

Both vegetable gardens and orchards are called *bahçe*. Both are always located near a source of water, either a *çeşme* (fountain) or a stream

31. A man in our quarter planted 52 fruit trees and a vegetable garden next to his house. The next spring these were eaten by a goat!

that can be diverted briefly to water the garden by the ingenious method of shifting a mud "wall" and then reforming it. In the *bahçe* the division between the sexes is not so rigid as elsewhere, nor is the division of labor. The barrier is lowered, permitting relaxation and a certain amount of freedom in interaction. Vegetables and fruits are almost "neuter" foods, and women and men can do the same jobs. Labor is minimal for large returns. Vegetables ripen by themselves, and fruit drops from the trees like manna from heaven.

The *bahçe* is the one place that people want to have their photographs taken, a clue to its more than mundane significance. Such a photograph is an idealized portrait, a snapshot of eternity, for the *bahçe* represents an earthly paradise, a reflection of the heavenly Garden.

When villagers are in *gurbet*, that is, outside the village, the village itself is remembered as a garden. Poems speak of its water like *abuhayat* (the elixir of life), its luscious fruits, its clear, clean air, the scents of oregano and thyme on the mountain, the birds playing, the rabbits leaping, the green fields, and the mountain like a big brother. "Garibin yatağı gurbet ellerdir, köyümün hasreti yakıyor beni"—[When] my exile's bed is in strange lands, the longing for my village burns me. Being outside the village is like being in hell; the remembrance of the village is heaven.

Sitting in the garden is an intimation of Paradise and an earthly experience of it. Certain old men of the village, referring to themselves as the *emekli* (retired), gather and sit on a bench near the mosque under a huge shade tree, near an ever-flowing fountain, passing the time in pleasant conversation. They claim this is the coolest place in the village because breezes blow from all directions. The goal of life is to sit, to arrive at the point where one can control the movement of others, the point where work can be delegated.

In any case, work of all sorts takes place at a leisurely pace; there is no hurry and no time clock. When I went to work in the fields, I always had the impression that an outsider who saw us would think we were involved in backbreaking peasant labor, but it was not so. Just when I thought we were really beginning, it was time for a tea break, and the work throughout the day was leisurely. I do not assume that it was like this in the past, or that the pace is this slow in other parts of Turkey or for migrant laborers. But for ordinary villagers, the only taskmaster is themselves. Villagers commented to me: "çok harcıyorsun"—you're

Emekli: "the retired"

exerting yourself too much, you're wasting energy, you're spending yourself. It is not time one spends or wastes, but oneself. Time has not been objectified; it has not yet become a commodity like money that one spends wisely or squanders.[32]

Inwardly felt, as the very movement of life rather than as a constraining limit, time cannot be dissociated from the experience of activity and of the space in which that activity takes place. Duration and space are described by reference to the performance of a concrete task, e.g., the unit of duration is the time one

32. E. P. Thompson's article "Time, Work-Discipline, and Industrial Capitalism" (1967) is a fascinating analysis of the transformation in the sense and meaning of time. For the notion of time as a commodity that can be bought, sold, wasted, etc., see especially pp. 56–92. Bourdieu (1979), Leach (1961), and Whorf (1956), among others, have written perceptively about the different understandings of time.

needs to do a job, to work a piece of land. . . . Equally space is evaluated in terms of duration, or better, by reference to the activity occupying a definite lapse of time, for example, a day at the plough or a day's walk. . . . Time experienced, just like space perceived, is discontinuous, made up of a series of heterogeneous islets of differing duration. (Bourdieu 1963: 60; cf. Massignon 1957 [1951])

Given this attitude to life and work, it is not difficult to imagine the ambivalence generated by the shift from subsistence to production for the market. The changes are subtle, and villagers had no way of knowing what the consequences would be. Machines, which helped to facilitate this change, are valued not because they decrease the overall time spent working—which they do not—but primarily because they reduce the arduousness of the work. They can also greatly increase the amount of land under cultivation, which creates a surplus that can be sold for cash income.

Before proceeding to describe the village's economy, let me say a few words about the system of land tenure in Turkey. During the Ottoman Empire all land belonged to the state; nevertheless most of it was cultivated on small allotments by family units from whom the state exacted a tax. Except in the southeast, a number of factors prevented the consolidation of large estates, so that at the dawn of the Republic "small family holdings still remained the predominant unit of agrarian production" (Margulies and Yildizoğlu 1987: 270). The same authors also report that as of 1977 almost 90 percent of all holdings were under ten hectares, and the great majority were under five hectares.[33] More surprisingly, perhaps, "83.5 percent of all holdings, covering 76.7 percent of total land area, were totally owner-cultivated, while a further 8.2 percent of holdings were more than half owned by the cultivator" (ibid.: 285). In addition, "holdings fully rented or sharecropped were insignificant both in terms of numbers (0.8 percent rented, 3.0 percent sharecropped) and of area" (ibid.). This landholding pattern fits our village very well and gives some context to its economy.

Villagers talk in terms of *dönüm* rather than hectares; a *dönüm* is one-tenth of a hectare, or about a quarter of an acre. A *dönüm* was

33. This percentage is slightly higher than in previous surveys: 86.8 percent in 1963, and 84 percent in 1952. Although the information was taken from the State Planning Organization, the authors expressed some skepticism about the reliability and commensurability of the earlier census material.

thought to be the amount of land a man could work in a day with traditional methods. One man could reasonably be expected to work only ten to fifteen *dönüm* total, but that was enough for subsistence. Since half a man's land must be fallow, twenty to thirty *dönüm* were needed in all, or between two and three hectares. These were still the estimates given to supply family needs when I was in the village.

The land that could formerly be plowed by a man in a day can now be done by a tractor in an hour. Whereas it used to take fifteen men a day to harvest one hectare (ten *dönüm*), now one combine can harvest fifteen hectares a day. Tractors are a considerable improvement over ox-drawn plows, but turning the heavy, wet soil is arduous and time-consuming even with a tractor. The combine, by contrast, is a spectacular improvement, rapidly skimming the hard surface of the field, cutting down the wheat, and separating the kernels from the straw.

The rapid and dramatic change from subsistence to production for the market seems to coincide with a shift from "procreation" to "reproduction." These changes, which are not just economic but social and symbolic as well, will be taken up shortly. In order to get an idea of the kind of surplus available, we need to consider the needs of a household in comparison with the total land under cultivation in the village.

Economic Geography

Cultivation of Grain. Villagers need grain for different purposes: in the form of flour for bread and noodles, as bulghur, and in small amounts for making the basis of *tarhana* soup. They estimate that the annual quantity needed for subsistence is about ten *yarım* (160 kilograms) per person. A small household of five persons would need only about 800 kilograms a year; but many households consist of more than five persons, and a wide margin must be allowed for visitors and for animal fodder. Thus the villagers' estimate of between one and two tons per household seems accurate. (A Turkish ton is one thousand kilograms.) If each *dönüm* of land yields ten to fifteen *yarım* of grain by dry farming, ten to fifteen *dönüm* would be enough to yield the amount of grain estimated as the yearly need. Given the fact that every year 20,000 *dönüm* are seeded, each yielding ten to fifteen *yarım* of grain, then theoretically there are twenty-three *dönüm* for each man, woman, and child in the village (or 230–345 *yarım*), more than twenty times what is needed for subsistence. If one subtracts 2,000 *dönüm* from the total to allow for both subsistence and animal fodder, 18,000 *dönüm* are left that can be used for profit.

Between 1979 and 1982 the government price for *buğday* went from 12 to 18.50 TL per kilo, which does not reflect the enormous rise in the rate of inflation (over 100 percent), making an assessment in terms of real income exceedingly difficult. Similarly, prices for *gubre* (fertilizer) and gasoline also changed. What follows can only be considered a very rough estimate.

If each *dönüm* yields ten *yarım* at a minimum, then the total amount of grain available for sale is 180,000 *yarım* or 2,880,000 kilograms. At 18 TL per kilo this would bring in 51,840,000 TL: approximately $518,400, or about $610 per person. From this figure one needs to subtract the cost of production. It is said that ten kilos of European/American fertilizer, at 20 TL per kilo, is needed for each *dönüm*; thus for 18,000 *dönüm* the cost of fertilizer would be 3,600,000 TL. An additional 3,600,000 TL is needed for the *biçer* (combine), since the rental charge is 200 TL per *dönüm*. Taking into account the cost of the fuel for the *biçer* and for the tractor that turns the soil, seeds the fields, and spreads the *gubre* twice, as well as the amount of grain to be kept aside for the next year's seeding, the net total would be about 40 million TL or about $470 per person.

There is clearly enough land to feed all the people and animals in the village as well as to make a comfortable profit for each household. Needless to say, however, land and income are not so equitably distributed as our calculations have assumed. Landholdings are about the most difficult matter on which to gain reliable information. During the period I was in Turkey, access to such documents was curtailed; but even if it had not been, there would be serious problems because not all land is registered. Even with the help of a Turkish assistant, I was unable to procure any but vague estimates. The *muhtar* claimed that most of the land was owned by fifty *hane*, but only a few owned as much as 500–600 *dönüm* (50–60 hectares); but this was no real clue to the real state of affairs. When Ibrahim and Ali said they owned no land, that was true because the land they farm is owned by their father. They work it for him, dividing the produce between him and themselves and giving a small percentage to their sister. In fact, that family was one of the few large landholders, with about 600 *dönüm* in all. Upon the death of their father, the land will be divided according to Muslim law; however, the two brothers may decide to continue to farm together.

Very few people have no land at all for their use. Ahmet, whom I knew well, was deprived of access to land because of a quarrel with his father, but in 1985, when his father died, he received his portion.[34] Landholdings range from 20 to 600 *dönüm*, most in the range of 50 to 500. Translated into hectares, this shows that our village was somewhat above the average and therefore a relatively prosperous one. An outside survey[35] of the village conducted in the spring of 1982 yielded the following figures: 0–25 *dönüm*, 19 households; 25–50 *dönüm*, 25; 50–100 *dönüm*, 27; 100–200 *dönüm*, 25; 300–500 *dönüm*, 1. But these figures cannot be trusted. When I compared them to my own information, they were clearly inaccurate. First, calculating the number of *dönüm* at the highest amount at each level would give a total of only 9,925, or only about half of the total amount seeded every year. Second, the survey figures show there is only one man who owns 300–500 *dönüm* when I know there are at least seven. Third, the surveyors assumed they had counted all households and population, but they came up with a figure of 609 when there are at least 850 people. Finally, even if most villagers were willing to give outsiders an accurate report, which they are not, probably only a few members of the family know exactly the amount of land it owns.

Until such time as accurate land surveys are conducted, all land is registered, and documents are made accessible, a situation of dubious advantage to villagers, a researcher must be satisfied with making rough estimates, informed by what people say about themselves and their neighbors and adjusted in the light of personal observations and calculations.

34. Ahmet's portion included wheat fields, a number of fruit trees, and enough land for growing melons and vegetables. The fortune of his brother, who had been benefiting for years from the quarrel, was proportionally diminished, a situation that naturally caused conflict. When I returned for a visit in the summer of 1986, I arrived just in time for Ahmet's first harvest (cf. Delaney 1989).

35. A friend in Ankara was teaching a course on rural sociology at Middle East Technical University and conducting a survey of "fringe" villages around Ankara. As a comparison, she asked if she could bring her class to survey our more remote village. Proper permissions were obtained from the government and the *muhtar,* and the class arrived on a rainy day with the mountain shrouded in mist. For many of the students, it was the first time they had ever been to a real village, and I heard that the experience helped to change their stereotypes of village life. One student returned later for a weekend with me, and drew the house plans that are contained in this volume.

Animal Husbandry. Wheat is not the only source of income; animals also provide an important portion. In 1981 the *muhtar* claimed that villagers owned 1,000 cows, 7,000 sheep, and 3,000 goats. Total village capital in animals was approximately 50 million TL in cows, 43 million TL in sheep, and 6.5 million TL in goats. Cows are kept primarily for milk and for producing calves which are sold as veal, but are eventually slaughtered for meat. One cow provides enough meat for a year in the form of *kavurma* (a kind of hamburger cooked and preserved in its own fat) and *sucuk* (sausage made with cumin and garlic). Sheep and goats are kept for their milk, which is used for yoghurt and cheese, for their offspring, and for their hair or wool. Most families have a couple of cows and from 20 to 50 sheep, but a few families have flocks numbering in the hundreds. The cost of maintaining a large flock increases with the number. Most importantly, more fodder will be required, which assumes a large landholding. But also a special corral outside the village is needed; and if there is no son of appropriate age, a private *çoban* must be hired at an average yearly wage of about 200,000 TL ($2,000) and provided for. Smaller flocks are kept in the village. Several owners cooperate to hire a *çoban*, usually an unmarried youth. The *çoban* collects the animals in the morning and returns them in the evening; during the night they are sheltered within the household compound on the ground level.

Villagers depend on these animals to supply many of their needs. All yield milk that is made into yoghurt and cheese, and that of cows and sheep is also used for *yağ* (butter or tallow). The wool is used to fill *yorgan* (quilts) and *döşek* (mattresses), and *tiftik* (goat hair) is spun into yarn for socks. Villagers in general do not eat much meat. Some may slaughter a sheep a month, but many slaughter only six or seven a year in addition to those sacrificed at Kurban Bayramı. Surplus animals are reared chiefly for the market.

Sheep are sold throughout the year, most often in the fall to avoid the expense of keeping old ones through another winter. Lambs are sold in the spring to middlemen from slaughterhouses in Milas and Ambarlı, who come to the village with trucks to transport them. Wool is also sold. Merino sheep yield high-quality wool that sold in 1981 for about 500 TL per kilo; the coarser wool of the *yerli* (native) fat-tailed Anatolian sheep sells for about 250 TL per kilo. If each sheep yields about five kilos, this is considerable extra income. But it is the Anatolian goat, prized for its world-famous angora (Ankara) hair, that brings in the most. Each animal yields between two and three kilos of hair, which fetches between 700 and 1,000 TL per kilo.

In order to get some idea of the kinds of income available to villagers, let us consider two examples, a man who owned 200 *dönüm* and a large flock, and a man who worked as a *çoban* and had no land. The first, Hasan, jointly owned a combine and flocks with his three brothers, though their land was kept separate. Between them they had 200 sheep and 120 *kuzu* (lambs), which sold for a total of 360,000 TL. Wool from the sheep brought in 300,000 TL, and *tiftik* (goat hair) 430,000 TL. In addition to providing fodder, they had to pay a *çoban*. The combine, which they rented out in our village and the surrounding villages, yielded 800,000 TL; when expenses of 300,000 TL were subtracted, 500,000 TL of *temiz parası* (clean, pure money) was left. Hasan planted 100 *dönüm* of his land in any given year; after subtracting 20 *dönüm* for family and animal needs, the remaining 80 would yield an additional income of about 236,800 TL. Hasan's total income from his animals and grain was about 700,000 TL; after subtracting about 60,000 TL for fertilizer, spread twice, and the use of a tractor and a combine, his net income was approximately 640,000 TL or $6,400 for his family of five.

Our second example, Ahmet, worked as a *çoban* and herded his own flock, built up over the years, of 50 sheep, along with 75 belonging to his employers. Ahmet sold 40 lambs at 3,000 TL each for a total of 120,000 TL, and wool yielded another 62,500 TL. In addition, he was paid 50 TL per head for each of the nine months he was able to take his employers' sheep to pasture, which amounted to 33,750 TL. His employers also paid him in grain (200 *yarım*), enough for both his family and his animals. His total cash income was about 216,250 TL, or about $2,163 for his family of nine.

The range of income in the village was somewhere between these two, although there were a few families who made more money and a few families who had very little money coming in. In order to get some idea of what this means, let us compare these incomes with the teacher's salary. Teachers at village schools are paid 9,000 TL per month, with small increments for each dependent: typically, then, about 110,000 TL ($1,100 a year). Their lodging is free, but they must supply their own food. At Middle East Technical University, the most prestigious university in the country, a full-time instructor's salary is about 25,000 TL per month or 300,000 TL per annum ($3,000). A lawyer working at a national bank is paid only 20,000 TL per month ($2,400 per annum). Both of these last figures are net income after compulsory taxes, health insurance, and social security are deducted. In other words, these villagers are relatively well off compared to many people with civil service jobs, especially when one considers that they produce their own food and build their own houses on their own property.

Until very recently, vegetables were grown only for home consumption. To produce for the market requires a lot of extra work just at the time when wheat labor is intensive. One man who had grown tomatoes in 1980 for profit decided against it in 1981. It was simply too much work at the time, though his garden remains a resource that can generate extra income when necessary. Nevertheless, a few people were beginning to produce for the market. Several began with melons, which, I was told, require the least amount of work: the planting is easy, they require no maintenance, and labor is needed only for the brief period of gathering. And they are profitable. One man made 200,000 TL ($2,000), and it was rumored that a man in a neighboring village made over a million. Those who have a number of fruit trees—especially mulberry or pear, for which this area is famous—sell their surplus fruit to the market.[36] Apparently, these trees also require little labor, only what is necessary to gather, pack, and transport the fruit. When there are surpluses, vegetables and fruit are sold either to wholesalers who come from Istanbul or Ankara to the depot town, or to the licensed *pazar* (bazaar, market) sellers. Villagers can sell their own crops directly, but not on *pazar* day and only away from the main market area.

Women also produce some income. Yoghurt is produced by the women in the household during the summer months, when there is an ample supply of milk; the occasional surplus was sold either in the *pazar* or to the yoghurt dealer mentioned above. Yoghurt is women's produce, and women were allowed to keep the income; but it is like the *ağız*—the creamy first milk of the season, something relished as a treat but not enough to sustain one. Most milk is consumed in the home in the form of yoghurt or cheese. Sometimes as much as ten kilos can accumulate in a week, but at 10 TL per kilo or 200 TL total, this is not very much income.

36. When I returned in the summer of 1986, several families were packing and selling significant quantities of apricots and peaches.

Putting final touches on a *yorgan*

Women also make some money by selling their handwork: *oya* (trim for scarves), lace for trimming sheets and pillowcases, knitted goat-hair socks, and *yorgan* (quilts). There was no handwork cooperative for marketing these items; they were usually sold among themselves, to relatives in the city, and to the occasional visitor. The income generated was minimal.

The mechanization of agriculture has greatly changed the economy of the village, but it is a mixed blessing. First and most obvious, by reducing the number of laborers required to do a given job, machines have left many men underemployed, if not altogether without work. Although there is more than enough land to sustain the village, there is not enough to fully occupy the village's men and machines. Since all the land in the village is owned, there is no place to get more land except from neighboring villages. Just before I left, a group of men were trying to buy a large tract of land from a nearby village with a view to farming it cooperatively for the market and sharing the profits. I do not know if this venture has succeeded.

Another result of the mechanization of agriculture has been a massive countrywide rural-to-urban migration. Our village was affected, though the out-migration has not been drastic. In 1950 the population was 1,073; in 1960, 983; in 1970, 1,009; in 1980, 850. Some of this decrease can be attributed to the increase in the use of contraceptives. Partly in response to the decrease in employment opportunities, many Turks have gone abroad. No one from our village went directly from the village to Europe, but a few villagers already living in Ankara did emigrate. Out-migration continues, but has slowed owing to the lack of opportunities in the city, the introduction of a few services to the village, and the fact that the surplus can support more people.

Some political analysts (cf. Turan 1982) have suggested that villages should be "capitalized," meaning that small holdings should be consolidated into large farms. Any such change would drive even more villagers out of the village. Some of these plans come, I believe, from a particular kind of education in which the village way of life is seen as an impediment to modernization and Westernization. Understandable as this view may be, the village way of life is a valuable one in many respects, not least of which is the social integration and emotional support it provides. More than half of the newlyweds in my time there chose to remain in the village, and others would have done so had it been feasible.[37]

37. What might make it feasible? I have a few suggestions, some of which I discussed with the villagers. The first and easiest is to use the village *dolmuş* for a school bus that would transport children to town for high school. Parents would not have to find relatives for them to live with, would not lose their labor or companionship, and would still have some control over them. Small milk, yoghurt, and cheese factories could be built in each village and the produce sold to the town; another possible product is ice cream. In a village the size of ours, there could be a grocery shop, a pharmacy, a real teahouse, a bakery, a tailor and dressmaker, a cooperative for women's handmade articles, and a photographer. Middlemen would be needed to transport and sell village produce to buyers in the city. There could be more intervillage cooperation and communication, both socially and financially; several villages together could sustain a larger enterprise, such as a movie theater. One day there might even be a need for a preschool or play group for small children. Another area that needs improvement is plumbing, which is technically not very difficult: running water could easily be piped not just to the courtyard but into the houses. A village generator could produce electricity and energy for heating water. In addition, large drums could be placed on rooftops to collect and heat water in the summer, and a shower would be very easy to make.

Village tailor

Some attempts have been made to diversify sources of income in the village. Several men, in addition to farming, keep a *bakkal* (small shop); and, as we have seen, the few who own combines have rented them to other villagers and other villages. One enterprising young man who was sent to *sanat okulu* (trade school) returned and opened an *atölye* (workshop for the maintenance and repair of machines). An older man served as the village *terzi* (tailor), but after his death in the spring of 1982 no successor could be found.

Three others continued to keep their households in the village but sought employment outside. One man worked as a laborer on the construction of a train tunnel to go through the mountain, commuting several hours each way by donkey. When construction stopped in the winter of 1981 owing to lack of funds, he became the village *bekçi* (watchman). Another worked as a recruiter for a sugar factory and was gone from the village several days a week. (No one from the village worked in the factory.) A third owned a truck and worked on construction projects all over the province, returning to the village to visit his family only a few times a year.

The village is too remote to make daily commuting feasible, especially with transportation undependable and roads impassable several months during the year. Transportation to and from the village was provided by three *dolmuş* (shared taxis: in this case Ford or Chevrolet vans), which provided additional income to their owner-drivers. Except for tractors with wagons that can be attached to carry people, these were the only vehicles in the village. Not all three of the *dolmuş* went to town every day; how many went depended on the weather and the number of passengers. When they did go, they would leave sometime in the morning and return sometime after noon.

All other men in the village were employed in the traditional occupations. Yet, as we have seen, these have changed dramatically. Not only does machinery decrease the amount of work and the number of laborers required, but men's work becomes more narrowly focused—on a brief few weeks in the fall to plow, fertilize, and plant, a second fertilization in the spring, and a few weeks of intensive labor in the summer.

There is less work for enormously greater profits, which are largely converted into consumer goods. The household is the beneficiary, of course, but its most treasured goods now come from the largesse of men rather than the cooperative labor of women and men. The more balanced reciprocity between the sexes that has been in existence for a long time is quickly being destroyed.

Procreation or Reproduction/Production?

All these changes have their effect on the meaning of the household and men's relation to it. The household was, and continues to be, the primary center and focus of attention for both men and women. The divisions of labor, time, and space between the sexes cannot be broken into a simple dichotomy of domestic-public or reproductive-productive. Rather the spheres of activity and expertise are complementary and reflect the symbolically constituted and perceived roles of men and women in procreation.

In most social scientific analyses, as we have seen, reproduction and production are seen as interdependent but separate domains of activity, one associated with men and the other with women. It is further argued that women's involvement with the "natural" processes of reproduction, and their relative confinement to the domestic sphere, are reasons for their devaluation in relation to men, who are thought to gain their value from occupying the public sphere of cultural productive activities. Women are seen as reproducing mere species life, whereas men are engaged in creating the lasting monuments of culture (cf. Ortner 1974: 75).

In conventional Marxist analyses, women are viewed as the means for reproducing human labor and hardly anything else; because of the "natural" facts of reproduction, the sexual division of labor is presumed to be self-evident. "The division of labor [was] originally nothing but the division of labor in the sex act" (Marx and Engels 1970 [1846]: 51). I have always been mystified by this sentence. Did they assume a particular position in the act and that it automatically implied certain meanings and roles? They seem not to have taken into account that sexual intercourse (the sex act?) and reproduction take place within different systems of meaning wherein there are different allocations of power. How *are* persons conceived, literally as well as conceptually? Under what conditions does intercourse take place, what are its meanings, how is reproduction integrated into an ongoing system of relations and meanings?

This Marxist view of reproduction also enters into the work of those who analyze "primitive" and nonmarket societies. Thus Meillassoux, in his article "From Reproduction to Production" (as if this were a natural progression), states that "self-sustaining agricultural communities are dominated by the production and reproduction of the material conditions of existence" (1972: 92). But why are both terms necessary when "reproduction of the material conditions of existence" would suffice? This is not a semantic quibble but is, I suggest, essential to his whole program, which emphasizes the separateness of the two domains. The assumption is not only that men are the producers and women essentially the reproducers, but also that reproduction is a kind of bedrock on which culture depends.

But rather than a universal substratum of society, reproduction, I have argued, is a culturally constituted and differentially valued activity. The dichotomization between reproduction and production is, I believe, a transformation and development of the ideology of procreation that has informed our own society as well as the Turkish village. In the village, it is not "reproduction" that is devalued, but only women's perceived secondary, derivative role. The creative, generative, "productive" role is attributed to men, and it is from this that their power and authority derive. Thus whatever else they set their hands (and minds) to is already validated. No matter how much of the productive work women do, and in Turkey the amount is considerable, its value is always secondary.[38] The value derives not from the work but from their gender, whose value in turn derives from their perceived role in procreation.

I suggest that the more overarching symbolic structure of coming-into-being encompasses both production and reproduction. The ideology of procreation encompasses both the production of children and the reproduction—creation and continuation—of the household. At present these are still the salient terms by which villagers conceptualize the household and their relation to it. Yet signs of very significant changes are also in evidence.

Implications of Symbolic Change

As the household rapidly becomes subordinated to the demands of production for the market, it is losing its hold as the center of gravity and the primary unit of "production." More than one woman told me "Men do the earning; all we do is consume," a statement that conceals women's tremendous economic contribution. A different concept of self is also involved. The idea of a woman as a housewife rather than a full partner in the household is also beginning to be heard. This label of self-identification is learned not only from television but also from the marriage register, where men generally enter their occupation as "farmer" and women have been instructed to enter "housewife."

Because of the cost of the machines, men must make formalized sharing arrangements called *ortak* (partnerships) with other men—not

38. I heard a very poignant confirmation of this phenomenon by Morvaridi (n.d.) at a conference in London on Turkish villages in May 1990.

necessarily family members or *akraba*—in order to purchase and utilize them. Because of this huge investment and the resulting production of income, grain, always the domain of men and asymmetrically valued as such, has completely overshadowed women's sphere of activity.

The methods, varieties, and organization of women's work have changed very little in the process of "development." But many of the products produced by women are becoming obsolete, and others can now be purchased so cheaply that it is pointless to go on making them. Although the village is still in a stage of transition, the changes in the social and economic relations between men and women can only intensify. All indications are that the gap between them, rather than closing, will widen even further, as has happened in other developing countries.[39]

A less well explored area involves symbolic changes and the meanings and values encoded in them. Land and women have long been symbolically associated and imagined as the nurturers and sustainers of life. In this capacity, women's role, though always secondary to men's, was nevertheless necessary, important, and valued. In peasant societies, says Bourdieu, "land cannot be treated as a mere raw material but rather as a foster-mother. . . . The land is an end in itself and not a mere means of existence, and work is not a way of earning a living but a way of life" (1962: 103–4).

As men's relation to the land changes, so too does their relation to women. No longer is land imagined as the source of sustenance, a power that demands respect and needs to be placated; now it is seen as a resource to be controlled and exploited. The balance and harmony are destroyed. Women's symbolic value becomes even more secondary and inferior. As men can buy more and more of the items necessary for the provision and maintenance of the household, women are more and more confined to the home, no longer co-(re)producers but consumers. In the process of mechanization or development, men's focus is being drawn outward; women are being left behind, more than ever enclosed

---

39. Rogers (1980) explores the way that purveyors of international aid for development have consistently ignored the role of women in the developing nations and have tried to impose the values and structures of their own society, i.e. those of the developed industrial nations. In addition, some development projects are profit-oriented and do not improve the quality of life for a village as a whole. There is a need for alternative development strategies that utilize traditional forms of organization as well as local psychological and social factors. See also Moore 1988 and Hill 1986.

in the house. This becomes evident in Turkey's small towns, where women, rather than becoming more open and integrated into the society, are more covered up and shut up in the house, now a small apartment. Even in the cities, a great number of women rarely go out.

It is at this juncture—that is, at the point where subsistence production gives way to producing for the market—that women tend to become identified with the "domestic" private realm of reproduction and men with the public realm of production. Although women had always been identified with the "inside" and men with the "outside," these terms were not isomorphic with reproduction and production. Rather, both men and women contributed differently to the creation, sustenance, and perpetuation of the household. Social scientists from industrial and postindustrial societies have grown up with the production-reproduction dichotomy and have tended to impose it upon peasant societies, *a priori* dividing their reality into the separate domains of production and reproduction and missing both the integrated foundation and the process by which it becomes divided. At the same time, they have excluded the possibility of any positive planning that would alleviate the divisions and dislocations exacerbated by development.

Outside Relations

Men's dependence upon the town for machinery and the market further involves them in "outside" relations. The inside-outside dichotomy, with its sexual derivation and gender significance, is becoming intensified rather than diminished. Although ties between village and town are increasing and becoming stronger every year, traffic between the two is far from constant. Some people never leave the village, some leave only a few times a year, and others, especially the *dolmuş* drivers, go much more frequently. As we have seen, women as well as men go to town—usually for social or medical reasons—and some women go to town more often than some men. However, in general, the major connections with the outside world are made and maintained by men.

One other factor that legitimates and consolidates the involvement of men with outside relations and the outside world is military service, to which all men are subject at age 20. Although the young men in the village looked forward to seeing other parts of Turkey, they did not look forward to military duty. The army provides some education and vocational training, but conscripts stressed the hardship and the torturous physical regime. They complained of the food, long hours, arduous exercise, and lack of money. The government paid them only 40 TL (or about 50 cents) per month, though it provided for such needs as cigarettes. And if their assignment was in a distant province, the cost of the journey to and from was borne by the family.

In order to provide conscripts with pocket money or so-called *yol parası* (road money) an interesting custom has evolved. Each November and May a number of men are conscripted for two years of military service. In the fall of 1980 fifteen youths were called up. Starting fifteen days before they were to leave, a nightly dinner party was given in rotation at each of their homes. These affairs were private and included only the fifteen enlisted men and the host family, though I was fortunate enough to be invited to several in my *mahalle*. Indeed, since I was leaving to return to the United States for a couple of months, it was thought that I too needed *yol parası*! The best food was prepared, and afterwards the men danced for and with each other. At the end of the evening, the hosts gave each conscript a 100 TL note (at that time worth about $1.50). In addition, friends and relatives would bring small gifts or money; thus, before leaving, each man had about $25 in pocket money. Their first forty days of military service were spent in Ankara at a training center, forty once again signifying a period of maturation and transition. A the end of the training period, they received *izin* (leave, permission) to return home for a brief visit. After that they were sent to various posts all over the country and generally did not get leave again until after a year had passed.

When their tour of duty was over and the men had returned to the village, they gave a round of lunch parties for each other and shared their various experiences. Although military service is not remembered with pleasure, it is a common experience undergone and endured, another test and symbol of pride and honor. Each conscript forms a bond not only with his fellow conscripts in the village, but also with friends from other areas who did their service at the same time and with whom he continues to keep in contact. This male bonding and camaraderie is comparable at a different level to the male bond of Islam, a faith in which military virtues are prized. To be a champion or fighter for the faith (*gazi*) means also to be a protector of the community. The purpose is to keep out infidels and outsiders whose incursion is felt as pollution of the purity and integrity of insiders; thus military service can be seen as an almost sacred duty. The title of *gazi* was bestowed on Mustafa Kemal after the decisive battle at the Sakarya River that opened the way to victory and independence. In secular Turkey these virtues and associations are presumed to be transferred to the state, but in the minds of the villagers the separation is not so clear-cut.

For all the forces pulling men away from the household and village, there are also very strong ones pulling them back. At present, the two kinds of forces seem fairly equal in strength, a situation that brings into the open the dilemmas of orientation. It is not possible to go in two directions at once. A stand must be taken, but what stand? In the words of Yeats,

> Things fall apart, the center cannot hold,
> Mere anarchy is loosed upon the world.[40]

From the village's position on the mountain, the landscape itself daily holds up a mirror of this conflict. Shall its people be drawn toward Ankara, capital of the secular Republic, whose glittering lights at night seem to beckon to all kinds of material attractions? Or toward that unseen point on the horizon suggestive of other values no less powerful because invisible?

To choose one seems automatically to exclude the other. Villagers' primary identity and loyalty are to the village and to Islam. Bernard Lewis's statement seems as applicable to the contemporary period as it did in 1968: "Loyalty to a place was known, but it was to a village or quarter, at most to a province, not a country; loyalty to one's kin was ancient and potent, but it was to the family or tribe not to the nation. The ultimate loyalty . . . was religion" (1968: 329). The notion of Turkey as an alternative that would encompass these loyalties has not yet been fully embraced.

Rhetoric of the Nation

In this world, a villager's native land is his or her natal soil, that place where he or she was born. Although the word *memleket* can be used to

---

40. William Safire, in *The New York Times Magazine*, July 24, 1988, claimed that this quotation comes to mind "whenever political polarization takes place and centrists disappear," which was just what was happening in the period I am describing in Turkey.

refer to one's native country, for most people it means a very specific piece of earth—one's natal village. One's native soil is as much a part of one's being as the milk one suckled at one's mother's breast. Certain characteristics are imbibed with both and are carried always. If one leaves the village, one is still identified not just as a villager (*köylü*) but as a particular kind of villager, in this case a Göklerli. If one is working or living outside one's natal village, one must return there for marriage papers, and most people are returned to be buried there, including even those who have migrated to Europe. One cannot adopt a different village or country any more than one can truly adopt a child. At best, residence outside the village is seen as a matter of convenience and mutual accommodation; at worst it is felt as exile, the unenviable condition of *gurbet*.

The idea of a nation as land coterminous with the people living upon its soil came relatively late to Turkey. Under the Ottomans "nations were classified according to churches" (Adivar 1935: 24), that is, according to their religious beliefs. The territory was controlled by the Ottomans, but within its boundaries were many nations: the Islamic nation, the Orthodox nation, the Gregorian-Armenian nation, the Jewish nation, etc. (see also B. Lewis 1988: 39ff). The word Turk did not refer to a nationality, but was a derogatory term for the Anatolian peasants (Hotham 1972: 104). People did not identify themselves as Turks: instead "they regarded themselves solely as Muslims and Ottomans" (Ağaoğulları 1987: 178).

At the turn of the century European-type nationalism was being discussed by the intellectuals of Istanbul as a means for building community solidarity. Two other concepts were also being considered, namely Pan-Islamism and Pan-Turkism. Territorially based nationalism was victorious, but the other two notions did not disappear; indeed, they resurfaced and were incorporated in the agendas of two political parties during the period just prior to this study. Both parties came to be seen as threats to the nation-state established by Atatürk, and it was for that reason that the army intervened in 1980.

The spark that made European-type nationalism catch on came from the embers of World War I. After that war, when Asia Minor was to be partitioned by the Allied Powers, Mustafa Kemal was ordered to Samsun to demobilize his troops and to relinquish his commission. Instead he made a whirlwind tour of the country igniting the spirits of the peasants and the exhausted armies to resist the partition and to claim the country as their own. The appeal was made to defend the honor of the motherland,[41] which had been prostituted under the Ottoman capitulations and was about to be further soiled and mutilated by the partition. Adapting a poem of Namik Kemal,

> The foe thrusts his knife into the heart of the land
> There was none to save our ill-fated mother,

Mustafa Kemal (no relation to Namik) changed the last line to read "But yes, one is found to save our ill-fated mother" (from Kinross 1965: 199).

Not only was Mustafa Kemal a brilliant soldier, but more importantly he was acquainted with and knew how to manipulate the symbols dear to the peasant heart. Once people's spirits were fired by the notion of the defense of honor, there was no stopping the conflagration that spread over the land. In what was perhaps one of the most unequally matched battles in modern history, Kemal's tattered "army" prevailed over several forces on different fronts who were trying to claim a piece of Anatolia and ejected the foreign bodies from their land.[42] What is rarely attended to, however, is the symbolism in which the notion of the nation was conceived and delivered to the people. The *birth* of a nation is not merely a colorful way of describing the creation of a new state, for the symbols and meanings of procreation form an integral part of its conceptualization.[43] Mustafa Kemal capitalized on peasants' deep relation to the soil—their own *memleket*. They did not have to understand the concept of nation-state to be motivated to protect their own

41. These images were activated once again by Turgut Özal, whose Motherland (Anavatan) Party in November 1983 won the first election after three years of military rule, despite predictions to the contrary and lack of endorsement from General Evren.

42. Gawrych (1988) gives a good account of the Turkish War of Independence. See also Kinross 1965, Volkan and Itzkowitz 1984, and B. Lewis 1968.

43. Although the symbolism may be more apparent in the case of Turkey, we too conceive of the creation of states (and other things) in the language of procreation. The raw material that needs to be given form is symbolically female, as are the "labor pains" and the "birth," but the ideas that bring them into being are "seminal." These are not idle metaphors but structure consciously and unconsciously the way real men and women are perceived, what kinds of relations ought to obtain between them, and what activities they are thought capable of. According to Vico, "A 'nation' is etymologically a 'birth,' or a 'being born' and hence a race, a kin or kind having a common origin or, more loosely, a common language and other institutions" (1986 [1744]: xx). This is what we would call a culture. My argument has been that the way origins are *represented* incorporates major categories and values of a culture.

threatened soil, conceived as a mother who was being raped or sold into captivity.

Once her virtue was restored and the boundaries between inside and outside were fixed, the land was henceforth to be one *memleket*. All those born upon and nurtured by her soil were henceforth to be related as one people. By decree of the Grand National Assembly, the founder of the Republic was to be called Atatürk, "father of the Turks."[44] The people could trace their descent to the *ata* (ancestor-father) and recognize their consubstantiality by being born on and nurtured by the same soil. Yet for all Atatürk's brilliant use of the symbols of descent and origin to forge a national consciousness and pride, some of the people were not convinced. Some never lost their pride in their own ethnic identities and resented being included under the label "Turk."[45] Others, although of Turkish origin, resented the shift in orientation from Mecca to Ankara. Oppositions, contradictions, and resentments remained to confound the modernizers' efforts.

That identity as a Turk is intimately related to gender and procreation is further suggested by two symbols that stand for the country: the flag and the *ocak* (hearth). The flag, a white crescent moon and star upon a red ground, is at the most overt level meant to represent the reflection of the moon and star in a pool of blood spilled at the first Turkish victory on Anatolian soil, the battle of Malazgirt (sometimes Manzikert) in 1071, which opened the way for the influx of Selcuk Turks to Anatolia.

The colors of red and white, however, are very important in Turkish culture and appear to symbolize aspects of procreative sexuality. They are prominent at *sünnet* (circumcision) and at marriage, two ceremonies whose expressed aim is procreation. A red and white flag is planted at weddings and at the completion of a new house; both occasions have to do with the creation of a new procreative unit. Red stands for *kızlık* (virginity) as well as menstruation, childbirth, and the procreative potential that is represented by henna (sacred soil) in the wedding ceremony. It also symbolizes the blood that nurtures the child in the womb. Those nurtured in the same womb are *kardeş*, the closest relation.

44. Atatürk never had any sons, only adopted daughters. Muhammed also had no sons.

45. Atatürk himself seems to have vacillated in what he meant by "Turk." Occasionally, it seems, he had in mind something like "American," but more often ethnic identity and nationality were intermingled (see also Ağaoğulları 1987).

Red symbolizes both the nurturing ground of sustenance (the land) and the consubstantiality (*kardeşlik*, siblingship) of those born upon Turkey's soil. But red also symbolizes the blood shed in sacrifice: the foreskin in *sünnet*, the sheep that stands for the child at Kurban, and the soldier who dies in battle in order that the country may live.

White, the color of milk, is another symbol of nurture and sustenance, for those nursed from the same breast are also *kardeş*. *Aybaşı*, the word for menstruation, means literally the beginning of the moon; thus the crescent moon forms a symbolic association between the white of the moon and blood. White is also the color of semen and thus can represent the male's generative or creative power, which is allied with the divine. Finally, white is the color of purity and honor. It is the color of the cloth people don while on the hajj at Mecca and of the shroud in which the corpse is buried.

That colors have gender relevance is also suggested by the fact that white skin is valued for women and red (sunburned) skin is acceptable for men. Similarly, white foods are associated with women and red with men; foods representing both combine to form a meal. The colors representing male and female are, however, not fixed. Red can symbolize the purity of virginity as well as impurity of menstruation and childbirth, kinship as well as the blood shed in battle or sacrifice. Similarly, white can symbolize the physical procreative elements of milk and semen, but also spiritual purity and death, the purer birth. The colors can represent the distinctions between the sexes as well as the necessity of both for procreation.[46] But perhaps they represent an ontological distinction as well. The physical world can be represented by blood of both men and women in relation to the white transcendent elements, but in other contexts red appears to carry transcendent elements in comparison with milk and the physical aspects of semen. My purpose is not to fix colors and meanings immutably but to stimulate a sensitivity to their significance.

The other symbol of the country, the *ocak* (hearth), is also the symbol of the household and the continuity of the patriline. The *ocak* as symbol of the nation was incorporated into the national anthem, whose first two lines are

---

46. The point is not to make a rigid classification of color, but to draw attention to the significance, especially the gendered significance, of color.

Korkma, sonmez bu safakları yuzen al sancak
Sonmeden, yurdumu ustunde tuten en son ocak—

which translates as "Don't be afraid, the vermilion [al][47] banner that flies in these dawns will not become slack, the last *ocak* that draws over my country will not be extinguished."

Individual identity comes from the *ata* and is passed by men. Although women were given the right to vote and made full citizens in Turkey before they were in many European countries, nationality, like the patriline and Islam, is perpetuated and represented by men. Material enclosures are symbolically female, which men cover and protect and at the same time represent. The nation as land, soil, territory, resource, is also symbolically female. Those nurtured by it have been given identity as Turkish citizens from the *ata* (father-founder). Men symbolize and represent the nation as they do the *aile* (cf. Sirman 1990). The defense of its honor and the protection of its borders—that is, of the line between inside and outside—are the primary duty of all men and the official duty of the military, which, in some sense, could be seen as Atatürk's agnatic lineage. Men are those who count and are counted. As General Kenan Evren stated on television six months after the military took control of the government in 1980: "Turkey is a nation of men, not women."

In the early years of the Republic, the authority and spirit of Atatürk held the nation together. He, who had been a military man, became the symbol of the new state, which the military loyally served,[48] regarding both the state and the modernist reforms as Atatürk's legacy (Karpat 1981: 10). After his death the "brothers," as in many villages, fought over the inheritance, and several times this struggle threatened to become an internal blood feud. It was in this situation and with this

47. Laude-Cirtautas (1961) says that color words of foreign origin refer to the physical color; thus *kırmızı* specifies the color crimson. *Kızıl* is Turkish and has many other connotations. Similarly, *al* means red or vermilion but implies also terrifying or horrific. Vermilion was the color of the battle flags of old Turkish tribes.

48. The army is dedicated to preserving Kemalist ideals. "It is important to understand the value attributed by the Turkish army to the democratic idea. The army is strongly Kemalist: Kemalism equals Westernization; Westernization, in its political expression means democracy. The army is thus impelled by a double, perhaps contradictory, motive. It is the watchdog of Kemalism. But it has a genuine passion for democracy. These two motives make it oscillate constantly between intervention and refraining from intervention" (Hotham 1972: 56). See also Vaner 1987.

understanding that the military stepped in to assume control of Turkey in his name on September 12, 1980.[49]

Unlike the armies of many third world nations, the Turkish army "has not sought to overthrow the system itself—and to impose, say, an authoritarian military or single-party regime. The Turkish military is frequently regarded as the guardian of democracy. . . . [Army spokesmen] have invariably declared an intention to return to democracy at the time of the take-over and, moreover and unusually, they have stuck to their word" (Dodd 1983: 1). We can thus accept that the army acted in good faith according to Atatürk's bequest, even though one may dispute what it did in his name. However, the issue is more complex than this. In one way or another, all the problems that led up to the intervention have to do with the question of legitimacy—that is, with origins and orientations. In particular, they have to do with the legitimacy of the founder and the customs laid down by him.

The notion of legitimacy for the Turk relates to origins. At the personal level the origin of the seed must be known if the person is to have a legitimate identity. Similarly, if the seed is good, so too is the offspring. With regard to individual identity, Turks are clear. With regard to the world, Turkish Muslims are also clear: it originated with God and its order was revealed by Muhammed. From that perspective, the only legitimate world order is Islamic and its claim to legitimacy is divine.

But what about democracy? "Where did it come from? Who established it?" These were the salient questions villagers asked me, by asking about the founding of the United States, the oldest democracy. I tried to explain that ideas about democracy had been around for a long time, and that the United States represented an effort to put them into action. The problem for them was that these ideas originated with men; they assumed George Washington was the founder and were disappointed to learn that he was only the first President. I do not know how much of this they understood, because for them the only source of legitimacy is God. When we watched the inauguration of Ronald Reagan on television, they were quick to point out not only that the President swore an

---

49. Recruited from the middle and lower classes, and to a small extent from the peasantry, the military is identified politically only with the state. "When the military have stepped in to exercise government power, they have done so not for their own sake or on behalf of a particular social group, but for the purpose of maintaining the integrity of the state" (Karpat 1981: 10). See also Vaner 1987.

oath on the Bible, but that the minister opened and closed the ceremony with a prayer. Could these parts be omitted from the ceremony without a murmur? I doubt it, yet Turkish government ceremonies are 100 percent secular. Despite our separation of church and state, we too—symbolically, at least—attribute the government's legitimacy to God. This was an important point, especially coming from an uneducated peasant.

During Ottoman times, the roles of Sultan and Caliph were often filled by one person. The Sultan-Caliph represented God's rule on earth. When Atatürk took power he abolished the Sultanate; sometime later the Caliphate was also abolished. Many Turks consider this to have been a mistake, for now there is no central religious authority; had the office been retained, they believe, it would have added to Turkey's prestige and power. In modern Turkey there is no appeal to religious authority as a source of legitimacy. This is what offends the villagers; it is also what prevents them from embracing Communism.

Borrowing ideas developed by Ziya Gökalp about the distinction between civilization and culture,[50] Atatürk believed that the salvation and development of his country depended on adopting certain Western ideas and customs while still retaining its cultural heritage. When Atatürk talked about civilization in the Turkish context, "he was talking to a large extent about relations between the sexes and the general attitude of his people to women. It was not merely a matter of polygamy or monogamy, it was more a matter of the wild, almost insane jealousy and sense of honor which most ordinary Turks have about women" (Hotham 1972: 193).[51]

50. Gökalp thought that civilization could be separated from culture, the former being a matter of technical advances and the latter a matter of mores or lifestyles, what Geertz would call "ethos." Most people would disagree, I think, arguing instead that much of the technical superiority of the West, or of Japan, is inseparable from a particular ethos. To adopt certain aspects of Western civilization entails, at least partially, the adoption of a whole range of attitudes, values, and customs that are part of the culture. For example, for efficiency to become a value, people's attitudes toward time and work must change. Cf. Gökalp 1968 and Berkes 1954.

51. Such attitudes are apparently of long standing. According to a letter of Ogier deBusbecq, an attaché at the court of Süleyman in the sixteenth century, "The Turks set greater store than any other nation on the chastity of their wives. Hence they keep them shut up at home, and so hide them that they hardly see the light of day. . . . The Turks are convinced that no woman who possesses the slightest attractions of beauty or youth can be seen by a man without exciting his desires and consequently being contaminated by his thoughts" (1968: 117).

As everything in this book has been arguing, the relation between the sexes symbolically represents the nature and order of their world. To change the relation between the sexes threatens the nature and order of the entire universe. Villagers are clearly aware of the immensity of the threat. There is a range of variation in differences of opinion over some issues, but all are joined on the "covering" of women. When issues are discussed on the level of East versus West or Islam versus secularism, it is the purity of the Eastern-Islamic women that marks the difference. The purity, of course, is controlled and enforced by men. At another level, however, women can be associated with the West. In their own cultural view, vis-à-vis men, women represent the seductive, attractive material aspects of this world, and since these aspects have been associated with the materialism of the West, women can come to symbolize the West. As the seductive attractions of the West are felt to be corrupting their country and must be controlled, so too must the seductiveness and attractiveness of women be controlled.

Boundaries thus become a focus of anxiety, and exits and entrances are controlled and under surveillance. This is true no matter whether the boundaries are those of the nation, the village, the house, or the woman's body. Mary Douglas, in her now classic study of pollution beliefs, thought that "to understand body pollution we should try to argue back from the known dangers of society to the known selection of bodily themes" (1966: 121). From the evidence in Turkey, one could cogently argue that the particular cultural understanding of the body generates the anxieties or dangers felt to be impinging on the society. In place of a simple cause-and-effect equation, and regardless of direction, I propose that the perceived dangers and bodily pollutants are both expressions of the same worldview, that is, a culturally specific way of construing the world. Boundaries are also expressions of the inside-outside distinction as it functions at a variety of levels of social discourse. These distinctions are one form of ordering society, of keeping clear who's who. In this life maintaining a boundary between inside and outside is as impossible as maintaining a boundary between purity and pollution. In order for life to be perpetuated there must be transactions between inside and outside, and in the messy flux of these transactions the pure become defiled.

Turkey as land is symbolically female. Given the particular social construction of femaleness, it must be protected from the influx of corrupting influences from outside, just as the village and finally the *aile* must be protected from outside influence. But the symbolism can be turned inside out. Proceeding from the inside out, the corrupting influences can be symbolized as male. It is other men who can potentially despoil one's wife, as it is other men who can tarnish the honor of the village and other men who militarily or commercially threaten the integrity of the nation. Although these appear to be contradictory beliefs, they are resolved when one keeps in mind the perceived differences in nature between men and women. Women represent the diffuse aspects of materiality and thus can symbolize the sensual qualities associated with seduction and attraction as well as corruption, whereas men in their persons represent the domains they have circumscribed. When a threat is conceived in terms of persons, it is from men; when a threat is conceived in terms of influences or material quality, it is from women. In a sense men are the figures, women the ground. This raises the interesting question that has been at the root of the feminist movement in the West: are women really persons in their own right or only as they are attached to and defined by men? If asked this question, Turks, like most Westerners, would be quick to answer that women are persons in their own right, but the logic implicit in their system of beliefs supports the other answer.

A capitulation to the West can, in the traditional worldview, be interpreted as a capitulation to women, that is, as an orientation to this-worldly, material attractions. People so oriented feminize the spirit of the nation, now conceived in its masculine form as the men who represent, control, and protect it. A capitulation to Communism also represents an orientation to materialism; the difference is one of degree, not kind. Jane Smith (1980: 22) has raised the very interesting question of whether the rise of Islamic fundamentalist movements can be considered a re-masculinization of Islam.[52]

Atatürk's orientation to the West and his feminism[53] are allied in the

52. My experience among Turkish immigrants in Europe suggest that it can. Many men were out of work and therefore unable to fulfill the male role of providing for their families. Symbolically "castrated" by their failure to provide, they turned to the other way of asserting their virility: controlling "their" women. Girls were being kept from school, "covered," and confined to the home.

53. His feminism, though a distinct departure from tradition, was a far cry from contemporary feminism. Villagers, however, do not make such distinctions. Support for the rights of women and changes in their position, status, and role in society was seen above all as an effort to change perceptions of women. That is what men with conservative views resent, for it threatens a worldview founded on their supposed superiority to women.

village imagination, and reactions against one entail reactions against the other. These reactions simultaneously call into question his legitimacy as *ata* and the principles on which the Republic was founded.

One man in the village, not by any means the most extreme, wanted to see a reinstatement of Şeriat law (Islamic law) to replace the Swiss code. He also argued for a return to Arabic script, in which revelation was inscribed. It is important to convey something of the meaning that Arabic script has for many Turkish Muslims. Revelation, or God's word, is whole, and this notion is symbolized by writing that is fluidly strung together, not separated as it is with Latin orthography. Instead of using the script of God, calligraphy that is of itself holy, they are forced to use that of *Rum* (literally Rome but also meaning Constantinople), the archetypal enemy. Furthermore, this man resents Turkey's adoption of the Christian yearly calendar and the Christian day of rest, i.e. Sunday instead of the Muslim holy day, Friday.[54]

To have to conduct one's life and adjust the rhythm of one's day according to the laws and schedules of the *gavur* (infidel) is understandably a bitter pill for many Turks to swallow. Many, like the man just mentioned, seek to rid themselves of this poison by a complete purge. In the interim, they try to reverse these trends in the one sphere over which they have control: the bodies of their women. To be sure, some women willingly participate in their own "covering" to demonstrate their solidarity with the Muslim "brothers" against the West; what they fail to see is that, covered or not, they are still being defined by their bodies in ways that men are not.

Some extremists favor ejecting outsiders from their midst, banning certain television programs, eliminating the production and consumption of alcohol, proscribing the uncovering of women, outlawing Western dress and the use of cosmetics, and purging all foreign words. This last is unusual and unexpected and deserves some notice.

Many intellectuals who embrace certain Western ideas and attitudes nevertheless wish to purify the Turkish language by purging it of all foreign words, which means Arabic and Persian words as well as those of German, French, English, or Italian derivation. They wish to make the *anadil* (mother-tongue) *temiz* (clean and pure). When possible, per-

---

54. For a fascinating account of the tremendous importance and psychological effect of calendars and attempted changes, see Zerubavel 1985.

sons of this persuasion substitute Turkish words for foreign words; when this is not possible, they invent new words using Turkish roots. Each year the government language society publishes volumes of vocabularies informing the public of *öz Türkçe* (literally the real, true, pure Turkish), which in practice means new Turkish. But a consequence of this practice is to further alienate people from their history, since "the difference between the Turkish used in 1920 and in 1982 is greater than that between Chaucer's English and ours" (Henze 1982: 108).

Disappointingly, antiforeign views of that sort were held by the teachers in the village, trained though they were to uphold the spirit of Atatürk and to be a "civilizing" influence. A Turkish friend of mine gave me a huge collection of Turkish children's magazines, which I distributed to children in the village. The teachers learned of this and confiscated the magazines. Incensed, I went to inquire the reason. "They are filled with *yabancı şey*" (that is, foreign or *outside* things): short articles about Beethoven, Einstein, Galileo, Lincoln, and others that were interspersed among articles about Turkey. "If they learn about all the great things of the West, how will they develop pride in being Turkish?" Atatürk, the first to say "How happy is the person who can say I am a Turk," would be appalled at such a distortion of his views.

Atatürk as "father of the Turks" is symbolically allied with both God and the Prophet. He has been referred to as *Tek Adam*, "A Singular Man" (Aydemir 1969). *Tek* means single, alone, unique, solitary, without a partner, an attribute that we have seen belongs only to God. Even in official documents "He" is always capitalized when it refers to Atatürk.

Like the Prophet, he brought the Turks the message of their origin and orientations, to recall them to their true heritage. They were to make the land a place where his laws and customs would prevail. The national *bayrams* (holidays) compare with the religious ones. For example, May 19 commemorates the date Atatürk arrived at Samsun in 1919 from the capital, Istanbul, where he would surely have been arrested. This movement could be considered his *hicret* (hijra, hegira), analogous to Muhammed's exodus from Mecca to Medina; alternatively, it might be imagined as the time he received his "call" to begin a *cihat* (holy war) to cast off the yoke of the infidels (the Allied Powers). October 29 commemorates the proclamation of the Republic (1923), the beginning of the new nation living under new laws. April 23, Children's Holiday, commemorates the opening of Parliament, which might be inversely comparable to Şeker Bayramı, the Candy Holiday, which closes the period of fasting.

In addition, statues and pictures of him are ubiquitous, an obvious contrast with Islam's aniconic tendency and the invisibility of God. His death date (November 10, 1938) is remembered every year by several minutes of silence at 9:04 A.M., but all children must learn a song that begins "Atatürk is not dead, he still lives." General Evren, after the military intervention in 1980, placed a wreath at his tomb and spoke to him as if he were alive. An eternal flame burns at his tomb, Anıtkabir, a large square structure dominating Ankara that is referred to even by taxi drivers as "our *kabe*" (Ka'ba), implying that Ankara is a new Mecca. Like its Meccan counterpart, Anıtkabir is also a place of pilgrimage. Many children are taken there on finishing primary school; others go whenever means and opportunity allow. It was the first place I, as a Fulbright grantee, was taken.

The symbolics of political geography reinforce the belief that secularism in Turkey cannot mean merely a separation of religion and state. Rather, the state has taken over the symbols and the structure of the authority of Islam but changed the referents. The secularism Turks are confronted with is a mirror image of the religious worldview reflected back to this world. But is the nation a sacred state or a secular religion?

FIVE

The Embracing Context
of Islam

In the preceding chapters we have seen how ideas of procreation are essential for understanding the structure and meaning of family, marriage, kinship, village, and nation. The important distinctions between inside and outside, open and closed, encompassed and encompassing, close and distant, are symbolically integrated in the conceptual model of the female body, which represents and expresses the lateral, spatial, and material dimensions of existence. The male role, conceptualized as generative, originating, essential, and linear, defines these various dimensions. Who you are is related to where you came from. Identity is a function of origin, and origin is the source of legitimacy. This is as true at the social level as at the personal, for the social order is felt to be dependent on and legitimized by the founder-father (*ata*).

The most inclusive and fundamental context in which identity, origin, and the social order are discussed is Islam. God is creator, author, and founder of the world, and as such "God is the sole Head of the Community and therefore sole Legislator" (Gibb 1978 [1949]: 67–68; see also B. Lewis 1988: 46). Islam, though simple in theology, penetrates every aspect of life down to the paring of the fingernails. "The conception of law in Islam is thus authoritarian to the last degree. . . . To violate the law, or even to neglect the law, is not simply to infringe a rule of social order—it is an act of religious disobedience, a sin and involves a religious penalty" (Gibb 1978 [1949]: 67–68).

In Turkey, for more than five centuries Islam and the State were one; Anatolian people knew who they were. They were Muslims and members of the Ottoman Empire, ruled by the Sultan/Caliph, God's regent on earth.[1] One lived either inside Islam (Dar al Islam) or outside (Dar al Harb, the Abode of War). Outsiders were infidels (*gavur*).

Since 1923, by contrast, the nation of Turkey has consciously tried to separate itself from Islam, causing a tear in what many had imagined as the seamless fabric of social life. Atatürk's desire to modernize Turkey meant following a Western model in which the state was 'a secular democracy and religion was privatized, a matter of individual conscience.[2] In his view there were two sources of legitimacy, each applicable to a different domain: in effect, people would "render unto Caesar the things that are Caesar's and unto God the things that are God's" (Matthew 22:21). Yet this kind of separation is not exactly what happened in Turkey; instead, religion was put under the control of the state. The change was not so much a separation between the two realms as a change in the balance of power between them. In a way, this arrangement reinforces the Islamic model that "the two cannot be separated but . . . one must be subservient to the other" (Toprak 1981: 57); but the subservience runs the other way. The symbols and structure of Islam persisted, but with a this-worldly orientation. This has not been sufficiently recognized by analysts who have stressed total rupture and discontinuity (cf. Yalman 1973) instead of persistence and continuity.[3]

The nation-state confronts people as a competitor for their loyalty and affiliation, making it very difficult for them to keep religion and the state in their separate domains. Both are competing for total allegiance. The conflict occurs not because they are in total opposition, but rather because there has been a symbolic transfer from the realm of God, not only to earth but specifically to the nation of Turkey;[4] not be-

---

1. See B. Lewis 1988 for an excellent discussion of the terms "sultan" and "caliph."

2. Apparently he also envisaged Westernizing religion, which implied drastic changes in the style of worship: for example, sitting in pews, wearing shoes, liturgical music, and learned sermons about contemporary affairs (B. Lewis 1968 [1961]: 414). These recommendations were never put into effect. Toprak states that Atatürk's secularizing policy succeeded in "relegating Islam to the position of a purely individualistic faith" (1987: 221), yet a few years earlier she herself took the opposite position: "instead of relegating religion to the private sphere, the Kemalist regime assumed the responsibility of supervising and controlling religious activity through maintaining, in modified form, the organizational links between the religious institution and the state bureaucracy" (1981: 1).

3. Toprak's analysis that "the Kemalists opted for a continuity of tradition between the Ottoman Empire and the new Republic" (1981: 1) supports my interpretation of events.

4. Toprak also talks about this conflict in her notion of symbolic secularization, by

cause secularism has been empowered, but because nationalism has become the secular religion of the sacred state. The juxtaposition of nationalism with Islam has caused villagers to become more reflective about their faith. "Dinimizde" (in our religion) has become the justification for certain practices and customs as opposed to alternatives offered by foreigners or urban (and often atheist) Turks. For some, like my neighbor Nazim, it has meant a more zealous affirmation of faith. In the village (and I believe elsewhere) this conflict is at the forefront of people's lives and is pulling them in different directions.

"Nereden geliyorsunuz? Nereye gidiyorsunuz?" Where do you come from? Where are you going? These questions, repeated incessantly, became a kind of Greek chorus underlining the drama of days. At first these appear to be the most mundane of questions, an attempt to locate a person's activity in the social world; but the repetition became a clue to their more than mundane significance.[5] They are part of a religious wall hanging found in many village homes that features a saying attributed to al-Ghazali: "Whether your life span be short or long, the world is but a brief lodging [misafirhane, guest house], so take care to make provisions for the eternal home." The questions are a reminder to think about one's ultimate origin and destination, which in Islam are both Cennet (Paradise).

This reminder raises the question of orientation in life. To what shall people be devoted? To what shall they commit their energies? The constant repetition seems to point to a growing insecurity about where people came from and where they are going. Since 1923 they are no longer quite so sure. But the religious answer is clear: the world is but a guest house; make provisions for the eternal life.

Any discussion of origins involves a discussion of procreation, which also entails that of Creation. "The sexual relation of the couple takes up and amplifies a cosmic order that spills over on all sides: procreation repeats creation. Love is a mimicry of the creative act of God" (Bouhdiba 1985: 8). Not only are intimate and ultimate concerns articulated, but the structure of both is the same. The two major themes

---

which she means "the transformation in the connotations of a set of symbols from the sacred to the profane" (1981: 40). What she has not seen is that the gendered meanings of the symbols are the vehicle of continuity.

5. Atatürk was also concerned with these questions. According to G. L. Lewis (1984: 203), they were part of the motivation behind his linguistic and historical research.

"Where do you come from? Where are you going?"

of the Qur'an are Creation and the Last Days; God is Creator as well as Lord of the Hour, that moment when the entire creation is to be wrapped up. The recognition of this power entails the surrender and obedience of mankind to God; it means that they are *muslim*. The creative power of God suffuses the Qur'an and especially the creation of man.

The first revelation to Muhammed is thought to have been "Recite in the name of thy God who created, created man from a clod of blood. Recite" (Qur'an, Sura 96: 1–2; Khan 1962: 25). Among the more often cited passages is the following: "Verily, we created man from a product of wet earth; then placed him as a drop of seed in a safe lodging, then fashioned we the clot a little lump, then fashioned we the little lump bones, then clothed the bones with flesh, and then produced it as another creation. So blessed be Allah, the Wisest of Creators" (Qur'an, Sura 23: 12–14; Khan 1962: 187). Again: "Does not man see that We have created him from a mere drop of seed? Yet, behold, he is given to constant arguing. He coins similitudes for us and forgets the processes of his own creation" (Qur'an, Sura 36: 77–78; Khan 1962: 186).

It is important for the thesis of this work to have a clear picture of villagers' understanding of this process. According to them, God created the first man, Adam (*Adem*), in Paradise (*Cennet*). His fleshly parts were made of mud or soil: not earthly soil but the *kutsal* (sacred) soil of Paradise, the soil that is symbolized by *kına* in the wedding ceremony. Since Adam was hand-crafted by God in Paradise, he is not *tabiat tarafından* (made by nature) but *Allahin tarafından* (made by God). This understanding parallels certain tendencies in European and American thought. Many Christians in the nineteenth century were opposed to the theory of evolution because it implied a wholly natural origination. Villagers, like the Creationists, believe that all species, including the human species, were created in the beginning by God and that they are immutable.

When I spoke with villagers about a related preoccupation of nineteenth-century anthropology, namely the origin of the different races, I was told that God took four different colors of sacred soil—red, black, yellow, and white—and mixed them together to form Adam. In Adam's offspring these resolved into the separate races; but since they came from the same source, this view implies the ultimate and essential unity of all *man*kind. "While still in Paradise, God made all of Adam's offspring come forth from him and obtained from him the contract that they would recognize Him, God, as their master. This implicitly justifies the further claim of the Qur'an that man by nature is orthodox and that only by secondary influences is he misdirected to one or another heresy. This belief further constitutes an argument for considering infidels guilty of breach or forgetfulness of contract" (Meier 1971: 98).

In other words, not only is humanity unified, but all are essentially Muslim. Humanity is united because all races derive from Adam and Adam was made by God. God is One; this is the fundamental article of faith. "The central pivot around which the whole doctrine and teaching of Islam revolves is the unity of the Godhead. From this concept proceeds the fundamental unity of the universe, man, and of life" (Khan 1962: 91).

Monotheism implies a monogenetic rather than polygenetic view of the creation of mankind: that is, all peoples stem from one source. What has not been recognized, however, is that it also implies a monogenetic view of procreation, that there is one source of origination. God created the first man and created in men the means of transmitting life. "Procreation is primarily the transmission of existence in the form of an immanent *thrust* in which God himself participates" (Bouhdiba 1985: 12, emphasis mine). Procreation is a "sacred mission," but the divine life-giving element is transmitted in the seminal emission. The view of another Islamic scholar appears to support such a claim: "The flesh, the bones, the muscles, the blood, the brain, and indeed all the faculties and the whole complicated and yet wonderfully coordinated machinery of the human body constituting a complete microcosm is all potentially contained in less than a millionth part of a drop of fluid" (Khan 1962: 186–87).

In other words, educated scholars like Bouhdiba and Khan continue to see the entire human creation as contained in the seed-sperm. So, too, apparently did al-Ghazali, who recommended that men at the moment of ejaculation recite Sura 25: 54: "Praise be to God, who created man from [a drop of] water" (Sabbah 1984: 107).

Eve was created differently. She was taken from Adam's rib or, as one villager told me, from his left palm. She was taken from man and was thus, like all women after her, if not quite an appendage, dependent. By the circumstances of her creation she was constituted differently. "Woman proceeds from man. Woman is chronologically secondary" (Bouhdiba 1985: 11).[6] This was also one of the villagers' rationales for women's inferior status: whatever or whoever is first has precedence. This is held to be true no matter what the context; in this case it implies that woman is not only different from but also "naturally" subordinate to man.

The difference in creation implies different values and meanings that

6. Sabbah notes that "Chronology determines the degree of power" and goes on to say that "the one who exists first, God, possesses what comes into existence afterwards" (1984: 73). She adds (p. 78) that the same rationale is used to determine the power and position of male and female in relation to each other.

prescribe and circumscribe different domains, complementary but asymmetrically ordered, of activity and expertise:

A different education for women is necessitated not only by the roles they have to assume, but also by the fact of basic differences between the sexes. These differences are not culturally conditioned, rather they are of the essence of Creation, part of God's wisdom as He provided for balance and harmony in life. Male and Female complement each other, each to fulfill the role for which they were preordained, each to uphold the other in their areas of weakness. It then becomes incumbent on Muslim society, not only to refrain from tampering with God's order by introducing innovations, but also to maintain the differences. (Haddad 1980: 65)

Adam, divinely created, has the power of human creation (procreation) within him. From Adam this spark is carried to his sons, by whom the tribes of mankind are established. From father to son, father to son, this ability is transferred. The procession of the generations is conceived as linear; indeed, it is my belief that the linear understanding of time and history is intimately related to this ideology of procreation. There is a notion of segmentation by generation but also a notion of some essence that perdures (cf. Leach 1961). History as we know it has been primarily the record of the events of one people, one religious tradition, and one sex. The pan-human patrilineage is exemplified by that of the six major prophets who precede Muhammed: Adam, Noah, Abraham, Moses, David, and Jesus. As the last in this divinely inspired line, Muhammed is considered the Seal of the Prophets.

Villagers believe that the Book, meaning the word of God, came with Adam. After the flood, people dispersed and forgot; all except the people of Abraham. Turks after Atatürk have been taught that the Hittites[7] were their ancestors. Yet when I asked if that meant they were Muslim, villagers, with expressions of embarrassment and shame, said no, they had forgotten. All come into the world *muslim*: it is the fault of the parents if they do not teach this truth.

The Qur'an is thus seen not as a new Book with a new doctrine for its time, but as embodying the one true faith given in the beginning. Islam is not a new and separate religion, but a reassertion of the one true faith of Abraham: not Moses, the founder of Judaism, or Jesus, the founder of Christianity, but Abraham, the predecessor and foundation

7. A group of Indo-European-speaking people who inhabited Anatolia from the second millennium B.C., long before the Turks arrived. See Gurney 1952.

of all three. Some suggest this is the reason that Friday was declared the Muslim day of prayer, preceding Saturday and Sunday, the days sacred to Jews and Christians, respectively. In any case, this emphasis on Abraham does point to a tendency in Islam to a kind of recursiveness, a looking back to foundations.

The Biblical prophets are esteemed in Islam, and Muslim children are named after them, but they are thought to represent only partial revelations compared to the one vouchsafed to Muhammed. Villagers' knowledge and understanding of the New Testament is limited to the Gospels, which, since there are four versions, implies that the Word is mutable and therefore *bozulmuş* (ruined, tainted). I tried to explain that the four gospels were views of Jesus by four friends, just as four villagers would have somewhat different, but also somewhat similar, views about a fellow villager. This they understood, but it was still unacceptable. Lloyd and Margaret Fallers (1974) have suggested why: the Qur'an, they argue, is structurally and symbolically the equivalent of Jesus in Christianity, that is, the Word become manifest. Muhammed was not divine, as Jesus is to Christians, but the human transmitter of the Word of God, which is the Qur'an. For villagers the criterion of the authority, truth, and legitimacy of the Qur'an is that it has not changed—it is immutable. It is the same now as it always was. And that is why, according to villagers, it is important to memorize the exact words in Arabic for they are *the* Word of God. A translation into Turkish, which they would be able to understand, is not the same; in fact, it is not considered a translation but an interpretation.

The immutability of God, the Word, and eternity is in stark contrast to the growth and decay of life and the earth. *Bu dünya* (this world) is the locale for man's brief sojourn called life. Not only is one's life span on earth brief, but the earth itself is ultimately perishable; both are encompassed by and dependent on God. *Öbür dünya* (the other world) is a constant presence in villagers' lives. When they speak of it they generally mean *Cennet* (Paradise), for that is where they believe their dead children are, as well as other relatives and friends. Nevertheless, like everything else, *öbür dünya* is divided: into *Cennet* and *Cehennem* (Hell). For each earthly transgression, one will burn so many days in Hell. Hell seems to be populated mainly by women, for it is felt they are morally weaker and more easily seduced into transgression. However, it may not be eternal, for even those in *Cehennem* can earn admission to *Cennet*.

In any case, although villagers live in this world, they are not entirely of it. The practices of Islam help to keep the mind's eye on the other world. Particularly does the structuring and regulation of time function to reinforce this, during the day, the year, and a life.[8]

Diurnal rhythms are in accordance with the sun, but the yearly calendar is tied to the moon. The Muslim year consists of twelve months of 29 or 30 days each, and the year consists of only 354 or 355 days. This means that religious holidays move relative to the solar year; they are celebrated ten days earlier every year and thus are not tied to any particular season of the agricultural cycle as are Christmas, Easter, Yom Kippur, and Passover. The Islamic calendar is also cyclical, making a complete rotation every 33 years. This contrapuntal rhythm emphasizes the separation between the things of the earth and those of the spirit. While one's feet are on the ground, one is oriented to the other world. Even though the *ezan* (call to prayer) is in harmony with the daily round, it recalls people five times a day to the world of the spirit.

Prayer

About an hour before dawn, when a black thread can be distinguished from a white,[9] one is awakened by the *ezan* floating over the rooftops and reminded that prayer is better than sleep.

The day begins gently, unlike the rude jolt of an alarm clock. Some men get up and go to the mosque; others perform their *namaz* (prayer ritual) at home. Women always perform theirs at home. Performing *namaz* is one of the five *şart* (conditions or "pillars") of faith. The others are the testimony of faith ("There is no God but God, and Muhammed is his messenger"); *oruç,* the fast of Ramazan; payment of *zekat* or alms;

8. According to Sabbah (1984: 83), time is felt by Muslims to be a divine monopoly; humans have no control over it. This supposedly reinforces their feeling of dependence on God and causes them to believe that they cannot plan, make an impact on their environment, or make their own history because these things are in God's hands. Cf. Massignon 1957 and Walker 1978.

9. Sura 2: 187. The context of this passage is a discussion of Ramazan and fasting, but it also states that men may have intercourse with their wives until the white thread can be distinguished from the black. This is the way dawn is described in the Turkish epic, *Dede Körküt*. Sexuality is also part of that context; men with sons are placed in white tents, those with daughters in red tents, and those with no children in black tents. I have been unable to find any material on the Muslim meaning of the black and white threads, but we must be cautious in attributing our associations to other cultures. In countries where the sun is merciless, shade and dark of night can have more positive associations.

and making the hajj to Mecca. The *namaz* is more than simply prayer (*dua*); it is also a series of ritualized actions that accompany the prayer. In order to perform the *namaz*, a special prayer rug, often made and embroidered by the women of the house, is laid out in the direction of Mecca. There is no special place where this is done; rather, wherever the rug is placed becomes the sacred space in which *namaz kılmak* (to perform *namaz*); in a sense, it is a "magic carpet" transporting the person to the realm of God. *Namaz* is also likened to a stream of pure water into which the believer plunges and cleanses himself, and the performance of it five times a day is felt to guarantee admission to Paradise. During this brief time no one may interrupt the person praying, for that would cause a change in focus from the spiritual world to the earthly one and thus profane and invalidate the *namaz*. Even small children learn to keep their peace. Although this is one of the few times women are left alone and can withdraw into themselves, it is not a time to devote to their own thoughts but a time for these thoughts to be directed to God.

After this, women light the *soba* (heater-stove), make tea, and feed and milk the animals. When they return, the children get up and breakfast is served. After breakfast the village is divided between the sexes. Men leave to talk, work on machinery, or at certain times of the year to work in the fields. Women are at home sweeping, cleaning, washing dishes and laundry, making bread, and in the summer churning milk and making butter, cheese, and yoghurt. Mornings are not good times to visit unless one wishes to be involved or watch.

The second *ezan*, known as *öğle*, comes sometime around midday—earlier in winter, later in summer—after which lunch is served. Women wait for men to return from their activities or from the mosque, or both. Another *ezan* is in mid-afternoon (*ikindi*) and another one after sunset (*akşam*). It is only after this that the evening meal is served; in summer this may be as late as 8:30 P.M. The last *ezan*, referred to as *yatsı*, is called approximately an hour later. This is the prayer to which many of the men go, joining their friends either before or afterwards in the tearoom. Although the new day actually begins at midnight, just as it does for us, "tonight" means not the night ahead but the one just past, perhaps again exemplifying the backward glance, the tendency to recursive structures.

The day is not evenly divided. Time is not portioned out equally; it is not calibrated to identical measures as on a clock. Instead, there is a long space in the morning and four of the five *ezan* come in the second part of the day. Originally, it is believed, there were only two *ezan* (morning and evening), then three (morning, sunset, and nighttime). One explanation is that the two midday *ezan* were added to give people a clearer idea of what time it was. In any case, the five *ezan* have been called since before the beginning of the eighth century. Originally, the *ezan* may have been designed to mark the boundary between the day, devoted to earthly concerns, and the evening, when one's attention can be turned to spiritual matters.

Although the present schedule of the *ezan* does punctuate the work day, perhaps it is also a recognition that the times of the day are not uniform: that a day, like a life, has its own rhythms. Perhaps it is an icon marking life's stages. The long morning period may represent the blank, sinless period of childhood until marriage, the noontime of life, after which it becomes more important to consider the things of the spirit, for one becomes accountable and sins are more likely to accumulate. The last two *ezan*, close together in the evening, may be a reminder that at the end of life, before one enters the long sleep,[10] one's mind ought to be even more turned to God. The notion of "turning" is important in Turkish Islam, and is given physical expression in the movements of the Mevlana or Whirling Dervishes.

During prayers people are turned toward Mecca, a kind of lodestar toward which all Muslims are oriented, guiding the spirit in the proper direction.[11] The spiritual center of their lives is in Mecca, the holy city where Muhammed first established a Muslim community. But it is not holy just because of Muhammed. It is felt to be the navel of the world; "it was created before the rest of the earth" (von Grunebaum 1951: 20). Muslims believe that Adam went there after leaving Paradise, and also that many other prophets were born and died there. "Mecca, as the center of the earth, is the natural place of origin of any prophet, and

10. Although some believe that people go directly to Heaven or Hell after death, others believe the dead are essentially asleep until the Final Day of Judgment.

11. Recently many Muslims living outside a Muslim country have acquired a watch, designed by a company in California, that indicates the precise direction of Mecca from any point on the globe. The watch can also be programmed to adjust the schedules of the daily *namaz* according to season and to announce the time with a tiny beep.

therefore, in the logic of legends, also the place where he must meet his end" (ibid.). It is not just the geographical center but also the cosmo-logical center, the *axis mundi*, creating a link between heaven and earth. In the village the minaret performs a similar function; not only is the mosque in the center of the village, but the tall minaret linking heaven to earth is a means of transmitting the divine message. I do not think it is insignificant that the minaret is a phallic-shaped structure.

Mecca is believed to be the first dry land, from which the rest of the world spread out. It is referred to as the "mother of towns," and the Ka'ba, the huge square structure at its center, is called God's dwelling place. It is also the meeting place of the physical and spiritual. Upon Mecca's soil the Word of God took root and then was broadcast to the rest of the world. Once again we see that orientation in life is deter-mined by origins, directed toward the foundation, toward the *ata* (ances-tors) who established the customs. In turning toward Mecca in prayer one ostensibly turns toward the holy city of Muhammed, the founder of Islam; but Muhammed, as the last of the prophets, is only the con-nection through which one is put in touch with the spiritual line ex-tending back to Adam and ultimately to God. Turning toward Mecca affirms an image that cuts across the boundaries of nationalism.

Ramazan

Ramazan, like *namaz*, is an occasion during which believers are thought to be closer to God. Ramazan is a month-long period of fasting, somewhat like Lent only more stringent. It is a time of atonement. It is the month in which the Qur'an was allegedly revealed to Muhammed. It is said: "When the noble time of Ramazan comes, the doors of heaven are opened, the doors of hell closed, and the devils tied down." In other words, people's souls are opened to God and closed to *şeytan* (devils); they are sustained by God as by food.

During Ramazan the faithful keep a fast (*oruç*). All day, from before sunrise to after sunset, one must abstain from food and drink as well as sexual intercourse. Here the association between sex and eating is made explicit. It is also not permissible to smoke, take medicine, or chew gum; in other words, no substance may enter the body. One must be separated from those things which promote and sustain life in its material earthly form; fasting is a way to remind people of their dependence on God for these things.[12] *Oruç* is felt to be a great *sevap* (good work) by which God is pleased; if faithfully performed, it is believed to bring a remission of sins.

Because of the rotation of the Islamic calendar, Ramazan can for a period of years fall in summer,[13] when the days are longer and hotter. During the two summers I was in the village (1980–81), Ramazan fell in August and July, respectively, the most grueling times for the fast.

The fast begins after a meal that must be finished before the sky begins to lighten. This meal, called *imsak*, was taken in the summer at about 2:30 A.M. I recall my first *imsak* meal. I was sound asleep, but was awakened by sounds of people moving about and talking. It was pitch dark outside, but lights were on in all the houses, as if some unwanted prowler had awakened the entire village. Old Ali called to me from across the street to invite me to partake of his family's *imsak* meal. Nuriye had made sweet, puffy doughnut-type pastries—"oruçun tatli olsun"—so that your *oruç* may be sweet. Upon drinking the last glass of water before returning to bed, people make known their intention to keep the fast: "Allah rızası için bugünku oruçumu tutmaya niyet ettim"—I intend to keep my *oruç* today for God's approval.

Most people sleep late during Ramazan to make the day pass quicker, but a few men looked upon the fast as an opportunity for virile display. "Khomeini," for example, purposely took his whole family off to work in the fields in the hot sun all day. In general, no projects are planned for this period beyond what is absolutely necessary. "İş tutmuyoruz, oruç tutuyoruz" (we are not working, we are keeping *oruç*)—the two things are mutually exclusive. But it was also harvest time and thus some work was necessary. Many of the men working in the fields did not keep the fast. Occasional nonfasting days can be made up at a later time, such as during the short days of winter; but some men, especially the younger ones, did not keep the fast at all. By contrast, most of the women, including young girls who had finished fifth grade, did keep it,

12. Sabbah argues that this dependence on God for all material things creates an atmosphere in which human work is denigrated and is in some sense seen as irrelevant; instead "one acquires wealth by submission to him who possesses that wealth: God" (1984: 80). As I have noted earlier, Turkish villagers do not define themselves in terms of work.

13. Apparently the word Ramazan is thought to be related to the root for "heat of summer," "the Scorcher," and it is thought that in pre-Islamic Arabia a fast was held in summer.

as did pregnant women and nursing mothers, despite their exemption from the requirement. It is almost as if the women do the spiritual work for the men and the men do the physical work for the women. At the same time, women have internalized a view that they are more sinful and therefore need to do whatever they can to help themselves attain heaven. In the hierarchy of being, men are closer to God; representing Him in the family as they do, they may think they do not need to continually prove their worth by such practices. The men who did not keep the fast nevertheless made sure that their women did.

Normally villagers are rather vague and unconcerned about time: *şimdi* (now) can mean anything from now to a few minutes from now to several hours from now. However, at Ramazan the breaking of the fast at the evening meal (*iftar*) is timed to the exact minute. In our village, this occurred two minutes after Ankara. Some people watched television to hear the Ankara *ezan* and then waited two minutes before breaking the fast. Others watched until the lights of the village minaret were turned on and then waited for the first notes of the *ezan*. This is especially moving if one is sitting outside on the rooftop waiting for the *iftar* meal. The sun has set, but it is not yet dark. The fields below are burnished and purple shadows move across, echoing the melancholy sound. The cloth is spread; the water jug is close by. As soon as the first words of the prayer are heard, people take a glass of water, the first in 18 hours. After that the *iftar* meal is served. This is always a special meal and especially so in the summer, when fresh produce is bountiful. The fast is not broken, but opened to receive God's food. The *iftar* prayer: "Oh Allah, I hold *oruç* for your approval. I believe in you only, and I trust in you only. I open my *oruç* with the daily food that you give. To all the blessings that you give, let it be with thanksgiving. Amen."

Three days before Ramazan ends is Kadir Gecesi (the Night of Power), believed to be the night on which the Qur'an first began to be revealed. In 1980, making this night especially dramatic, there was a strange conjunction of crescent moon and star, exactly as on the Turkish flag. It is believed that all the spirits of the dead are abroad that night. On Arife Günü, the day before Ramazan ends, people go to the *mezar* (cemetery) to offer prayer.

The last *iftar* of Ramazan is a special feast. Often relatives from outside come to spend this night and the next day, Şeker Bayramı, with their families. The feast during the summer usually included *tarhana* çorbası (*tarhana* soup with tomatoes and *güvey çiçeği,* wild thyme), *ço-ban salatası* (salad of tomatoes, cucumbers, and green onions), *tavuk* (chicken), *dolma biber* (stuffed peppers), green beans, bread, yoghurt, watermelon, cantaloupe, grapes, plums, pears, and later, sweets with tea. Sometimes a whole sunflower (called moonflower, *ayçiçeği,* in Turkish) is torn to pieces for the seeds.

The next day, Şeker Bayramı (Sugar or Candy Holiday), is a happy day after the hardships of the fast. The day starts by paying respects to the oldest male of the family as a means of reconstituting the norms of social relations in a purified world. Thus before breakfast one might dress in new clothes made or bought for the occasion and go to the house of one's grandfather. He will be sitting in the place of honor, away from the door, in the corner next to the window. Next to him on the divan are his adult sons. On the floor next to him are adult male visitors; on the opposite side are the women and children. His wife would be either helping guests or sitting with the women. Occasionally, she might sit next to her husband.

Shoes are removed upon entering the house; one goes directly to the *ata* (father-founder), bows, kisses his hand, and then raises it to one's forehead. Finally, one says "Bayramınız mübarek olsun" (may your *bayram* be blessed), after which one kisses or shakes the hands of all present. Lemon cologne is offered and a few drops are sprinkled into outstretched hands, rather like receiving the communion wafer. The cologne is rubbed over the face, neck, and lower arms, creating a communion of scent and refreshment. Candies (*şeker*) are passed, and later children visit lots of houses to collect candy, as do American children at Halloween.

After this leisurely greeting, men leave and go to the neighborhood tearoom for a communal breakfast. The women eat theirs at home. On this important religious occasion not only are men and women separated, but men are gathered together while women celebrate separately in their separate homes. Breakfast was more like an evening meal: *imam bayıldı* (a baked stuffed eggplant dish), green beans, yoghurt, cheese, *yaprak dolması* (stuffed grape leaves), tea, and baklava.

During this repast the *zekat* (the collection and distribution of alms to the poor) was discussed.[14] Appropriate amounts to be given (usually

14. Lazarus-Yafeh (1981: 41) claims that the *zekat* is an integral part of this particular holiday. If so, the association of this *şart* of faith with one of the two major festival days would reinforce the importance and holiness of that day.

one-fortieth of income) are listed in the newspaper. Şeker Bayramı is a time of reconciliation and peacemaking. If there have been fights or grievances, these will be annulled by a visit, as when my neighbor brought me a bowl of olives after our altercation.

Ramazan has been a testing of the faithful, and Şeker Bayramı, also known as Küçük (Little) Bayram, is the happy reward. But the most important and sacred day of the year is Kurban Bayramı, which is also called Büyük (Big) Bayram, commemorating the testing of Abraham's faith.

Kurban Bayramı

Kurban Bayramı falls ten weeks after Şeker Bayramı. Villagers who plan to go on the hajj (Turkish *hac*) to Mecca, the timing of which coincides with Kurban Bayramı, would leave about a month before it. Shortly before the *bayram*, houses are cleaned, *badana* (whitewash) is applied, and new clothes are made. Relatives from outside also came for this holday. So did gypsies, who camped near the village in order to be present for the distribution of meat.

A minor *oruç* (fast) is kept until after the sheep representing Abraham's son has been sacrificed, which occurs after men have returned from a special service at the mosque. Thus the fast is kept only from the night before until midmorning. On the morning of Kurban Bayramı all of the men went to the mosque to perform their *namaz*. When they came outside they formed a large circle, facing inward; the younger men went all around the circle kissing the hands of their elders and thereby paying them obeisance or respect. The men then dispersed to their homes to perform individually the communal tribal ritual "cutting" of the sheep.

In the courtyard a small hole was dug to collect the blood. The animal's legs were bound, and it was laid on its side with its neck over the hole. The head of the household softly stroked its throat while simultaneously intoning "Allah is great, I testify there is no god but Allah, I testify that Muhammed is his prophet." This soft chanting seems to calm the animal. A quick slash was made across the neck, and the blood gushed forth with a sound like a fountain. There was far more blood than I had imagined, and after a few minutes it became a gurgling sound. The sheep made a few last bleats, shivered, and was dead. This is not a pleasant thing to watch, but I think the unpleasantness of watching is part of the point.

Before the meat can be cut, distributed, and cooked, the skin must be removed. I found this even more difficult to watch than the actual sacrifice. A small rubber hose attached to a kind of bicycle pump is inserted in the leg of the sheep, just under the skin. As air is pumped under the skin it creates a kind of pocket that helps to separate the skin from the body so that it can be removed easily and in one piece. The skins are supposed to be collected and donated to the Turkish Red Cross—Kızılay (Red Crescent)—which sells them to raise money. Prior to September 1980, villagers refused to donate the skins to Kızılay, for they believed the money was being used to establish houses of prostitution; but after the military takeover, donation was mandatory. Money from the sale of the skins is used by both Kızılay and the Türk Hava Kuruma (Air Society) to buy parts for planes.

Some of the meat of the Kurban is eaten on that day by the family; the rest is distributed to the poor and sometimes to neighbors. I was the beneficiary of several choice pieces of meat from my neighbors. "Is it because I am poor?" "Well, you are a *dul kadin.*" This expression normally refers to a widow, but here meant that I was a woman without a husband or family to support me. Because generosity on this occasion is felt to bring great *sevap* (blessings in the next world), even gypsies got a share.

Kurban Bayramı, like Şeker Bayramı, is preeminently a family holiday, and though I was invited to several homes to partake, as an outsider I could not really participate. On this day, just as at Şeker Bayramı, men celebrated separately. They ate a communal meal in the tearoom while the women remained in their homes and thus separated from each other. However, at the house where I witnessed the sacrifice, Ali stayed home complaining of a sore throat. I jokingly told him it must be in sympathy for the sheep!

After the sacrifice and the meal, the rest of the day is spent visiting and exchanging small gifts such as scarves and costume jewelry for women, socks and shirts for men, and candy for children. Yet for all the holiday spirit, Kurban Bayramı seemed to be a sober and somber day.[15]

---

15. The austerity of Muslim holidays has been noted by numerous scholars. Lazarus-Yafeh (1981) attributes it to the fact that Muslim holidays do not commemorate any his-

When I asked about the meaning of the Kurban, the answers I got were fairly uniform: "In ancient times we used to cut our sons. If God hadn't given us a ram [koç], we would still be cutting children." A child's answer was similar: "Allah wanted a child every year. Every year a boy was cut. One of the prophets [Abraham] gave his son, but this time Allah sent a sheep with an angel. Now at Bayram we don't cut people."

The scene of Abraham's intended sacrifice is visually prominent throughout Turkey, being displayed on posters, wall hangings, and postcards. In all these representations, a boy[16] is tied hand and foot, like the sheep, while his father stands over him brandishing a knife in upraised hand. One wonders how this is internalized, what kinds of sentiments are generated. Parents often said jokingly to a misbehaving child: "I will make a Kurban out of you if you don't obey." Children are permitted to witness this bloody spectacle, and they clearly know what it means, but what passes through their minds? Were their jokes and giggles a way of releasing suppressed anxiety? Were they imagining that if fathers were once capable of such a deed, they might be capable of doing it again? Does witnessing the sacrifice help to strengthen and reinforce authoritarian values?

While I was in Turkey, a film documenting a true story that had taken place in eastern Turkey in the 1970s was released. It was called *Adak*, a word that refers to the sacrifice made in fulfillment of a vow previously made with God. A man, portrayed in the film as highly religious if ignorant, had apparently killed his infant son in fulfillment of such a vow. The legal and ethical controversy that ensued never once questioned the morality of the original story, that of Abraham, on which the defendant modeled his action and based his case.

It was not questioned because that story is almost beyond question. It represents the foundation of faith of the three monotheistic religions, and is explicitly the foundation of Islam. Muhammed's mission was to recall the people to the faith of Abraham, who is referred to as *hanif*, a

---

torical events or events in the life of Muhammed, nor are they associated with any season. The austerity of the holidays, she believes, has encouraged the incorporation of certain pre-Islamic or folk festivities into popular religious practice.

16. Apparently there is some disagreement about whether the son to be sacrificed was Isaac, as in Judaism and Christianity, or Ismail (see Lazarus-Yafeh 1981: 44–45), since the Qur'an does not mention the son by name in that context (Sura 37: 100–113). It does mention Isaac immediately afterwards, but all the Muslims I knew in Turkey believed Ismail to be the son in this story.

true, devout monotheist. To question that story is to question the foundation not just of faith, but also of the society and values derived from it.[17] In that story God tests Abraham's faith by demanding that he sacrifice his son, the very one who would continue the line of seed. Abraham becomes the model of faith precisely because he was *willing* to sacrifice his child; because he submitted to God's will in so central a matter, a tremendous amount of power was conferred upon him.

Note that Abraham assumed the right to dispose of his son without consulting his wife, Sarah, or asking for her consent. Nor did God speak to her. Clearly, the child was not hers in the same sense; in other words, once again the theory of procreation is crucial to understanding the story. In Jewish, Christian, and philosophical commentaries on this story the child is talked about as Abraham's dearest *possession*. Clearly, if the child was a possession, Abraham did not need permission to dispose of him as he wished; he had the *patria potestas*, the power and right of the father. The story represents, to me, a "cutting" of that power, but also, simultaneously, an affirmation of it. In this symbolic transfer of power to God, to whom all people must be *muslim* (in submission), men's lordship on earth is reinforced. In performing the Kurban, men ritually reproduce this metaphor of power over life and death.

Women are never allowed to perform the Kurban, nor may they slaughter animals for ordinary purposes until after menopause. Generally these prohibitions have been interpreted as menstrual taboos, but they are more than that; women are forbidden to slaughter not only while menstruating but throughout their entire reproductive lives and, for Kurban, all their lives. To focus narrowly on the physical event of menstruation misses the point that menstruation also indexes fertility, the capacity to bring forth life and sustain it. Nevertheless, as we have seen, menstruation in both its positive and negative aspects symbolizes earthly life, its materiality and mortality.

It is also for this reason, I believe, that menstruating women are forbidden to enter the sacred precincts of Mecca during the hajj. Yet to make the journey and not be able to perform the rituals is ultimately not to have made the hajj; such a journey would not fulfill the requirement of faith. No doubt this is one reason that most women who go on

17. Given the strategic and theological significance of this story, surprisingly little has been written about it. See Delaney 1977.

the hajj are postmenopausal. Every precaution is taken to ensure that the minds and bodies of the faithful are purified. The exclusion of menstruating women is, I suggest, motivated by a belief that menstruation as a symbol and reminder of fertility, process, and mutability has no place in an unchanging ritual directed to the eternal.

Women, whose blood forms the closest *physical* ties, represent the eventual dissolution of earthly life, and thus stand in stark contrast to those who share an enduring, spiritual bond. Women, like the earth, symbolize the womb and the tomb. They are the physical portals, men the spark that passes through and does not die. In the menstrual restrictions the notion of pollution is undoubtedly operating; it is not, however, simply pollution by menstrual blood, but contamination of the spiritual realm by the physical. Women's exclusion, I suggest, expresses the incommensurability between earthly life and eternal life. I cannot agree with the Ferneas, who claim that "women are an equal but different half of the Islamic universe" and that women's exclusion from the central symbols and rites is merely "a slight tailoring of practice to suit the special circumstances of womanhood" (1972: 385). It is true that women are required to fulfill the basic obligations of the believer: profession of faith, prayer, fasting, giving of alms, and the pilgrimage. However, the symbolic focus on the male generative organ as a vehicle for power and authority automatically excludes them. The differences between men and women are not incidental, but are fundamental to the system.[18] The values assigned the two sexes are asymmetrically and hierarchically ordered, and this ordering is reinforced by the practices of Islam.

The Muslim God is a jealous God, particularly with regard to anything that might diminish a believer's devotion to Him (Sura 2: 165ff). But there is a difference between men and women believers. It is considered appropriate for a woman to be totally devoted to her husband, since he is considered a second god and represents God in the world and in the family; but for a man to succumb to passion for a woman would be a sign of weakness and a capitulation to his baser instincts.

---

18. This is also the main point made by both Sabbah (1984: 69) and Bouhdiba (1985), although each takes a very different stance toward this phenomenon. I do not mean to single out Islam for special opprobrium. I believe that gender is central to Judaism and Christianity in a very similar way.

This, of course, reinforces the association of woman with sex. Both are to be used to clear the mind and spirit to focus on God.[19]

Neither the love of one's wife nor even the love of one's son, though a son is the aim and pride of every man, is to interfere with a man's devotion and allegiance to God. At the overt level, this is what the story of the Kurban is meant to demonstrate. At another level it supports and represents male dominance.

The Hajj[20]

Kurban Bayramı is associated not only with Abraham but also with the hajj, since it coincides with and culminates the rituals of the hajj. To make the hajj is not only to fulfill one of the obligations of faith, but also, at least in theory, to signal a devotion reminiscent of Abraham's; it is the ultimate expression of a life of faith. Both the hajj and the sacred city of Mecca are inextricably bound up with the story of Abraham. He is thought to have raised the foundation of the Ka'ba or Temple of the Lord (Sura 2: 137–38) around the black stone nestled in its eastern wall, which in turn is said to have been sent from heaven in the time of Adam.[21] The institution of the pilgrimage (Sura 22: 27–28) is also attributed to Abraham. Plainly Mecca's pedigree as a holy city goes back to the beginning of time, and it is on this account the quintessential pilgrimage city.

In Muhammed's time Mecca was already a pilgrimage city, but many gods, and especially goddesses, were worshiped there.[22] In Islam this

19. See Mernissi 1975, Sabbah 1984, Bouhdiba 1985, Farah 1984, and numerous other studies.

20. This section has been elaborated in my article "The Hajj: Sacred and Secular" (1990).

21. Another tradition says that Adam built the Ka'ba (T. kabe) beneath an identical building in Heaven, and still another says that God built it, then Mecca, then the rest of the world. The black stone within the Ka'ba is said to be the eye of God on earth; or alternatively his hand, which blesses all that touch it. Others say that the black stone was given to Abraham by Gabriel, who was later to transmit the Qur'an to Muhammed. See Esin 1963 and Lazarus-Yafeh 1981 for various stories and interpretations of the hajj, the black stone, Abraham, and Mecca.

22. See Lazarus-Yafeh 1981 for a good analysis of pre-Islamic pilgrimage and attempts to Islamize it. Sabbah (1984) describes the goddesses worshiped in Mecca prior to Islam. These goddesses are mentioned in the Qur'an (Sura 53: 19). Some Muslim and Western scholars believe that verses indicating that Muhammed recognized them have been left out of the Qur'an. These verses are known as the "satanic verses," a term recently revived by the publication of Salman Rushdie's novel of that title.

difference is explained in terms reminiscent of those used by nine-teenth-century anthropologists of the monogenetic persuasion when confronted with the phenomenon of primitives. It is said that the orig-inal faith had degenerated because the people had forgotten. The sacred city had been desecrated, and thus Muhammed's mission is set in a wider cosmological frame. Muhammed purified the Ka'ba and recalled the people to the one true faith established by God in the beginning. The journey to Mecca is thus a journey not only to the physical center of Islam, but to the origin and foundation of the faith.

"The pilgrim should realize that he is journeying to his Lord when he sets out for the Lord's house. Allah has promised that those who see His house may hope after death to see His face. It is the intense longing to behold the face of God in the next world which causes the pilgrim to leave his home and to make the long, arduous journey to Mecca" (Partin 1967: 192–93). This may be the legitimate religious reason for making the hajj; what propels individual pilgrims to undertake this journey can, of course, be quite variable. In the village, the hajj is a journey that is undertaken only toward the end of one's life, for it is only then that one may have accumulated enough money or, as in the case of one couple, that one can sell one's entire flock with equanimity. In 1981 the trip from Turkey to Mecca on one of the organized bus tours cost between 125,000 and 150,000 TL ($1,500). In 1980 Turks were not permitted to go on the hajj because departure time coincided with the military intervention and all travel was suspended. When permission was given in 1981, eight people (five men and three women) from our village joined a group formed from the surrounding villages that would leave from Milas. (When I returned in 1986 for a brief visit, six people, three men and three women, were preparing to go.) This modern-day caravan would make a trip of 32 days.

Before leaving on the journey to Mecca, it is necessary to leave one's estate in order (for one may not return) and to give a feast for the entire village. The eight people in 1981 cooperated in planning the feast and sharing expenses. For this occasion they needed 100 kilos of rice, 8 sheep (120 kilos of meat), soup, bread, and 26 kilos of *hoşaf* (dried fruit compote).

September 13, 1981, was a cold morning and threatened rain. Co-incidentally, it was the day after the anniversary of the 1980 military intervention. Two of the men supervised the cooking of the pilav (rice dish);[23] however, when the rain began, the cauldron was moved inside to a laundry house and the women took over.

An open space above the village (*harman*) was the site for the feast. Canvases were spread on the ground, and people donated *sofras* (low table-trays). After the noon *namaz* a long line of men, led by the imam and the men going on the hajj, proceeded from the mosque chanting "Allah is Great." As men represent the village to the outside world, so too will the male *haçı*[24] represent the village, as well as Turkey, in Mecca. They were dressed in special light blue suits with the insignia of the Turkish flag on the breast pocket. The women who were going on the hajj also had special long light blue dresses and head coverings, but they were not included in this march, or, of course, in the prayer in the mosque. All the older men ate first, then younger men and boys, and finally the women, including the three female *haçı*.

On the morning of departure, everyone gathered in the *meydan* (square) for the blessing and farewell. All the men of the village (over a hundred) formed a huge circle, and the five male *haçı* went around the circle and kissed their hands or embraced them. The three women were excluded; outside the circle they kissed and embraced their friends, but they were not included in the ritual of communion and blessing.

It was an emotional moment, for everyone was aware that some of these pilgrims might not return. The journey is arduous and people are liable to get sick, especially since they will be drinking unfamiliar water and eating unfamiliar food when their own provisions run out. At the same time it is felt to be a great blessing to die in Mecca. The imam intoned a special blessing for the men leaving for the hajj, but only after the circle had broken up and dispersed did he come over to the three women to wish them a safe journey.

This ritual, more than anything else, displayed to me the peripheral character of women and their exclusion from a major communion of the

23. Men did cooking when it was done outdoors. For example, when they were working in the fields, men occasionally cooked the midday meal. They also supervised cooking for weddings if there were a large number of guests, for the cooking then was done outdoors. Also shepherds who spent days at a time in Küçükler or in the cave on the mountain, as Isa did, would sometimes do their own cooking, though often food was brought to them from home. Within the home, cooking is women's task.

24. Theoretically the term *haçı* is used only for those who have already made the hajj, but in the village it was a convenient label to designate those preparing to make it.

faithful.[25] The circle of men with their backs to the women not only excluded them, but made them invisible. There is no "special circumstance of womanhood" to exclude them from this. Rather, the physical and symbolic separation points all the more to the notion that Islam is a brotherhood; the essential bond is between men.

Details of the rites to be performed in Mecca can be found elsewhere[26] and will only be touched upon here. Before entering the area of the Ka'ba, pilgrims must perform a *güsül aptes* (a total ablution) that includes paring the nails and removing body hair. A man then dons the *ihram,* the special pilgrim's garment to be worn in Mecca. This garment, composed of only two lengths of seamless cloth, is usually interpreted as a symbol of the equality of men before God. Women are exempted from wearing the *ihram.* They retain their conventional clothes and thus continue to display ethnic or national differences as well as the status and rank of the husbands or fathers who accompany them. Some rationalize the difference in dress by explaining that men symbolize the unity of Islam and women the diversity.

The *ihram* has another meaning: "Even as the believer will some day meet God in a garment he does not wear in life, that is, the shroud, so the pilgrim goes to the House in an unusual garment—the *ihram.* Both are alike in that they are unsewn" (von Grunebaum 1976: 45). Many pilgrims do in fact save the *ihram* to be used as their shroud. The fact that male pilgrims must wear a special garment seems understandable enough, but what is the significance of its being unsewn? Villagers did not know, and I have been unable to find an answer elsewhere. The following are my own speculations.

This garment is seamless and all of a piece, as is God's world. It cannot be stitched, for stitching implies joining things that are separated.

25. This exclusion is replicated in Mecca also. Women are not permitted inside the mosques during prayer time, but perform their prayers outside around the periphery; nor are they permitted to visit the cemetery of the prophets in Medina. An excellent film, often difficult to obtain, called *Mecca: The Forbidden City* (produced and directed by Abolghasem Rezai, no date) visually conveys the impact of their exclusion and distinctiveness, while its commentary supplies the rhetoric of unity and brotherhood.

26. Especially useful and beautifully recounted are Emel Esin's *Mecca the Blessed, Madina the Radiant* (1963) and David Long's *The Hajj Today* (1979). An excellent contemporary account by Antoun (1989) also discusses the hajj in relation to the villagers with whom he worked in Jordan. Muhammed Abdul-Rauf (1978) has written a popular, personal account accompanied by beautiful photographs. See also von Grunebaum 1981 [1951], *Encyclopedia of Islam* 1965, and Lazarus-Yafeh 1981.

Dikmek means to sew, or to stitch, but also to plant (basically to stick something into), and is used for the planting of flags at weddings and upon the completion of a new house, symbolizing the establishment of a conjugal unit. It is also one of the words that can be used for sexual intromission, to plant the seed. Thus the garment seems to imply not only the unity of God's creation but the fact that it was accomplished without sex and without a partner. Women's status is clearly ambiguous.

The catalogue of proscriptions during the hajj is usually given as follows: the pilgrim must abstain from wearing sewn clothes, covering the head, bathing and bodily care, sexual activity, marriage, using perfume, engaging in personal combat or shedding blood, hunting wild animals, and uprooting plants. Making a sacrifice or fasting can atone for any violation except sexual intercourse, which voids the entire hajj (Long 1979: 16). But the list applies mostly to men; women are exempted not only from wearing the *ihram* but from uncovering their heads—the proscription of covering is taken to mean only that they need not cover their faces. Finally, as we shall see shortly, a significant difference obtains with regard to sexual intercourse.

Upon entering the area of the Ka'ba, pilgrims circumambulate the sacred stone seven times in the counterclockwise direction, as angels are thought to do around the throne of God. The goal of pilgrims is to be able to touch and kiss the black stone in the eastern corner of the Ka'ba. In some traditions this stone is thought to incorporate the souls of all people; others hold that it is given power to judge people on Judgment Day, still others that it was white in Adam's time and has been turned dark by accumulated sin. Photographs brought back by villagers showed this stone to have a remarkable resemblance to a vagina, complete with labial folds and a clitoris. No doubt villagers, and Muslims in general, would be shocked by this association. Nevertheless, there is evidence that the Ka'ba is symbolically female.[27] From the photograph, at least, the black stone reminded me of the dark place on village wall hangings that villagers said was meant to be the womb.

27. The earthly dwelling or *house* of God could be considered symbolically female like other houses, and the Kiswa or covering could be interpreted as a veil. Lazarus-Yafeh notes that some Muslims, at least, personify the Ka'ba as female: "On the Day of Judgement the Ka'ba shall also arise from the dead and be led to paradise as a *bride* to *her* wedding and those who ever performed the pilgrimage—shall hold on to *her* covers on that day and thus enter paradise with *her*" (Lazarus-Yafeh 1981: 30, emphases mine).

While pilgrims are inside the sacred precincts they go to the well of Zemzem, where it is said God revealed a spring to Hagar, Ismail's mother, when they were sent into the desert by Abraham.[28] Villagers filled containers with the sacred water to bring back to share with fellow villagers. The day before the Kurban, pilgrims proceed to Arafat for the "Standing," in which all assemble and stand together in prayer from noon to sunset. Many consider this to be the central event of the hajj. The last important rite of the hajj proper is the stoning of the devils at Mina, where Abraham is supposed to have attempted the sacrifice of his son. "The son was brought to Mina to be offered as a sacrifice. It was here that the devil came to tempt, in the name of paternal love, to tempt to disobey. This was only to know that the man's love for his Creator was greater. It was at this stage of human submission to Almighty Allah that Ibrahim (peace be upon him) took pebbles and cast them at the Devil" (Matthews 1977: 24).

After this rite the hajj proper is at an end, but to many pilgrims, including the villagers, the Kurban is an integral part, indeed the consummation, of the hajj. After the stoning, the Kurban is made:

An estimated 800,000 to 1,000,000 sheep, goats, and camels are annually slaughtered in the three day period. The magnitude of this slaughtering is staggering. . . . In order to prevent the spread of disease from such a large number of slaughtered animals, no one is allowed to keep from the animals he slaughters more than meat which he and those with him can actually cook and eat (an estimated 10–20 pounds per animal). The animals, covered with lime or other disinfectant, are then pushed by tractors and bulldozers into huge pits prepared beforehand and buried. (Long 1979: 85)[29]

Considering the millions of poor and starving people in the world who should, according to Muslim tradition, be the beneficiaries of the sacrificial meat, this slaughter seems an extravagant demonstration of faith. If a sheep can symbolically stand for a person, why not have one sheep, ritually slaughtered in some central place, stand for all pilgrims, and use the money saved to feed the poor? Apparently others are also beginning to think in these terms; there is some talk of freezing the

28. Readers interested in the debates about the place of Hagar in Islam and differences between the Muslim story of Abraham and that found in Judaism and Christianity should consult Crone and Cook 1977.

29. What will some future archaeologist, coming upon these pits filled with skeletons of millions upon millions of animals, make of the culture of the people responsible?

extra meat and shipping it to other Muslim nations, or even of establishing a cannery on the site (Lazarus-Yafeh 1981: 126).

When the hajj is over, a man can shave his hair and a woman often cuts off a lock of hair. Normal activities and clothes can be resumed. Many pilgrims stay on for a few days or make a trip to the city of Medina.

For the return, pilgrims bring back gifts by which they hope to share some of the luster of Mecca with family members and fellow villagers. In addition to the Zemzem water and dates, villagers brought back special vials of myrrh, frankincense, and shiny baubles, reminiscent of the gifts that the Three Wise Men took to Jesus. As soon as the *hacılar* arrived in the village, they went directly to their homes to receive visitors.

I went with a group to see Halil and Semiha, a couple in their sixties. After distributing gifts, they talked of the sights and the hardships they had endured; several villagers had been quite ill, and the oldest man went to the hospital upon his return, dying shortly afterwards. Their talk and the stories they brought back were as exotic as their journey itself, especially to villagers who hardly ever left the village. Their accounts opened up a horizon of possibility for others. Such travel was given sanction as a legitimate goal of a lifetime.

In addition to the extraordinary heat in Mecca, the fact that there were no trees except date palms, and the cheap cost of fuel, the aspects that struck them most vividly were two. First, they had never before been with so many different kinds of people speaking languages they could not understand and eating different kinds of food. Because the hajj is supposed to be an expression of unity and communion, they had gone believing, at least to a certain extent, that all Muslims would be able to understand each other. But they could not even understand Turks from other countries and they felt lost. This gave them some insight and appreciation of my situation in their village. "Look, we brought all our own food and didn't try anything there, but Carol *teyze* tries everything here." Or again, "We hadn't realized how hard it is to go to a place where you don't know the language and the customs."

Second, and most puzzling, was the revelation that when one is at the center one is disoriented. All their lives people face toward Mecca in one straight line,[30] but once there they can face the sacred precinct

---

30. The notion of the "straight path" is very important in Islam and for some is syn-

from any direction. This collapse of linearity the village *hacılar* were totally unprepared for; expecting to be more oriented, they instead found themselves profoundly disoriented. In retrospect, their experience provided a means for thinking about eternity.

In *Cennet* (Paradise) there is no begetting and no birth. Procreation involves ideas of linear time; not only does life have a beginning and an end, but also a lineage (or line) is established by male seed. On earth, sexual intercourse is inseparable from procreation. The sanction against intercourse during the hajj is surely related to ideas of pollution, but also, I believe, it is considered appropriate because intercourse brings with it a focus on bodiliness and procreation, and thus on time. By means of seed, men provide the link between the eternal and the earthly; nevertheless, it is lineal, across time. Women, by contrast, as an ever-present but perishable ground for life's perpetuation, embody the nonlinear aspect of time and thus paradoxically seem nearer the notion of the eternal. *Cennet* combines both aspects—the spiritual and unchanging with the nonlinear. Sexual intercourse, however, implies procreation through time and for this reason is not only inappropriate but also voids the entire experience. One's mind and body during the brief period of the hajj are supposed to be devoted to God; the actions one performs are directed not to this life, but to the one to come. Bodily adornments, whether of dress or perfume, not only distract the attention but imply a seduction by the attractions of this world rather than heaven, a submission to the flesh rather than to God.

Given the association of bodiliness and sex with women, the injunction against intercourse is directed primarily to men; it is up to them to abstain from women. In this regard, since a woman may not refuse her husband, the fulfillment of a pure and proper hajj for a woman is dependent on her husband or other men whom she is with, a situation that further undermines her autonomy in the one area, worship, in which she is alleged to have it.

Having been on the hajj confers a certain status on the *hacılar*, but the outward signs were exhibited by and to men. Although the hajj also confers status on a woman who has made it, there are no outward signs

---

onymous with Islam. Şeriat, Muslim law, is considered the straight path. Sometimes this path is symbolized by *Sirat*, the razor-sharp bridge that leads the devout into heaven but forces the sinful into hell. The straight path is also the line to Mecca faced by Muslims when they pray. See also Rahman 1980, Nasr 1985, and B. Lewis 1988.

to distinguish her and she must resume her normal routine. At home as in Mecca she displays her attachment to and immersion in the physical world. By contrast, men who have been on the hajj may let their beards grow, as they were required to do in Mecca; though long hair has unwelcome connotations of sexuality, men old enough to be *hacı* have presumably overcome the entanglements of the flesh and are therefore permitted to grow beards. This distance from sexuality is further symbolized by not allowing women to shake the hand of a male *hacı*.

Further, a male *hacı* may expect to spend the rest of his days sitting, not working. In theory, his former work should be delegated to others, leaving him free to concentrate on spiritual activities such as prayer and reading the Qur'an. In practice, what happens depends on the man's age, wealth, and inclination. Most of the older men, not all of whom have been on the hajj, do participate in more of the daily prayers than younger men, and spend much of the day sitting in the courtyard of the mosque.

The reward of a long life is to be able to sit out one's days waiting for death. One's death is written, but when it will come only God knows. Still, if possible, it is best to be prepared, to have set one's life in order and to have left nothing undone. Then there is nothing to do but wait.

Death

In the village, as in the city, one learns that a death has occurred by hearing an *ezan* outside of the normal prayer times. Shortly after I heard such an *ezan* one morning, my neighbor Nuriye came over and informed me matter-of-factly "Our *bakkalcı* is gone." Thus I learned that my next door neighbor, the *bakkalcı* (small shop owner) and *terzi* (tailor), had died in the hospital after an operation that no one thought would be very serious.

If a person dies in the hospital or outside the village, word is sent ahead and the *cenaze* (corpse) is brought back, accompanied by relatives and friends from town. Most people wish to be buried in their native soil, to be next to kin; to be buried elsewhere is to be consigned to eternal *gurbet* (exile). My neighbor Fatma said she would not come to visit me in the United States in case she should die there. There is a tradition that when a person is born, God instructs an angel to put into the semen in a mother's womb a speck of soil of the territory in which the person is destined to die (Smith and Haddad 1981: 35). I did not hear this view expressed by villagers, but any who might hold it would surely expect the soil to be from the village of their birth. Not only would this be in accord with the Muslim notion that the original and eventual homes are the same, but it would also confirm that earth is for the physical body and heaven for the spiritual one.

It is important to bury the body on the day of death. Villagers' concern about the treatment of the body after death was made clear by the insistence with which they asked about customs in the United States. "Do you wash the bodies?" "Do you burn them?" "Do you put them in the freezer to await a cure?" "How are they placed in the grave?" "What do they wear?" Some questions I could not answer. In the United States, not only is the subject of death generally avoided, but the details of burial tend to be left to professionals; in the village, everyone was knowledgeable on this subject. I realized also that their questions were a way of asking what they should do with me if I should die in the village. During my first six months in the village, I became quite morbid because their questions forced me to confront that ever-present possibility.

Washing the body after death is as important as washing a baby after birth and washing after sexual intercourse. The profane residues of bodiliness must be removed so that the body may enter the next world pure and clean. The imam washes men's bodies; women wash women's bodies. There is no special woman assigned to do this; usually it is some woman in the family. Not every woman will take on this task, as I learned when Fatma told me she was too afraid to wash her mother's body.

After the body is washed, cotton is placed in the eyes, nose, and ears, the avenues of sensual and social engagement with the world, the places where the boundaries of personhood are permeable. The body is left naked and wrapped in a seamless white cloth (*kefen*) much the way a baby is wrapped in *kundak* (swaddling cloth). The body of a man is removed from the house, a female symbol of earthly dwelling, and taken to the mosque—the house of God, a spiritual dwelling—to be joined for one last time in the communal fellowship of Islam. A woman's body is taken directly from the house to the *mezar* (cemetery). Her exclusion from the *cemaat*, the congregation or religious community, reflects her lack of a socially ratified spiritual identity.

As soon as the *ezan* is heard, all work ceases. The men perform ablutions and rush off to the mosque. The *Yasin surası* (Sura 36) is recited, ending with "Glory be to Him whose Hand is the dominion over all things. Unto Him ye will be brought back." This is very close to the Christian prayer "Into Thy hand I commend my spirit." The men proceed en masse to the cemetery to bury the body. Women are not allowed to be present. Some women explained that this is because the *nikâh* (engagement or marriage) is broken at death, because death releases the couple from the bonds of marriage. It would seem to follow that women are not reunited with their husbands in Heaven (cf. Saadawi 1989: 56–57). Other women believed not only that the *nikâh* survived death, but that they would be reunited with their husbands in the other world. In either event, a prohibition based on *nikâh* considerations would apply only to the burial of one's husband, not to that of one's father, brother, uncle, son, or other male relative or fellow villager. Clearly something else is involved.

Since death is the means to the second or higher birth (Sura 2: 28; 40: 11),[31] it is not surprising to find that the practices surrounding death are intimately related to ideas of procreation and birth. Women nurture and transform the seed in the soil of the womb and bring it forth embodied. Birth is an affair of women. Death and entombment of the body in the earth's soil are men's affairs. If birth is the coming forth of embodied seed, the dead body is the symbolic equivalent of seed planted in the earth to be born in the other world. Men, invoking the assistance of God as they do during insemination, officiate at the ritual of burial; women are symbolically identified with the tomb, the earth. Some would see the process as procreation in reverse; the corpse becomes disembodied in the grave and the seed-soul, like semen, "spurts out like a jet of water" to be born into the next world (Smith and Haddad 1981: 37). Yet even this birth must be achieved through a symbolically female medium, the earth. "At death, with reference to the fuller life

31. In Christianity baptism is considered to be a "second birth," a means of washing away the signs (or sins) of the profane birth from woman and rebirth into the spiritual community of God the father. In Islam there is no comparable ritual, but death takes on much the same meaning. This was made clear to me by my total misinterpretation of the wall hanging previously discussed: what I had assumed was the birth of a person into the beauties of the world turned out to be the birth of a person into *Cennet*. This interpretation is further affirmed by the practice of reciting the "Mevlidi Şerifi," a poem about Muhammed's birth, on the occasion or the anniversary of a death.

awaiting it, the soul is, so to speak, in the condition of a sperm drop. It passes through a stage which may be compared metaphorically to the womb, where it develops the faculties that may be needed in, and would be appropriate to, the conditions of the Hereafter. Its birth into a new life after passing through the process of developing its faculties to a certain degree is the resurrection" (Khan 1962: 187).

The earth, like a woman's body, is merely a temporary place of incubation; the essential person is neither of woman nor of the earth. Some villagers thought that the person would be born whole in the next world, others that just the soul persisted. In either case the second birth was imagined as spiritual, not physical; the physical body is left behind.

From the mosque, men accompany the body in procession to the cemetery; women gather at the house of the deceased to pay respects to the surviving female relatives. In contrast to the formality and dignity of the men's procession, women's gatherings were emotional scenes. Women are expected to cry; their free-flowing tears correspond to the free-flowing expression of emotion. A woman cries when a daughter marries and leaves home; on the occasion of a death it is more likely to be a daughter crying for her mother. I participated in one gathering of a neighbor whose mother had died. She cried and moaned "Mother, why did you leave me?" Her tears brimmed over her eyes and flowed down her face; like all other transgressions of bodily boundaries, crying was considered, at least by the men, to be shameful and sometimes even *günah* (sinful). What should be contained and kept inside was moving outside. Men said it showed that women are *vadık*, meaning animal-like, having emotion but no intelligence; in other words, without spirit.[32] Recalling that the power of discernment, the age of reason, is intimately linked to sexuality may help to give another view on women's crying. Semen as the spiritual essence of a man is connected in some way to the head, the locus of reason; it is conducted via the man's spinal column into creative production, and it is also under his control. The attainment of sexual maturity for women is signaled by menstrua-

---

32. Sabbah (1984: 32–33) discusses the "keen intelligence" of women in terms that seem to imply something nearer to animal-like cunning than to what is usually meant by intelligence. Turks have a saying about women that is relevant: "Saçı uzun, aklı kısa"—hair long, intelligence (or wisdom) short. Boddy (1986) discusses a similar view among Sudanese Muslims; women are thought to have more *nafs* (animal-like force), men more *'aqel* (reason, rationality, and the ability to control emotions). *'Aqel* is the Arabic form of *akil*.

tion, something not under their control and also without "spirit."[33] One might imagine that women's *akıl* (intelligence, discernment) is not contained and channeled, but seeps out through many openings and is diffused. Women are more embodied than men, and are more attached to their bodies and to those of others.

During the "wakes" I observed and participated in, women packed close together, supporting the grieving woman and each other; they wiped the bereaved's tears and face with lemon cologne, and brought her a glass of water with a twist of lemon. Others picked up the moaning in sympathy, and recounted events of the dead person's life including those that led up to the death—when the deceased first felt ill, if and when he or she consulted a doctor or went to the hospital. At the wake of our *bakkalcı*, I, though a *gavur* (infidel), was given the place of honor next to the widow. She was pleased to have the likeness of her deceased husband in the form of a photograph I had taken, and later we had an enlargement made. Strangely enough, though a grandchild was born at just the time of his death, the death completely overshadowed the birth.

For a few days following the burial the widow was surrounded by relatives, but all her children, except for a daughter with whom she did not get along, lived in the city and soon she was left alone. They invited her to come with them, but she did not want to leave the village. She couched her wishes in terms of her duties: "I have a cow to look after." Three months later, when she and another widow came to my house for coffee, she was still grieving and in tears. She confided that she had married at 14, had been married 43 years, and could not remember what it was like to be alone. After a time, however, she adjusted to her new situation and seemed to be fairly content. Other widows became quite revitalized, especially if they had children living in the village. But one sad woman, immediately after her husband died, took to her bed to await her own death, for which she had even bought an extra supply of *kefen* (shroud).

On their return from the cemetery men congregate in front of the house of the deceased while the imam gives a benediction. Money from

33. Eilberg-Schwartz (1990) notes similar connections between these bodily substances and processes and their relation to control in ancient Judaism. He goes on to discuss the shift from the focus on procreation via semen to the dissemination of knowledge via teaching, which in Judaism even up to the present, as well as Islam, has been a male enterprise. My own feeling is that these associations are behind centuries of prejudice against permitting women to study and teach.

the person's estate and/or collected from among relatives is distributed to the poor. These alms, called *iskat*, are meant to compensate for any religious duties the dead person may have left undone, such as not saying prayers, missing days of *oruç*, or not reconciling with persons with whom he or she may have fought. These lapses or transgressions were said to be *cevir*, a hindrance to the soul's progress into the next world.

After the corpse is buried and the men have left the cemetery, villagers believe that the dead person is questioned. Some thought the questioning began immediately in the grave; others opined that the soul first went to *ahret*, where all the people in the other world assemble to hear the questioning by a *melek* (angel). Men's verbal capacity and power no doubt help them answer, whereas women's imputed lack of this power is a handicap. At this time, dead friends and relatives should also speak up for the deceased. It is typically women who make an *ahretlik arkadaşı*, a bond of friendship such that whoever first enters the other world can intercede for the other. The questions are simple: What is your religion? Who is your prophet? Did you keep *oruç*? Did you perform *namaz*? Did you keep your hair covered? It is said that for even one strand of hair exposed, women will burn ninety days in hell. The fact that hair can be very difficult to control may be part of the reason hell is pictured as being mainly occupied by women.

If the questions are answered satisfactorily, *Sirat*, the razor-sharp bridge leading to *Cennet*, opens out to allow the person to cross. If they are not, he or she falls into *Cehennem* (hell). Because hell is envisioned as a place of burning and fire, villagers contemplated cremation with horror. Cremation would not only preclude the questioning ritual and the decomposition of the body in the earth/womb, but would be equivalent to consigning someone to burn in hell. When I asked whether people who die in airplane crashes go to heaven, the answer was a hesitant no. Most villagers seemed to think that the decision between heaven and hell is made directly after death, though there is also a tradition that it is made only after the Last Days, until which time the dead are as if asleep. Villagers' discourse about the Last Days, the resurrection, and final judgment was not consistent with their apparent belief that deceased relatives and friends go directly to Paradise at death. This inconsistency they have in common with many others of all religions.

Mevlud

Birthdays are forgotten, but death as the more valued birth is re-membered and commemorated. Forty days after death, and then on some anniversaries of a death, a *mevlud* is held: a special ceremony at which the "Mevlidi Şerifi," a poem by Süleyman Celebi (d. 1421) about Muhammed's birth, is recited in the mosque. This was the only other occasion, besides evenings during Ramazan, that women were allowed in the mosque; and perhaps partly on this account women were quite enthusiastic about *mevluds*.[34]

Before going to a *mevlud*, as before any other service in the mosque, an *aptes* (ablution) must be performed. The hands are washed, the mouth is rinsed three times with water, water is taken into the nose and blown out three times, then water is smoothed over the head, arms, ears, and lastly the feet. In our village I, though *gavur*, was permitted to attend a *mevlud* if I performed the *aptes*. At another *mevlud* in a neighboring village, the men objected to my attending; but they were overruled by the women, who said I had made a proper *aptes*.

Women were permitted upstairs in a screened balcony; it was often very hot there, and we could not see the service. We sat in neat rows, and one woman who assumed the role of prayer leader stood in front facing us. She would indicate when prostrations should be made, and when it was time to turn to a neighbor and embrace her. Many of the women were softly crying; whether this was in memory of the dead, in sympathy with the bereaved, or simply because it is expected be-havior I do not know. No doubt it is a combination of sentiments and expectations.

In the balcony, and while the service was going on, young girls dis-tributed rose-flavored *lokum* (Turkish Delight) or cones of candy with *lokum* on top. These were meant to be taken home as mementoes. Rose water was sprinkled on outstretched hands, and at the end of the service the remainder was sprinkled on the floor.

Here again scent plays an important role not only in disguising the sensuality of body odors, but also in drawing a perfumed boundary between sacred and profane activity and in establishing a communion

34. In our village *mevluds* were for both men and women simultaneously, as they were not in a town in Eğirdir described by Tapper and Tapper (1987).

of believers. It is also believed that Muhammed's tears turned to roses. Thus the sprinkling of rose water at a *mevlud* may help to transmute the salty tears to perfumed ones, whose scent when wafted to the dead will bring pleasure. The practice may also be related to a few lines from the "Mevlidi Şerifi": "O Thou, the seal and warrant of the Prophets, whose light did make the whole world shine in brilliance, Whose rose-like beauty filled the world with roses."[35]

This poem is primarily an emotional and archetypal account of the miraculous birth of Muhammed, the signs of his precociousness, and his ascent to heaven, where he sees God face to face and returns with His message. It is neither factual nor realistic in tone, but characteristic of stories of the divine hero and perhaps especially reminiscent of Jesus:

> This night foretold in song and story
> In which the worlds rejoice to see his glory
> This night the world a paradise he maketh
> The Light God's mercy on mankind awaketh.

In orthodox Islam, Muhammed is not divine and should neither be worshiped nor be imagined as an intercessor with God on behalf of the dead. Yet the poem is suffused throughout with just these ideas:

> In that night when he *descended*
> A host of herald signs bespoke his coming

The heavens opened, the sun revolved around the house of his birth, and angels bearing banners announced the glad tidings of his birth:

> No son like thine, such strength and grace possessing
> Hath God to earth *sent down* for its redressing.

His birth is divine, he is seen as the last of the long line of divinely inspired prophets beginning with Adam on whom God has set the spark of light:

> From brow to brow, in linked chain unbroken
> The Light at last attained its goal, Muhammed.

And finally he is seen as Intercessor:

> Welcome since thou of both worlds are the Blessor
> Welcome to thee, the sinner's Intercessor.

35. This passage and those following are taken from the *Mevlidi Sherif*, translated by F. Lyman MacCallum (London: John Murray, 1943). The emphases are mine.

Toward the end of the poem a prayer of petition is said:

We make a gift of the merit and reward of this recitation to the honoured soul of our Master and Prophet; accept it we pray thee O Lord God. . . . Let thy mercy rejoice all the spirits of such as are departed from among the friends who have been responsible for this recitation of the Mevlidi Sherif, O Lord God.

The "Mevlidi Şerifi" is a joyous poem about birth, specifically about the "divine" birth of Muhammed; yet it is recited, not on the occasion of a birth of a child, but at death. This ceremony points clearly to the belief that human birth is profane and that death is the second and higher-order birth.[36] It also supports my argument that procreation and birth are the most encompassing ideas, the key symbols by which and through which the world is represented, perceived, and ordered.

Cennet, the Heavenly Garden

Villagers believe that persons are born into the other world not as babies, but in the prime of life or about thirty. *Cennet* is conceived as a Garden in which there is always cool water nearby and gentle breezes to refresh, where the inhabitants can eat and drink of the celestial victuals without defecation or urination, and where voluptuous pleasures abound. However, in Heaven as on Earth these benefits and joys are primarily for men.

Each man is believed to have 40, or 70, or in one delirious vision 4,900, houris (Sabbah 1984: 108) to attend him. Houris are voluptuous but virginal maidens who never were human earthly flesh. The Believer is imagined as surrounded by splendor and comfort and as spending his time making love. The Believer, it must be noted, is always imaged as male. According to Bouhdiba (1985), who has written a great deal about the Muslim vision of Paradise, the Believer is never fatigued and is able to maintain an eternal erection. Indeed, Bouhdiba describes Paradise as "the infinite orgasm"! Although men in heaven are continually

36. For a different emphasis see Tapper and Tapper 1987. My experience of village *mevluds* does not support these authors' interpretation that the ritual represents an exaltation of birth and motherhood and is therefore affirming of women. I would argue instead that it reinforces the dominant ideology of women's role and place. It is an exaltation of one birth, namely Muhammed's, just as Christianity exalts one birth, that of Jesus. If the *mevlud* were truly an exaltation of birth and motherhood, one would expect these to be more revered and valued in everyday life. In addition, the *mevlud* commemorates a death and normal births are not commemorated.

making love, there is no issue and no birth—intercourse without responsibility. A man's ultimate pleasure appears to consist of an endless supply of virgins to deflower, for after intercourse a houri becomes a virgin again.[37] Transposed and elaborated from earth to heaven is the idea that sexual pleasure for a man is intimately related to his being able to be the first to possess a woman. It is not mature sexual love, but a matter of being able to control a woman and have her devoted solely to the satisfaction of his needs. The houri has no personality or desire of her own; she is the projection and symbol of male desire. Woman is objectified and depersonalized. She is Pleasure.

It is not surprising, therefore, to find that there is great ambiguity surrounding the status of "real" women—the women who have died, the women who were wives of men—in heaven. Although Paradise seems to be populated by myriad maidens, there seems to be no room for women. When I asked village men if women would have a houri in heaven, a few of them grudgingly admitted that perhaps a woman might have a houri, but her houri would be a handmaiden, not a sexual partner. Indeed, there was ambiguity about whether women even go to heaven. When confronted directly, villagers equivocate. On the one hand, they say that women will join their husbands in *Cennet*; on the other hand, they say that although women can go to heaven, it is much more difficult.

The ambiguity about whether women go to heaven seems clearly related to the question of whether women have souls, and what "soul" means. In some contexts villagers will say that women do have souls; yet in others it is implied that they do not. *Can* is the word they use for soul, and as noted earlier it also means "life"; since it is *can* that the male transmits via seed, women do not have *can* in the same way that

37. No doubt this heavenly infibulation is less painful than the earthly variety. According to Bouhdiba (1985: 76), the bodies of the 70 houris that wait upon each man "are so diaphanous, so transparent that one can see the bones through the flesh and the marrow through the bones"; he does not explain why this should be so attractive. In the extraordinary detail expended on this celebration of sexuality Bouhdiba sees evidence of a positive attitude toward sexuality in Islam. It does not occur to him that he means a positive sexuality for men. The beautiful houri has no autonomy, no mind or feelings of her own; she is passive, an object created solely for the satisfaction of the male believer. The human female is not dissimilar: "She is made for his pleasure, his repose, his fulfillment" (ibid.: 11); she is never allowed to refuse her husband (ibid.: 89). Although Bouhdiba claims to base his view of women and the hierarchy between the sexes on the Qur'an, he has the audacity to claim that "one would seek in vain for the slightest trace of misogyny in the whole of the Quran."

men do.[38] If women do have souls, it is clear that those souls are more embedded in the carnal aspects of life than men's, making it more difficult to extricate women from the physical, material world and release them to heaven. This view, which no doubt accounts for the paucity of women in *Cennet*, is reinforced by a number of *hadith* (codified traditions), one of which states:

The majority of them [women] will be consigned to the Fire. This is said to have come from a vision of the Prophet about which he related, "I passed by the Fire and when I noted the intensity of its heat, I tarried; the most of those I saw therein were women who, if you put your trust in them, tell that with which they had been entrusted, and if you ask them (about something) they hide it, and if they are given (many things) they are ungrateful." (Smith and Haddad 1981: 162, translating from Ahmad ibn Hanbal's *Musnad*)

The ambivalence toward Woman is clearly drawn. On the one side she is pure pleasure, but only when depersonalized; conversely, "real" women are the means through which the sacred, creative fire of men is perpetuated. Once a woman has served this purpose, her gross body can be discarded, perhaps to be refined by the fires of hell. No doubt these views serve the ideological purpose of inspiring fear in women and keeping them in their place. Most women appear to internalize the male model while not identifying with the fate of women portrayed in it.[39] Nor have women generated a model of their own. The ambivalence about women is also projected onto the world—*bu dünya*—with which they are associated.

The other world, with all its delights and pleasures as well as the absence of work, appears as a vivid reality in the minds of villagers.[40]

38. "There is much evidence that amongst Turks, at least, and these not only of the uneducated masses, women are regarded as not having souls, at any rate on the same footing as men" (MacDonald 1922: 316). Admittedly, this was written some time ago, but the ambiguity remains, and not just among villagers but also among scholars of Muslim societies. For some conflicting views, see Smith and Haddad 1981: 234, n. 2; Boddy 1988: 5; Massignon 1968: 319; Rahman 1980: 17.

39. This is a very common experience among women. It is similar, for example, to the way women in Western culture have identified with male heroes of myths or novels or everyday life, only to be accused of resisting their feminine role. I believe that the resulting feeling of betrayal is what underlies much of the feminists' anger and fuels their critique. Few feminists anymore wish only to realize the male model; most question the entire system of beliefs that valorizes that model.

40. Sabbah (1984) calls it an "economy of gatherers," but even that implies some kind of work. She goes on to call it a consumer society in which all are dependent on the beneficence of God.

It not only offers a reward for hardships in this world, but functions to create a detachment from it. Neither this life nor this world is a thing in which to put one's faith or trust. Yet the promise of another life in the other world implies a devaluation or sacrifice, at least emotionally, of the only life and only world we know. Such an attitude has consequences for one's life and for the world that are rarely taken into consideration in development projects. In a word, why should villagers commit themselves to transforming this world into a garden when their major concern is with entering the Garden in the next world? This focus on heaven precludes certain kinds of discussions, and perhaps even certain kinds of thoughts. Indeed, the whole idea of attempting to transform this world into a garden would surely be interpreted as heretical, not only because the other world takes precedence but because transforming this world would require work. Since the Garden is symbolized as a place of rest, any such notion is *ters* (reversed, backwards), a contradiction.

Villagers are, of course, dependent on the earth and quite attached to their bit of soil. It is the only thing (besides women) that men will fight over and kill for. Yet this has far more to do with rights and possession than with the virtues of the land itself. Indeed, those who show too much devotion or commitment to their land, or become too involved in efforts to make profits, are felt to be in league with the Devil. Their priorities and orientation are also considered *ters*.

Although villagers would like their lot to be easier, I believe the seduction of the other world and the dispositions it inspires (cf. Geertz 1973; Bourdieu 1977) are a major obstacle to change. The attractions of this world are clearly luring some in that direction, but the change is accompanied by much displacement, alienation, ambivalence, and often sharp reaction.

At the center of this reaction is woman. She is both a symbol and a site of conflict. She symbolizes the seductions of the physical world; as men become more involved in it, many become even more zealous in their protection and control over women. This may be interpreted as a way of keeping control over a symbol of their cultural identity that they feel is slipping away. Men who are gradually being integrated into the modern world and becoming somewhat more progressive with regard to women are viewed by others as becoming less and less Muslim. Urban

Turks, most of whom dress and behave like Europeans, are considered to be, and often are, atheists.[41]

From the traditional perspective, it appears that woman is the linchpin keeping the cosmos on its ordered course, a function she accomplishes by being invisible and staying in her place. To change her place and thus the perception of her nature would be equivalent to unhinging the world and letting it spin off into chaos. In a sense, woman is like a cosmic "black hole" from which all things flow and toward which all things gravitate; like her cosmic model, she too is invisible. The entire religious system could be interpreted as an elaborate denial and "covering" of the power of women to bring forth life and sustain it, as well as an attempt to appropriate, channel, and control this power. But repressions return, projected in different forms that nevertheless reveal the source. The centrality of procreation and birth both in the system of symbols and in the preoccupation of life seems to confirm this. Even in the Hereafter, transcendent bliss is conceived in terms of the sensual/sexual pleasures of the female body. Heaven as well as earth is woman!

Finally, I close with the most commonly seen and heard blessing, one that in fact opens many human activities: *Bismillahirrahmanirrahim*— In the Name of God, The Compassionate, The Merciful. The last part of the word-phrase, *rahim*, means merciful; it is also a word for womb. As woman encloses the child in the womb, so does God embrace Creation.

41. The opposition between believer and atheist is itself created by the monotheistic traditions. As there is only one God, so there can be only two alternatives: belief and disbelief. Such a view forecloses other spiritual and moral options, leaving a void in those who no longer believe. This either-or view of things, I believe, is not unrelated to the rise of fundamentalist sentiments in the monotheistic faiths.

Selected Bibliography

Abadan-Unat, Nermin. 1978. "The Modernization of Turkish Woman." *Middle East Journal* 3: 291–306.

———, ed. 1979. *Türk Toplumunda Kadın.* Ankara: Turkish Social Science Association.

Abdul-Rauf, Muhammed. 1978. "Pilgrimage to Mecca." *National Geographic,* November: 581–607.

Abu-Lughod, Lila. 1986. *Veiled Sentiments.* Berkeley: University of California Press.

Abu-Zahra, Nadia. 1970. "Reply to Antoun." *American Anthropologist* 72: 1079–87.

An Account of the Activities of the Etimesgut Rural Health District, 1970–74. 1975. Ankara: Hacettepe University, Institute of Community Medicine.

Acıpayamlı, Orhan. 1974. *Türkiyede Doğumlu ilgili adet ve inanmaların etudu.* Erzurum: Atatürk Universitesi yayınları.

Adivar, Halide Edip. 1935. *Conflict of East and West in Turkey.* Lahore: Kashmir Bazar.

Ağaoğulları, Mehmet Ali. 1987. "The Ultranationalist Right." In *Turkey in Transition,* ed. Irvin C. Schick and Ertugrul Ahmet Tonak, 177–217. Oxford: Oxford University Press.

Ahmad, Feroz. 1977. *The Turkish Experiment in Democracy, 1950–1975.* Boulder, CO: Westview Press.

Ahmed, Akbar. 1986. *Toward Islamic Anthropology.* Herndon, VA: International Institute of Islamic Thought.

Ahmed, Leila. 1989. "Arab Culture and Writing Women's Bodies." *Feminist Issues* 9(1): 41–55.

Allman, James, ed. 1978. *Women's Status and Fertility in the Muslim World.* New York: Praeger Publishers.

Altorki, Soraya. 1980. "Milk Kinship in Arab Society: An Unexplored Problem in the Ethnography of Marriage." *Ethnology* 19: 233–44.

And, Metin. 1981. "Permanence des civilisations Anatoliennes." *Objets et Monde* 21: 5–11.

Anderson, J. G. C. 1897 and 1899. *Annual of the British School of Athens.* London: Macmillan.

Antoun, Richard. 1968. "On the Modesty of Women in Arab Muslim Villages:

A Study in the Accommodation of Tradition." *American Anthropologist* 70: 671–97.

———. 1989. *Muslim Preacher in the Modern World.* Princeton: Princeton University Press.

Ardener, Edwin. 1981*a* [1975]. "Belief and the Problem of Women." In *Perceiving Women,* ed. Shirley Ardener, 1–17. New York: John Wiley and Sons.

———. 1981*b* [1975]. "The Problem Revisited." Ibid., 19–27.

Ardener, Shirley, ed. 1978. *Defining Female: The Nature of Women in Society.* New York: John Wiley and Sons.

———, ed. 1981. *Women and Space: Ground Rules and Social Maps.* New York: St. Martin's Press.

Arı, Oğuz. 1977. *Readings in Rural Sociology.* Istanbul: Boğaziçi University Publication.

Aristotle. 1979. *Generation of Animals,* trans. A. L. Peck. Cambridge, MA: Harvard University Press.

Armstrong, Harold C. 1933. *Gray Wolf: Mustafa Kemal, An Intimate Study of a Dictator.* New York: Minton, Balch.

Ashley-Montagu, M. F. 1974 [1937]. *Coming into Being among the Australian Aborigines.* London: George Routledge and Sons.

Aswad, Barbara. 1967. "Key and Peripheral Roles of Noble Women in a Middle East Plains Village." *Anthropological Quarterly* 40: 139–52.

———. 1974. "Visiting Patterns among Women of the Elite in a Small Turkish City." *Anthropological Quarterly* 47: 9–27.

Austin, R. W. J. 1983. "Islam and the Feminine." In *Islam in the Modern World,* ed. Denis MacEoin and Ahmed al-Shahi. New York: St. Martin's Press.

Aydemir, S. S. 1969. *Tek Adam.* Istanbul: Remzi Kitabevi.

Ayoub, Millicent. 1959. "Parallel Cousin Marriage and Endogamy: A Study in Sociometry." *Southwestern Journal of Anthropology* 15: 266–75.

Balçı, Mustafa. 1980. "Ana katliama: kürtaj yasağının kurbanları" (Mother Massacre: The Forbidden Sacrifices of Abortion). *Cümhüriyet,* January 22–29.

Barnes, J. A. 1973. "Genetrix : Genitor :: Nature : Culture." In *The Character of Kinship,* ed. Jack Goody, 61–87. Cambridge, Eng.: Cambridge University Press.

Barth, Frederick. 1954. "Father's Brother's Daughter Marriage in Kurdistan." *Southwestern Journal of Anthropology* 10: 164–71.

Başgöz, İlhan. 1983. "The Name and Society: A Case Study of Personal Names in Turkey." Paper presented at Center for Middle East Studies, University of Chicago.

Bates, Daniel. 1970. "Normative and Alternative Systems of Marriage among the Yoruk of SE Turkey." *Anthropological Quarterly* 47: 270–87.

Beck, Lois. 1980. "The Religious Lives of Muslim Women." In *Women in Contemporary Muslim Societies,* ed. Jane Smith, 27–60. Lewisburg, PA: Bucknell University Press.

Beck, Lois, and Nikki Keddie, eds. 1978. *Women in the Muslim World*. Cambridge, MA: Harvard University Press.

Benedict, Peter. 1974. "The Kabul Günü: Structured Visiting in an Anatolian Provincial Town." *Anthropological Quarterly* 47: 28–47.

———. 1976. "Aspects of the Domestic Cycle in a Turkish Provincial Town." In *Mediterranean Family Structures*, ed. J. G. Peristiany. Cambridge, Eng.: Cambridge University Press.

Benveniste, Emile. 1971. *Problems in General Linguistics*. Coral Gables, FL: University of Miami Press.

Berg, Charles. 1951. *The Unconscious Significance of Hair*. London: George Allen and Unwin.

Berger, John. 1979. *Pig Earth*. New York: Pantheon Books.

Berkes, Niyazı. 1954. "Ziya Gökalp: His Contribution to Turkish Nationalism." *Middle East Journal* 8: 375–90.

———. 1964. *The Development of Secularism in Turkey*. Montreal: McGill University Press.

Blacking, John, ed. 1977. *The Anthropology of the Body*. London: Academic Press.

Blok, Anton. 1981. "Rams and Billy-Goats: A Key to the Mediterranean Code of Honour." *Man* 16(3): 427–40.

Blunt, Mrs. John E. 1878. *The People of Turkey*. London: John Murray.

Boddy, Janice. 1982. "Womb as Oasis: The Symbolic Context of Circumcision in Rural Northern Sudan." *American Ethnologist* 9: 682–98.

———. 1986. "Spirits and Selves in Northern Sudan: The Cultural Therapeutics of Possession and Trance." *American Ethnologist* 15:1, 4–27.

———. 1989. *Wombs and Alien Spirits: Women, Men, and the Zar Cults in Northern Sudan*. Madison, WI: University of Wisconsin Press.

Boissevain, Jeremy. 1979. "Towards a Social Anthropology of the Mediterranean." *Current Anthropology* 20(1): 81–85.

Bouhdiba, Abdelwahab. 1985 [1975]. *Sexuality in Islam*, trans. Alan Sheridan. London: Routledge and Kegan Paul.

Bourdieu, Pierre. 1962. *The Algerians*. Boston: Beacon Press.

———. 1963. "The Attitude of the Algerian Peasant toward Time." In *Mediterranean Countrymen*, ed. Julian Pitt-Rivers, 55–72. Paris: Mouton.

———. 1966. "The Sentiment of Honour in Kabyle Society." In *Honour and Shame: The Values of Mediterranean Society*, ed. J. G. Peristiany. London: Weidenfeld and Nicolson.

———. 1977. *Outline of a Theory of Practice*. Cambridge Studies in Social Anthropology. Cambridge, Eng.: Cambridge University Press.

———. 1979. *Algeria 1960*. Cambridge, Eng.: Cambridge University Press.

Brandes, Stanley. 1980. *Metaphors of Masculinity: Sex and Status in Andalusian Folklore*. Philadelphia: University of Pennsylvania Press.

———. 1987. *Forty: The Age and the Symbol*. Knoxville, TN: University of Tennessee Press.

Briefing Paper for the UNFPA Basic Needs Mission, 1979. Ankara: Office of the UNFPA.

328   Bibliography

Burdick, Eugene, and H. Wheeler. 1962. *Fail-Safe*. New York: McGraw-Hill.

deBusbecq, Ogier G. 1968. *The Turkish Letters of Ogier deBusbecq*, trans. Edward Forster. Oxford: Clarendon Press.

Butler, Judith. 1990. *Gender Trouble*. New York: Routledge.

Campbell, John Kennedy. 1964. *Honour, Family and Patronage*. New York: Oxford University Press.

Cansever, Gocke. 1965. "Psychological Effects of Circumcision." *British Journal of Medical Psychiatry* 38: 321–26.

Casson, Ronald, and Banu Özertuğ. 1974. "Semantic Structure and Social Structure in a Central Anatolian Village." *Anthropological Quarterly* 47: 347–73.

Celebi, Suleyman. 1943. *Mevlidi Sherif*, trans. F. Lyman MacCallum. London: John Murray.

Chodorow, Nancy. 1978. *The Reproduction of Mothering: Psychoanalysis and the Sociology of Gender*. Berkeley: University of California Press.

Collier, Jane. 1986. "From Mary to Modern Woman: The Material Basis of Marianismo and Its Transformation in a Spanish Village." *American Ethnologist* 13(1): 100–107.

Collier, Jane, and Sylvia Yanagisako, eds. 1987. *Gender and Kinship: Essays toward a Unified Analysis*. Stanford: Stanford University Press.

Comaroff, Jean. 1985. "Bodily Reform as Historical Practice: The Semantics of Resistance in Modern South Africa." *International Journal of Psychology* 20: 541–67.

Coward, Rosalind. 1983. *Patriarchal Precedents: Sexuality and Social Relations*. London: Routledge and Kegan Paul.

Crone, Patricia, and Michael Cook. 1977. *Hagarism*. Cambridge, Eng.: Cambridge University Press.

Cuisenier, Jean. 1964. "Matériaux et hypothèses pour une étude des structures de la parenté en Turquie." *L'Homme* 4: 71–89.

Cunningham, Clark E. 1974. "Order in the Atoni House." In *Right and Left*, ed. Rodney Needham, 204–38. Chicago: University of Chicago Press.

Daniel, E. Valentine. 1984. *Fluid Signs: Being a Person the Tamil Way*. Berkeley: University of California Press.

Dankoff, Robert. 1972. "Kasari on the Tribal and Kinship Organization of the Turks." *Archivum Ottomanicum* 4: 27–44.

Davis, Fanny E. 1968. "Two Centuries of the Ottoman Lady." Ph.D. diss., Columbia University.

Davis, John. 1977. *People of the Mediterranean*. London: Routledge and Kegan Paul.

de Beauvoir, Simone. 1968 [1949]. *The Second Sex*, trans. H. M. Parshley. New York: Random House.

Dede Körküt, trans. Geoffrey. 1974. London: Penguin Books.

Delaney, Carol. 1977. "The Legacy of Abraham." In *Beyond Androcentrism*, ed. Rita Gross. Missoula, MT: Scholars Press.

————. 1986. "The Meaning of Paternity and the Virgin Birth Debate." *Man* 21(3): 494–513.

————. 1987. "Seeds of Honor, Fields of Shame." In *Honor and Shame and the Unity of the Mediterranean,* ed. David Gilmore, 35–48. Special Publication #22, American Anthropological Association, Washington, DC.

————. 1988. "Mortal Flow: Menstruation in Turkish Village Society." In *Blood Magic: The Anthropology of Menstruation,* ed. Thomas Buckley and Alma Gottlieb, 75–93. Berkeley: University of California Press.

————. 1989. "Participant-Observation: The Razor's Edge." *Dialectical Anthropology* 13(3): 291–300.

————. 1990. "The Hajj: Sacred and Secular." *American Ethnologist* 17(3): 513–30.

Devisch, Renaat. 1981. "Semantic Patterning of Fertility and Gynaecological Healing: Some Anthropological Perspectives." In *Reversibility of Sterilization: Psycho(patho)logical Aspects,* ed. P. Nijs˘and I. Brosnens. Leuven, Belgium: Acco.

————. 1983. "Space-Time and Bodiliness: A Semantic-Praxiological Approach." In *New Perspectives in Belgian Anthropology,* ed. R. Pinxten. Gottingen: Herodot.

Dittemore, Margaret. 1983. "Zemzemiye: An Ethno-Archeological Study of a Turkish Village." Ph.D. diss., University of Chicago.

Dobkin, Marlene. 1967. "Social Ranking in the Women's World of Purdah: A Turkish Example." *Anthropological Quarterly* 40: 65–72.

Dodd, C. H. 1983. *The Crisis of Turkish Democracy.* Beverly, U.K.: Eothen Press.

Douglas, Mary. 1966. *Purity and Danger.* London: Routledge and Kegan Paul.

————. 1970. *Natural Symbols.* New York: Random House.

Duben, Alan. 1985. "Nineteenth and Twentieth Century Ottoman-Turkish Family and Household Structures." In *Family in Turkish Society,* ed. Turkoz Erder. Ankara: Turkish Social Science Association.

Dubetsky, A. 1973. "A New Community in Istanbul." Ph.D. diss., University of Chicago.

Dubisch, Jill, ed. 1986. *Gender and Power in Rural Greece.* Princeton: Princeton University Press.

duBois, Page. 1988. *Sowing the Body.* Chicago: University of Chicago Press.

DuBoulay, Juliet. 1974. *Portrait of a Greek Mountain Village.* Oxford: Clarendon Press.

————. 1986. "Women—Images of Their Nature and Destiny in Rural Greece." In *Gender and Power in Rural Greece,* ed. Jill Dubisch, 139–68. Princeton: Princeton University Press.

Dumont, Paul. 1984. "The Origins of Kemalist Ideology." In *Atatürk and the Modernization of Turkey,* ed. Jacob Landau, 25–44. Boulder, CO: Westview Press.

Dundes, Alan, Jerry Leach, and Bora Özkök. 1972. "The Strategy of Turkish Dueling Rhymes." In *Directions in Sociolinguistics,* ed. J. Gumperz and Dell Hymes, 130–60. New York: Holt, Rinehart and Winston.

Durkheim, Emile. 1965 [1915]. *The Elementary Forms of the Religious Life.* New York: Free Press.

Dwyer, Daisy Hilse. 1978. *Images and Self Images: Men and Women in Morocco.* New York: Columbia University Press.

Edholm, F., O. Harris, and K. Young. 1977. "Conceptualizing Women." *Critique of Anthropology* 9–10: 101–30.

Ehrenreich, Barbara, and Deirdre English. 1973. *Witches, Midwives and Nurses: A History of Women Healers.* New York: Feminist Press.

Eickelman, Dale. 1978. "The Art of Memory: Islamic Education and Its Social Reproduction." *Comparative Studies in Society and History* 20(4): 485–516.

———. 1989 [1981]. *The Middle East: An Anthropological Approach.* Englewood Cliffs, NJ: Prentice-Hall.

Eilberg-Schwartz, Howard. 1990. *The Savage in Judaism.* Bloomington: Indiana University Press.

Eliade, Mircea. 1971. "Spirit, Seed and Light." *History of Religions* 11(1): 1–30.

el-Zein, Abdul Hamid. 1977. "Beyond Ideology and Theology: The Search for the Anthropology of Islam." *Annual Review of Anthropology* 6: 227–54.

Encyclopedia of Islam. 1965. Leiden: E. J. Brill.

Engelbrektsson, Ulla-Britt. 1978. *The Force of Tradition: Turkish Migrants at Home and Abroad.* Göteborg: Acta Universitatis Gothoburgensis.

Engels, Frederick. 1972 [1884]. *The Origin of the Family, Private Property and the State.* New York: International Publishers.

Erdentuğ, Nermin. 1956. *Hal Koyunun Etnolojik Tetkiki.* Ankara: Turk Tarıh Kurumu Basımevi.

———. 1959. *A Study on the Social Structure of a Turkish Village.* Ankara: Ayyildiz Matbaası.

Erder, Turköz. 1985. *Family in Turkish Society.* Ankara: Turkish Social Science Association.

Esin, Emel. 1963. *Mecca the Blessed, Madina the Radiant.* London: Elek Books.

Evans-Pritchard, E. E. 1940. *The Nuer.* Oxford: Oxford University Press.

———. 1962. "Heredity and Gestation as the Azande See Them." In *Essays in Social Anthropology,* 117–30. London: Faber.

———. 1963. *The Position of Women in Primitive Society and Other Essays in Social Anthropology.* London: Faber and Faber.

Fallers, Lloyd, and Margaret Fallers. 1974. "Notes on an Advent Ramadan." *Journal of the American Academy of Religion* 42: 35–52.

———. 1976. "Sex Roles in Edremit." In *Mediterranean Family Structures,* ed. J. Peristiany, 243–260. Cambridge, Eng.: Cambridge University Press.

Farah, Madelain. 1984. *Marriage and Sexuality in Islam.* Salt Lake City: University of Utah Press.

Fernea, Robert A., and Elizabeth W. Fernea. 1972. "Variation in Religious Observance among Islamic Women." In *Scholars, Saints and Sufis: Muslim Religious Institutions since 1500,* ed. Nikki R. Keddie. Berkeley: University of California Press.

Ford, Clellan Stearns. 1945. *A Comparative Study of Human Reproduction*. New Haven: Yale University Publications in Anthropology.

Foucault, Michel. 1980. *The History of Sexuality*. New York: Vintage Books.

Fox, Greer L. 1975. "Love Match and Arranged Marriage in a Modernizing Nation: Mate Selection in Ankara, Turkey." *Journal of Marriage and the Family* 32: 180–93.

Freud, Sigmund. 1907. "On the Sexual Enlightenment of Children." In *The Standard Edition of the Complete Psychological Works of Sigmund Freud*. London: Hogarth Press, 1959.

———. 1908. "On the Sexual Theories of Children." In *The Standard Edition*.

———. 1910. "Leonardo da Vinci and a Memory of His Childhood." In *The Standard Edition*.

———. 1913. *Totem and Taboo*. In *The Standard Edition*.

———. 1939. *Moses and Monotheism*. In *The Standard Edition*.

Friedl, Ernestine. 1962. *Vasilika: A Village in Modern Greece*. New York: Holt, Rinehart and Winston.

———. 1967. "The Position of Women: Appearance and Reality." *Anthropological Quarterly* 40: 97–108.

Friedrich, Paul. 1979. *Language, Context and the Imagination*. Stanford: Stanford University Press.

Fruzzetti, Lina, and Akos Östör. 1984. "Seed and Earth: A Cultural Analysis of a Bengali Town." In *Kinship and Ritual in Bengal: Anthropological Essays*, 79–124. New Delhi: South Asian Publishers.

Fustel de Coulanges, Numa Denis. 1956 [1864]. *The Ancient City*, trans. Willard Small (1873). Reprinted New York: Doubleday Anchor Books.

Gaffney, Patrick. 1982. "Shaykh, Khutba and Masjid: The Role of the Local Islamic Preacher in Upper Egypt." Ph.D. diss., University of Chicago.

Garnett, Lucy. 1909. *Home Life in Turkey*. New York: MacMillan Co.

Gawrych, George. 1988. "Kemal Atatürk's Politico-Military Strategy in the Turkish War of Independence, 1919–22." *Journal of Strategic Studies* 11(3): 318–41.

Geertz, Clifford. 1973. "Religion as a Cultural System." In *The Interpretation of Cultures*. New York: Basic Books.

———. 1975 [1968]. *Islam Observed*. Chicago: University of Chicago Press.

———. 1976. "From the Native's Point of View: On the Nature of Anthropological Understanding." In *Meaning in Anthropology*, ed. Keith H. Basso and Henry A. Selby. Albuquerque, NM: University of New Mexico Press.

Gibb, H. A. R. 1978 [1949]. *Mohammedanism*. Oxford: Oxford University Press.

Gilligan, Carol. 1982. *In a Different Voice*. Cambridge, MA: Harvard University Press.

Gilmore, David D. 1982. "Anthropology of the Mediterranean Area." *Annual Review of Anthropology* 11: 175–205.

———, ed. 1987. *Honor and Shame and the Unity of the Mediterranean*. Washington, DC: American Anthropological Association.

————. 1990. *Manhood in the Making.* New Haven, CT: Yale University Press.

Gimbutas, Marija. 1982. *The Goddesses and Gods of Old Europe.* Berkeley: University of California Press.

Gökalp, Ziya. 1968. *The Principles of Turkism,* trans. Robert Devereux. Leiden: E. J. Brill.

Good, Mary Jo DelVecchio. 1980. "Of Blood and Babies: The Relationship of Popular Islamic Physiology to Fertility." *Social Science and Medicine* 14: 147–56.

Goody, Jack, ed. 1973. *The Character of Kinship.* Cambridge, Eng.: Cambridge University Press.

————. 1976. *Production and Reproduction: A Comparative Study of the Domestic Domain.* Cambridge, Eng.: Cambridge University Press.

Grandquist, Hilma. 1947. *Birth and Childhood among the Arabs.* Helsingfors: Soderstrom.

Gulick, John. 1955. *Social Structure and Culture Change in a Lebanese Village.* New York: Viking Fund Publications in Anthropology.

Güntekin, Reşat Nuri. 1949. *The Autobiography of a Turkish Girl,* trans. Wyndham Deedes. London: George Allen and Unwin.

Gurney, Oliver. 1952. *The Hittites.* London: Penguin Books.

Haddad, Yvonne Yazbeck. 1980. "Traditional Affirmations Concerning the Role of Women as Found in Contemporary Arab Islamic Literature." In *Women in Contemporary Muslim Societies,* ed. Jane Smith, 61–86. Lewisburg, PA: Bucknell University Press.

Haire, Doris B. 1973. "The Cultural Warping of Childbirth." *Journal of Tropical Pediatrics and Environmental Health* 19: 171–91.

Hallpike, C. R. 1969. "Social Hair." *Man* 4: 256–64.

Harding, Sandra. 1986. *The Science Question in Feminism.* Ithaca, NY: Cornell University Press.

Harris, Olivia, and Kate Young. 1981. "Engendered Structures: Some Problems in the Analysis of Reproduction." In *Anthropology of Pre-capitalist Societies,* ed. Joel S. Kahn and Joseph R. Llobera. London: Macmillan Press.

Henze, Paul B. 1982. "Turkey: On the Rebound." *The Wilson Quarterly* 6(5): 108–25.

Hertz, Robert. 1973. "The Pre-eminence of the Right Hand." In *Right and Left,* ed. Rodney Needham, 3–31. Chicago: University of Chicago Press.

Herzfeld, Michael. 1980. "Honor and Shame: Problems in the Comparative Analysis of Moral Systems." *Man* 15: 339–51.

————. 1985. *The Poetics of Manhood: Contest and Identity in a Cretan Mountain Village.* Princeton: Princeton University Press.

————. 1986. "Within and Without: The Category of 'Female' in the Ethnography of Modern Greece." In *Gender and Power in Rural Greece,* ed. Jill Dubisch, 215–33. Princeton: Princeton University Press.

Hewson, M. Anthony. 1975. *Giles of Rome and the Medieval Theory of Conception.* London: Athlone Press.

Hilal, Jamil. 1971. "The Management of Male Dominance in Traditional Arab Culture: A Tentative Model." *Civilizations* 19: 85–95.

Hill, Polly. 1986. *Development Economics on Trial.* Cambridge, Eng.: Cambridge University Press.

Hirschon, Renée. 1978. "Open Body/Closed Space: The Transformation of Female Sexuality." In *Defining Female*, ed. Shirley Ardener, 66–88. New York: John Wiley and Sons.

——. 1981. "Essential Objects and the Sacred: Interior and Exterior Space in an Urban Greek Locality." In *Women and Space: Ground Rules and Social Maps*, ed. Shirley Ardener, 72–88. New York: St. Martin's Press.

Hodgson, Marshall G. S. 1974. *The Venture of Islam.* Chicago: University of Chicago Press.

Hotham, David. 1972. *The Turks.* London: John Murray.

International Social Science Bulletin. 1957. Special Issue: "The Reception of Foreign Law in Turkey."

Jeffrey, Patricia. 1979. *Frogs in a Well.* London: Zed Press.

Jody, Nina. 1978. "Production and Reproduction and the Status of Women." Ph.D. diss., University of New York, Stony Brook.

Jordan, Brigitte. 1978. *Birth in Four Cultures.* St. Albans, VT: Eden Press.

Kağıtçıbaşı, Çiğdem. 1977. *Cultural Values and Population Action Programs in Turkey.* United Nations Publication.

——, ed. 1982. *Sex Roles, Family, and Community in Turkey.* Bloomington, IN: Indiana University Press.

Kandiyoti, Deniz. 1974. "Social Change and Social Stratification in a Turkish Village." *Journal of Peasant Studies* 2: 206–19.

——. 1977. "Sex Roles and Social Change: A Comparative Appraisal of Turkey's Women." *Signs* 3: 57–73.

——. 1980. *Major Issues on the Status of Women in Turkey: Approaches and Priorities.* Ankara: Çağ Matbaası.

Karpat, Kemal. 1981. "Turkish Democracy at Impasse: Ideology, Party Politics and the Third Military Intervention." *International Journal of Turkish Studies* 2: 1–43.

Keddie, Nikki, ed. 1972. *Scholars, Saints and Sufis.* Berkeley: University of California Press.

Keller, Evelyn Fox. 1985. *Reflections on Gender and Science.* New Haven, CT: Yale University Press.

Keyser, James M. B. 1974. "The Middle Eastern Case: Is There a Marriage Rule?" *Ethnology* 42: 293–309.

Khan, Muhammad Z. 1962. *Islam: Its Meaning for Modern Man.* New York: Harper and Row.

Khuri, Fuat. 1970. "Parallel Cousin Marriage Reconsidered: A Middle Eastern Practice That Nullifies the Effects of Marriage on the Intensity of Family Relations." *Man* 4: 597–618.

Kinross, Lord. 1965. *Atatürk: A Biography of Mustafa Kemal, Father of Modern Turkey.* New York: William Morrow.

Kiray, Mübuccel. 1976. "The New Role of Mothers: Changing Intra-Familial Relationships in a Small Town in Turkey." In *Mediterranean Family Structures*, ed. J. Peristiany, 261–71. Cambridge, Eng.: Cambridge University Press.

Kudat, Ayşe. 1974. "Institutional Rigidity and Individual Initiative in Marriage of Turkish Peasants." *Anthropological Quarterly* 47: 288–303.

Landau, Jacob. 1974. *Radical Politics in Modern Turkey.* Leiden: E. J. Brill.

————, ed. 1984. *Atatürk and the Modernization of Turkey.* Boulder, CO: Westview Press.

Langer, Suzanne K. 1979 [1942]. *Philosophy in a New Key.* Cambridge, MA: Harvard University Press.

Laude-Cirtautas, Ilse. 1961. *Der Debrauch der Farbbezeichnungen in den Turdialekten.* Weisbaden: Ural-Altaic Bibliotek, No. 10.

Lawrence, Denise. 1988. "Menstrual Politics: Women and Pigs in Rural Portugal." In *Blood Magic: The Anthropology of Menstruation,* ed. Thomas Buckley and Alma Gottlieb. Berkeley: University of California Press.

Lazarus-Yafeh, Hava. 1981. *Some Religious Aspects of Islam.* Leiden: E. J. Brill.

Leach, Edmund. 1958. "Magical Hair." *Journal of the Royal Anthropological Institute* 88: 147–64.

————. 1961. "Two Essays Concerning the Symbolic Representation of Time." In *Rethinking Anthropology,* 124–36. London: Athlone Press.

————. 1966. *Genesis as Myth.* London: Jonathan Cape.

————. 1967. "Virgin Birth." In *Proceedings of the Royal Anthropological Institute, 1966–67,* 39–48.

Leach, Edmund, and D. Alan Aycock. 1983. *Structuralist Interpretations of Biblical Myth.* Cambridge, Eng.: Cambridge University Press.

Leder, Arnold. 1976. *Catalysts of Change: Marxist vs Muslim in a Turkish Community.* Austin: University of Texas Press.

Lévi-Strauss, Claude. 1983*a* [1958]. *Structural Anthropology,* trans. Claire Jacobson and Brooke Grundfest Schoepf. New York: Basic Books.

————. 1963*b* [1962]. *Totemism,* trans. Rodney Needham. Boston: Beacon Press.

————. 1969 [1949]. *Elementary Structures of Kinship,* trans. James Harle Belle, John Richard Von Sturmer, and Rodney Needham. Boston: Beacon Press.

————. 1973 [1962]. *The Savage Mind.* Chicago: University of Chicago Press.

————. 1975 [1955]. *Tristes Tropiques,* trans. John and Doreen Weightman. New York: Atheneum.

Lewis, Bernard. 1968 [1961]. *The Emergence of Modern Turkey.* Oxford: Oxford University Press.

————. 1988. *The Political Language of Islam.* Chicago: University of Chicago Press.

Lewis, G. L. 1975 [1967]. *Turkish Grammar.* Oxford: Clarendon Press.

————. 1984. "Atatürk's Language Reform as an Aspect of Modernization in the Republic of Turkey." In *Atatürk and the Modernization of Turkey,* ed. Jacob Landau, 295–320. Boulder, CO: Westview Press.

Lewis, Geoffrey. 1955. *Turkey.* New York: Frederick A. Praeger.

Lewis, Raphaela. 1971. *Everyday Life in Ottoman Turkey.* London: Batsford.

Lloyd, Genevieve. 1984. *The Man of Reason: "Male" and "Female" in Western Philosophy.* Minneapolis, MN: University of Minnesota Press.

Loeffler, Reinhold. 1988. *Islam in Practice: Religious Beliefs in a Persian Village.* Albany, NY: State University of New York Press.

Long, David Edwin. 1979. *The Hajj Today.* Albany, NY: State University of New York Press.

MacCormack, Carol, and Marilyn Strathern, eds. 1980. *Nature, Culture and Gender.* Cambridge, Eng.: Cambridge University Press.

MacDonald, D. B. 1922. "Immortality in Mohammedanism." In *Religion and the Future Life,* ed. E. H. Sneath, 295–320. New York: Fleming H. Revell.

Mackinnon, Catherine. 1981. "Feminism, Marxism, Method and the State: An Agenda for Theory." In *Feminist Theory: A Critique of Ideology,* ed. N. Keohane, M. Rosaldo, and B. Gelpi, 1–30. Chicago: University of Chicago Press.

Mackintosh, M. 1977. "Reproduction and Patriarchy: A Critique of Claude Meillassoux, *Femmes, Greniers et Capitaux." Capital and Class* 2: 119–27.

Magnarella, Paul. 1969. "Turkish Bridewealth Practice in Transition." *The Muslim World* 9: 142–52.

———. 1973. "The Reception of Swiss Family Law in Turkey." *Anthropological Quarterly* 46: 100–116.

———. 1974. *Tradition and Change in a Turkish Town.* Cambridge, MA: Schenkman.

———. 1979. *The Peasant Venture.* Cambridge, MA: Schenkman.

Magnarella, Paul, and Orhan Turkdoğan. 1973. "Descent, Affinity and Ritual Relations in Eastern Turkey." *American Anthropologist* 75: 1626–33.

Makal, Mahmut. 1954. *A Village in Anatolia,* trans. Sir Wyndham Deedes. London: Valentine, Mitchell.

Malinowski, Bronislaw. 1927. *The Father in Primitive Psychology.* London: Kegan Paul, Trench, Trubner.

———. 1954 [1948]. "Balima: The Spirits of the Dead in the Trobriand Islands." In *Magic, Science and Religion.* New York: Doubleday Anchor Books.

———. 1961 [1922]. *Argonauts of the Western Pacific.* New York: E. P. Dutton.

———. 1982 [1929]. *Sexual Life of Savages in Northwestern Melanesia.* London: Routledge and Kegan Paul.

Mandel, Ruth. 1989. "Turkish Headscarves and the Foreigner Problem." *The New German Critique* 46: 27–46.

Mansur, Fatma. 1972. *Bodrum: A Town in the Aegean.* Leiden: E. J. Brill.

Marcus, Julie. 1984. "Islam Women and Pollution in Turkey." *Journal of the Anthropological Association of Oxford* 15(3): 204–18.

Mardin, Şerif. 1962. *Genesis of Young Ottoman Thought.* Princeton: Princeton University Press.

———. 1973. "Center and Periphery Relations: A Key to Turkish Politics." *Daedalus* 102: 169–90.

Margulies, Ronnie, and Ergin Yildizoğlu. 1987. "Agrarian Change: 1923–70." In *Turkey in Transition*, ed. Irvin C. Schick and Ertuğrul Ahmet Tonak, 269–92. Oxford: Oxford University Press.

Martin, Emily. 1987. *The Woman in the Body*. Boston: Beacon Press.

Marx, Karl, and Frederick Engels. 1970 [1846]. *The German Ideology*, ed. C. J. Arthur. New York: International Publishers.

Massignon, Louis. 1957 [1951]. "Time in Islamic Thought." In *Papers from Eranos Yearbooks*, Vol. 3. Bollingen Series XXX. Princeton: Princeton University Press.

———. 1968. "Nature in Islamic Thought" and "Idea of the Spirit in Islam." In *Papers from Eranos Yearbooks*, Vol. 6. Bollingen Series XXX. Princeton: Princeton University Press.

Matthews, Anis David. 1977. *A Guide for Hajj and 'Umra*. Lahore: Kazi Publishers.

Mauss, Marcel. 1973. "Techniques of the Body." *Economy and Society* 2: 70–88.

Mead, Margaret. 1980. "On the Viability of Villages." In *Village Viability in Contemporary Society*, ed. Priscilla C. Reining and Barbara Lenherd, 19–31. Boulder, CO: Westview Press.

Meeker, Michael. 1970. "The Black Sea Turks: A Study of Honor, Descent and Marriage." Ph.D. diss., University of Chicago.

———. 1976. "Meaning and Society in the Middle East: The Black Sea Turks and the Levantine Arabs." *International Journal of Middle East Studies* 7: 243–70, 383–422.

Meier, Fritz. 1964 [1954]. "The Transformation of Man in Mystical Islam." In *Papers from Eranos Yearbooks*, Vol. 5. Bollingen Series XXX. Princeton: Princeton University Press.

———. 1971. "The Ultimate Origin and Hereafter in Islam." In *Islam and Its Cultural Divergence*, ed. G. L. Tikku, 96–112. Urbana, IL: University of Illinois Press.

Meillassoux, Claude. 1972. "From Reproduction to Production: A Marxist Approach to Economic Anthropology." *Economy and Society* 1: 93–105.

———. 1981 [1975]. *Maidens, Meal and Money: Capitalism and the Domestic Community*. Cambridge, Eng.: Cambridge University Press.

Mellaart, James. 1962–64. "Excavations at Çatal Hüyük." *Anatolian Studies*, Vols. 12–14.

———. 1965. *Earliest Civilizations of the Near East*. New York: McGraw-Hill.

Mernissi, Fatma. 1975. *Beyond the Veil: Male-Female Dynamics in a Modern Muslim Society*. Cambridge, MA: Schenkman.

Minai, Naila. 1981. *Woman in Islam*. London: John Murray.

Modernization in Turkish Villages. 1974. Ankara: Turkish Republic State Planning Organization.

Moore, Henrietta. 1988. *Feminism and Anthropology*. Minneapolis, MN: University of Minnesota Press.

Mopsik, Charles. 1989. "The Body of Engenderment in the Hebrew Bible, the

Rabbinic Tradition and the Kabbalah." *Zone: Fragments for a History of the Human Body* 3(1): 49–73.

Morgan, Lewis Henry. 1871. *Systems of Consanguinity and Affinity in the Human Family.* Washington, DC: Smithsonian Contributions to Knowledge, No. 17.

———. 1877. *Ancient Society.* New York: Henry Holt.

Morsy, Soheir. 1978. "Sex Roles, Power and Illness in an Egyptian Village." *American Ethnologist* 5: 137–50.

Morvaridi, Behrooz. n.d. "Gender Relations in Agriculture: Women in Turkey." Paper presented at conference on "Culture and Economy: Changes in Turkish Villages," London, May 1990.

Munson, Henry, Jr. 1986. "Geertz on Religion: The Theory and the Practice." *Religion* 16: 19–32.

Murphy, R., and L. Kasdan. 1959. "The Structure of Parallel Cousin Marriage." *American Anthropologist* 61: 17–29.

Musallam, Basim. 1983. *Sex and Society in Islam.* Cambridge, Eng.: Cambridge University Press.

Nasr, Seyyed Hossein. 1985 [1966]. *Ideals and Realities of Islam.* London: George Allen and Unwin.

Needham, Rodney, ed. 1973. *Right and Left.* Chicago: University of Chicago Press.

Noonan, John T. 1986 [1965]. *Contraception.* Cambridge, MA: Harvard University Press.

Obeyesekere, Gananath. 1981. *Medusa's Hair: An Essay on Personal Symbols and Religious Experience.* Chicago: University of Chicago Press.

O'Brien, Mary. 1979. "Reproducing Marxist Man." In *The Sexism of Social and Political Theory,* ed. Lorenne Clark and Lynda Lange. Toronto: University of Toronto Press.

———. 1981. *The Politics of Reproduction.* London: Routledge and Kegan Paul.

Olson, Emelie. 1985. "Muslim Identity and Secularism in Contemporary Turkey." *Anthropological Quarterly* 58(4): 161–71.

Ong, Walter. 1982. *Orality and Literacy: The Technologizing of the Word.* London: Methuen.

Onians, R. B. 1951. *The Origins of European Thought.* Cambridge, Eng.: Cambridge University Press.

Orga, Irfan. 1950. *Portrait of a Turkish Family.* New York: Macmillan.

Örnek, Sedat Veyis. 1971. *Anadolu folklorunde ölüm.* Ankara: Ankara Üniversitesi Basımevi.

———. 1979. *Geleneksel kulturumuzde çocuk.* Ankara: Türkiye Iş Bankası kultur yayınları.

Ortner, Sherry. 1973. "On Key Symbols." *American Anthropologist* 75: 1338–46.

———. 1974. "Is Female to Male as Nature Is to Culture?" In *Women, Culture and Society,* ed. M. Rosaldo and L. Lamphere, 67–87. Stanford: Stanford University Press.

———. 1984. "Theory in Anthropology since the Sixties." *Comparative Studies in Society and History* 26(1): 126–66.

Ortner, Sherry, and Harriet Whitehead. 1981. *Sexual Meanings: The Cultural Construction of Gender and Sexuality.* Cambridge, Eng.: Cambridge University Press.

Ott, Sandra. 1979. "Aristotle among the Basques: The Cheese Analogy of Conception." *Man* 14: 699–711.

Özbay, Ferhunde. 1982. "Women's Education in Rural Turkey." In *Sex Roles, Family, and Community in Turkey,* ed. Çiğdem Kağıtçıbaşı. Bloomington, IN: Indiana University Press.

Özbel, Kenan. 1976. *Türk Köylu Çorapları.* Ankara: Türkiye İş Bankası kultur yayınları.

Özertuğ, Banu. 1973. "Household Composition in a Turkish Village." Ph.D. diss., Stanford University.

Öztürk, Orhan. 1963. "Psychological Effects of Circumcision as Practised in Turkey." *Turkish Journal of Pediatrics,* No. 5.

————. 1964. "Folk Treatment of Mental Illness in Turkey." In *Magic, Faith and Healing,* ed. A. Kieve, 343–63. New York: Free Press.

————. 1965. "Childrearing Practices in Turkish Villages and the Major Area of Intra-psychic Conflict." *Turkish Journal of Pediatrics,* No. 7.

————. 1973. "Ritual Circumcision and Castration Anxiety." *Psychiatry* 36: 49–59.

Paige, Karen, and Jeffrey M. Paige. 1981. *The Politics of Reproductive Ritual.* Berkeley: University of California Press.

Papanek, Hanna. 1964. "The Woman Field Worker in a Purdah Society." *Human Organization* 23(2): 160–63.

————. 1973. "Purdah: Separate Worlds and Symbolic Shelter." *Comparative Studies in Society and History* 15(3): 289–325.

Partin, Harry Baxter. 1967. "The Muslim Pilgrimage: Journey to the Center." Ph.D. diss., University of Chicago.

Peck, A. L. 1979 [1942]. Preface to Aristotle's *Generation of Animals.* Cambridge, MA: Harvard University Press.

Peristiany, J. G. 1966. *Honour and Shame: The Values of Mediterranean Society.* London: Weidenfeld and Nicolson.

————, ed. 1976. *Mediterranean Family Structures.* Cambridge, Eng.: Cambridge University Press.

Pickthall, Mohammed Marmaduke. n.d. *The Meaning of the Glorious Koran.* New York: Mentor Books.

Pierce, Joe E. 1964. *Life in a Turkish Village.* New York: Holt, Rinehart and Winston.

Pitt-Rivers, Julian, ed. 1963. *Mediterranean Countrymen.* Paris: Mouton.

————. 1966. "Honour and Social Status." In *Honour and Shame: The Values of Mediterranean Society,* ed. J. G. Peristiany. London: Weidenfeld and Nicolson.

————. 1977. *The Fate of Shechem or the Politics of Sex: Essays in the Anthropology of the Mediterranean.* Cambridge, Eng.: Cambridge University Press.

Rahman, Fazlur. 1980. *Major Themes of the Qur'an.* Minneapolis, MN: Bibliotheca Islamica.

Ramsay, W. M. 1890. *Historical Geography of Asia Minor.* Supplementary Papers of the Royal Geographical Society, No. 4. London: John Murray.

Rapp, Rayna. 1988. "Chromosomes and Communication: The Discourse of Genetic Counseling." *Medical Anthropology Quarterly* 2: 143–57.

Rathbun, Carole. 1972. *The Village in the Turkish Novel and Short Story: 1920–1955.* Paris: Mouton.

Redfield, Robert. 1956. *Peasant Society and Culture.* Chicago: University of Chicago Press.

Reinhart, Kevin. 1990. "Impurity/No Danger." *History of Religions* 30(1): 1–24.

Ricoeur, Paul. 1976. *Interpretation Theory.* Fort Worth, TX: Texas Christian University Press.

Robinson, Richard. 1965. *Letters from Turkey.* Printed for the Peace Corps by permission of the Institute for Current World Affairs. Istanbul: Files of Roberts College.

Rogers, Barbara. 1980. *The Domestication of Women: Discrimination in Developing Societies.* New York: St. Martin's Press.

Rogers, Susan Carol. 1978. "Women's Place: A Critical Review of Anthropological Theory." *Comparative Studies in Society and History* 20: 123–62.

Roper, Joyce. 1974. *The Women of Nar.* London: Faber and Faber.

Rosaldo, Michelle Zimbalist. 1974. "Women, Culture, and Society: A Theoretical Overview." In *Women, Culture, and Society,* ed. Michelle Zimbalist Rosaldo and Louise Lamphere, 17–42. Stanford, CA: Stanford University Press.

Saadawi, Nawal El. 1980. *The Hidden Face of Eve.* London: Zed Press.

Sabbah, Fatna. 1984. *Woman in the Muslim Unconscious.* New York: Pergamon Press.

Sahlins, Marshall. 1976. *Culture and Practical Reason.* Chicago: University of Chicago Press.

Sapir, Edward. 1951. *Culture, Language and Personality,* ed. David G. Mandelbaum. Berkeley: University of California Press.

Schick, Irvin C., and Ertuğrul Ahmet Tonak, eds. 1987. *Turkey in Transition.* Oxford: Oxford University Press.

Schimmel, Annemarie. 1975. *Mystical Dimensions of Islam.* Chapel Hill, NC: University of North Carolina Press.

Schneider, David M. 1965. "Kinship and Biology." In *Aspects of the Analysis of Family Structure,* ed. A. Coale et al., 83–101. Princeton: Princeton University Press.

———. 1968. *American Kinship: A Cultural Account.* Englewood Cliffs, NJ: Prentice-Hall.

———. 1972. "What Is Kinship All About?" In *Kinship Studies in the Morgan Centennial Year,* ed. P. Reining, 32–63. Washington, DC: The Anthropological Society.

———. 1976. "Notes Toward a Theory of Culture." In *Meaning in Anthropology,* ed. Keith H. Basso and Henry A. Selby, 197–220. Albuquerque, NM: University of New Mexico Press.

————. 1977. "Kinship, Nationality and Religion: Toward a Definition of Kinship." In *Symbolic Anthropology*, ed. J. Dolgin, D. Kemnitzer, and D. Schneider, 63–71. New York: Columbia University Press.

————. 1984. *A Critique of the Study of Kinship*. Ann Arbor: The University of Michigan Press.

Schneider, Jane. 1971. "Of Vigilance and Virgins: Honor and Shame and Access to Resources in Mediterranean Society." *Ethnology* 10: 1–24.

————. 1980. "Trousseau as Treasure: Some Contradictions of Late Nineteenth-century Change in Sicily." In *Beyond the Myths of Culture*. New York: Academic Press.

Settle, Mary Lee. 1977. *The Blood Tie*. Boston: Houghton Mifflin.

Shiloh, Ailon. 1961. "The System of Medicine in Middle East Culture." *Middle East Journal* 15: 277–88.

Sirman, Nükhet. 1990. "State, Village and Gender in Western Turkey." In *Turkish State, Turkish Society*, ed. Andrew Finkel and Nükhet Sirman, pp. 21–51. London: Routledge.

Sissa, Giulia. 1989. "Subtle Bodies." *Zone: Fragments for a History of the Human Body* 3(3): 133–56.

Smith, Jane. 1980. *Women in Contemporary Muslim Societies*. Lewisburg, PA: Bucknell University Press.

Smith, Jane, and Yvonne Haddad. 1975. "Women in the Afterlife: The Islamic View as Seen from the Qur'an and Tradition." *Journal of the American Academy of Religion* 18: 39–50.

————. 1981. *The Islamic Understanding of Death and Resurrection*. Albany, NY: State University of New York Press.

Smith, Wilfred Cantwell. 1957. *Islam in Modern History*. Princeton: Princeton University Press.

Spencer, Robert. 1954. "Aspects of Turkish Kinship and Social Structure." *Anthropological Quarterly* 27: 40–50.

Spencer, W. B., and F. J. Gillen. 1899. *The Native Tribes of Central Australia*. London: Macmillan.

Starr, June. 1978. *Dispute and Settlement in Rural Turkey*. Leiden: E. J. Brill.

————. 1989. "The Role of Turkish Secular Law in Changing the Lives of Rural Muslim Women, 1950–1970." *Law and Society Review* 23(3): 497–523.

Stirling, Paul. 1957. "Land, Marriage and the Law in Turkish Villages." *International Social Science Bulletin* 9: 21–33.

————. 1963. "The Domestic Cycle and the Distribution of Power in Turkish Villages." In *Mediterranean Countrymen*, ed. J. Pitt-Rivers, 201–13. Paris: Mouton.

————. 1965. *Turkish Village*. New York: John Wiley and Sons.

————. 1974. "Cause, Knowledge and Change: Turkish Village Re-visited." In *Choice and Change*, ed. John Davis, 191–229. London: Athlone Press.

Stolcke, Verena. 1986. "New Reproductive Technologies—Same Old Fatherhood." *Critique of Anthropology* 6(3): 5–31.

Stone, Frank. 1970. "A Pioneer in Turkish Village Revitalization." *Hacettepe Bulletin of Social Sciences and Humanities* 2: 220–34.

Strathern, Marilyn. 1980. "No Nature, No Culture: The Hagen Case." In *Nature, Culture and Gender,* ed. Carol MacCormack and Marilyn Strathern, 174–222. Cambridge, Eng.: Cambridge University Press.

Szyliowicz, Joseph. 1966. *Political Change in Rural Turkey: Erdemli.* Paris: Mouton.

Tachau, Frank. 1984. "The Political Culture of Kemalist Turkey." In *Atatürk and the Modernization of Turkey,* ed. Jacob Landau, 57–76. Boulder, CO: Westview Press.

Tapper, Nancy, and Richard Tapper. 1987. "The Birth of the Prophet: Ritual and Gender in Turkish Islam." *Man* 22(1): 69–92.

Taşkıran, Tezer. 1976. *Women in Turkey.* Istanbul: Redhouse Press.

Taylor, Gordon. 1975. *Place of the Dawn.* New York: Holt, Rinehart and Winston.

Tezcan, Sabahat, Carol Carpenter-Yaman, and Nüsret Fişek. 1980. *Abortion in Turkey.* Ankara: Hacettepe University Institute of Community Medicine.

Thompson, E. P. 1967. "Time, Work-Discipline and Industrial Capitalism." *Past and Present* 38: 56–97.

Timur, Serim. 1978. "Socioeconomic Determinants of Differential Fertility in Turkey." In *Women's Status and Fertility in the Muslim World,* ed. J. Allman, 54–76. New York: Praeger Publishers.

Toprak, Binnaz. 1981. *Islam and Political Development: Turkey.* Leiden: E. J. Brill.

———. 1987. "The Religious Right." In *Turkey in Transition,* ed. Irvin C. Schick and Ertuğrul Ahmet Tonak, 218–35. Oxford: Oxford University Press.

Toynbee, Arnold. 1917. *Turkey: A Past and a Future.* London: George H. Doran.

Tuana, Nancy. 1988. "The Weaker Seed: The Sexist Bias of Reproductive Theory." *Hypatia* 3(1): 35–59.

———. 1989. *Feminism and Science.* Bloomington, IN: Indiana University Press.

Turan, Ilter. 1982. "Villages, Village Organization and the Government in Rural Development." Occasional Paper No. 20. Iowa City: University of Iowa.

Turner, Terence. 1980. "The Social Skin: Bodily Adornment, Social Meaning and Personal Identity." In *Not Work Alone,* ed. J. Cherfas and R. Lewis, 112–40. London: Temple Smith.

Turner, Victor. 1967. *The Forest of Symbols.* Ithaca, NY: Cornell University Press.

Van Dusen, Roxan. 1976. "The Study of Women in the Middle East: Some Thoughts." *Middle East Studies Association Bulletin* 10: 1–19.

Van Gennep, Arnold. 1960 [1909]. *The Rites of Passage.* Chicago: University of Chicago Press.

Van Nieuwenhuijze, C. O. 1977. "Near Eastern Village: A Profile." In *Readings in Rural Sociology,* ed. Oğuz Arı, 10–24. Istanbul: Boğaziçi University Publication.

Vance, Carole. 1984. *Pleasure and Danger.* Boston: Routledge and Kegan Paul.

Vaner, Semih. 1987. "The Army." In *Turkey in Transition,* ed. Irvin C. Schick and Ertuğrul Ahmet Tonak, 236–65. Oxford: Oxford University Press.

Vico, Giambattista. 1986 [1744]. *The New Science of Giambattista Vico,* trans. Thomas G. Bergin and Max H. Fisch. Ithaca, NY: Cornell University Press.

Volkan, Vamik D., and Norman Itzkowitz. 1984. *The Immortal Atatürk: A Psychobiography.* Chicago: University of Chicago Press.

von Grunebaum, Gustave E. 1981 [1951]. *Mohammadan Festivals.* London: Curzon Press.

———. 1969 [1946]. *Medieval Islam.* Chicago: University of Chicago Press.

Walker, Paul E. 1978. "Eternal Cosmos and the Womb of History: Time in Early Ismaili Thought." *International Journal of Middle East Studies* 9: 355–66.

Weigle, Marta. 1989. *Creation and Procreation.* Philadelphia: University of Pennsylvania Press.

Weiner, Annette. 1976. *Women of Value, Men of Renown.* Austin, TX: University of Texas Press.

———. 1978. "The Reproductive Model in Trobriand Society." *Mankind* 11: 175–86.

———. 1979. "Trobriand Kinship from Another View: The Reproductive Power of Men and Women." *Man* 14: 328–48.

———. 1980. "Reproduction: A Replacement for Reciprocity." *American Ethnologist* 7: 71–85.

———. 1982. "Sexuality among the Anthropologists and Reproduction among the Informants." *Social Analysis* 12: 52–65.

Whorf, Benjamin. 1956. "The Relation of Habitual Thought and Behavior to Language." *Language, Thought and Reality.* Cambridge, MA: MIT Press.

Wikan, Unni. 1982. *Behind the Veil in Arabia.* Baltimore: Johns Hopkins University Press.

———. 1984. "Shame and Honour: A Contestable Pair." *Man* 19: 635–52.

Winter, Michael. 1984. "The Modernization of Education in Kemalist Turkey." In *Atatürk and the Modernization of Turkey,* ed. Jacob Landau, 183–94. Boulder, CO: Westview Press.

Yalman, Nur. 1973. "Some Observations on Secularism in Islam: The Cultural Revolution in Turkey." *Daedalus* 102: 139–68.

Yanagisako, Sylvia. 1979. "Family and Household: The Analysis of Domestic Groups." *Annual Review of Anthropology* 8: 161–205.

Yanagisako, Sylvia, and Jane Collier. 1987. "Toward a Unified Analysis of Gender and Kinship." In *Gender and Kinship: Essays toward a Unified Analysis,* ed. Jane Collier and Sylvia Yanagisako, 14–50. Stanford: Stanford University Press.

Yasa, Ibrahim. 1957. *Hasanoğlan.* Ankara: Yeni Matbaa.

Yassihöyük: Bir Köy Incelemesi. 1965. A group project in the Architecture Faculty. Ankara: Orta Doğu Teknik Üniversitesi yayınları.

Yerasimos, Stephane. 1987. "The Monoparty Period." In *Turkey in Transition,* ed. Irvin C. Schick and Ertuğrul Ahmet Tonak, 66–100. Oxford: Oxford University Press.

Zafar, S. M. 1978. *Haj—a Journey in Obedience.* London: Repon Printing Press.

Zerubavel, Eviatar. 1985. *The Seven Day Circle. The History and Meaning of the Week.* Chicago: University of Chicago Press.

Index

Ablutions: of corpse, 312–13; and hajj,
306; and Mevlud, 317; places for,
128–29, 234; after sex, menstruation, childbirth, 41, 46, 48–49, 71,
95; and the wedding, 128–29. *See
also* Bathing; Cleanliness; Dirt; Pollution

Abortion, 58–59

Abraham: and circumcision, 85; as father of monotheistic religions, 21,
34, 289–90, 300–301; and the hajj,
303, 303n, 308; sacrifice, 6–7, 68,
68n, 298–303. *See also* Kurban
Bayramı

Abu-Lughod, Lila, 18, 49n, 103, 143n,
218n

Abu-Zahra, Nadia, 39n

Adak, 300

Adam, 41, 93, 287, 289, 293–94, 318;
and Mecca, 303, 307

Adulthood, meaning of, 76, 112

Ağaoğulları, Mehmet Ali, 271, 273n

Agriculture, 255–57, 261–62; crops,
209–10, 260; and relations of de-
pendency, 170

Ahmad, Feroz, 221

Aile, see Family

Akraba, see Kinship; Marriage; Relatives

Alms: and death, 315–16; and faith,
291, 297; Kurban Bayramı, 299

America: adolescence in, 98; birth in,
69; democracy in, 276–77; hospitality in, 194–95; marriage in,
116–17; notions of, 115n, 273n;
and presidential election, 276–77;
U.S. surplus food, 171

Anatolia/Anadolu, 202–4

Anatolian Turks as ethnic group, 21,
149, 204

And, Metin, 80

Animals: and humans, 210–11; husbandry of, 22, 243–48, 258–59;
Süleyman and, 211n; women and,
246, 314–15

Anthropological theory: and cultural
imperialism, 19–20; and fieldwork,
as practice, 4–5, 24, 28, 88–89,
163n, 189; and gender, 3, 9–17, 27,
217–18; and kinship, 14–16, 43,
99–102, 147–64; and language, 8,
31–34, 36; marxist approaches, 17,
40, 166–67, 170, 265–66; and religion, 3, 7, 18–21, 25; and reproduction, 3, 9–13, 17, 26; Virgin
birth debate, 7, 10–12

Antoun, Richard, 18, 39n, 40, 65n,
96n, 101, 103, 171n, 306n

Aristotle, 8, 48n; *Generation of Animals*,
37n, 211n; seed and soil, 47, 54,
58n, 154; and soul, 211n

Ashley-Montagu, M. F., 14–15, 37,
46n, 52n, 147

Atatürk, Kemal: and education, 221,
232; father of Turks, 68, 88n, 153,
179, 273, 273n, 281; founder of
Republic, 221–23, 271–82; Kemalism, 222, 222n, 224; and the military, 275–76; modernization/
Westernization, 221–23, 227, 277,
284–85, 284n; research of, 224,
285n; resistance to reforms, 226,
280; and the state, 224–25, 271–82

Austin, R. W. J., 35

Authority: of Atatürk, 221–32; diagram of, 199; from God, 221, 275–
77, 301; men's/father's, 33–34, 39,
112, 170–72, 221, 231, 275–77,
301; of *muhtar,* 173, 179, 212; and
procreation, 231–32, 266; relations

Authority (*continued*)
of, 170–200; religious, 221, 223, 275–77, 282

Balçı, Mustafa, 58
Barnes, J. A., 12
Başer, Tevfik, 42n
Başgöz, Ilhan, 70, 70n
Bathing: of babies, 65, 71; of brides, 128; description of, 128–29; places for, 234. *See also* Ablutions
Bed: as paternal endowment, 171; wedding, 144
Benveniste, Emile, 31
Bible, 36n; circumcision, 85; Gospels, 290; and Noah, 80, 289; notion of witness, 69n; and procreation, 27; Prophets, 289–90; verses in, 87, 95, 284. *See also* Abraham; Book; Christianity; Creation
Biology: and gender, 13, 35; genetics, 13; and kinship, 150; and procreation, 3, 30; as science, 12, 96
Birth, 23, 45–46, 59–64, 67, 313, 319–20, 319n; afterbirth, 64; and Cennet, 319; *loğusalık* period, 64–72; of Muhammed, 313n, 317–19; of nation, 272; relation to marriage, 130, 187, 273–74; spiritual, 313–14, 317–23; statistics of, 59, 61; symbol of women's openness, 87; and washing, 312; and world order, 323
Blok, Anton, 38n
Blood: and babies, 93; and circumcision, 86; "crazyblood," 112; feud, 275–76; and flag, 273–74; and marriage, 86, 96, 101; menstrual, 26, 54, 85, 95, 302–3; nutrient, 54; and politics, 198–200, 228–32, 273–76; as polluting, 54, 85; as sacred, 54, 298–99; and seed, 168; and sex, 96, 112; symbolic bond, 14–15, 73, 147, 154–57, 168, 198–200, 228–32, 302–3; and weddings, 86; and women, mortality, physicality, 26, 93–94, 302–3. *See also* Colors; Kinship; Menstruation
Boddy, Janice, 56, 96, 314n, 321n
Bodiliness: concepts of, 26, 99; associated with women, 310

Body: as book, 28, 82; as culturally constructed, 23, 25–30, 65; at death, 67, 312–14, 316; man's, 28, 30, 38, 97, 287; as open/closed, 38, 86, 88, 116, 198; in Paradise, 319; at puberty, 92–98; as signifier, 25; symbolism of woman's, 35, 48n, 138–40, 198–200, 238, 278, 283, 322–23; training of, 79, 82, 97–98; village as, 192, 198. *See also* Boundaries; Covering
Boissevain, Jeremy, 38n
Book: meaning of The, 29, 289; village as, 82
Bouhdiba, Abdelwahab, 25, 37, 47, 48n, 96, 96n, 97, 285, 288, 302n, 303n, 319, 320n
Boundaries: of body, 86–88, 114–15, 278, 312; of fields of study, 17; of house, 114–15, 238–39; of nation, 273, 275, 278, 294; personal/social, 82; rituals of, 80, 317–18; and smells, 79, 195; transgressions of, 80, 86–88, 107, 314–15; and women, 86–88, 107, 114–15, 188–99, 278, 314–15. *See also* Body; Hospitality; Nation; Pollution; Village
Bourdieu, Pierre: and anthropology, 19–20; on change, 322; on covering, 38n; on education, 230; on embodiment, 58n, 82, 166; on marriage strategy, 101–5; on sexual difference, 20, 267; on time, 253–54
Brandes, Stanley, 218n
Bread: and diet, 243; making, 240–43; and menstruation, 95; relation to procreation, 95, 159–61, 240–48; and sexual division of labor, 240–48; sustains life, 81, 239, 243. *See also* Eating
Breast feeding: and fasting, 295–96; and gender, 72–73; material substance, 155–58; milk and milk bond, 70–73; symbolic of women, 73, 87; weaning, 81–82. *See also* Femininity; Milk; Women
Brideprice: changes in tradition, 118–22; description of, 104, 110–11, 119–21; and son's dependence on father for, 171

Caliph, 277, 283–84
Campbell, John Kennedy, 31n, 218n
Cansever, Gocke, 85
Capitalism, state, 227. *See also* Commu-
    nism; Market; Modernization;
    Westernization
Carpenter-Yaman, Carol, 58
Casson, Ronald, 150–51, 161–62,
    167
Çatal Hüyük, 81, 203, 234n
Categories: of kinship and procreation,
    147–48; of religion and reproduc-
    tion, 17–18, 27; usefulness across
    cultures, 18. *See also* Boundaries
Cats, 210–11
Celebi, Süleyman, 317; "Mevlidi
    Şerifi," 317–19. *See also* Mevlud
Cemetery: village relation to, 67, 199,
    211, 311–16; women excluded,
    313. *See also* Death
Cennet: and birth, 293, 310; and con-
    sumption, 321n; description of, 41,
    58, 93, 153, 251–52, 285, 287,
    290, 293, 310, 319; and henna,
    137; and menstruation, 93; as ori-
    gin and destination, 285, 287; and
    prayer, 292; and rebirth, 313n,
    316–23; as spiritual and nonlinear,
    310; and women, 293, 310, 313n,
    316–17, 319–23. *See also* Death;
    Garden; Heaven; Origins; Other
    world
Census: problems with data, 75;
    household, 162; land survey, 257
Çeyiz, *see* Trousseau
Children: and Kurban Bayramı, 300;
    linguistic gender distinctions, 159;
    meaning of childhood, 75–84, 77,
    82, 84, 293; morality, 84; and
    movement, 82; and procreation, 86,
    266; relation to father, 156, 171,
    176, 179–81; relation to marriage,
    146, 158–61, 186; relation to
    mother, 23, 156, 301
Christianity: baptism, 313n; and The
    Book, 289–90; calendar, 280; as
    enemy, 280; gender, 34–35, 47–48,
    87n, 301n, 308n, 319n; God the
    father, 11, 33n, 34; and marriage,
    116; medieval debates on women,
    47–48; men's role, 33n, 34; sacred

and secular, 18–19; and women,
    87n, 319n
Circumcision: and Abraham, 85; age
    of, 84; meaning, 71, 85–86, 141,
    273–74; and men's relation to sex
    and religion, 85, 141; women's
    view of, 141
City: for drinking, 182; as open,
    tainted, 207; relation to village, 208
Cleanliness/purity: and circumcision,
    84; of house, 237; and Islam, 84;
    and morality, 42, 84–85; mother
    tongue as, 280–81; village as, 207;
    woman's body, 200, 230, 277–80,
    277n. *See also* Covering; Open/
    closed; Pollution
Close/distant: relatives, 153–54, 156–
    60, 169–70; structured vis-à-vis fe-
    male body, 156–61, 169
Clothing: children's, 82; on hajj, 306–
    7; making of, 177; men's, 121, 132,
    144, 253; and school, 83–84, 88;
    for wedding, 120–21, 129, 134–35;
    women's, 44, 97, 120, 133–36. *See
    also* Covering; Swaddling
Collier, Jane, 14, 15, 57, 170–71n
Colors: black, 291, 291n, 307; red, 92,
    140, 142–43, 273–74; white, 92,
    109, 273–74. *See also* Blood; Flag;
    Henna; Nation
Coming-into-being: importance of be-
    liefs in, 13, 21, 147; and kinship,
    16, 147; notion of, 10, 16, 21, 27,
    36–37, 42, 57, 75, 266; relation to
    masculinity, 37, 57. *See also* Kin-
    ship; Procreation; Reproduction
Communism: accusations of, 90, 227–
    28; relation to capitalism, 227, 277;
    understandings of, 90–91, 105,
    277; women as material in, 91,
    225, 279–80
Community: description of, 107, 218–
    19; divisions, 219–21; men's rela-
    tion to, 269–70; and nation, 271–
    73; of women, 139–42, 316–17. *See
    also* Neighborhood; Village
Conception: and contraception, 52;
    notions of, 11, 32–38, 47–49, 52–
    54. *See also* Procreation; Reproduc-
    tion

Consanguinity: problems with notions of, 148, 154. *See also* Anthropological theory; Blood; Kinship

Contraception: government policy of, 74, 262; methods of, 52–54

Control: of animals, 246; of land, 267–68; as life goal, 252; men's, of women, 39–40, 42, 44, 54, 267–68, 278, 279n, 280, 314–15, 320–23; of sexuality, 42, 54, 57, 96, 96n, 314–15, 314n; of slaughter, 246; of sperm, 57, 96; in the village, 206–9; women's lack of, 54, 77, 96. *See also* Authority; Covering; Femininity; Masculinity; Menstruation; Open/closed

Conversation: as art form, 196–97; as male prerogative, 57, 197, 316; relation to television, 251; women's, 43. *See also* Verbal power

Cooperation: between brothers, 186; men's partnerships, 266–67; in village, 105, 191, 218; among women, 187–88

Cooperatives: collapse of, 226; development of, 219; lack of, 261

Cosmic order: as divided (dual), 225–26; in Islam, 24; relation to procreation, 9, 15, 147–48; relation to science, 27; and women, 323

Covering: of baby, 65–67; of bride, 143, 146; of children, 75, 77, 181; of corpse, 67, 312–16; among emigrants, 279n; of girls, 87–92; on hajj, 306–7, 310; house as, 97, 114–15, 145, 162; of ka'ba, 307n; linguistically, 75; men "covering" woman, house, field, village, 38, 42, 97, 114–15, 145, 162, 181, 211–12; and modesty, 40, 101–2, 109; prohibited in school, 88, 230; as resistance to uncovering, 90, 278–80; trousseau as, 128; of valuables, 65, 145; and veiling, 38–41, 67, 97; of village, 42, 211–12; of women, 40–42, 67, 162, 230, 237–39, 267–68, 278, 323. *See also* Education; Femininity; Open/closed; Veiling

Coward, Rosalind, 14, 17, 43

Cows, 243–48, 258

Creation: as analogous to breadmaking, 95; relation to procreation, 21, 95,

248; theme of Qur'an, 285–86; villagers' understandings of, 286–91; women symbolize, 8, 37, 40, 225. *See also* Origins; Procreation

Cutting: of animals, associated with men, 240, 298, 301; a promise, 122

Dancing: and community of women, 135–37, 142; by men, 269; at wedding, 122–23, 129, 131

Daniel, E. Valentine, 232

Dankoff, Robert, 148, 154n, 160n

Daughter, 53n; concealed linguistically, 75; as field, 102; and Oedipal complex, 175. *See also* Father; Femininity; Masculinity; Mother; Paternity; Puberty

Davis, John, 38n

Death: and burial, 271, 312–16; as men's affair, 246, 313–16; relation to living, 60, 67, 187, 199–208, 211, 274; like sleep, 293; as spiritual birth, 313–14, 317–19; womb and tomb, 68, 302, 313, 316–17; women and, after birth, 67–68; women's insurance against, 120

de Busbecq, Ogier G., 210, 277n

Delaney, Carol, 26, 39, 41n, 88, 93, 117, 172n, 198n, 301n, 303n

Democracy, 105, 221–24, 228; and the military, 275–76, 275n; and religion, 276–77. *See also* Political parties

Descent: ancestors, 202–8; from Hittites, 289; as male, generative, allied with God, 151–53, 157, 168–70; relation to ethnic identity, 152; relation to national identity, 152, 198–200; symbols of, 273; how traced, 152, 202–8; unity of identity through time, 153; woman's role, 151–53. *See also* Kinship; Paternity

Development: and beliefs, 322; divisions and dislocations, 268; in village, 262–68; role of women in, 267n. *See also* Education; Government in village life; Modernization; Westernization

Devisch, Renaat, 99

Dictatorship, 221

Dirt: and women, 79; menstruation as, 93–96; sex as, 97. *See also* Pollution

Disputes: between husband and wife, 179–81; between kin and neighbors, 187–90; and outside intervention, 180–90; between political associations, 219–20; reconciliation, 189–90

Distribution of wealth: in the village, 22; and inheritance, 104

Dittemore, Margaret, 112, 232–34

Divinity/the divine: association with gold, 120n; as male, 16, 36, 199–200, 274; metaphors for human-, 20; procreation as, 5; woman's barrenness as punishment, 53; determination of sex, 57. *See also* God; Masculinity; Religion

Divorce, 53; and Islam, 179–81; like weaning, 81; women's insurance against, 120

Dodd, C. H., 219, 220, 276n

Dogs, 210

Domesticity/the domestic: as analytic category, 17; the domestic cycle, 163; domestic violence, 176–81; problems with domestic-public categories, 264–66; women as domestic, 268. *See also* Anthropological theory; House; Work

Douglas, Mary, 26, 37, 79, 278

Dream symbolism, 6; and boys' puberty, 96

Drink: alcohol as Western, 280; in city, 182

Dualism: in conception, 53–54; of cosmos, 60, 116, 225–26; of marriage, 116, 125, 132; separate things not joined, 306–7; suspicionn of, 222. *See also* Cosmic order; Procreation; Singleness; Union

Dubetsky, A., 107

Dubisch, Jill, 208n

duBois, Page, 49

DuBoulay, Juliet, 38n, 211n, 218n

Dumont, Paul, 222n

Dundes, Allen, 51, 85

Durkheim, Emile, 4, 9; relation to Atatürk, 223n

Eating: etiquette of, 251; fasting, 294–98; holiday feasts, 296–98, 304–5;

meal brings together male and female, 247–51; and sex, 138–39, 248, 251; and sexual divisions, 176. *See also* Bread; Food; Gender; Ramazan

Education: attitudes toward, 228–30, 281; for men, 230n; relation to politics, religion, 232; for women, 228–30, 289. *See also* Covering; Knowledge; School

Eickelman, Dale, 18, 29, 228

Eilberg-Schwartz, Howard, 41n, 85n, 96n, 230n, 315n

Eliade, Mircea, 36

el-Zein, Abdul Hamin, 18–20

Embodiment: children and women as, of world, 82, 157; human existence as, 26; of Islam, 25; kinship as, of ancestors, 153. *See also* Body; Femininity

Engelbrektsson, Ulla-Britt, 30, 41n, 151n, 152, 186

Engels, Frederick, 112–13n, 166, 265

Enlightenment, 229, 229n

Erdentug, Nermin, 30, 85, 116, 119, 158

Erder, Türköz, 102n

Erotic literature, 25, 150n; denied to women, 231

Esin, Emel, 303n, 306n

Ethnicity: displayed by women on hajj, 306; relation to kinship, 149–50, 153; relation to nationality, 273n; Turkish as superior, 149

Evans-Pritchard, E. E., 107n

Eve, 41; menstruation given to women because of, 93; creation of, 228

Evil eye, 42, 65, 121, 130

Evolution, 231, 287

Evren, General Kenan, 23, 272n, 275, 282

Exile: as burial away from village, 311; as hell, 199, 252; marriage as, 117; this world as, 117

Fallers, Lloyd and Margaret, 186, 290

Family: and the domestic cycle, 163, 186–88; extended, 161–70, 239; and household, 112–14; Kurban Bayramı as family holiday, 299–300; and marriage strategies, 101–

Family (*continued*)
3; meanings of, 112, 264–66; symbolized by hearth, 243, 274–75
Farah, Madelain, 33, 36, 47, 67, 303n
Fasting, 73. *See also* Eating; Ramazan
Father: and authority, 35, 172; as creator of child, 26–27, 32, 36, 69, 167; as head of family, like god, 16, 33, 35, 301, 303; relation to children, 69, 91, 171; role in marriage, 118–19. *See also* Paternity; Permission; Seed
Femininity/the feminine: animal-like, 96n, 314; and cosmic order, 16, 28, 32, 37, 225, 278, 288, 323; and death, 68, 302, 313; like earth, land, 8, 37–38, 40, 48n, 102, 156, 278, 313–14; and emotion, 314–15; and evil, left, 225–26; Heaven as, 323; as this-worldly, 35, 37, 198. *See also* Body; Covering; Masculinity; Sex; Soil; Women
Feminism, 13, 279, 312n; anthropology and, 17, 54; Atatürk's, 279–80; and critiques of Meillassoux, 170–71n; Socialist, 17
Fernea, Robert and Elizabeth, 302
Fertility: and female figurines, 203; links women to fields, 8, 30–31, 37, 115; and menopause, 184; and menstruation, 93, 301–2; women's, transferred between men, 143; and women's status, 40, 74, 75
Fişek, Nüsret, 58
Five Pillars of Faith, 23, 222, 291–92
Flag, 273–75. *See also* Nation
Food: ambrosial, in Cennet, 79; bread as quintessential, 243; crops, 209–10; at feasts, 296–97, 304–5; as gendered, 145, 249–52, 274; on hajj, 309; and hospitality, 194–97; and house plan, 233; at meals, 249–52; meat, 22, 243; at wedding, 132–33, 144; as women's work, 196–97, 197n. *See also* Eating
Foucault, Michel, 43
Fountains, 83, 128, 209; as public place for women, 214, 216
Freud, Sigmund, 5–8, 174–75; and Oedipus myth, 6
Friedrich, Paul, 8

Fustel de Coulanges, Numa Denis, 162n

Galen, 47, 48n, 154
Garden: description of, 251; intimation of Paradise, 252. *See also* Cennet; Sexual division of labor
Geertz, Clifford, 7, 9, 18; and change, 322; on identity, 107n; on Islam, 25; on worldview and "ethos," 19–20, 277n
Gender: of children, 58, 84–92, 177, 186–88; and colors, 274; and cosmology, 8–9, 15, 32, 35; as culturally constructed, 13–14, 27, 30, 37, 76, 84–92, 170–200, 238–39 (of food, 58, 145–46, 249–51); and death, 312–16; and the division of labor, 239–55; and education, 230n, 232; effects of mechanization, 264; and identity, 30, 36–37, 153, 232, 239–55, 266; and kinship, 14, 23, 36, 153, 186–88; and marriage, 116, 135–37; of nation, 273, 275, 278; not reducible to biology, 13; relation to monotheism, 5–8; relation to procreation, 3–4, 13, 30, 98; relation to religion, 195, 232, 300–303, 302n, 304–11; and secularism, 284–85n; and space, 211n. *See also* Colors; Education; Femininity; Male-female roles; Masculinity; Procreation; Religion; School; Space; Time
Generativity, 23. *See also* Aristotle; Femininity; Masculinity
Genesis, 3, 288–89. *See also* Bible; Creation; Procreation; Verbal power
Genetics: blood as cover for, 156; Lamarck, 46n; and male authority, 231; Mendel, 13. *See also* Biology; Evolution
Genitals, *see* Body; Penis; Women's genitals
Gibb, H. A. R., 283
Gillen, F. J., 9
Gilmore, David, 218
Gimbutas, Marija, 81
Girl: as less valuable, outsider, 77–78, 114. *See also* Daughter; Femininity; Gender; Puberty; School

God: as creator, 11, 33, 37, 89, 94, 225, 276, 285–97, 290–91, 294, 323; and faith, prayer, 290–94; and the hajj, 303–11; as invisible, 282; and Kurban Bayramı, 298–303; as masculine, 5, 11, 33, 34–35, 37, 94, 156, 168–69; and procreation, 248; and Ramazan, 294–98; and sex, love, and marriage, 108, 175, 248; singleness of, 99. *See also* Masculinity; Muhammed; Procreation; Religion; Verbal power

Gökalp, Ziya, 27, 277n

Gold: insurance against divorce, 120; jewelry as endowment of bride, 120, 123; symbol of divinity, 120n; theft of, 183

Good, Mary Jo DelVecchio, 55, 93

Goody, Jack, 166

Government in village life: blood tests, 154–55; campaign against close kin marriage, 155; courts, 226–27; library, 213; officials, 192–94, 212; political divisions, 220–32; population policy, 74, 262; school, 83–84; settlement of immigrants, 191; view of peasants, 220. *See also* Development; Military coup; Political parties; School

Grandparents, 160–61

Greek legend, 6–7, 80n, 211; and semen, 96; tragedy, 180. *See also* Oedipus complex

Gurbet, see Exile

Gurney, Oliver, 289n

Gypsies, 192; and Kurban Bayramı, 298

Haddad, Yvonne, 312, 313, 321, 321n

Hadith, 20, 321

Hagar, 308, 308n

Hair: anthropological literature on, 130n; as fleece, 246, 258–59; and the hajj, 309, 311, 314n; and Heaven, 316; pubic, 87, 128; and sexuality, 41, 86–92, 129–31. *See also* Body; Covering; Head; Pollution

Hajj: experience of, 291, 298, 303–11; and food, 195, 214; *ıhram* and the color white, 274; and women, 94, 301–2, 305–7

Hands: represent genitals, 138, 141–42. *See also* Body; Henna

Handwork: photograph of, 126; as women's work, 88, 98, 112, 144, 231, 261. See also Femininity; Trousseau

Hane, see Household

Harem, 39n, 40

Head: and genitals, 196n, 230; and men's work, 231, 314–15. *See also* Body; Covering; Femininity; Honor; Knowledge; Masculinity; Semen

Headman: represents the village, 211–12; role in village, 105, 133–34, 162, 173, 179–81, 190–91, 212, 218–21. *See also* Alms; Development; Marriage; Permission; Violence

Headscarf: and covering, 38, 42, 45, 238; and puberty, 87–92, 88n. *See also* Covering; Femininity; Head

Health system: analysis of, 17, 55–56; and development, 219; hospital births, 61–62; national, 55, 213. *See also* Contraception; Midwife

Hearth: as meeting place of male and female, 243; and nation, 273–75; relation to descent and identity, 158–70, 243. *See also* Femininity; House; Household

Heaven: and hospitality, 195, 293n; and men's sexual pleasure, 139, 313, 315–17; as origin of Turks, 149; path to, 310n, 316–17; and Ramazan, 294; and women, 67, 139, 296, 320–22. *See also* Cennet; Garden; Origins; Other world

Hell: path to, 310n, 316–17; and Ramazan, 294; women and, 290–91, 293n, 316, 321

Henna: and community of women, 139–42; as red, 143; as sacred soil, 137–42, 273, 287; and wedding ritual, 125–26, 137–42. *See also* Colors; Hands; Heaven; Soil

Henze, Paul B., 281

Herzfeld, Michael, 38n, 211n, 218n

Hewson, M. Anthony, 47

Hill, Polly, 267n

Hirschon, Renée, 116, 211n

History: Atatürk and, 224, 285n; and paternity, 289; of village, 202–5

Hittites, 289

Hodgson, Marshall G. S., 20

Holidays: Muslim, 296–99; national, 281–82

Homosexuality, 50, 50n, 96

Honor: and hospitality, 180–81, 194–98; and marriage, 39, 101, 107, 167; as masculine, 39, 113, 171n; and nation/motherland, 269–70, 272–73, 275; relation to religion, 19; and women's virtue, 38–39, 107, 143, 230, 272–73, 273–75, 277–80. See also Covering; Education; Femininity; Masculinity; Military service; Paternity; Shame

Honor/shame complex, 32, 38–39; relation to paternity, 39, 101–2

Hospitality: and headman, 212; and nomadic past, 233; to outsiders, 192; as protection, 233; as representation of world, 192–98; at weddings, 188. See also Cennet; Femininity; Heaven; Tea

Hotham, David, 105, 208, 223–24, 271, 275n, 277

Houris, 319–20. See also Cennet; Femininity; Heaven; Masculinity; Sex

House: as clean, 232; description of, 232–39; as enclosing women, 97, 112–14, 188, 237–38, 267–68; and family, 113–14, 164; as feminine, 32, 114–15, 278, 307n, 312; as inside-outside boundary, 32, 107, 112–14, 232, 278; and paternity, 159, 166–67. See also Covering; Household; Femininity; Inheritance; Masculinity; Nation; Soil; Village

Household: and aile, 113; critique of concept, 112–14; as hane, 113–14, 162–70; and loyalty, 264–66, 270; man's relation to, 264–66; perpetuation and increase of, 163, 186–88, 239, 264–66; relation to government, 162; relation to house and hearth, 162, 243, 274–75. See also Family; Hearth; House; Procreation

Humor, 20; between men and women, 177; verbal dueling rhymes, 50; wedding pranks, 129–31, 134, 137, 141. See also Conversation

Identity: Atatürk and, 224; from father, 32–33, 36; and gender roles, 232, 275, 322; and Islam, 270–71; and marriage register, 266; and naming, 152; and origins, 4, 60, 204, 276, 283, 294; as Turk, 273–82; and village, 207–8, 232, 270; woman's, 37, 232, 312, 322–23. See also Nation; Orientation; Origins; Paternity; Seed; Village

Ihram: and the hajj, 306–7. See also Clothing; Death

Imam, 182, 192, 305; role in community politics, 226–27, 239

Immigrants, Bulgarian, 191

Incest, 103, 111

Income: agricultural, 11, 260; household, 259; from lambs, 259; other sources of, 111, 263–64; as shepherd, 111, 258–59; teachers', 259–60; from wheat, 256; women's, 260–61; from wool, 258–59. See also Distribution of wealth; Market; Money

Independence, War of, 271–73, 272n

Individuality: of men, 105; of women, 238. See also Community; Identity

Infant mortality, 59

Inflation, 256

Inheritance: of hereditary leadership, 105; of land, 102n, 104–5, 186–87; of nation-state, 275–76; and procreation, 167; relation to religion, 19; and women, 102n, 166–67. See also Islam; Law; Wealth

In-law: critique of concept, 110, 160–61; mother-in-law to daughter-in-law, 178, 184–85; son-in-law, 167–69. See also Kinship

Inside/outside: and cooking, 305n; ethnic group as inside, 149, 273; and female body, 114–15, 157, 200, 267–68, 273, 278–80; house versus street, 114–15, 197–98; outside as source of threat, 183, 206–8, 220–21, 269–70, 283–84; and procreation, 32, 80, 83, 107–8, 114–15; village, national boundaries, 238–39, 273. See also Covering; Femininity; House; Nation; Outsiders; Village

Islam, 283–323; calendar, 124, 291, 295; and cleanliness, 23, 46, 84–85, 94–96; as community/brotherhood of faith, 35, 85, 269–70, 306; and death, 312, 313n; embodied, 25; and the hajj, 303–4; and inheritance, 166, 256–57; and the military, 269–79; monotheism, 21, 34, 300; and the nation-state, 116, 222–25, 248, 271, 283–85; as "orthopraxy," 25; relation to men, paternity, 36, 70, 78, 181, 269–70, 275, 279–80; relation to women, 35, 47–48, 94–96, 181, 301–2, 306–7, 312–13, 319–20, 319n, 320n; and secularism, 222–23, 227, 284; the study of, 18–21, 25. *See also* Abraham; God; Law; Muhammed; Muslims; Secularism

Itzkowitz, Norman, 272n

Izin, see Permission

Jeffrey, Patricia, 218

Jesus, 289–90, 318

Judaism: and gender, 33n, 69n, 85n, 300–301, 301n, 308n; relation to Islam, 5, 29, 289–90, 300, 315n; villagers' views of, 29

Jung, Carl, 5

Ka'ba: meaning of black stone, 303n; secular Ka'ba, 282; as symbolically female, 307; temple of the lord, 294, 303–16. *See also* Mecca

Kağıtçıbaşı, Çiğdem, 74, 85

Kandiyoti, Deniz, 74

Karaosmanoğlu, Yakup Kadir, 208n

Karpat, Kemal, 228

Keller, Evelyn Fox, 13, 230n

Kemal, Mustafa, 269–70, 271–73. *See also* Atatürk

Kemal, Namik, 272

Kemalism, 222–24, 222n; relation to religion, 223; as Westernizing, 275n, 284n. *See also* Nation; Secularism; Westernization

Keyser, James M. B., 102n

Khan, Muhammad Z., 288, 314

Kına, see Henna; Soil

Kinross, Lord, 272n

Kinship: and anthropological theory, 10, 14, 147–48, 168–70; as blood relations, 154–63; and color, 274; as cultural logic, structure and relation, 25, 147–53; established through nursing, 72–73; and gender, 13–16, 156–57; and marriage, 124; and nation, 16; and neighbors, 187–91; and procreation, 10, 13; and religion, 10, 15, 19; terminology, 9, 157–61, 167–70, 198–200; villagers' notions of, 110, 157, 187–91, 198–200. *See also* Blood; Breast feeding; Family; Household; Identity; Marriage

Knowledge: of body, 98; and girls, 88; and masculinity, 231, 315n; midwife's, 56; traditional, versus modern education, 228. *See also* Education; School

Kurban Bayramı: and the hajj, 303, 308–10; relation to Abraham and sacrifice, 7, 68, 189, 258, 298–303; as representation of male domination, 303. *See also* Abraham; Family; Father; Hajj; Sacrifice

Land: and endogamy, 102; and the nation, 271–82, 322; and orientation, 228; relation to women, 203, 267; tenure, 102, 210, 254–57, 261–62. *See also* Animals; Femininity; Inheritance; Mother; Nation; Soil; Production; Wealth

Langer, Suzanne K., 8, 32

Laski, Harold, 221

Laude-Cirtautas, Ilse, 275

Laundry house: as bathhouse, 128–29; for cooking, 214; description of, 128; location of, 128, 214–16. *See also* Cleanliness/purity; Ablutions

Law: court settlements, 186–87; in Islam, 256–57, 281, 283; *Şeriat,* 32, 53, 280, 310n; *Soyadı* (last name), 152, 169; Swiss civil code, 179, 280; and women in school, 230. *See also* Divorce; Education; Government in village life; Islam; School; Violence

Lazarus-Yafeh, Hava, 297n, 299–300n, 303n, 306n, 307n, 309

Leach, Edmund, 10, 85, 87n, 130n, 253n, 289

Leder, Arnold, 220, 223

Left/right: as gendered, 57, 225; Islam
and spiritual as right, secular and
sexual as left, 46n, 227, 230. *See
also* Dualism; Gender
Legitimacy: of birth, 133–34; as dual,
224; God as source of, 225, 276–
77; and origins, 276; and paternity,
39–40, 39n; political, 224–25, 276;
of Republic, through Atatürk, 224,
275–76, 279–82. *See also* Authority;
God; Nation; Origins; Paternity
Lewis, Bernard, 222–23, 227, 270,
271, 272n, 283, 284n, 310n
Lewis, G. L., 285n
Library, village, 213, 218, 220; women
excluded, 231. *See also* Education;
Government in village life; Knowledge
Life cycle: birth, 59–64; circumcision,
84–87; death, 311–16; and domestic cycle, 163; first tooth, 80–81;
and gender, 70, 99; girls', 86–88;
marriage, 124–46; stages of life, 72
Logos spermatikos as seminal word of
God, 11, 34, 35. *See also* Verbal
power
Loğusalık, see Birth

MacDonald, D. B., 321n
Machines: and agricultural production,
254–55; effects of mechanization,
255, 261–64; and the market, 254–
57, 261–64; and men, 240, 264,
266–68. *See also* Development; Market; Modernization; Money; Wealth
MacKinnon, Catherine, 17, 170–71n
Mackintosh, M., 17, 170–71n
Magic: attitude toward words, 108,
229; spirits, 183, 211
Magnarella, Paul, 30, 119
Mahalle, see Neighborhood
Makal, Mahmut, 202n
Male-female roles: and biological reproduction, 35–36, 75, 155; as
closed/open, 37–38, 42, 46; as
complementary and asymmetrical,
239–55, 264–66, 278–80, 288–89,
288n, 302; and cosmic and social
order, 28–29, 34, 99, 156, 225,
238–55, 264–66, 277–80, 288–89,
302; epitomized in seed/soil, 32;
husband's rights over wife, 34, 42,

46, 177–81, 305–7; and social
change, 264, 266–68, 278–80. *See
also* Authority; Food; Household
Malinowski, Bronislaw, 9–13, 46n,
52n, 189n
Mandel, Ruth, 88n
Mansur, Fatma, 65n, 77, 85, 97, 109
Map of village, 215
Marcus, Julie, 41n, 47
Market: local, 214–16; nonmarket
societies, 265–66; shift to production for, 254–55, 258–59, 266–68.
See also Machines; Male-female
roles; Money
Marriage: age of, 109; until death,
134, 313; as economic relation,
102–9, 118–24, 146; endogamous,
100–108, 114–15; for men, 108–9,
177–81, 271, 273; and menstruation, 95; practices, 42–43, 95, 98–
149, 238; and procreation, 75,
100–108, 130; register and identity,
271; women's experience of, 54,
75, 111–12, 116–18, 130, 177–81,
184–85, 187; uxorilocal, 167. *See
also* Brideprice; Trousseau; Wedding
Marx, Karl, 265
Marxism: and anthropology, 17, 40,
166–67, 265–66; and village teachers, 223
Mary: in Islam, 35; as Mother, 34; as
the Virgin, 70n, 139n
Masculinity/the masculine: as creative,
generative, rational, 3, 26–27, 32–
33, 36, 38, 96n, 150, 153, 170–71,
212–13, 274–75, 283, 288–91,
314–15, 321–22; as divine, spiritual, related to God, 5, 16, 26–27,
33, 35–36, 138, 199–200, 225–26,
296, 302–3, 306, 311; as insemina-
tor, 33, 38, 49, 69, 69n, 80–81,
138, 158, 167, 239–55; and production, 80–81, 239–55, 264, 265–
68, 295–96; as public, active, 38,
50, 173, 175, 212–13, 265, 279,
302–3, 305, 310; Ramazan and virility, 295–96; related to descent,
linear time, 16, 153, 283, 310; as
self-contained, closed, 38, 82, 85–
86, 96, 96n, 178
Massignon, Louis, 254, 291n, 321n

Maternity: as material sustenance, like
earth, 8, 12–13, 39, 73, 156–61;
meanings of, 12–13, 15, 39
Mead, Margaret, 201
Mecca: and Cennet, 139; and hajj,
274, 301–11; and menstruation,
301–2; as orientation, 82, 293–94
Meeker, Michael, 30, 33, 39, 41n, 86n,
96n, 105n, 171n, 218n
Meier, Fritz, 116, 287
Meillassoux, Claude, 167, 170, 170–
71n, 265. See also Feminism; Marxism
Mellaart, James, 81, 203, 234n
Men: body as self-contained, 28, 30,
38, 96–97, 199–200, 287, 310; desire and sexuality of, 65, 96n, 146,
320; jealousy, 277n; as head of
family, state, and church, 16, 33,
35, 197, 212–13, 225–26, 239–55,
301, 303, 305, 319–20; represent
unity of Islam, 85, 195, 306; weakness of, 72. See also Authority; God;
Legitimacy; Masculinity; Paternity;
Seed; Sex
Menstruation: and conception, 49, 94;
and covering, 87–92; as dirty, sinful, 54, 92; menopause, 55, 93,
184, 302; power of, 95; and red,
273–74; and sex, 45, 49; and
slaughter, 301–2; symbolizes
woman as uncontrolled, 87–92; taboos, 41, 45–46, 49, 93–94, 301–
2, 314–15; understandings of, 55–
56, 92–93. See also Ablutions; Hajj;
Pollution; Puberty
Mernissi, Fatma, 40, 91, 96, 97n, 174–
75, 218n, 303n
Metaphor: of gender, 16, 34; relation to
beliefs, 31–32; seed and soil as, 30;
and social theory, 30; verbal imagery, 8, 37, 115
Mevlud, 313n, 317–19
Mezar, see Cemetery
Midwife: government-appointed, 55–
56, 60, 77, 133, 191–92, 213, 220–
32; local, 61–64. See also Birth;
Health system; Outsiders
Migration: as exile, 117; before marriage, 111–12; and mechanization,
262–64; and prayer, 279n, 293n;
for work, 21, 75, 178, 271

Military coup of September 11, 1980,
23; and the hajj, 304; and marriage, 76; martial law, 104, 217,
219, 226, 227; and the nation-state,
269–70, 275–76, 275n, 282; and
political associations, 217, 219; relation to Atatürk, 275–76, 282. See
also Democracy; Evren; Nation
Military service: age of, 69; customs
related to, 269–70; as exile, 117,
133; relation to Atatürk, 275; relation to household, 163–65, 175,
180; women as prize for completion
of, 109
Milk: and blood bonds, 155, 198–200;
and diet, 22, 247; products, 246–
48, 258–59; as substance of kinship, 157–58, 198–200; and wom-
en's income, 260–61; women's
work, 246–48. See also Animals;
Breast feeding; Colors; Femininity
Modernization/the modern: associated
with this world, women, 219, 322–
23; Atatürk and, 221–23, 275–76;
bottle feeding as, 73; education,
230; hospital births as, 61; and village life, 262–64. See also Atatürk;
Secularism; Westernization
Money: as income, 254–55, 259–64;
for musicians, 127; symbolizes reproductive wealth, 140; and time,
253; and weddings, 111, 119, 122,
140, 142; and women, 238. See also
Income; Wealth
Monogenesis: versus duogenesis, 47–
48, 156; relation to monotheism,
34, 288; relation to state authority,
221–22; as theory of procreation, 3,
11, 26, 34; and women's monogamy, 39n. See also Monotheism; Paternity; Procreation
Monotheism: and Abraham, 6, 300,
301; and atheism, 323n; and fatherhood, 5, 6, 34, 37, 288; and
monogenesis, 34, 37, 221–22, 288;
and the state, 221–23. See also Abraham; Gender; Paternity; Religion
Moore, Henrietta, 17, 115n, 170n,
267n
Morgan, Lewis Henry, 9, 147, 161
Moses, 6, 139; one of prophets, 239.
See also Freud

Mosque: and masculinity, 78; as place of men, 135, 212–13, 251, 312–13; symbolism of minaret, 294; and women, 317

Mother: "Anadolu" as, 203; bond as physical, of this world, 73, 156–61, 203, 319n; and daughter, 110, 175; motherland, 272; Motherland Party, 272n; respect owed to, 174; and son, 52, 174–75. See also Father; Nation

Movement: as controlled, 82–83, 83n, 237–39; through military service, 268–70; sitting (and hajj), 115, 252; to town, 268; turning (Whirling Dervish), 293; of women, 83n, 237–39. See also Covering; Migration; Permission

Muhammed, the Prophet: and Abraham, 300–301; and Atatürk, 281; birth of, Mevlud, 313n, 317–19; and cats, 210–11; and daughters, 139n, 273n; and Mecca, 293–94, 303–4, 303n; relation to God, 20, 29, 276, 286, 289–91; and women, 321. See also God; Islam; Religion

Muhtar, see Headman

Musallam, Basim, 48, 48n

Musicians at wedding, 127, 131, 137, 142. See also Dancing

Muslims/muslim: Alevis, 21; all people are, 287–88; Sufis, 35; Sunnis, 21, 204, 222–23; world is to God, woman is to man, 171. See also Five Pillars of Faith; God; Hajj; Islam; Kurban Bayramı; Masculinity; Mecca; Religion

Naming: of children, 70, 181; last name law, 152, 169; nicknames, 152; tribal, 153. See also Identity; Verbal power

Nasr, Seyyed Hossein, 33, 318n

Nation, 25, 107, 207–82; and anthem, 274; construction of, 221–23, 225–26, 278–80; as gendered, 68, 199, 275–80; and identity, 273, 278–80; nation-state, 271–72; and procreation, 201, 270–73, 272n, 275–80; relation to body, family, village, 206, 207; and religion, 68, 225, 248, 271, 283–85; symbolism of, 201, 272–82. See also Atatürk; Land; Secularism; State

Nationalism: conflict with Islam, 248, 285; and ethnic identity, 273n; European-type, 223n, 271–73; rhetoric of, 16, 24. See also Identity; Religion; State

Nature: biology and biological reproduction as, 3, 17, 27, 60; as culturally constructed, 14, 16, 26, 31; and women, 17, 27, 156, 265. See also Anthropological theory; Gender

Needham, Rodney, 46n

Neighborhood: and divisions in village, 227–32; relations among neighbors, 107, 187–92, 237–39. See also Kinship; Village

Noonan, John T., 47, 52n

Obeyesekere, Gananath, 130n

O'Brien, Mary, 17

Ocak, see Hearth

Oedipus complex: and Abraham, 6; and Muslim marriage, 174–75

Olson, Emelie, 88n

Ong, Walter, 29

Onians, R. B., 96n

Open/closed: and endogamy, 107; and house, 172–74; men as closed, socially enclosing women, 32, 42, 107, 172–74, 267–68; relation to clean/dirty, 42; and village, 198–200, 206–8; women as naturally open, 32, 38, 77, 86–88, 116, 145, 198–200, 207, 230, 237–39. See also Boundaries; Covering; Femininity; House; Masculinity; Sex; Village

Orientalism, 20

Orientation: toward Ankara, 282; Atatürk and, 281–82; of book, 23–24; conflict over, 74, 228–29, 232, 322; through kinship, 149, 310; to Mecca, 18, 293–94, 309, 310; political, 224–25, 278; sexual, 50, 50n; through structures and practices, 4, 19, 24, 285–91. See also Identity; Left/right; Space; Time

Origins: Atatürk and, 281–82; and destination, 149, 204, 285–91, 312; and identity, 4, 60, 276, 283, 294; and nation, 273–82; and procreation, 4, 60, 147, 285. *See also* Identity; Procreation

Ortner, Sherry, 17, 26, 32, 43, 265

Other world: 26, 32, 290; Mecca as link to, 293–94, 315–17; as more valued, 59, 74, 79, 228, 291; sex in, 79, 319–20; and women, 37, 321–22. *See also* Cennet; Heaven; This world

Ottoman empire, 283–84, 284n

Outsiders: as agents of change, 220–22; brides as, 184–85; as dangerous, 183, 269–70, 280; in village, 191–94, 220–32

Özbay, Ferhunde, 74

Özertuğ, Banu, 150–51, 161–62, 163, 167

Öztürk, Orhan, 72n, 85

Paige, Karen and Jeffrey, 96

Pan-Islamism, 271

Pan-Turkism, 271

Papanek, Hanna, 29, 218

Parallel cousin marriage: and endogamy, 102–7, 119–20; and religion, 19

Paternity: gives rights to child, 39–40, 53, 148–49, 301; and identity, 33, 39–40, 148–50, 155, 275, 289–91; meanings of, 8, 11–12, 15, 39, 53; and monotheism, 34, 294; and the nation-state, 221–22, 273–82; related to honor/shame complex, 39–40, 102; and roots, 143; and Virgin Birth debate, 10, 12. *See also* Atatürk; Father; God; Masculinity; Monogenesis; Monotheism; Procreation; Seed; Semen

Patriarchal power, symbols and practices of, 7, 11, 35, 170–200. *See also* Abraham; Islam; Kurban Bayramı; Masculinity; Religion

Patriline: and Adam, 289; and marriage strategy, 101–4; meanings of, 36, 101–4, 110, 150, 161; and naming, 152; and the nation, 275; and *ocak*, 162, 274; and procreation, 11, 36, 53n; and social life, 167–200; through time, 73, 289–91; women's relation to, 150–52. *See also* Seed

Peasants: called Turk, 271; government's view of, 220, 262–64; and symbol, 272, 276

Penis: emphasis on, 50–51, 78–79, 85, 141; and minaret, 294; and patriline, 150, 150n; vehicle of relation with the divine, 34, 78, 302–3. *See also* Circumcision; Father; Masculinity; Men; Paternity; Sex

Peristiany, J. G., 38n

Permission: and authority, 172–73; and military service, 269; and women, 69, 238–39

Pierce, Joe E., 161

Pilgrimage, 7, 282, 303–11. *See also* Hajj

Pis, see Dirt

Pitt-Rivers, Julian, 38n, 101, 103

Political parties: associations in village, 216–17, 219–20, 221; Democratic party, 222–23, 272n; and military coup, 23; monoparty, 221–32; Motherland Party, 272n; questions of legitimacy, 224. *See also* Legitimacy; State

Politics. *See* Education; Orientation; Religion; Sex

Pollution, 278, 310; as mixing, 41–42, 46, 232, 233–39, 251, 278; outsiders, 269–70; sexual fluids as, 41, 46, 64, 84–85, 251; streets as, 233–39; and women, 41, 68, 87, 200, 232. *See also* Blood; Boundaries; Dirt; House

Polygamy, 53, 277

Population, 59; Family Planning Law, 74; of village, 21–23, 204. *See also* Contraception; Government in village life

Power: as gendered, 3, 5, 32, 153, 221–22; and monotheism, 5, 32, 153. *See also* Authority; God; Legitimacy; Masculinity; Military coup; Verbal power

Prayer, 291–94; and women, 291, 306n. *See also* God; Islam; Mosque; Religion

Pregnancy, 53–59, 80, 95, 185, 295–96

Procreation: according to villagers, 27–30; and Adam, 289; analogous to breadmaking, 95; as coming-into-

Procreation (*continued*)
being, 3, 27, 147; contrasted with
reproduction, 3, 13–14, 16, 27, 35,
264–66; and cosmology, 3, 8–9,
15, 24, 29–30, 33–35, 37, 74, 323;
and Creation, 5, 37, 225, 285–89;
and death, 313–14; definition of, 3,
14, 16, 26–28; as divine mission,
29, 60, 288; as engendering, 4, 98,
201, 238–39; folk theory of, 8, 12,
16–17, 31–33; as genesis, 3, 37;
and honor/shame complex, 102; human purpose as, 146; and inheritance, 167; and kinship, 147, 157;
and lineage, 36; male-female roles
in, 8, 12, 16, 28–30, 35, 54; and
marriage, 99; as monogenetic, 3,
34, 288–91; and nation, 201, 272–
82; and religion, 4–5; symbolized
by seed and soil, 8, 12, 30–41. *See
also* Creation; Reproduction; Seed;
Soil
Production: changes in gender roles,
267–68; and reproduction, 27, 239,
264–68; from subsistence to market, 254. *See also* Feminism; Machines; Marxism; Reproduction;
Sexual division of labor; Work
Prostitution, 91, 96, 182, 299; symbolism of, 91, 272
Puberty, 23, 42; for boys, 84–87, 96–
98; for girls, 87–96; rituals of, 86,
92–98. *See also* Circumcision; Covering; Life cycle; Menstruation
Public as masculine, 212. *See also* Pollution

Qur'an: as God's word, 20, 229–30,
280, 285–91, 294–96; and inheritance, 102n; marriage partners,
103; as miracle, 29; seed and soil,
30; *sura*, verses in, 30, 49, 49n, 57,
287–88, 291n, 300, 302, 303,
303n, 313; and women, 94, 172,
303n, 320n. *See also* Islam; Muhammed; Ramazan

Race, Muslim unity of, 287–90
Rahman, Fazlur, 49n, 310n, 321n
Ramazan: and menstruation, 94; and
Muhammed, 294; Night of Power,
211, 296; observance of, 73, 213,

291, 294–98, 317; and Qur'an,
294; Şeker Bayramı (Candy Holiday), 296–98. *See also* Eating; Islam
Ramsay, W. M., 202n
Rape, 183; of nation/mother, 272–73
Reason: and men, 314–15, 314n; and
puberty, 92. *See also* Knowledge;
Masculinity; Men
Red Crescent (Turkish Red Cross), 299
Reinhart, Kevin, 41n, 47, 128
Relatives, 147–61; blood and milk,
155–60; close and far, 153–61; kin
terms, 159–61; and neighbors,
187–88; as patrilineal system, 151,
167
Religion: as category of study, 17–23;
fundamentalist, 323n; and hair, 87–
88; and paternity, descent, 10–11,
141; relation to the nation-state and
secularism, 16, 23, 222–32, 271,
276–77, 284–85, 289; and reproduction, 3–4, 17–21; and sexuality,
10, 23, 51–52, 85, 91–92, 140; and
women, 51–52, 141, 310, 323
Reproduction: critique of category, 3,
8, 16, 20, 27, 170–71, 264, 266; as
natural, 5, 14, 26–27, 40, 75; and
production, 27, 239, 255, 264;
Turkish words for, 27–28, 33, 60;
and women's devaluation, 3–5, 26–
27, 40, 75, 170–71n, 198–200. *See
also* Feminism; Procreation; Production
Resistance, 20; women's, 141
Ricoeur, Paul, 31
Right/left, *see* Left/right
Roper, Joyce, 49n, 60, 131, 135, 142
Rosaldo, Michelle Zimbalist, 17
Rushdie, Salman, 303n

Saadawi, Nawal, 87, 93, 96, 97, 313
Sabbah, Fatna, 47, 139n, 288, 291n,
295n, 302n, 303n, 314n, 321n
Sacrifice: and Abraham, 6, 308; and
authoritarian values, 300; and circumcision, 86; and Kurban Bayramı, 308; and motherhood, 67; and
the nation, 273–74; in popular
imagination, 300–303, 321. *See also*
Abraham; Kurban Bayramı
Safire, William, 270n
Sahlins, Marshall, 19

Sapir, Edward, 8
Satan, 322; and eating, 249; and hajj, 308; and women, 41, 93, 96
Satanic verses, 303
Schimmel, Annemarie, 38
Schneider, David M., 7; culture as system of symbols and meanings, 14–15; on kinship, 15–16, 147
School: attendance, 213n; buildings, 213, 215, 218; and conflict, 91–92, 248; and girls, 88; and nation-building, 220–32, 248; teachers, 163, 191, 223, 226, 259, 281; uniforms, 83–84, 89–90; in village, 83, 88, 90–91, 213. See also Education
Science as value-laden, 12–13, 30. See also Biology; Evolution; Genetics
Secularism: association with woman, left, sexuality, 225–26, 230; and authority, 223, 223n, 270–82; symbolics of, 276–77, 282, 284–85n. See also Islam; Kemalism; Modernization; Religion
Seed: creative spark, generative of child, 32, 35–37, 47, 76, 156, 198–200, 225, 276, 287, 288, 310, 320–21; as male, 30, 32, 36, 48, 80, 161–62, 170–76, 301, 310; and reproduction, 8, 12, 32, 53–54, 76, 154–55, 225, 310; in rituals of planting, weddings, sacrifice, 115, 230–40, 301, 307; and women, 39, 41, 47–48; wheat, 239–43. See also Blood; Descent; Kinship; Masculinity; Seed and soil; Time
Seed and soil: and birth and death, 313–14; and endogamy, 102–7; as symbols of gender and the cosmos, 30–36, 49, 146, 155, 311–12
Semen: and the color white, 274; as divine, life-giving, 49, 96, 288, 314–15; and the head, 96, 315n; as polluting, 41, 64, 92; relation to blood, 85, 154; and soil, 311–12. See also Seed
Sex/sexuality: as culturally constructed, 43; as dirty, 92, 97; and eating, 248, 251, 294–95; and hair, 86–92, 311; and honor/shame, 39–41, 43–52; initiation into, 87, 145; without issue, 79, 319–22; and

love, 174–75; men's, 41, 65, 96n, 97, 139, 146, 285–91, 319–22; and politics, 23, 85, 90, 232; and procreation, 3, 13, 15, 30; as related to religion, 23, 85, 140, 232; and seed/soil, 32; women's, 39–41, 310–11. See also Sexual activity
Sexual activity: in Cennet, 79, 310, 319–20; marital and extramarital, 43–44, 130, 181–84; masturbation, 46, 78, 96; orgasm, 46–47, 319–20; proscribed on hajj, 307; and social relations, 16, 23, 41–43, 57, 265; styles, 49–52, 94, 251; taboos on, 68–69, 94, 294; and washing, 48–49, 312; woman as pleasure, 320–23; women's lack of autonomy and, 45–46, 310
Sexual division of labor: as hierarchized, 239, 244–51, 296; and prayer, 292; and social spheres, 176–77, 217–18, 238–55; symbolic logic of, 20, 24, 76, 103, 166, 176–77. See also Machines; Procreation; Work
Shame: as attribute of women, 39–40, 59; and birth, 61–63; children and, 77; and covering, 87–92; and kinship, 169; and ostracism, 190. See also Covering; Tears
Sheep: and Abraham, 298–99; as livelihood, 239–55; shepherds, 210, 258–59
Sibling relations, 186–88; and inheritance, 233
Signs: bodies as, 25; procreation as, 29; words as, 29. See also Symbols
Singleness: of Atatürk, 281; attribute of God, 99, 116, 307; author's, 64, 99; not prized, 64, 108; and vulnerability, 183
Sirat, bridge to Paradise, 316
Sirman, Nükhet, 197n, 275
Smell: categories of, 79–80; and Cennet, 137–38, 317–18; cologne, 80, 195; menstrual blood, 95
Smith, Jane, 9, 279, 312, 313, 321, 321n
Smith, Wilfred Cantwell, 25
Social change: difficulty of, 20, 226, 322; from subsistence to market, 254–55, 266–68

Social organization: and complementary, asymmetrical gender relations, 238–39, 262, 278–80, 279n; in context of Islam, 276, 283; and kinship, 15, 147, 161. *See also* Male/female roles

Soil: henna as sacred, 137–40; house made of, and related to woman, 112, 199–200, 232; and nation, 271–75; native, 148–49, 157, 204, 270–75, 311, 322; and procreation, 12; woman as field, 30, 38, 40–41, 49, 51–52, 54, 157, 199–200, 213, 239–40, 322. *See also* Seed and soil

Son: and descent, 53, 75–76, 301; and marriage, 64, 110, 146; relation to father, 171. *See also* Abraham; Kurban Bayramı

Soul: at death, 313–14; from God, 60; opens, 58; progress of, 316; seed as, 36, 47; women's, 320–21, 321n

Space: divided by gender, 82–83, 153, 211–13, 211n, 264; nearness and distance, 24; sense of place, 153, 201–2

Spencer, W. B., 9

Spirit: encloses and enclosed by material world, 156–57; as male creativity, identity, 43, 80, 156, 183. *See also* Birth

Spirits, 183, 211

Starr, June, 105n

State: as gendered, 221–22; ideal of, 223–32; relation to religion and authority, 224, 226, 270, 282–85, 284n. *See also* Democracy; Nation; Religion

Status/prestige: change in women's, 264, 266–68, 307; and telephones, 194n; in the village, 22

Stirling, Paul, 104–5, 109, 119, 151, 163, 171, 187, 189, 202, 202n

Stolcke, Verena, 12, 39n

Strathern, Marilyn, 16

Street: as wild, polluted, 233, 239. *See also* Inside/outside; Masculinity

Submission: and circumcision, 85; of man and world to God, 171, 286, 301; as meaning of *muslim*, 171, 286; of son to father, 174–75; of women to men, 46, 50, 195. *See also* Authority; Femininity; Muslims/*muslim*

Sülale, see Descent; Kinship; Patriline

Sultan/caliph, 277; union of religion and state, 283–84

Sura, see Qur'an

Swaddling, 65–67; and shroud, 306–7, 312, 315. *See also* Clothing

Symbols: biology as, 14; as engendering and ordering the world, 3, 19, 26, 29–30, 34–35, 224, 323; key, 32; kinship as, 14–15. *See also* Metaphor; Signs; Social organization

Tachau, Frank, 222

Tailor, village, 263

Tapper, Nancy and Richard, 317n, 319n

Taxes, 162, 212

Taylor, Gordon, 203n

Tea: break, 197, 252; and hospitality, 194, 217–18; making of, 195; tearooms as male space, 176, 217, 251, 292; and weddings, 125, 127, 133, 137; women's tea parties, 44, 98, 112

Teachers, *see* School

Tears: Muhammed's, 318; symbolize women as physical, 130–31, 314–15

Teeth, 80, 196, 196n

Television, 121, 155, 176–77, 212, 217, 276; as clock, 296; Colombo, 152; effects of, 251, 266, 275, 288; and space in house, 236–37; tax on, 212

Temiz, see Cleanliness

Tezcan, Sabahat, 58

Theft, 183

This world: 25, 32, 310, 322; as corruptible, 79, 290–91; encompassed by other world, 225; and Mecca, 293–94; and menstruation, 93–95; as woman, material, seductive, 59, 73, 74, 93, 228

Thompson, E. P., 253n

Time: calendars, 115, 124, 177n, 280, 280n; and call to prayer, 248; descent and identity through, 24, 73, 153, 157; as gendered, 264, 296; and other world, 291–93; and pro-

creation, 289; rhythm of life, 248,
252–55
Timur, Serim, 59, 74
Toilet training, 79
Toprak, Binnaz, 102n, 222, 223n, 225,
227, 284, 284n
Trousseau, 104, 119–24, 125–27, 142,
144; as covering, 237; and divorce,
179, 181
Tuana, Nancy, 12, 13, 28
Turan, Ilter, 262
Turkey, Republic of: 21, 189, 202, 270,
275, 284n; established, 153; gov-
ernment, 221–32. See also Atatürk
Turner, Victor, 128

Uncovered: men as, 65, 86, 97, 310;
resistance to being, 90, 278–80
Union: conception not a, 53–54; marriage not a, 116, 125, 132; and
mysticism, 116
Uterine unit, 157–61, 168. See also
Kinship

Van Gennep, Arnold, 87
Veiling: of house, 97; of the ka'ba,
307; of nature, 60; of women, see
Covering
Vendors, 192–93
Verbal power: of God's word, 11, 17,
33, 89, 94, 225, 285–87, 290–91,
323; as male, 34–36, 57, 70;
women lack, 316. See also Logos spermatikos
Village: as closed, clean, 42, 211–12,
218, 232, 278; divisions in, 220–
32; as female body, 192, 198, 204,
207; history and description of, 21,
22, 202–11; and identity, 82, 202,
206–7, 270–71; structure of, 107,
201–2; as symbolic womb, 199
Village Institutes, 221, 221n
Violence: domestic, 176–81; political,
220, 220n
Virgin birth debate, see Anthropological
theory
Virginity: and the color red, 142–43,
274; and houris, 319–20; women's,
40, 97, 146. See also Honor/shame
complex; Soil
Volkan, Vamik D., 272n

von Grunebaum, Gustave E., 20, 293,
306, 306n

Walker, Paul, 291n
Water, 208–9, 214, 309; and prayer,
292; semen as, 49; at weddings,
128
Wealth: and community divisions,
228; displayed by women, 56–57;
distribution of, 22, 104; God as
source of, 295n; and power, 105.
See also Gold; Income
Wedding, 24, 71, 86, 124–47; timing
of, 115; transactions, 237; and soil,
81, 287
Weiner, Annette, 17, 27
Westernization: beliefs and values of,
53, 155–56, 284, 287; and civilization, 272n, 277; as model, 227,
284; as modern, material, symbolized by woman, 13, 21, 88n, 278–
80; and status, 120–21, 194n; and
village life, 262–64, 277, 277n,
279–82
Wheat, 22, 210; as livelihood, 239–55;
as seed, male, 80–81; at wedding,
143
Whitehead, Harriet, 43
Widow/widower, 53, 163–67, 182,
190–91; widow's inheritance, 104,
166
Women: bear children, 27, 33, 48, 52,
59, 63, 265; community of, 106,
187–90; as consumers, 267; dependent on men, 54, 93, 225, 288,
310; guarantee paternity, 40; in
Heaven, 319–20; in Hell, 290, 321;
as housewives, 266; income of,
260–61; and Islam, 291–92, 295–
96, 305–7, 317–18, 319n; as lack,
54, 141, 320–21; nurture children,
73, 146, 239–55; serve men, on
earth, in heaven, 195, 319; as sexual objects, 45, 97, 320; as strong,
238; as symbol and site of conflict,
278, 322–23. See also Birth; Body;
Femininity; Land; Procreation
Women's genitals, 59, 307; and birth,
61–62, 69; and hair, 87–88; and
hands, 138–39; and head, 196n;
and shame, 78, 87, 128–29

Wool: animals kept for, 243; and henna, 140; income from, 258–59; knitted items, 126, 261; mattresses and quilts, 121, 261; shearing of, 246

Work: attitudes toward, 115, 252–54, 277n, 295n; and children, 84, 98; handwork versus headwork, 115; and marriage, 98, 111–12, 163–65, 184–86; men's, 111, 239–40; pace of, 252–55, 267; and the "retired," 253; theories of, 20, 115n; women's, 239–55, 260–61, 266–67. *See also* Income; Machines; Sexual division of labor

Yalman, Nur, 39n, 284
Yanagisako, Sylvia, 14, 15, 162, 170–71n
Yeats, William Butler, 270
Yerasimos, Stephane, 221

Zemzem, waters of, 308–9
Zerubavel, Eviatar, 280n